Extreme Cities

Extreme Cities

*The Peril and Promise of Urban Life
in the Age of Climate Change*

Ashley Dawson

VERSO

London • New York

First published by Verso 2017
© Ashley Dawson 2017

1 3 5 7 9 10 8 6 4 2

Verso
UK: 6 Meard Street, London W1F 0EG
US: 20 Jay Street, Suite 1010, Brooklyn, NY 11201
versobooks.com

Verso is the imprint of New Left Books

ISBN-13: 978-1-78478-036-4
ISBN-13: 978-1-78478-038-8 (UK EBK)
ISBN-13: 978-1-78478-037-1 (US EBK)

British Library Cataloguing in Publication Data
A catalogue record for this book is available from the British Library

Library of Congress Cataloging-in-Publication Data
A catalog record for this book is available from the Library of Congress

Typeset in Sabon LT by Hewer Text UK Ltd, Edinburgh
Printed in the US by Maple Press

Contents

Jetstar Rollercoaster in Seaside Heights, New Jersey, after Hurricane Sandy. Photo by Hypnotica Studios Infinite, 2012.

Introduction

Extreme City

I found a huge blister of water forming on my bedroom wall when the wind woke me in the middle of the night. Hurricane Sandy had been buffeting the city all day, and as nightfall approached I hunkered down in my apartment in Jackson Heights, Queens, hoping that my neighborhood's elevation would bring a degree of safety. The previous day New York City Mayor Michael Bloomberg had ordered the evacuation of everyone living in flood Zone A, a total of 375,000 people, and by evening the city halted all subway service, marooning people without cars in their neighborhoods. There was little to do the following day, Monday, 29 October, other than to fill the bathtub with water, stock up on batteries, and watch the sky over the city ominously darken. When the full force of the storm hit that night, the intensifying winds drove rain into the bricks and mortar of my building, which age had rendered all too permeable to such a sustained onslaught, producing a threatening bulge in the paint of my bedroom wall. I prodded the blister gingerly and mopped, slept fitfully, and then was awoken by the winds raging outside to find the blister growing larger again, in what seemed like an endless cycle. By morning, I felt exhausted but fortunate to have escaped the hurricane relatively lightly. We still had power, and taxis and delivery trucks rolled through the streets.

But other portions of the city had sustained major damage. The superstorm drove a wall of water into the financial district of Manhattan, capitalism's great citadel. Sandy's fourteen-foot surge had flooded a power substation in Manhattan's Lower East Side, causing a catastrophic short circuit that cut off electricity to all of Lower Manhattan. The surge had also inundated many low-lying areas: Red Hook, the Navy Yard, Brighton Beach, and Coney Island in Brooklyn; areas around Jamaica Bay in Queens, including the Rockaways, a barrier island where the community of Breezy Point was utterly destroyed by a fire started by short-circuiting electrical equipment. On Staten Island, a borough still mourning losses from 9/11, beachside communities like Ocean Breeze and Oakwood Beach had flooded catastrophically.

In the days following Sandy's landfall, it became clear that it had been one of the most destructive storms ever to hit the United States. The storm killed 160 people in the New York metropolitan region and caused $65 billion in damage. New York City suffered cataclysmic breakdowns in basic infrastructure and services, including the flooding of the subway system and most major roads entering Manhattan; the destruction of hundreds of homes and a quarter million vehicles; and a power outage that plunged all of Manhattan below 14th Street into an eerie darkness for days. Hurricane Sandy accomplished what the Occupy Wall Street protests had been unable to do the previous autumn: it shut down the world's preeminent financial hub, the New York Stock Exchange. The uncanny sight of downtown Manhattan's spires plunged into darkness was an unmistakable signal that something had gone deeply awry.

The prostration of New York left me with turbulent emotions. I felt fortunate (as I had on 9/11) that my neighborhood escaped almost totally unscathed, but the city itself suddenly seemed vulnerable: the sense of certainty that underlies quotidian urban life had been dramatically interrupted.[1] I also felt disconnected from the rest of the city: the subways did not start running again for days; I couldn't reach friends who lived in downtown Manhattan, since their power was out and their cell phones weren't working; and without a car, I didn't know what was being done to help people in the most damaged areas. The city's immense size, and its disconnected and disjointed character, became painfully evident as life unfolded in my neighborhood with striking placidity, while in some other neighborhoods, those who lived above the 5th floor had no access to drinking water.

I would later discover that people I knew had been displaced by the hurricane. My colleague Fred Kaufman, a resident of downtown Manhattan, had already spent years struggling with the disruption caused by 9/11: being forced to move out, then dealing with endless construction and associated pollution once he was able to move back in.[2] Hurricane Sandy devastated the neighborhood afresh. Many of the small businesses Fred frequented were inundated by a fifteen-foot storm surge. Billions of dollars of property had been damaged. The FDR Tunnel, not far from Fred's apartment, was completely filled with water, as were most basements in the area. The noise of diesel generators pumping that water out was constant, day and night. But when I asked Fred about the psychological impact of this experience, he seemed relatively resigned. The experience of Sandy was frightening, he said, but in many ways it is constantly frightening to live in downtown New York. When disaster strikes, no amount of money or advance preparation is going to save you; at the end of the day, you have to be able to walk out of the disaster zone on foot. What matters most is knowing how to get out and having friends who can support you once you do. Yet life returned to normal for him in a matter of days.

Just across the harbor, the people of Red Hook, Brooklyn, had a different experience. Sheryl Nash-Chisholm, a Red Hook resident, watched with trepidation as the water advanced up Columbia Street toward her home on Monday night.[3] Scenes of people on rooftops after Hurricane Katrina were not far from her mind, but she put on a brave face for her family. Still, when the lights went out, they were all terrified. How far would the floodwaters rise? They lit some candles and huddled, sleepless, until dawn. Once the storm passed and they were able to leave home, her son discovered that his car, the pride of his life, was totally submerged, a complete write-off. Sheryl did her best to console him.

The devastation in Red Hook was vast. When Hurricane Sandy struck, the New York City Housing Authority (NYCHA) had shut down elevators, boilers, and electrical systems in public housing complexes across the city, including those in Zone A neighborhoods like Red Hook. With roughly 8,000 residents, NYCHA's Red Hook Houses complex is the largest public housing development in Brooklyn. When the power went down, the heat turned off and the water stopped running, leaving the residents of Red Hook Houses in life-threatening conditions.

The morning after the storm, Sheryl headed over to the Red Hook Initiative (RHI), a community organization dedicated to empowering the youth of the neighborhood. She is one of their key organizers. The building, unlike many others in Red Hook, was largely spared flooding during the storm and had also kept its power supply, so after failing to reach the Federal Emergency Management Agency (FEMA) on the phone, Sheryl began coordinating with residents of Red Hook Houses to turn RHI into a hub for the community. Within hours, RHI was providing power for charging cell phones, so that community members could let family members elsewhere know that they were okay. The building also provided a warm space, where residents of the chilly public housing complex could escape hypothermia. By the end of the day, hundreds of volunteers with what would become known as Occupy Sandy had arrived at RHI on bicycles, bringing much needed donations of batteries, candles, blankets, and canned food. A colleague of Sheryl's organized medical delegations to Red Hook Houses to check on elderly residents who needed medical attention, fresh medical supplies, and even basic needs like drinking water and food. For the next three days, RHI was the principal center for organizing the community, gathering donations from around the city and delivering food and other supplies to needy people living in public housing and other parts of Red Hook. For Sheryl, it was an exhausting but exhilarating sequence of days, a time in which her personal energies were strained but her faith in the solidarity of her community was reaffirmed. The federal government and relief agencies like the Red Cross would not arrive in the neighborhood with supplies for many days.

The stories of Sheryl, Fred, and myself highlight the precariousness of urban life in the face of climate change–induced disasters like Hurricane Sandy. After Sandy, endemic subway delays from heavy rain would no longer seem like mere temporary inconveniences, but rather prologues to a permanently drowned city. We wait anxiously for the next superstorm, fearing that the efforts of officials to prepare the city will turn out to be inadequate. And these Sandy narratives also dramatize the diversity and disparity of experiences of urban space and community during a disaster.

In *Extreme Cities*, I place Hurricane Sandy in a broader context, weaving together stories of cities around the world that are threatened by climate chaos. *Extreme Cities* draws on interviews with researchers at the cutting edge of climate science, landscape architects whose work uses natural processes to build our capacity to endure extreme weather, and activists fighting to diminish the inequalities that render cities vulnerable to climate chaos. Cities, I contend, are at the forefront of the coming climate chaos, their natural vulnerabilities heightened by social injustice. Cities are the defining social and ecological phenomena of the twenty-first century: they house the majority of humanity, they contribute the lion's share of carbon to the atmosphere, and they are peculiarly vulnerable to climate chaos.

New York City is not alone in its vulnerability to flooding: almost all of the world's great cities are sited on or near bodies of water. This should come as no surprise, since rivers, lakes, and the ocean have always been key to the economic and ecological health of cities. Thirteen of the world's twenty largest cities are port cities. But this has generated a deadly contradiction that is one of the most-overlooked facts of the twenty-first century: the majority of the world's megacities are in coastal zones threatened by sea level rise. Today, more than 50 percent of the world's population lives within 120 miles of the sea; by

2025, it is estimated that this figure will reach 75 percent. In addition, urbanites all over the world are particularly vulnerable to deadly heat waves, whose intensity and frequency are increasing as a result of global warming, because of the "heat island" effect that makes urban areas hotter than their rural surroundings. Several decades of evidence suggests that people are migrating out of drought-prone areas in the developing world and into coastal cities that are prone to floods and cyclones.[4] Whether we like it or not, anthropogenic climate disruption is going to dramatically alter the world's cities, and it is here that the effects of climate change will be of most consequence.

The New York that Hurricane Sandy struck was experiencing a second Gilded Age. It was a city presided over by Michael Bloomberg, the consummate corporate insider and power broker, who embodied nearly four decades of big business–friendly neoliberal urban policies. During that period, as Occupy Wall Street activists tirelessly pointed out, the city became a place of extreme economic and social inequality. It was also a site in which a variety of high-profile initiatives were undertaken to turn the city into a green metropolis. Yet inequality in the city continued to spiral. Today, New York is the consummate example of the prototypical social form of our age: the extreme city.

The extreme city is not a city of a certain size, like the megacity or metacity, which designate, respectively, metropolitan areas with populations in excess of 10 and 20 million. Instead, it describes the specific character of the urban fabric.[5] For instance, Tokyo and Lagos are both metacities, but the two are often taken as opposing poles in the contemporary urban imaginary, one a paradigm of technological sophistication and orderliness, and the other a sprawl of decaying infrastructure and informal settlements. By contrast, "extreme city" refers to an urban space of stark economic inequality, the defining urban characteristic of our time, and one of the greatest threats to the sustainability of urban existence. How a city copes with stratifications of race, class, and gender (or how such inequalities are left to fester) has everything to do with how well it will weather the storms that are bearing down upon humanity. It is in the extreme city that the most important struggles for human survival will take place.[6]

Nevertheless, this global convergence of urbanization and climate change, which I call the extreme city, has remained surprisingly invisible. Scientific literature on climate change has largely ignored the disproportionate contributions of cities to global warming, while climatology tends to assess the threat on a global scale and in the future tense, often in terms of how much the planet as a whole will warm by 2100, for instance. As a result, scientists actively suppress specific information about climate change in cities, statistically adjusting data collected from urban weather stations in global temperature datasets.[7] In seeking to record the overall fluctuations of a planetary environment, science ignores the specific places where most of us live—cities—which also happen to be the sites of the most extreme transformation. This makes climate change seem distant and abstract, something that will happen in a remote future on a scale far removed from that of individual experience.[8]

But climate change is happening right now, and above all in the cities where the majority of humanity now lives. Many have already exceeded the magnitude of warming projected for the planet as a whole over the current century.[9] Take São Paolo, the Brazilian metacity of over 20 million. São Paolo lies in a region that typically receives four times as much rainfall as Los Angeles, in a country that, with more than 12 percent of the world's renewable fresh water, is often referred to as "the Saudi Arabia of water."[10] Yet São Paolo has suffered from a deep drought in recent years that is tied to anthropogenic climate change. The city's main water reserves are perilously low, and in recent years the authorities have introduced water rationing. The origin of São Paolo's water crisis is no mystery. Since 1984, researchers have linked potential declines in precipitation in southern Brazil to the deforestation of the Amazon. The rain forest transformed what would otherwise have been a desert into a lush environment, by releasing massive quantities of water vapor into the air. Yet 224,000 square miles of the rain forest—an area nearly one-and-a-half times the size of California—have been clear-cut since 1980.[11] This unchecked deforestation, which disrupts the rain forest's ability to recycle precipitation from the Atlantic, is one of the primary causes of São Paolo's drought. Without adequate supplies of water, a city shuts down in a matter of days, and São Paolo has seen an exodus of "water refugees" as well as the proliferation of wildcat drilling for water that is polluting groundwater, a development that worsens the drought's long-term impact. There is still much that the city can do to conserve water, but São Paolo's plight makes the crisis tendencies of the extreme city dramatically evident.

Despite this, the predominant outlook on urbanization remains surprisingly sunny, even utopian.[12] Numerous paeans have been devoted to the economic and civic benefits of urban development, penned by writers who are frequently economists by training and consultants by profession.[13] Most of them recognize the inequalities that have generated what Mike Davis calls our "planet of slums," but they also characterize cities as the breeding grounds for new entrepreneurship that will provide solutions to the "challenge" of poverty. Their "smart," technologically enhanced forms of urbanism will usher capitalism into a new era of "green" urban growth and produce a "city fix" for climate change: a new era of efficiency and resilience based on compact green cities. But these blithe predictions elide the glaring contradiction of capitalism's destruction of nature, its material base. The perils of climate change in the city are either totally ignored in this literature, or cast as a mouthwatering opportunity for entrepreneurs to usher in the next wave of green technology.[14]

Neither "smart" urbanism nor good design alone will provide safe harbor from the storms increasingly breaking on our shores. "Tactical urbanist" interventions, however noble, will remain isolated oases in the vast desert of neoliberal urbanization.[15] We certainly need technology and planning to help adapt to the coming climate chaos, but under present social conditions, these tools are more likely to be employed by elites to create architectures of apartheid and exclusionary zones of refuge. The War on

Terror has shown us that the computer networks that are supposed to make cities efficient and green can be used not only against dissident groups and targeted populations, such as Muslims, but against the entire US population.[16] The oppressive character of surveillance in the "smart" city is sure to be stepped up as climate chaos intensifies.

Urban growth is driven at bottom by capitalism. As urban critics Henri Lefebvre and David Harvey have emphasized, the city plays a central role in solving the economic crashes that periodically wrack the capitalist system.[17] The shiny new buildings and spiffy developments that are constantly popping up in cities are a fantastic sink for the surplus capital that builds up in this economic system. In other words, profits are not left idle in bank accounts; they are always reinvested in other profit-generating schemes, like urban development. But the city is also the primary site for the feckless depletion of natural resources that characterizes this economic system, which is founded on unbridled compound growth. There is consequently no "city fix" without addressing overproduction. The city is where capitalism's central contradictions play out and consequently where revolutionary movements have often been pushed into existence. This means that the movement for climate justice, which builds on anti-imperialist, antiracist, and feminist movements of the past, will necessarily grow through solidarities forged in urban terrain. To suggest this is to challenge the notion that the city is the antithesis of "nature." We need to abandon such stale preconceptions. Not only are cities dependent upon nature, but they also structure our increasingly chaotic natural world. Climate change will unleash the greatest havoc in cities, but cities will also produce the most ferocious struggles against the inequalities of our urban age.

There is no green capitalist exit from the extreme city, when capitalism is founded on the principle of "grow or die." The world does not have a limitless supply of resources for humans to exploit. Urbanization and climate change are the two great products of this dysfunctional system, the central contradictions that define our age. And while the urban dwellers of the global

South are the most vulnerable in the face of the gathering storms, climate extremes will affect all of humanity, albeit unevenly.

After Hurricane Katrina struck New Orleans, geographer Neil Smith wrote that there is no such thing as a natural disaster: "In every phase and aspect of a disaster—causes, vulnerability, preparedness, results and response, and reconstruction—the contours of disaster and the difference between who lives and who dies is to a greater or lesser extent a social calculus."[18] "Disaster" connotes an unpredictable calamity that falls from the stars, but Smith suggests that so-called natural disasters are actually the product of all-too-tangible social inequalities. In New Orleans, for example, poor people (who are predominantly black) tend to live in low-lying, flood-prone areas, while the city's wealthy (and mainly white) residents live in the most elevated (and safe) areas. Similarly, in New York, in true American form, many impoverished and predominantly black neighborhoods are isolated from the rest of the city, thanks to housing discrimination and segregation, and continue to be starved of resources and targeted by the criminal justice apparatus.[19] Today, climate change bites down on these neighborhoods with particular ferocity, both in the form of dramatic disasters like Katrina and Sandy, as well as more subtle, protracted forms of environmental injustice like elevated mortality rates caused by increasing summer temperatures in cities.

And the unevenness also extends beyond the confines of the city; after all, extreme weather is oblivious to political boundaries. Before Hurricane Sandy hit the eastern United States, it began life, as most hurricanes do, in the warm waters of the Caribbean. Gestating in the hot waters of the Antilles, Sandy knocked out power for 70 percent of Jamaicans and destroyed thousands of homes in Cuba and the Bahamas. But it was in Haiti that Sandy was most devastating: fifty-four Haitians were killed by the storm, more than the number of dead in New York City. With 99 percent of Haiti's landmass already deforested, the rainfall quickly produced flash flooding, with death-dealing torrents of water rushing down denuded hillsides, washing away homes and burying people alive.[20] Sandy also destroyed the island's staple crops of banana, plantain, sugar cane, bean, and breadfruit, placing hundreds of thousands of Haitians at risk of malnutrition and famine in the following days and weeks.[21]

The extent of this damage was made possible by the destruction of social infrastructure (housing, schools, hospitals) on the island, a disaster that unfolded over many years rather than in the course of a single stormy night.[22] When Sandy arrived, almost 400,000 Haitians remained homeless following the devastating earthquake of 2010,[23] and many thousands were still sick from the cholera epidemic that UN peacekeeping troops brought to Haiti. Sandy made matters worse by destroying sixty-one cholera treatment clinics, while also flooding the streets of cities like Port-au-Prince, worsening the cholera outbreak by polluting water supplies. But the conditions that laid the ground for Sandy's impact on Haiti reach back much further, troubling neat lines between anthropogenic (or man-made) and "natural" calamities. Ever since the Haitian Revolution at the end of the eighteenth century, when the country's enslaved populace rose up and demanded that the "Rights of Man" of the French revolutionaries apply to all human beings rather than simply to Europeans, Haiti has been punished by the world's ruling powers. This began when the French insisted in 1825 that the newly independent Haitian state indemnify slaveholders for the capital lost when the island's slaves freed themselves. It extends as far as 1991, when the United States used the language of human rights to help block loans to the democratically elected government of Jean-Bertrand Aristide for clean water systems for the poor.[24] Indeed, for years the US insisted on sending aid for Haiti exclusively to NGOs, which currently provide 70 percent of health care and 80 percent of essential services on the island. And US-backed dictators like François and Jean-Claude Duvalier were only too happy to oblige these demands to dismantle public services.[25] But NGOs do not build infrastructure or public works, and, as a result, basic services in Haiti are now nearly totally privatized. Sandy's high death toll resulted from the liquidation of public infrastructure by corrupt domestic elites and the United States.

In addition, the threat of famine that loomed in Sandy's wake is also linked to decades of underdevelopment. Since the 1970s, Haiti has been subjected to some of the most stringent free market reforms ever imposed on a country by international financial institutions such as the World Bank and the International Monetary Fund. In the name of neoliberalism, Haiti became a supplier of the cheapest labor in the western hemisphere for foreign and domestic export assembly companies.[26] Public institutions providing education, water, and energy were privatized, and all obstacles to free trade were dismantled, including tariffs on food imports. This devastated Haitian agriculture, and the country went from producing 90 percent of its own food during the 1970s to importing more than 42 percent of its food today. Haitians are now the highest per capita consumers of subsidized US-imported rice in the Western Hemisphere. And as Haiti's agricultural sector was decimated, Haitians fled rural areas in ever-increasing numbers, with the capital city Port-au-Prince swelling to more than 2 million people. When Sandy hit, over 350,000 of these people were still living in emergency camps established after the earthquake of 2010. Despite the proliferation of NGOs in Haiti, the majority of the city's population lacks access to potable water, electricity, and health care. Haiti's vulnerability to natural disasters is a product of its subjection to the savage doctrines of neoliberalism.

Hurricane Sandy's effect on Haiti is a striking example of how disasters are "combined and uneven." Leon Trotsky used this phrase to describe capitalist development, a system that does not develop in a linear fashion but rather produces zones of abject poverty cheek-by-jowl with sites of shocking affluence.[27] Such extremes are not a temporary aberration but an inherent feature of capitalism. In today's neoliberal world system, gaping inequalities open up within and between countries. Hurricane Sandy's course from Haiti to New York rendered national boundaries nonsensical, although they continue to structure how we think about weather.[28] Haiti and New York were linked long before Sandy by centuries of imperialism and racial capitalism, but the hurricane wore the grooves of extreme inequality even deeper. If poverty is a kind of disaster, it is one that has been imposed on the people of Haiti. The plunder of Haiti, which left the island defenseless when Hurricane Sandy barreled down on it, is a product of the very same system that has amassed wealth, power, and a degree of insulation (for some) from disasters in global cities such as New York. Disasters such as Hurricane Sandy are combined and uneven, linking territories, cities, and nations whose fates are often diverse, and affecting their populations in highly unequal ways. Like capitalist development, combined and uneven disaster yokes together disparate stages, steps, and cultural forms.

Extreme Cities explores conditions of uneven development and disaster in cities around the globe, returning always to New York, the capital of capital and a microcosm of the challenges posed by climate change to global cities. The first chapter, "Capital Sinks," looks at the way in which real estate development, a key motor of contemporary capital accumulation, generates forms of irrational and unsustainable urbanization in cities like Miami, New York, and Jakarta. Chapter 2, "Environmental Blowback," surveys the historical "conquest" of nature that has attended urban growth, spawning increasingly unmanageable environmental contradictions in places like New York's Jamaica Bay and the Mississippi Delta south of New Orleans. This urban risk has been represented (and ignored) in different ways, which is the topic of Chapter 3, "Sea Change." How are the perilous conditions of global cities made invisible by the global scale of scientific calculations? And how does the recent wave of celebrations of urban living as the key to global upward mobility similarly downplay these hazards? Exploring what are often regarded as exemplary efforts to stormproof Dutch cities, the chapter underlines the massive challenges facing even the best-prepared cities. I examine this even more closely in Chapter 4, "The Jargon of Resilience," which casts a critical eye on cutting-edge efforts to adapt cities to the threats posed by climate change, looking in particular at the Rebuild By Design program in the New York region. If there are some good reasons for the buzz around the idea of resilience, we need nonetheless to question the extent to which free market ideology permeates the concept—and the adaptation efforts deployed in its name. In Chapter 5, "Climate Apartheid," I turn to one of the most significant ways that climate change is already reshaping humanity, examining contemporary accounts of so-called climate refugees and tracing the appropriation of this term from its origins in humanitarian and environmentalist discourse to its current deployment by the military-industrial-urban security complex in the wealthy nations of the European Union and the US. If current state-led efforts to cope with climate change are inadequate and often draconian, where one may find alternatives? In "Disaster Communism" (Chapter 6), I look at mutual aid efforts in cities struck by natural disasters in order to assess the viability of community self-help when the state falls away. Finally, "Urban Futures" broaches the taboo but ultimately inescapable topic of retreat from imperiled cities, which I argue must be accompanied by the dismantling of a feckless capitalist culture of ruinous growth whose epitome is the extreme city.

There is no better place to bear witness to these contradictions and shifts than New York City. As the world's preeminent financial hub, New York is not only the world's most iconic modern city, but also one of its most densely built and cosmopolitan urban spaces. While it has been surpassed in population by the megacities of the global South, it continues to be seen as the citadel of modern capitalism and to control key institutions of the global economy. Meteorites, flying saucers, giant radioactive monsters, and, of course, zombies—no other city in the world has been destroyed in as many ways and as many times in literature and films as New York.[29] The flooding of New York by Hurricane Sandy generated similarly spectacular images, not of an external threat laying waste to Gotham, but of capitalism's own self-destruction. Climate chaos brought one of the modern era's greatest cities to its knees, a city that has become synonymous with unbridled free market capitalism. With its massive carbon footprint and the outsize global impact of its financial institutions, New York bears a disproportionate responsibility for deepening climate chaos.

At the same time, New York can also make a strong claim for being the paradigmatic green city, thanks to New Yorkers' dense living patterns and use of public transportation, as well as recent initiatives like the creation of more than 400 miles of bike lanes.[30] But Hurricane Sandy revealed the hubris of celebrations of New York as a green metropolis, exposing a city completely unprepared for the larger threats posed by climate change. Like Hurricane Katrina before it, Sandy also showed the yawning social divisions that fissure cities, making a mockery of homogenizing accounts of urban resilience. Since the superstorm devastated us, much effort has been expended to help the city adapt to a warmer, more unstable world. Yet there has been relatively little discussion of the links between the city's vulnerability to climate change, and the economic and social inequalities New York embodies. There has been even less critical analysis of the model of untrammeled economic growth that New York incarnates. The world is watching. How New York City attempts to mitigate and adapt to climate change—and also to respond to climate justice more broadly—will set key precedents nationally and internationally.

THE STATUE OF LIBERTY

TORCH DAMAGE
Superman, 1980

AMPUTATION
A Man Called Hero, 1999

BURIED
Planet of the Apes, 1968
Oblivion, 2013

HEAD DAMAGE
Batman Forever, 1995
Judge Dredd, 1995
X-Men, 2000

DECAPITATED
Deep Impact, 1998
Cloverfield, 2008

SUBMERGED
Deluge, 1933
Artificial Intelligence, 2001
The Day After Tomorrow, 2004
Ice Age, 2011

Illustration by Feifei Ruan, from the series *Leave NYC Alone!*

Capital Sinks

Miami Vice

Phil Stoddard, the mayor of South Miami, lifted a trap door in his back yard, revealing a borehole that tunnels down through the porous limestone on which all of southeast Florida is based. Water was pooled just three feet below the surface. "That, my friend, is the Biscayne Aquifer," Stoddard said.[1] The water was so close to the surface, Stoddard explained, because salt water was pushing it up from underneath. The other day, he'd come across a large pool of water in a nearby park while walking his dog. There were fish swimming in the pool, fish from the ocean. "You can't find a clearer case of hydraulic connectivity," Stoddard said.

Stoddard is, uniquely, both a biology professor and a public official. Equally unique is his candor about the situation confronting his city and the surrounding region. "We're going underwater. There's enough heat in the oceans and CO_2 in the atmosphere to melt a lot of glacier. The science is uncertain on the height we've already got baked into the system, but no one will disagree with 20 feet of water, and some think 60 feet, and that's if we stop adding CO_2 right now. If we're going to build any infrastructure to ease people through this transition from *terra firma* to submerged lands, we better start financing it now. Because the financing won't be there in thirty years. This is our chance. This is the window."[2]

Of all the world cities threatened by climate change, Miami is faced with particularly daunting challenges. A report by the Organization for Economic Cooperation and Development listed it as the second most flood-imperiled city in the world, after the port city of Guangzhou in China.[3] A recent report on storm surge–threatened cities in the United States lists four in Florida among its eight most endangered.[4] Seventy-five percent of the 5.5 million people in South Florida live along the coast.[5]

Two key geophysical characteristics explain why Miami is uniquely endangered. The first is the flat topography of south Florida. With just 3 feet of sea level rise, more than a third of southern Florida will disappear below the waves. Once sea levels rise 6 feet, more than half the region will be gone. It's worth recalling that the National Oceanic and Atmospheric Administration (NOAA) is predicting up to 6.6 feet of sea level rise by 2100.[6]

The other major reason that Miami is particularly threatened has to do with the porous limestone bedrock that Phil Stoddard showed me in his backyard. Limestone is sedimentary rock formed from skeletal fragments of marine organisms like corals and mollusks. The ground under Miami is like a giant coral sponge. Both fresh water and salt water flow through it freely. As a result of this, it is impossible to build dikes or other barriers to keep out the ocean, as so many other cities threatened by sea level rise are contemplating doing. The seawater would just seep in under the dikes. Somewhere below Miami there is a boundary where fresh water meets seawater. As the sea level rises, this boundary gets pushed further inland by the increasing pressure of the sea, and the city's fresh water rises ever closer to the surface. When heavy rains pour down on Miami, a phenomenon that climate change is expected to intensify, the water bubbles up to the surface through drains and manholes, forming lakes like the one Stoddard saw near his house and flooding roads and any other low-lying spots. For Miami residents, wading through giant puddles of water has become an increasingly common experience in recent years.

But the city's problems don't end with keeping the sea out. There's also the question of dealing with fresh water. As salt water penetrates further inland, it contaminates wells supplying fresh water. Many of these wells have been moved further westward to escape the creeping ocean, but there is a limit to how far they can be shifted since salt water is also moving from the Everglades in the west toward Miami. According to Jayantha Obeysekera, the chief modeler for the South Florida Water Management District, there is therefore ultimately no retreat for Miami.[7] Obey, as local people know him, watches over one of the largest and the most complex water engineering systems in the world. South Florida is traversed by 2,300 miles of canals, sixty-one pump stations, and more than 2,000 sluice gates that prevent saltwater intrusion.[8] Much of this infrastructure was built in the 1950s in order to drain the water that flowed down from Lake Okeechobee to the Everglades, allowing reclamation of the land for agriculture and urbanization.[9] But this elaborate system is now imperiled by rising tides. Built at the end of canals and powered by gravity, the sluice gates that keep salt water out of Miami must now deal with an ocean that has risen six inches since they were built, increasing the water pressure of the incoming ocean. Already a few of the gates are inoperable as a result of the declining gradient between land and sea, and all of them must remain shut twice a day, during high tides. This is a particular problem during heavy rains since it makes it impossible to drain floodwaters. Obey's agency is installing extremely expensive pumps—each of which is slated to cost upwards of $70 million—to move this water out to the ocean, but this system will not fix Miami's underlying problems. Among these is the fact that Miami's growth is increasing demand for fresh water, which is draining the Biscayne Aquifer. As the freshwater pressure in the aquifer declines, more and more salt water penetrates it, poisoning the city's drinking supply. In an ironic situation for a city that seems to be surrounded on every side by water, Miami finds itself running low on fresh water and is consequently now struggling to impose dramatic water conservation measures.[10]

Reactions to the extreme environmental threats that confront Miami are, appropriately enough, strikingly extreme. Among those who pay attention to Miami's situation, no one is more alarmed than Hal Wanless, professor and chair of the Department of Geological Science at the University of Miami. A specialist in the history of coastal sedimentary strata in millennia past, Wanless bases his bleak assessment of Miami's future on his studies of the past, as captured in the sedimentary layers of the Biscayne Bay, which separates Miami from the barrier island–based city of Miami Beach. "I study the past," he said. "When we were in the last ice age, the coldest part of it, roughly 18–20,000 years ago, the seas were about 420 feet lower. Carbon dioxide levels rose from 180 to 280 parts per million before the Industrial Revolution, and the seas rose 420 feet, to where they are now. And they didn't do it in an even slow curve, but in a series of steps, rapid bumps and pauses. All across our continental shelf we have barrier reefs, old coastal mud flats and tidal delta complexes. The record of sea level change is there. This is why scientists are rightfully saying we're probably going to have 70 to 80 feet of sea level rise, because last time we were at the same CO_2 levels we have now, that was where the sea was. Pretty straightforward."[11] The burning question of the moment is how quickly the sea will rise to this level, but, according to Wanless, the historical record suggests it will get there not through the slow, smooth process that many current projections envisage, but through a series of abrupt and dramatic increments, interspersed with periods of relative stasis.

Although he serves on numerous local task forces focused on climate change, including the Miami-Dade County Climate Change Advisory Task Force and the Southeast Florida Regional Climate Change Compact, Wanless expresses frustration with the palatable projections they frequently offer in place of the unblemished science. "They don't want to scare people," said Wanless, referring to the Compact. "They got a group of people together to talk about sea level rise. Unfortunately they weren't all scientists. They'd say things like 'I'm not authorized to approve more than a 2 feet rise.'"[12] Not that his scientific colleagues are much better: the International Panel on Climate Change offers a scandalously low-ball projection for sea level rise in their 2007 report, according to Wanless. ("The problem is that a huge percentage of scientists are conservative by nature. They're very concerned about rocking the boat, and don't want to cry wolf," he said.) And adding to all this is the political pressure from governments not to alarm constituents and investors. "It's like the old mayor of Miami Beach, who gave a talk and explained that we have to work on solving this problem, but we can't let it hurt real estate prices, because this is their tax base," he said.[13] These fears of scaring investors produce false and ultimately harmful ideas about how to cope with sea level rise. Although Wanless thinks that sea levels are likely to rise 10–30 feet this century, he says that even NOAA's upper level projection of 6.6 feet by 2100 should force Miami politicians to stop "futzing around with expensive and ultimately futile defenses" and start thinking about how to help people relocate from the doomed city.

Considering the challenges Miami faces regarding its infrastructure, Wanless's Cassandra-like warnings do not seem overblown. Take the issue of sewage. In a 2013 settlement with the United States Department of Justice and the Environmental Protection Agency, Miami-Dade County agreed to upgrade its wastewater treatment plants and its sewage collection and transmission system within fifteen years in order to deal with overflows from the system's decrepit sewers. In the seven years before the settlement, such overflows had discharged 29 million gallons of raw sewage into the bright blue waters that surround some of the country's most popular beaches.[14] But the sewage has not gone away. In fact, expensive measures adopted by Miami Beach to cope with rising sea levels seem to be exacerbating the problem. The city installed massive pumps to direct high waters off the island, but while this has helped deal with flooding caused by King Tides it has worsened the city's sewage discharge problems. A recent study found that levels of fecal bacteria in the waters around Miami Beach were as much as 600 times above state mandated limits.[15] These high levels of waste in the water generate elevated levels of phosphorus, nitrogen, and other pollutants that can in turn trigger algae blooms toxic to marine life, a problem that led Florida to declare a state of emergency as an alarming guacamole-thick algae bloom clogged waters and washed up on beaches in the summer of 2016.[16] According to Henry Briceno, a hydrologist with Florida International University's Southeast Environmental Research Center, sea level rise will dramatically exacerbate this pollution, since these pumps will have to be continuously in operation.[17]

But Miami's sewage problem pales in comparison with the danger of the Turkey Point nuclear power station, which lies on a small barrier island just twenty-five miles south of Miami. Built in the early 1970s, the plant's operating license was extended by the Nuclear Regulatory Commission in 2002 from forty to sixty years, extending its life until 2032. Florida Power and Light, which operates Turkey Point, is planning to build two new reactors at the site. But controversy has swirled around the plant. For one thing, it lies right in the middle of Hurricane Alley. As Phil Stoddard puts it, "It is impossible to imagine a stupider place to build a nuclear plant than Turkey Point."[18] As sea levels rise, so of course do the storm surges that hurricanes push onto land. The implications for nuclear power plants around the world, many of which are sited in coastal areas because of abundant cooling waters, were made appallingly clear by the meltdown of Japan's Fukushima Daiichi plant in 2011.

Although most people assume that the danger of a meltdown at Fukushima is over, a full cleanup of the site—including removal of melted uranium fuel from the damaged reactor cores—will take at least forty years according to government projections.[19] In the meantime, Fukushima continues to leak radioactive water into the sea and remains vulnerable to another earthquake or tsunami. While the reactors at Turkey Point are designed differently from those at Fukushima, both rely on vulnerable backup systems to prevent meltdowns. If a hurricane-spurred storm surge from Turkey Point's neighboring Biscayne Bay were to knock out power from the mainland, the plant would be forced to rely on emergency diesel generators to keep cooling water flowing into the reactors. It was the failure of just such backup generators that led to the meltdowns at Fukushima. Turkey Point is only one of fourteen nuclear plants in the United States whose sites are expected to be partially if not completely underwater by 2030.[20] The Nuclear Regulatory Commission's (NRC) safety assessments for these plants were traditionally made using historical data concerning storms and flooding. Fukushima demonstrated the abject folly of this approach. The NRC has since issued new safety rules but fundamental questions remain about the security of the plants while in operation and about what will happen to the radioactive fuel rods after the plants are decommissioned. Will the looming problems at Turkey Point be addressed before the seas rise significantly?

Florida Power and Light, which runs Turkey Point, has responded to public concern by pointing out that the main reactors at the plant are elevated twenty feet above sea level, and by arguing that the plant's successful weathering of Hurricane Andrew in 1992 is evidence of its safety. Critics like Phil Stoddard respond that Andrew's peak storm surge actually passed far north of the plant, meaning that Turkey Point only actually faced a surge of three feet.[21] In addition, according to Stoddard the diesel-powered generators that keep cooling waters circulating when the power from the mainland fails—as it usually does during a hurricane—are significantly less elevated and less well insulated from rough weather than the main reactors.[22] But the real absurdity of Turkey Point becomes apparent when one considers even relatively conservative projections for sea level rise during the plant's sanctioned operating life. Nuclear cores must be constantly cooled to avoid meltdowns. Turkey Point uses a series of canals cut into the limestone base of the island to circulate water through the plant and leach heat off the reactors. As the fish near Phil Stoddard's house demonstrate, however, limestone is highly permeable. It was inevitable that the contaminated water circulating through Turkey Point's canals would leak back into Biscayne Bay and the Everglades, threatening nearby drinking water wells.[23] In fact, they were recently found to be pumping radioactive water into the Biscayne Bay.[24] In addition, the plant's cooling canals are cut into limestone only three feet above sea level at the moment. With only a small amount of sea level rise, Stoddard argues, these cooling canals will be regularly overtopped, spewing radioactive water into the surroundings.[25] Worse still, with only one foot of sea level rise, Turkey Point will be an island in the bay, accessible only by boat. How will the plant keep generating power safely under such conditions, and what will happen to the nuclear waste that is being stored onsite?

Public figures like Wanless and Stoddard, who are outspoken about Miami's dire situation, are very much in the minority in Florida. The state's governor, a Tea Party Republican, has said that he's "not convinced" that climate change is caused by human beings. Since becoming governor in 2011, Rick Scott has slashed budgets at the state's environmental protection agencies, including at the South Florida Water Management District for which Obey works.[26] He has also issued a gag order prohibiting state officials from discussing global warming.[27] Seeking to compensate for this atrocious abdication of responsibility, the four large counties of southeast Florida formed a regional compact dedicated to cutting carbon emissions and helping cities adapt to climate change. Drawing on the experience of New Orleans and New York, the group organized a series of design competitions—known in the world of architecture and design as *charrettes*—over the last several years to help local governments figure out how to upgrade their infrastructure and emergency preparedness.[28]

Notwithstanding these efforts, it is nearly impossible to get the real estate developers who are putting up gleaming skyscrapers along the state's threatened coastline to think about sea level rise, argues Jim Murley, head of the South Florida Regional Planning Council until he was made chief resiliency officer of Miami-Dade County. "It's not like they're avoiding the subject," he said, "but there are institutional places where we assume that risk is being analyzed. But what you realize is that it's not being analyzed from the standpoint of long-term trends like sea level rise. That is not in the equation. We have conversations as a group to get developers to think about the risks. And they say that they hire attorneys to think about risk."[29] It would help if there were some financial incentive to think about these long-term risks, something to offset the massive financial incentives to do the opposite: studiously ignoring it. In south Florida, such funds are nonexistent at present. According to Phil Stoddard, in the Miami-Dade budget of 2015 there was only one mention of sea level rise, and it was in an unfunded item relating to adaptation of parks to rising tides.[30]

For many in south Florida, these failures have to do with the timescales of sea level rise. "Decision makers have a hard time including the timeframe of sea level rise in their calculations. People are bound into the limitations of the worlds they're in: annual budgets, five-year work plans, 30-year mortgages," said Jim Murley.[31]

Hal Wanless echoed this sentiment. "I get Wall Street people calling me all the time, asking if they can get eight or nine years out of a condo on Miami Beach. I tell them they probably will. But to be an Iowa pig farmer and move down here to have a nice investment for your grandchildren. That's not gonna work. We're entering a real estate investment roulette."[32]

But Miami's powerbrokers also have a concrete incentive not to face up squarely to the inconvenient truths of climate change: admitting that the city is inevitably going to be submerged and that this will happen in a reasonably short timeframe might hurt real estate prices, which are nearly half of the city's main tax base, accounting for over $250 billion in revenues for Miami-Dade county in 2016.[33] The intentions behind this aren't all bad. The mayor of Miami Beach, Philip Levine, believes that if you bring in enough rich people, it'll expand your tax base sufficiently to allow you to pay for flood-proof infrastructure. But, according to his colleague Phil Stoddard, like any Ponzi scheme, this idea starts out well in the beginning but quickly goes bad. "I like to analogize it to running downhill," Stoddard says. "You go down faster and faster. If it's a small hill, you're fine by the time you get to the bottom. But if it's a big hill, your legs eventually can't keep up and you fall on your face. Sea level is like this: if we were going to get 10 feet in a slow curve, hey, we could outbuild it, and Levine's scheme works out. But what are you going to do with 60 feet? You can't outbuild that. It's like running down a really big hill—it ends badly."

But the refusal to speak openly and honestly about climate change and sea level rise isn't always driven by ethical motives. Miami is the center of a white-hot real estate boom, outstripping New York and Los Angeles in population growth in the years since the Great Recession of 2008.[34] Responding to this influx, more than 25,000 new condominium units were either proposed or under construction in downtown Miami in 2016.[35] This boom has partially been fueled by illicit sources of money that also transformed Florida into one of the major hubs of the world's shadow economy. Analysis of the Panama Papers, the massive trove of leaked confidential files from the secretive Panamanian law firm Mossack Fonseca, showed that nineteen foreign nationals have been buying high-end Miami real estate through shell companies, trusts, and limited liability corporations established in global tax havens like the Virgin Islands, with half of them linked to bribery, corruption, embezzlement, tax evasion, or other misdeeds in their home countries.[36] This is a tiny fraction of Miami's luxury condo market, but Mossack Fonseca is only one of the many law and accounting firms that set up offshore entities for real estate investors, capitalizing on the city's willingness to turn a blind eye to the shady origins of money. This is a lucrative business: one lawyer, Olga Santini, worked for Mossack Fonseca out of a bayside luxury condo high-rise once featured in an episode of *Miami Vice*.[37] According to the Chicago-based firm Jones Lang LaSalle, an investment management company that specializes in property, approximately $25 billion in cross-border residential real estate investment took place in Miami in 2014.[38] But foreigners are not the only ones engaging in real estate speculation in Miami. According to Miami realtors, New Yorkers have spent at least $586.5 million in property concentrated in one square mile of the city's downtown. Some joke that Miami has become New York's sixth borough.

Not all of this shadow economy is illegal: celebrities, for instance, have legitimate reasons for wishing to keep their identities secret. But cash deals accounted for 53 percent of all Miami-Dade home sales in 2015—double the national average—and 90 percent of new construction sales, according to the Miami Association of Realtors.[39] This spurred the US Treasury Department to start tracking shell companies buying homes for at least $1 million using cash. (They suspected that criminals were using Miami's gleaming waterfront towers to launder dirty money.[40]) In 2001, the USA PATRIOT Act mandated that everyone engaged in real-estate deals perform due diligence on their clients. But hard lobbying won the real estate industry a fifteen-year reprieve, based on the convenient argument that real-estate agents don't have the expertise to investigate their clients. The American Bar Association has also opposed disclosure requirements for real-estate lawyers, arguing that such stipulations would infringe attorney–client privilege.[41] As former assistant US Attorney Charles Intriago put it, "There is a wave of willful blindness about the source of a good portion of the money coming into real estate investments in South Florida."[42]

In Miami as in New York, this surge of speculative money from the global 1 percent has distorted home prices beyond the reach of most urban residents, whose median county income is $50,000. "It looks like a rich place, but the middle class is gasping for air because rent has been driven up, and we have a service economy that doesn't pay well. Never mind poor people," said Phil Stoddard.[43] But why even invest in such an unsustainable place as Miami? Some of these investors may not know about climate change or may even believe that it's a hoax. But, more fundamentally, for most wealthy speculators the threat of sea level rise one day submerging their luxury condos doesn't matter much. If they can pull their money out of a developing country, where the inflation rate is roughly 50 percent and park it in dollars in a Miami condo for five years, where it will appreciate 5–10 percent a year, it's not important what's going to happen in thirty years. "Everyone assumes that they're going to be the first one to sit down in this game of musical chairs. The problem with this mentality is that it creates an unstable market when things tip. And they tip suddenly," said Stoddard.[44]

This kind of short-term mentality is encouraged by federal insurance policies. The US government established the National Flood Insurance Program (NFIP) in 1968 to provide subsidized insurance in areas prone to flooding, since private insurance was too expensive in these areas for most. The intention behind NFIP was to encourage flood mitigation measures like building standards that required homeowners to elevate their houses on pilings. In exchange for access to flood insurance, communities were required to pass ordinances restricting additional development in flood zones.

But the NFIP also ensures that when storms wipe out houses in vulnerable coastal areas, they are repaired and replaced by even more expensive buildings, all bankrolled by US taxpayers,[45] and this has inadvertently fueled a fifty-year building boom in extremely vulnerable coastal areas around the United States. The Union of Concerned Scientists' report *Overwhelming Risk: Rethinking Flood Insurance in a World of Rising Seas* (2013) documented that NFIP has paid out nearly $9 billion to repetitive-loss properties, nearly 25 percent of total NFIP payments since 1978.[46] Such repetitive-loss properties constitute just 1.3 percent of all NFIP properties, but they are projected to account for as much as 15–20 percent of future losses. We are, in other words, paying people not simply to build in foolish places, but to do so over and over again. And these NFIP subsidies are dramatically skewed toward the rich. Nearly 79 percent of NFIP-subsidized policies are in counties that rank in the top 30 percent of home values, while fewer than 1 percent are in counties that rank in the bottom 20 percent.[47] Many of these subsidies are not for beach shacks where people have lived for generations, but rather for the second homes of the 1 percent.

This arrangement is now in crisis. After a particularly busy hurricane season in 2005, NFIP was $23 billion in arrears with just $2.2 billion in premiums.[48] The federal government has consequently begun to rethink subsidies for flood insurance. In 2012, Congress passed the Biggert-Waters Flood Insurance Reform Act, which required updating of flood-risk maps and raised insurance premiums to reflect true flood risks, but backed off after a public uproar. However, this showed clearly how disproportionate amounts of the subsidy go to rich investors who can easily afford increased premiums, but who have the political connections to sandbag reforms, while the increasing housing costs could displace many working-class families who have lived at the coast for generations. Like coastal cities themselves, the insurance program will eventually be brought into line with environmental realities or will face catastrophic collapse. The key question is whether this transition will happen in a way that does not further exacerbate the extreme inequalities of coastal cities like Miami.

Looking further down this road of coastal economic crisis, Phil Stoddard worries about the legal clauses built into the thirty-year mortgages that middle-class constituents depend on to subsidize their home purchases. The mortgages include a clause stating that the seller knows there's no problem with the property or the land. But what if you know the place is going to be flooding with increasing frequency? Is that something buyers have to reveal to the bank? Would the bank still support your purchase?[49] Old-timers have always known that Miami sits on shifting sands, Stoddard says. But younger generations are increasingly shocked to learn that the place isn't permanent. "For the past 6,000 years," Stoddard says, "mankind has lived in [a] period of remarkable sea level stasis. It's changed a negligible amount, so cities have been able to stay put on coastlines, and property has been handed down across the generations. It's been *the* way to accumulate wealth. But now that sea levels are shifting 20 feet a generation, that assumption falls apart. Coastal land is no longer a key to long term wealth."[50] Stoddard worries a lot about how the transition from *terra firma* to submerged lands will go. "There will be an exodus," he says. "The dynamics of how this exodus happens are important. And not just here but in every community adversely impacted by climate change. So we need to create an orderly transition. As people begin to leave you need to forestall collapse. This means that there needs to be a functioning economy that can scale down without producing depression or total collapse. How do you create that? We don't have it yet. Creating that order and structure requires a lot of thought. And there's virtually no one talking about this transition."[51]

A transition is inevitable. Like all coastal cities, Miami will have to engage in some strategic and, ultimately, wholesale retreat. After all, scientists estimate that when all of the planet's ice sheets and glaciers eventually melt, the sea will be sixty-five meters (or 212 feet) higher than at present.[52] We already have 50 feet of rise locked in given current levels of global warming, and the international community has yet to seriously commit to the diminution of emissions. Either way, the seas will rise. Ice sheets are rather like the Titanic: it takes a lot of energy to get them moving, but once they're on a certain trajectory they are carried forward by tremendous amounts of inertia. We cannot be sure how long this melting will take, but, according to scientists like James Hansen, much of it is likely to come during the next century and a half, or in other words, within one or two generations.[53] Given the highly vulnerable infrastructure that weaves through cities, once one part of the metropolis has to be abandoned because of the rising tides, the city will for all practical purposes cease to function. How, for example, would elevated portions of Miami continue to function without access to clean water or sewage? And what would be the sense of a central business district on a walled-off island like Manhattan that workers could not reach by mass transit from the outer boroughs? If political leaders had some foresight, the retreat would come sooner, when it can be on a planned footing rather than as an emergency response to extreme anthropogenic climate disaster.

New York City: Capital of Capital

Planning for climate disaster is not the path our politicians are currently following. On the tenth anniversary of the attacks on the World Trade Center, New York City Mayor Michael Bloomberg appeared at a gala breakfast sponsored by the real estate–backed Association for a Better New York to celebrate the rebirth of Lower Manhattan.[54] Referencing fears that had gripped the city after 9/11, Mayor Bloomberg said that many had worried that "the bad old days were coming back. That crime would return. Residents would move out. Businesses would flee to the suburbs. And the city would go to seed."[55] But such fears about a return to the New York of the 1970s and early 1980s, when the city underwent a fiscal crisis and cultural turmoil, had been thoroughly banished, the mayor said. The population of Lower Manhattan had doubled since the attacks of 9/11, adding more people than the entire cities of Atlanta, Dallas, and Philadelphia combined. This real estate–fueled transformation of Lower Manhattan was one of the "greatest comeback stories in American history," said Bloomberg, a rebirth that "will stand as our greatest monument to those we lost on 9/11 and to our unshakeable faith in the moral imperative of protecting and preserving a free, open, democratic society."[56]

Although his speech contained many references to commemorative sites such as the National September 11 Memorial, Bloomberg's celebration of Lower Manhattan focused on the revival of real estate development and businesses in the area, from the humble storefront of Minas Shoe Repair to the recently completed "New York by Gehry," a starchitect trophy building and the tallest residential tower in the western hemisphere. A testament to American resilience, the real estate–driven economic bonanza was synonymous for Bloomberg with the core elements of US democracy, in contrast to the "bad old days."

The mayor's speech was delivered scarcely one week after Hurricane Irene made landfall in New York. Mandatory evacuation orders were issued for low-lying areas of the city; the Metropolitan Transit Authority, the nation's largest mass transit system, shut down completely in anticipation of a storm surge; and portions of the Meatpacking District on Manhattan's West Side were flooded. Bloomberg made strikingly few references to the storm and its dramatic impact on the city, only mentioning it in a glancing allusion to the uncertain future. While admitting that there was no way to accurately see even ten days let alone ten years into the future, Bloomberg nonetheless asserted, "Over the next 10 years—come hell or high water—I fully expect that Lower Manhattan will continue to grow."[57] He did not reflect on the wisdom of continuing to build skyscrapers in the middle of Lower Manhattan's flood zone, or acknowledge how this waterfront development placed some communities more at risk than others. When Hurricane Sandy struck New York the following year, these oversights had deadly consequences.

This is not to say that the Bloomberg administration was unaware of the threats posed by climate change. In 2007, the city published *PlaNYC*, which broke the silence around environmental issues and the urban future at a moment characterized by climate change denial on the federal level and virtually total inaction on an international scale.[58] As part of *PlaNYC*, Bloomberg convened the New York City Panel on Climate Change, which issued its first report on urban adaptation to climate change in 2010.[59] One year later, the city introduced *Vision 2020*, a plan for the next decade of development along New York City's waterfront. "The rise in sea level and increased frequency and magnitude of coastal storms will likely cause more frequent coastal flooding and inundation of coastal wetlands as well as erosion of beaches, dunes, and bluffs," it stated.[60] Several weeks later, an updated version of *PlaNYC* was released, with an equally dramatic series of statements: "As a city with 520 miles of coastline—the most of any city in America—the potential for more frequent and intense coastal storms with increased impacts due to a rise in sea level is a serious threat to New York City."[61] After Hurricane Sandy devastated New York, far exceeding many of these official predictions, the Bloomberg administration convened a panel of experts entitled the Special Initiative for Rebuilding and Resiliency, which in 2013 released the report *A Stronger, More Resilient New York*.[62] This report lays out a remarkably detailed catalogue of 250 measures, with a price tag of over $19 billion, intended to help New York weather future storms. Two shorter reports were published by the Department of City Planning that same year, the first of which elaborates key design principles to guide flood-resistance construction in urban areas.[63] The second study, *Urban Waterfront Adaptive Strategies*, identifies a range of initiatives to increase the resilience of urban coastal areas to the hazards associated with sea level rise.[64] Taken together, these reports have established New York as the most forward-thinking city in the United States in addressing climate change in general and sea level rise in particular.[65]

Yet at the same time as city planners and expert consultants were issuing these increasingly stark warnings about climate change, the Bloomberg administration was spending hundreds of millions of public funds luring real estate developers to construct luxury apartment buildings in waterfront zones of the city. During his three terms in office, Mayor Bloomberg oversaw the rezoning of nearly 40 percent of New York City's total land. Much of this transformation was focused on derelict industrial zones along the waterfront in areas such as Williamsburg, in Brooklyn, and Hunter's Point, in Queens, which were reborn as upscale residential communities for the affluent professional class that had flocked to the city. A significant portion of this newly developed real estate was in areas threatened with inundation. Today, more than 400,000 New Yorkers live in flood zones; property at risk in these zones is estimated to be worth more than $129 billion.[66] Yet even in the face of dramatic evidence such as the flooding of many portions of the city by Hurricane Sandy, Bloomberg insisted that there would be no retreat from the city's waterfront. "As New Yorkers, we cannot and will not abandon our waterfront. It's one of our greatest assets. We must protect it, not retreat from it," he proclaimed at the press conference to announce the release of *A Stronger, More Resilient New York*, held at the Brooklyn Navy Yard, a site that was inundated by 4.5 feet of floodwater during the superstorm.[67]

Such rhetoric may make good political theater, and it certainly dovetails with the macho imperial masculinity that dominated the public sphere after the 9/11 attacks. But it is completely detached from reality, and perhaps a reflection of how the time-scale of rising sea levels far exceeds electoral terms.

The Special Initiative for Rebuilding and Resiliency was tasked with studying the impact of Hurricane Sandy and assessing risks in a medium term that extended to 2020 and a long term extending only to 2050—a scant few decades.[68] But the seas will not stop rising in 2050, despite Bloomberg's Canute-like defiance of the rising tides, and these short timeframes are particularly deceptive since the rate of sea level rise is expected to increase dramatically as the atmosphere and seas warm up and feedback effects begin to kick in.[69] The new buildings and infrastructure designed and built according to these projections are likely to be standing long after 2050, although they may be submerged.

This may partially be a case of political expediency. Retreat remains anathema in public discourse, a kind of admission of weakness that most contemporary politicians are unwilling to countenance.[70] But there is also another, deeper reason for this unwillingness to confront the magnitude of the climate crisis and its likely impact on cities over the course of coming centuries: capitalism's inherent need to grow. A "healthy" capitalist economy must expand at an annual rate of 3 percent, according to David Harvey. If it ceases to do so, it goes into crisis, as it did in 2008. Harvey, a theorist of capitalism, sees this as one of its most fundamental yet overlooked contradictions.[71] This contradiction has been intensifying for the last four decades. The International Monetary Fund has warned in recent years that the world is awash with "surplus liquidity," or excess capital.[72] In other words, it has become more and more difficult to find investment opportunities that can offer high rates of return, since global profit margins in production have declined substantially since the 1970s. Faced with such contradictions, capital turns to the city, where fixed plots of land promise to increase in value as more of the world's population migrates to urban centers—what Harvey calls a "spatio-temporal fix" for the contradictions of capitalism.[73] Real-estate speculation provides a way for economies to grow as production declines.[74] In other words, the city is a growth machine, and speculative real estate development functions as a sink for surplus capital. Sixty percent of global wealth today is invested in real estate.[75]

This dynamic is responsible for the rise of planetary urbanization. The past half century has seen a massive boom in building that has turned humanity into a predominantly city-dwelling species. Of course, there is much to be said for urban life in political, economic, and even environmental terms. The density of cities like New York has been touted as a particularly green form of living, fostering support for a mass transit system that allows half of the city's denizens not to own cars.[76] But this market-driven process of planetary urbanization is not a rational process, and it does not generate cities of sweetness and light. As the crash of the stock market in 2008 showed, speculation in property markets generates dramatic boom and bust cycles that destroy the few assets that vulnerable groups have been able to accumulate. Particularly hard hit by the crash of the mortgage-backed securities market—a boom that fueled the building spree in downtown Manhattan—were low-income African-Americans and single mothers across the United States. Mayor Bloomberg's celebration of the transformation of downtown into a land of luxury condos seems particularly tin-eared given the role of Wall Street in spurring the boom and then seeking to profit from the massive wave of foreclosures that followed the crash. If there was a real-estate fueled renaissance after 9/11, it was one that was distinctly uneven, generating unparalleled wealth for a few, alongside gentrification and displacement that, as the Right to the City Alliance puts it, amount to undeclared campaigns of state-sanctioned violence against low-income communities and people of color.

But this tale of two cities did not unfold in New York alone, or even solely in the United States. Around the globe, the wave of planetary urbanization has seen spectacularly lavish building projects constructed as investment vehicles for the affluent, who often do not actually live in these properties. Shadowy shell companies launder money from secretive celebrities and moguls from autocratic countries in the form of opulent skyscrapers like Manhattan's Time Warner Center.[77] Twenty-four percent of the apartments in New York are not used as primary residences, and this is equally true for other global cities such as London and Hong Kong. Perhaps the most extreme examples of this criminally absurd urbanization for the 1 percent have emerged in places like Dubai and Abu Dhabi, "evil paradises" where oil wealth is sunk into ultra-lavish air-conditioned high rises in the desert, built by legions of ill-paid migrant workers. With their passports routinely confiscated by employers, these latter-day helots are an indentured, invisible majority living subterranean lives amidst the glittering spires.[78] Such informal settlements of hyperexploited workers exist all around the world, constituting what Mike Davis calls a "planet of slums."[79] Here, luxury domiciles for the global 1 percent exist cheek-by-jowl with intense deprivation and dispossession, caused by the spiraling cost of real estate, and the extreme polarization of wealth and power. In these enclaves of astonishingly conspicuous consumption and fatuous spectacle, elites seldom have cause to think about the abject living conditions of those who build the city and keep it running. Over the last decade, these spiraling city-based inequalities have generated a succession of revolts in places like Istanbul's Taksim Gezi Park, El Alto and La Paz in Bolivia, and of course Zuccotti Park in New York, uprisings that David Harvey calls the crisis of planetary urbanization.[80]

But cities are not just sinks for "surplus capital." Capital is also sinking. This is true on a literal level, as the world's coastal cities confront the rising seas. In addition, as these coastal cities expand, the market-based forces driving development also produce greater risk, vulnerability, and environmental disasters globally.[81] In other words, cities are not just places where environmental crises wreak the most havoc; they are also one of the main drivers of climate change. United Nations-Habitat estimates that, as of 2011, cities are responsible for as much as 60–70 percent of total anthropogenic greenhouse gas emissions.[82] Heating and cooling cities like New York accounts for an estimated 35–45 percent of current carbon emissions, while urban industries and transportation contribute another 35–40 percent.[83] A recent scientific report demonstrates that urbanization and its increasing demand for commodities is the primary cause of deforestation in the planet's tropical rainforests, the great lungs of the planet.[84] As Mike Davis puts it, "City life is rapidly destroying the ecological niche—Holocene climate stability—which made its evolution into complexity possible."[85]

Why are cities so environmentally destructive? In his anatomy of the unsustainable city, Davis highlights the features that make contemporary cities peculiarly antiurban, of which the most prominent is massive sprawl that leads to "grotesquely oversize environmental footprints."[86] Davis also notes that "where urban forms are dictated by speculators and developers, bypassing democratic controls over planning and resources, the predictable social outcomes are extreme spatial segregation by income or ethnicity" (in other words, segregated neighborhoods).[87] For Davis, it is capitalist forms of urbanization that are making contemporary cities unsustainable. For this reason, anticapitalist struggles for social justice in the city and the question of urban sustainability are inherently linked.[88]

It is precisely the growth of the luxury city, hailed by Bloomberg not just as a symbol of economic dynamism but as a token of democratic renewal, that is responsible for the increasingly catastrophic forms of social and environmental disasters. This is true despite Bloomberg's efforts to create affordable housing. In a report entitled *Elite Emissions*, the Climate Works for All coalition notes that "a mere two percent of the city's one million buildings use 45 percent of all of the city's energy."[89] These dirty buildings are the largest ones in the city, composed primarily of luxury apartments and commercial buildings, where fat cats like Donald Trump, Alice Walton (heir of the Walmart fortune), and David Koch (an active climate denier) live and do business, beneficiaries of all the extravagant, energy guzzling amenities they can imagine. The majority of New Yorkers live in totally different circumstances, struggling to pay the rent on cramped spaces and using only enough energy to meet basic needs. Yet, as Hurricane Sandy demonstrated, they are the ones who ultimately pay for the unsustainable consumption of the 1 percent. Fifty-five percent of the storm-surge victims in New York, for example, were low-income renters, with incomes averaging $18,000 a year.[90] Although the wealthiest New Yorkers contribute disproportionately to emissions through their excessive consumption, it is the city's poorest and the dwindling middle classes who actually pay the bill for climate chaos. And what is true in New York is also true globally: the richest 7 percent of the world's population are responsible for 50 percent of carbon emissions.[91] But the global majority will be the ones who pay for the extreme consumption of the rich, in the form of increasing climate chaos and attendant social disruption.

New York and Miami represent different ways of responding to the climate crisis, yet both are also capital sinks and have deployed what I term "urban greenwashing," the effort to depict urban life under the reign of capital as sustainable, to continue attracting speculative real estate development. Green rhetoric has become an essential tool in urban branding and promotional strategies, as cities compete for investment.[92] Despite their many well-meaning and important components, reports like *PlaNYC* are also environmental branding mechanisms, designed to protect and enhance property values for elite property owners and transnational corporations. All too often, such plans promote processes of "environmental gentrification," where green living is used to attract wealthy professionals to luxury buildings in freshly developed urban neighborhoods, rather than fostering urban sustainability and environmental justice for the majority of citizens.[93] In the absence of policies designed to check gentrification, green buildings, parks, and other forms of environmental urbanism help drive up property values, displacing the long-time residents of such areas, who have often fought for decades against life-destroying concentrations of urban toxins. Top-down green development plans such as those issued by the Bloomberg administration do not fundamentally shift the socially and environmentally unsustainable nature of capitalist urbanization. If we wish to transform these cities, we have to abandon models of urban design based on ceaselessly augmented growth. And in some cases, we may have to acknowledge that such cities must be abandoned before they actually sink.

Mayor Bloomberg signaled his outsize ambitions for *PlaNYC* quite clearly by the way he announced it: from a stage at the American Museum of Natural History on Earth Day 2007. If the federal government was not going to take decisive action on climate change, then cities like New York would have to take the lead, he declared. Staking New York's place in a competition with cities like London and Paris, which had already unveiled urban sustainability plans, Mayor Bloomberg claimed that *PlaNYC* would transform NYC into the "first environmentally sustainable twenty-first century city."[94] It was akin to the first blueprints for Central Park and to the construction of Rockefeller Center during the Great Depression, he suggested, boldly proclaiming the capacity of cities and their mayors to tackle some of the most intractable problems of the contemporary age—problems that national governments have been unable or unwilling to address with any success.[95] But *PlaNYC* was perhaps most notable for how it departed from a long-standing refusal to engage in comprehensive urban planning in New York.

New York has never had a rational comprehensive plan for urban development.[96] Early in the city's history, surveyors were the primary planners, laying down the famous rectangular grid pattern of streets and lots in 1811 that defined the development of Manhattan north of Houston Street. Although this grid introduced a certain degree of order, it was ultimately animated by the dictates of real estate development and the liberal economic theory that supported it. The city's role was essentially to create a skeletal land-use policy that would facilitate land subdivision and development. After the city was consolidated into its present five-borough form in 1898, this fundamentally anticivic policy was reinforced, with the city government eschewing any comprehensive approach to its growth. While other industrializing cities crafted ambitious plans for development in this period, New York City allowed the market to lead, limiting its role to the restricted tool of zoning, which classifies buildings according to use (residential, industrial, or mixed-use) and density.[97] Zoning may allow for orderly growth, but it tends to codify patterns of inequality rather than reimagining significant public landscapes and social spaces.[98] Even Central Park, one of the paradigmatic public spaces of the modern city, was created primarily as a result of real estate speculation.[99] Although institutions like the Regional Plan Authority and figures like the city planner Robert Moses may seem an exception to this rule of real estate, the former was not an official government body and had no power to implement its proposals, and the latter, despite his much-lamented determination to hack his way through the city with a meat-ax, implemented his schemes in a relatively piecemeal, nonholistic manner.[100]

Of the many conflicts catalyzed in New York by Moses, the fight by Jane Jacobs to preserve her neighborhood in Greenwich Village is the most well known. Jacobs's denunciation of the overweening—and often purblind—claims of modernist urban designers in her renowned 1961 manifesto, *The Death and Life of Great American Cities,* ironically dovetailed with the growing resistance of the city's real estate elite to urban planning.[101] Jacobs opposed Moses and the "urban renewal" programs of the federal government, whose multibillion dollar Federal Highway Program had transformed the fabric of social life in the United States after 1945, bankrolling white flight into the sprawling suburbs and leaving inner city neighborhoods such as the Bronx devastated. Against such segregated spaces and the arrogant planning prerogatives that created them, Jacobs championed the "intricate sidewalk ballet" of Greenwich Village. For Jacobs, the street was not a space of anarchic disorder, as the architect and urban planner Le Corbusier and others had argued, but the matrix within which a complex, organic community formed, ensuring safe and notably democratic spaces.

Although Jacobs's work might have opened space for community planning processes in New York, just over a decade after she penned her paean to the complex choreography of urban street life, New York was convulsed by a fiscal crisis during which the city's business elite imposed a crisis regime that totally gutted democratic governance of the city.[102] Elites blamed the city's insolvency on everyone—unions, city workers, communities of color—except themselves, and set about implementing savage cuts to all aspects of New York's social democratic state. This crisis regime in New York laid the foundation for the roll-out of neoliberalism across the nation and around the globe, predicated on the idea that the role of the state is to stay out of the way of the market, cut back taxation in order to stimulate growth, and eschew all but the most basic provision of public infrastructure.[103] Neoliberalism consecrated the rule of New York's elites in the FIRE industries—finance, insurance, and real estate—draining social and economic capital from public spending, public works, and the creation of public spaces and institutions in the city. For the following two decades, although there was much resistance to the crisis regime, there were few social forces capable of mounting a systemic challenge to the power of pro-growth elites to shape the urban fabric as they chose.

PlaNYC was a significant departure from this history of militant resistance to comprehensive, long-range planning on the part of city elites. It is a testament to Naomi Klein's contention in *This Changes Everything* that the climate crisis lays bare the bankruptcy of free market ideology.[104] Here was the mayor of the capital of capital declaring that the unchecked free market system had set in train potentially cataclysmic processes of climate change. Given this unfolding disaster, Bloomberg proclaimed, the city had no choice but to plan how to mitigate its greenhouse gas emissions and how to adapt to the baleful forces unleashed by unrestrained capitalism. Yet if *PlaNYC* sought to address the climate crisis with a framework of 127 different initiatives designed to green the city in various ways, it was nonetheless shaped by New York elites' antipathy to planning. As the urban theorist Peter Marcuse remarked following the publication of *PlaNYC*, this blueprint for a "greener, greater New York" is not a comprehensive plan since it does not include an overall assessment of the city's physical, economic, and social needs.[105] For Marcuse, *PlaNYC* focuses on narrowly infrastructural needs and environmental threats and offers no attempt to engage with the city's economic and racial inequalities in relation to the many proposed transformations of the city. This may have stemmed from the fact that the document was drawn up through a blatantly undemocratic process. The New York City Charter mandates that plans for city development should be reviewed and voted on by affected community boards, borough presidents, the City Planning Commission, and the City Council. At each step in this process, a series of public hearings are required. None of this took place. Instead, the drafting of *PlaNYC* was overseen by a small group in the Mayor's Office of Operations, with the bulk of the work being done by the global consulting firm McKinsey and Company, which worked under contract for the city's Economic Development Corporation.[106] The future of the city was, in other words, entrusted to a private corporate entity, which concocted plans for three decades worth of future urban development without significant democratic consultation.

This failure to engage with the city's democratic planning process, not to mention with New York's myriad social and environmental advocacy groups, made it extremely difficult for the Bloomberg administration to win public support for *PlaNYC*. Public mistrust of Bloomberg's top-down, high-handed approach flared up particularly clearly around the proposal for a congestion pricing scheme that would have charged drivers coming from the outer boroughs for the right to drive in downtown Manhattan. If Bloomberg had purposely cultivated the reputation as a charismatic CEO mayor, capable of cutting through the city's snarled bureaucracy with his entrepreneurial leadership skills in order to implement technocratic solutions for the greater public good, he quickly found himself struggling to quell charges of elitism during the congestion charge debate unleashed by *PlaNYC*.[107] After all, while congestion charges would have cleaned Manhattan's air and raised money for the city, the scheme was easily cast as an iniquitous tax on the increasingly immiserated working class forced to commute to the city's central business districts from ever more remote parts of the outer boroughs.

Nevertheless, many of the initiatives proposed in *PlaNYC* have been implemented. Since the plan's publication, New York has planted over a million trees on the city's streets. More than 300 miles of those streets have also been painted with bike lanes, and the largest public bicycle sharing program in the United States has been established. Public plazas have been created in places like Times Square that were once the exclusive preserve of automobiles, helping to calm the city's hectic traffic. But the most successful aspect of *PlaNYC* has been in the sphere of the mitigation of greenhouse gas emissions. True to McKinsey's background in management consulting, the most detailed element in *PlaNYC*'s long-term plans for the city was the effort to promote energy efficiency.[108] To implement these plans, which did not require public approval, the city purchased hybrid cars to green its auto fleet and cut energy use in government buildings by installing insulation and updated lighting systems. The city also encouraged building owners throughout the city to replace dirty heating oil with cleaner natural gas. Just before leaving office in 2013, the Bloomberg administration issued a greenhouse gas inventory celebrating a 19 percent cut in the city's emissions, two-thirds of the way to *PlaNYC*'s goal of a 30-percent reduction by 2030.[109] The report credits these diminishing emissions to efficiency retrofits and energy-use monitoring, but also admits that nearly 60 percent of the reductions came from city power plants shifting from coal to natural gas as a fuel source.[110] But much of New York's supply of relatively clean-burning natural gas is derived from fracking, the controversial process of oil and gas extraction that the state has banned.[111] Mayor Bloomberg even supported construction of a pipeline, the first to be built in the city in decades, to bring fracked natural gas straight into downtown Manhattan from the Marcellus Shale in Pennsylvania, arguing that natural gas is a cleaner, greener alternative to dirty heating oil.[112] While the controversial pipeline may have helped the city produce impressively diminished greenhouse gas emissions, it underlined the city's failure to develop a comprehensive plan to move to renewable energy sources instead of creating more demand for another fossil fuel. As Heather Rogers puts it, this element of *PlaNYC* is part of a broader pattern in which New York "structurally saddles other people in other places with the detritus of the city's unequal and high-consuming class structure, aggravating the environmental instability we all fear."[113]

It should not be entirely surprising that New York's claims to sustainability hinge on offloading environmental destruction on other places and people. New York is, after all, the global city *par excellence*; its ecological history is linked not just to regional landscapes but to the globe-spanning circuits of US colonial and imperial power, which have a dramatic impact on the social and physical fabric of the city. From the days of Peter Stuyvesant and the Dutch West India Company, to those of the bankers, barristers, and sugar refiners who made outsize profits from the transatlantic slave trade, to the hedge fund managers who fueled the subprime mortgage crisis, the city's economic power brokers have always sunk the capital gained through speculative enterprises in far-flung locations into prime properties in the city.[114] They have equally consistently sought to externalize the social and ecological ramifications of these processes of accumulation onto others, whether they reside in the city or elsewhere. As finance became more central to capitalism during the neoliberal era, this dynamic has intensified, resulting in mammoth urban development projects in tandem with the imposition of savage austerity and new rounds of accumulation by dispossession and extreme extraction at home and around the world, with concomitant explosions of resistance and repression, from the IMF-fueled food riots of the 1980s, to the Arab Spring, to today's Black Lives Matter protests.[115] By the time of *PlaNYC*'s publication, the unsustainable character of this form of urban growth, in both environmental and social terms, was clear, a fact hammered home by the city's strong grassroots environmental justice movement.[116]

PlaNYC should be seen as an effort to promote an urban sustainability fix, a solution to capitalism's periodic crises of accumulation that combines rampant real estate speculation with a variety of enticing yet relatively superficial greening initiatives. For although *PlaNYC* is ostensibly devoted to preparing the city to weather climate change, it nonetheless puts real estate development front and center. If the need to curtail urban carbon emissions is part of this plan, there is no sign in *PlaNYC* of a recognition of the need to curb urban growth, with attendant forms of consumption of everything from cement to air conditioning. *PlaNYC* appropriates the language of sustainability, which was previously deployed by environmental justice organizations to challenge the uneven distribution of pollution in cities like New York. It transforms sustainability into a market-oriented doctrine for urban development. Indeed, of the three principal challenges that *PlaNYC* identifies—growth, an aging infrastructure, and an increasingly precarious environment—the plan tackles the issue of growth first, making its priorities patently clear.[117] "By 2030," the introduction to *PlaNYC* announces, "our population will surge past nine million, the equivalent of adding the entire population of Boston and Miami combined to the five boroughs."[118] It is not exactly clear where this projection comes from, but *PlaNYC* frames such population growth as part of a story of urban renaissance, attributing the collapse of the city's population during the 1970s to "rising crime and a plummeting quality of life" and the subsequent growth to efforts to revive this quality of life.[119] No mention is made in this upbeat account of the toll taken on the poor and communities of color in the city by the crackdown on "quality of life" crimes like panhandling by the homeless under the city's previous mayor, Rudy Giuliani.[120] The unremarked-upon use of code words such as "quality of life" in *PlaNYC*'s initial pages is a clear indication of the audience to whom the plan is addressed. It is certainly not directed to the communities subjected to heavy policing and mass incarceration and increasingly priced out of their own neighborhoods.

According to *PlaNYC*, the city's growth trends offer great opportunities:

Our employment force will grow by 750,000 jobs, with the largest gains among health care and education. New office jobs will generate needs for 60 million square feet of commercial space, which can be filled by the re-emergence of Lower Manhattan and new central business districts in Hudson Yards, Long Island City and Downtown Brooklyn.[121]

The basis for these projections are just as unclear as the report's population growth figures, as if the projected addition of nearly a million residents will magically produce three quarters of a million new jobs. Is this projection based on employment figures taken at the time of *PlaNYC's* publication, six months before the worst economic downturn since the Great Depression hit the city? And why do these new jobs, mostly slated to be in health care and education, necessitate the construction of 60 million square feet of commercial space? The answer to these questions lies not simply in the unstated assumptions behind the statistical projection—will today's rosy unemployment statistics still hold twenty-five years into the future?—but also on a specially tricked out tugboat cruising up the East River four years before the publication of *PlaNYC.*

As he chugged along in this tugboat in the winter of 2003, Daniel R. Tishman, co-chair of the New York Building Congress's Economic Development Committee and CEO of Tishman Realty and Construction, reflected on the future development bonanza unfurling around him, opining that, "New York City's waterfronts are indeed a new frontier, and the East River contains many of the best locations left in the City."[122] This language, reminiscent of America's settler colonial history, belies the racial dynamics that underlie gentrification: from the 1980s onward, real estate magazines have celebrated the "urban pioneers" and homesteaders looking for cheap apartments who ventured into communities of color previously shattered by the "urban renewal" programs of previous decades. These gentrifiers were celebrated as the modern-day equivalents of the settlers who "bravely" seized native lands.[123]

In fact, this was a tugboat tour of waterfront development opportunities, attended by some of the most powerful figures in the world of New York real estate, including New York City Planning Commission Chair Amanda Burden, one of Bloomberg's key appointees, who brought a blue-blood pedigree and the credibility of an Ivy League degree in planning to the post. Prior to working for Bloomberg, Burden had overseen the planning of public spaces in Battery Park City, the waterfront luxury enclave created (with state support) on landfill from the World Trade Center.[124] Speaking to the assembled guests, Burden described the Bloomberg administration's plans for waterfront areas in Brooklyn and Queens as "one of the most ambitious rezoning plans in the City's history."[125] The challenge, she said, would be to "respect the low scale of the neighborhood while giving local residents the access they desire to the waterfront." Such increased waterfront access would only be possible, Burden and Bloomberg believed, through private real estate development.

As part of the Bloomberg administration's plans, developers such as those aboard the tugboat would be obligated to construct and maintain parks adjacent to their properties, replicating the strategy of building waterfront ribbon parks behind a wall of luxury condos pioneered in Battery Park City. These development plans followed the blueprint laid out, at the urging of the powerful Real Estate Board of New York, by the Department of City Planning's *Comprehensive Waterfront Plan* of 1992.[126]

Waterfront development was a key priority for the Bloomberg administration since its inception, a fact made clear when the freshly elected mayor appointed Daniel Doctoroff as his deputy mayor for economic development and rebuilding in 2001. Doctoroff had no prior experience in government but had made his name in elite New York circles through his role heading New York's failed bid to host the Olympic Games in 2012. While overseeing the bid, Doctoroff became aware of the ties between environmental sustainability and urban development. This was reflected in the bid, which married amenities like parks and bike paths with megaprojects that, though spread across the city's five boroughs, centered on the redevelopment of the Hudson

Yards on Manhattan's so-called "Far West Side." Hudson Yards was essentially an extension of Midtown's Central Business District, an enlargement that New York elites had long dreamed of.[127] When Doctoroff was appointed by Bloomberg, these ideas became the core of the mayor's planning and development strategy.[128] It is impossible to overstate Doctoroff's impact on the city: not only did he lead the redevelopment of the Hudson Yards, but he also oversaw the rebuilding of Lower Manhattan following the attacks of 9/11, the rezoning of waterfront neighborhoods such as Greenpoint-Williamsburg in Brooklyn (now the upscale hipster capital of the world), and *PlaNYC*. The Bloomberg administration's own publicity documents celebrate Doctoroff and Burden, who "fundamentally changed the way that the City approaches the land-use process, by using zoning laws to foster new development, create mixed-use communities, improve the quality of life and to enhance tax revenues."[129] Doctoroff and Burden carried out the plans of the city's real estate elite, faithfully executing the goals laid out by entities like the Partnership for New York City, a powerful nonprofit founded by David Rockefeller whose *2005 Priorities* document set out a series of projects almost identical to those launched by Doctoroff. The Partnership document lays bare the economic interests driving these urban projects when it calls for "rezoning and public investment to encourage private development projects that strengthen secondary business districts" and "reclaim neglected waterfront land."[130]

Crucially, waterfront development ballooned under Bloomberg, not only in Lower Manhattan and the Far West Side, but also in Brooklyn neighborhoods like Williamsburg, DUMBO, Red Hook, Gowanus, and Coney Island, as well as the development of the Navy Yards for light industry and of the Atlantic Yards in downtown Brooklyn; and waterfront development in Long Island City in Queens.[131] Taken together, these projects constitute a wholesale transformation of New York's waterfront. With few exceptions, they were carried out under the umbrella of the Empire State Development Corporation (ESDC) and one of its many subsidiaries (e.g., the Lower

Manhattan Development Corporation, the Times Square Hudson River Park Trust, and the Atlantic Yards Area Redevelopment Project).[132] The ESDC is an outgrowth of the New York State Urban Development Corporation, one of many "public benefit corporations" created by Governor Nelson Rockefeller in the 1960s to impose "urban renewal" projects without legislative oversight and in the face of local opposition.[133] By the 1980s, the rechristened ESDC's mandate had shifted from the provision of public housing to economic development through megaprojects. Among these were the construction of controversial megaprojects such as Battery Park City and the Jacob Javits Convention Center in Manhattan's Far West Side, the "revitalization" of Times Square, and a doubling in the size of the New York State prison system.[134]

The extent to which the ESDC corrodes democratic control over the city's development is perhaps most evident with the case of the Lower Manhattan Development Corporation (LMDC), an ESDC subsidiary instituted by New York governor George Pataki to orchestrate the rebuilding of downtown Manhattan after 9/11. As an independent authority largely immune from public oversight, the LMDC was able to quash the calls of grassroots groups for a genuinely equitable rebuilding of downtown, one that would benefit economically devastated working-class neighborhoods populated predominantly by people of color, like Chinatown and the Lower East Side, as well as the far more affluent denizens of Wall Street and the surrounding area. The LMDC ensured that nearly half the government aid earmarked for small businesses in the area went to transnational corporations with hundreds of employees, and structured the area's affordable housing program in a manner so restrictive as to exclude virtually all of the neighborhood's poor residents.[135] By arguing that post-9/11 policies should come in the form of publicly subsidized (but market-oriented) redevelopment and growth, and by commandeering antidemocratic institutions such as the LMDC, city elites ensured that pre-crisis patterns of inequality would be significantly exacerbated by the recovery.[136] As we will see in Chapter 4, post-Sandy initiatives such as Rebuild by Design exemplify these same dynamics of urban disaster capitalism.

But beyond questions of the equity of the real estate development to which *PlaNYC* is fundamentally devoted is the striking irrationality of this development: almost all of the proposed development falls within Federal Emergency Management Agency-defined floodplains.[137] This suggests that the Bloomberg administration's devotion to coping with climate change was superficial at best. It certainly could not claim ignorance concerning sea level rise and cognate threats. After all, their hired scientific consultant, the Goddard Institute's Cynthia Rosenzweig, had authored numerous papers containing detailed projections of ominous amounts of sea level rise. In a 2001 paper co-authored with William Solecki, Rosenzweig argues that "climate change is already occurring in the New York City region" and that the previous two years witnessed "striking examples of the impacts of climate extremes, including heat waves, droughts, and floods."[138] Looking forward, Rosenzweig and Solecki warned that "the key threat of sea level rise is its effect on storm surges," and that "many of the region's most significant infrastructure facilities will be at increased risk to damage."[139] Citing the blackout during the summer of 1999, which affected the predominantly black and Latinx neighborhoods of Northern Manhattan and the South Bronx, they also argue that the increasing number and severity of heat waves brought by climate change are likely to place the city's marginalized populations at most risk. While noting that the New York metropolitan region is severely hampered in its efforts to deal with climate change by its fragmented governance structure, Rosenzweig and Solecki lay out a number of necessary adaptation strategies. Among these is "disinvestment in highly vulnerable coastal sites."[140] Serious adaptation, in other words, would involve moving people and buildings out of flood zones, a course of action diametrically opposed to Doctoroff and Bloomberg's ambitious—and lucrative—plans for developing the city's nearly 600 miles of waterfront. Indeed, Rosenzweig's most comprehensive study of urban adaptation recommended that the city buy up coastal properties to restrain development.[141]

Had Rosenzweig's recommendations been adopted, *PlaNYC* would have been predicated on a comprehensive plan to transform city-owned waterfront properties into parks, providing much-needed green spaces for adjoining working-class neighborhoods, and doubling as flood-absorption zones during storms. The model here would be the "water plazas" built by the Dutch city of Rotterdam. Under normal conditions these plazas function as attractive playgrounds for the surrounding community, but during heavy rains they temporarily hold water, discharging it slowly into the drainage system after the storm subsides.[142] More broadly, however, such a transformation of the city's waterfront would have generated a series of softer, more fluid edges to the city, sites very different from the armored levees and other forms of hardened infrastructure that modern engineering uses to divide urban spaces from the fluid environments they ultimately depend upon.[143] The significant addition of vegetation and wetlands through interlinked waterfront parks could also mitigate New York's heat island effect and, to a certain extent, its carbon emissions. As Brian Stone has argued, land-surface changes such as adding significant vegetation are the single most effective (not to mention the most economical) step that cities can take to counteract the threats of climate change.[144] Stone contrasts the planting of 11 million trees in Los Angeles, which the Lawrence Berkeley Heat Island Group predicts will lower summer temperatures in the city by three degrees, with the city's pledge, identical to New York's, to decrease carbon emissions by 30 percent by 2030, which would still result, Stone notes, in dramatically higher summer temperatures.[145]

Echoing the orientation of global climate policy, *PlaNYC* promises to reduce greenhouse gas emissions in a manner that produces no immediate protections for the city itself. While emissions cuts are clearly necessary, they will not diminish warming for centuries, even if they are ultimately adopted globally. Forms of adaptive mitigation such as the planting of trees and the mandating of green rooftops on buildings, by contrast, can cool the city dramatically in a relatively short amount of time. Had the city turned its waterfronts into expansive parks, it could have added to its green areas dramatically and also significantly abated storm surges. Tragically, the growth imperative that shaped *PlaNYC* led the city to squander a tremendous opportunity to make dramatic and relatively immediate improvements to the social and environmental terrain of New York.

The emaciated public esplanades created by NYC's waterfront developers over the last two decades are a far cry from such transformational green spaces. The well-heeled occupants of the adjacent luxury condos may have the means to flee the city in the face of storms, or to abandon New York entirely when its infrastructure is brought to the point of collapse by rising seas, but their outsize carbon footprints do a great deal to exacerbate climate change in the meantime. But when waterfront real estate is simply a sink for accumulated capital, there is no incentive for thinking in the longer term.[146] Nonetheless, advocates for this kind of waterfront development might argue that they transform disused—and often toxic—industrial zones into vibrant, mixed-income neighborhoods. "Reclamation of underutilized waterfronts" is, in fact, one of the key initiatives laid out in *PlaNYC*. To support this directive, the document weaves another narrative of decline and rebirth:

> Across New York, stretches of land—once teeming with life, action, activity, commerce— sat largely abandoned. As factories and ports closed down after World War II, the land stayed cut off from communities, the piers vacant, the old buildings empty. Our economy had evolved. Our land use did not.[147]

But thanks to a rezoning of the Greenpoint-Williamsburg waterfront, which replaced the empty manufacturing sites with a mixture of housing, business, and open space, this had begun to change, as *PlaNYC* stated. The plan adopted in 2005 was projected to produce about 10,000 new housing units—a third of them affordable. It is true that New York went through a wrenching wave of deindustrialization after 1945. Yet the story of New York's working waterfront is not one of natural evolution. To suggest this, as *PlaNYC* does, is a convenient form of mystification.

As in other cities, much manufacturing moved out of New York to the Sun Belt and then overseas in search of cheaper sites of production. The globalization of production was made possible because of the rise of the shipping container, which made cheap circulation of goods around the world possible.[148] But containerization handed immense power to capital, which became increasingly footloose while workers remained overwhelmingly tied to particular places. Containerization thus played a key but vastly under-acknowledged role in the dramatic erosion of wages and workers' power in advanced economies. In New York City, containerization destroyed the city's role as the country's single greatest port. In 1956, New York handled one third of all seaborne trade in the country, with a specialization in high-value goods meaning that its economic role far outweighed sheer numbers of items shipped. New York's docklands, which were located behind the finger-like piers that protruded into the Hudson and the East River along the waterfront in Manhattan and Brooklyn, were central to the city's economy. After World War II, for example, 100,000 workers were employed in various aspects of the shipping industry, and nearly as many manufacturing jobs in the city were linked directly to the port.[149] When subsidiary occupations such as insurance and banking are included, the tally of jobs for which the city's port was directly responsible reaches at least half a million. Despite its importance to the city's economy, New York's docks were weighed down by increasingly crippling problems by the 1960s. Among these was the corruption among dockworker unions that Elia Kazan's film *On the Waterfront* indicted. But also of issue was the city's failure to invest in the port infrastructure, including renovating decaying piers and building facilities to handle container-based shipping, which was gaining an increasing share of all waterborne freight by the early 1960s. While New York Mayor Robert Wagner reacted with alarm to the Port Authority's opening of Port Elizabeth in 1955, many city elites were more than happy to see the port relocate to the marshlands of New Jersey. Indeed, the city's own planning commission suggested in a report of 1959 that the city should not rebuild derelict piers but should instead use waterfront land in lower Manhattan for new office and residential buildings.[150]

In calling for the transformation of New York from a city that built and moved things to one based on real estate speculation and the immaterial flows of the finance industry, the planning commission was reiterating long-standing calls by elites, which went all the way back to the Regional Planning Association's initial blueprint of 1929, to replace the city's blue-collar workforce with white-collar office workers and luxury homes for the rich.[151] For the city's real estate dynasties, much more money was to be made through the sky-high rents to be gleaned from office buildings like the World Trade Center than from the small businesses and light industry that it displaced. In the decade before the fiscal crisis struck the city, New York's maritime industry disappeared almost completely, and, in tandem, the city lost a quarter of its factories and a third of its manufacturing jobs.[152] This transformation played an important role in the loss of city revenues that sparked the fiscal crisis, and it also laid the foundation for New York's lamentable and enduring status down to the present as the most unequal metropolis in the nation, a city of extremes in which there is a more than eightyfold difference between those at the top and bottom of the economic ladder.[153]

These citywide dynamics were certainly at play in the dereliction of the Greenpoint-Williamsburg waterfront that *PlaNYC* cites. But an equally key factor in the neighborhood's travails was the closure of the Brooklyn Navy Yard in 1966, which had been a mainstay of employment in the area and in the borough in general since its opening in 1801.[154] This closure was met with fierce but ultimately futile resistance, including protests inspired by the civil rights movement, such as a bus caravan to Washington.[155] The closure of the Navy Yard was of a piece with broader federal antiurban policies, including the construction of the national highway system and federally subsidized mortgage programs, both of which encouraged white flight to the suburbs in the postwar era. These policies were set in place at precisely the moment when large populations of African-Americans and Puerto Ricans were migrating to industrial cities in search of decent jobs.[156] Government disinvestment in cities in favor of suburbs effectively meant divestment from the lives of people of color in favor of whites.[157] These policies culminated in New York with the advocacy of Roger Starr, the city's chief housing administrator, for "planned shrinkage," the withdrawal of city services like garbage collection and subway stations from communities of color in order to "accelerate the drainage" of these communities. This policy of abandonment was twinned on the federal level by the attitude of "benign neglect" that Daniel Patrick Moynihan urged Richard Nixon to adopt in relation to the nation's cities in the 1970s.[158]

But predominantly black and Latinx neighborhoods were not simply abandoned—they were also actively targeted. Many of the waterfront neighborhoods where people of color had settled in the postwar era were characterized by a mix of housing and industry. In 1961, the city rezoned many of these mixed-use neighborhoods exclusively for industry. Waste facilities and other noxious uses could be located on waterfront land zoned for heavy manufacturing without public review or approval. The result of this zoning was an unparalleled concentration of toxic facilities in low-income communities of color along the city's waterfront. No fair-share principles were used in the distribution of such polluting facilities around the city. Instead, planners simply allowed toxic industries to accumulate in neighborhoods where land values were lowest, which was without exception in low-income communities of color. Williamsburg and Greenpoint, for example, have one of the largest concentrations of waste facilities in the city, with a nuclear waste transfer station, a sewage treatment plant, dozens of privately operated waste transfer stations, equal numbers of petroleum and natural gas storage facilities, hundreds of industries handling hazardous wastes, and the country's largest underground oil spill.[159] Similar dynamics leading to the clustering of toxic facilities in waterfront communities of color were at work around the rest of the city.

In 1992, recognizing but also exacerbating this dynamic, the Department of City Planning's Comprehensive Waterfront Plan set aside two areas in Williamsburg-Greenpoint, the Navy Yard and Newtown Creek, as part of the city's Significant Maritime and Industrial Areas (SMIA), zones designed to encourage the concentration of heavy industrial and polluting infrastructure uses. The other SMIAs designated by the city are in Brooklyn's Sunset Park and Red Hook neighborhoods, the South Bronx, and the North Shore of Staten Island. All of these are low-income communities of color. While the city was clustering such toxic facilities in vulnerable neighborhoods, it was transforming the waterfront in affluent areas like downtown Manhattan into attractive public spaces like the Hudson River Park. Indeed, these simultaneous transformations were explicitly planned for in the Comprehensive Waterfront Plan.

These transformations helped catalyze the city's environmental justice movement. In Williamsburg, opposition arose to city plans in the late 1980s to locate a garbage incinerator in the former Navy Yard. A coalition called the Community Alliance for the Environment (CAFE) united the erstwhile antagonistic Latinx and Hasidic communities of the neighborhood in opposition to the incinerator.[160] Despite the fact that it would produce tons of carcinogenic ash, the incinerator scheme had been supported by some national environmental groups since the city had pledged to impose strict emissions controls and to start a citywide recycling program. Real estate developers for their part were in favor of the project since it would generate an increased electricity supply, allowing them to power more buildings. By injecting civil rights and social justice issues into environmentalism and by organizing public pressure campaigns accordingly, CAFE was able to convince the city to drop support for the project by the mid-1990s. Framing the incinerator as a threat to a shared environment, CAFE succeeded by establishing a common ground upon which political solidarity and respect across cultural differences could be forged.

Yet, as with other communities that have witnessed successful struggles for environmental justice, gentrification followed hard on the heels of this victory.[161] As developers went in search a "new frontier" beyond Manhattan, they found it convenient to represent waterfront zones in neighborhoods like Williamsburg-Greenpoint as barren and uninhabited, or, in the terms of *PlaNYC,* as "largely abandoned." To suggest that the city's waterfronts were "empty" and that the land was "cut off" from surrounding communities is to engage in striking but convenient forms of ignorance about the struggles for environmental justice that unfolded along the waterfront over several decades. It erases the history of displacement, toxicity, and resistance, substituting for this rich history of community building a settler colonial discourse of *terra nullius,* in which the land to be colonized is treated as a vacant wilderness ripe for colonization.[162]

But what about *PlaNYC*'s pledge to create affordable housing along the waterfront? During the twelve years that Bloomberg was mayor, the median monthly gross rent for an apartment skyrocketed 54 percent while median household income increased only 2 percent.[163] No doubt there was a pressing need for affordable housing in New York. Unfortunately, the thousands of units of affordable housing promised to Greenpoint-Williamsburg were not built. A fervent campaign by community activists and local politicians had resulted in a reform to the city's 421-a tax subsidy to development,[164] requiring that 20 percent of the new housing units be set aside for low- to middle-income people. Prior to the development of Williamsburg, the city had allowed developers to put the affordable units they'd promised to build somewhere other than in the buildings they were constructing; the vast majority of such affordable units were built in the South Bronx rather than in fast-gentrifying areas like the Brooklyn waterfront. The compromise struck in Williamsburg was the first agreement to stipulate that poor and working-class people should be able to live in tax-subsidized developments.[165] But the hitch was that the construction of affordable housing was purely voluntary. In addition, as Maritza Silva-Farrel of Real Affordability for All argues, the criteria for affordability often end up amplifying rather than combating gentrification.[166] Affordability is determined according to a formula set by the federal government based on Area Median Income. In a city of economic extremes like New York, the median income is often far higher than the wages of people in a low-income neighborhood. So even if developers accept the deal of 20 percent affordable to 80 percent luxury housing, they end up displacing poor and working class people, while the construction of new market-rate apartments under inclusionary zoning guidelines inevitably ends up raising property values and rents in poor neighborhoods, destroying the existing affordable housing stock in the area.[167] Affordable housing as presently practiced constitutes an undeclared land grab, one that enriches unscrupulous speculators while displacing people in low-income communities of color who have already been subjected to decades of economic divestment and the slow violence of polluted neighborhoods.

The egalitarian-sounding promises of affordable housing in *PlaNYC* turned out to be just as hollow as the document's broader pledge to transform New York into the most sustainable city of the twenty-first century. But the elements of *PlaNYC* discussed here also remain central to the environmental plans of Bloomberg's successor, Mayor Bill de Blasio's *OneNYC*.[168] These plans' inability to adequately prepare the city for the onset of climate chaos is not for a lack of attention paid to this or that bit of vulnerable infrastructure. It is because they continue to encourage investors to sink ever greater sums of capital into city real estate. This capital will eventually sink, leaving the majority of citizens under water, struggling to hold onto land whose value is plummeting, when it is not also killing them slowly through its toxicity. Plans for fostering urban resiliency in the face of climate chaos may introduce welcome reforms like networks of bicycle paths, but as long as they continue to rest on the imperatives of capital accumulation and speculative urban development, they amount to nothing more than greenwashing. As the double meaning of "capital sinks" suggests, the crisis of planetary urbanism is inescapably a crisis of the urban environment. The solution to this crisis will not come from urban development that continues to subordinate the city to the disastrous reign of capital, but from plans for the urban future framed around values of anticapitalist climate justice.

Jakarta: Accumulation by Adaptation

Growing over the last decade at a blistering pace that outstrips the vertiginous development of Beijing and Bangkok, Jakarta is part of the world's second-largest metropolitan area, with a population of over thirty million. The capital of Indonesia, it also has the unhappy distinction of being one of the world's fastest sinking cities. According to a team of Dutch experts, Jakarta is an example of extreme subsidence: the city is sinking at an average rate of 3 inches (7.5 centimeters) each year, with some parts subsiding by up to 10 inches annually.[169] Forty percent of northern Jakarta currently lies below sea level; in fifteen years, this number will rise to as much as 80 percent. In 2007, a massive flood inundated almost half of the city in up to 13 feet of water, forcing 340,000 people to flee their homes and leading city authorities to build a seawall the following year. At high tide, parts of that seawall, atop which squatters have built scores of tin shacks, are already submerged.

To cope with this crisis, Jakarta is planning to build the world's biggest seawall. To be constructed with the aid of a consortium of Dutch companies over the course of three decades, it will include an exterior wall off the coast that will be 80 feet high—one third of it will protrude above the waters of Jakarta Bay—and will extend for 25 miles.[170] The project goes by various names, including the National Capital Integrated Coastal Development project and the Giant Sea Wall, but it is more popularly known as the Great Garuda since the seawall and its accompanying seventeen artificial islands will be designed in the form of the mythical birdlike creature that is the national symbol of Indonesia. If it does not quite rival the vertiginous phantasmagoria of Dubai's artificial "island world" and its accompanying megamalls, entertainment zones, and skyscrapers, the Great Garuda nonetheless aspires to a similar level of architectural gigantism and city branding.[171] Indeed, developers promise that the $40 billion project will pay for itself through the sale of luxury homes on the artificial islands, as well as the inevitable shopping malls and "Grade-A" office towers.[172] In addition to helping Jakarta distinguish itself in the urban branding melee, the Great Garuda "offers an integral solution for water safety with additional benefits for sanitation and urban regeneration," according to one of the Dutch construction companies involved in the project.[173] Unpacking this promise, a Dutch construction industry newsletter explains that the project would improve the city by "strengthening the existing sea defenses" as well as permitting "redevelopment of the slum district on the existing dike."[174] In other words, poor people's houses will be demolished and they will be forcibly removed to the distant hinterland so that wealthy citizens and international investors can settle in the desirable seaside setting of the Great Garuda.[175]

The Dutch physical geographer Victor Coenen touts the Great Garuda seawall city for being "completely new."[176] But while it may be history's largest seawall, it is not unique. Indeed, similar projects are in the works around the world, driven by studies suggesting that, despite their mammoth costs, seawalls are more economical than the costs of flooding.[177] Off the coast of the flood-plagued Nigerian city of Lagos, for instance, an artificial barrier island dubbed Eko Atlantic is currently under construction. Described in promotional videos as the future home of a "sustainable city, clean and energy efficient with minimal carbon emission" that will house 250,000 people in luxury skyscrapers, Eko Atlantic, developers promise, will benefit Lagos by acting as a defensive dike made up of 100,000 five-ton concrete blocks.[178] Like the Great Garuda, Eko Atlantic is being built by private developers, but it differs in that the evil underbelly of the extreme city is even more apparent since the developers in question, the Chagoury brothers, were advisors to the notoriously corrupt military dictator Sani Abacha, who looted Nigeria of billions of dollars and executed the environmental activist Ken Saro-Wiwa.[179]

Despite the unsavory history of Eko Atlantic's developers, owning a plot of land on the island has become a status symbol among Nigeria's upper class, a spectacular means of demonstrating wealth for local elites who tend to move much of their money out of the country.[180] An extension of Victoria Island, Eko Atlantic is surrounded by informal settlements like Makoko, a city of rickety shanties perched on stilts above the Lagos lagoon where the chefs, chauffeurs, doormen, nannies, and security workers who service the city's elite enclaves live.[181] Both Eko Atlantic and the Great Garuda offer visions of the extreme social injustice of emerging neoliberal urban phantasmagoria in a time of climate change. As the journalist Martin Lukacs puts it, "Eko Atlantic is where you can begin to see a possible future—a vision of privatized green enclaves for the ultra-rich ringed by slums lacking water or electricity, in which a surplus population scramble for depleting resources and shelter to fend off the coming floods and storms."[182] As Lukacs notes, Eko Atlantic is protected from the poor not just by well-armed private security forces but by the insurmountable barrier of real estate prices. Eko Atlantic allows elites to profit from the global environmental crisis while entrenching conditions that Lukacs aptly describes as a form of climate apartheid.

Even if these supposed "green enclaves" delivered on their environmental promises, the flagrant inequality they reproduced would still be monstrous. But no matter how many sophisticated environmental technologies are embedded in the designs, the rampant consumerism of green enclaves generates an outsize carbon footprint that vitiates the green branding that is used to promote them. In the case of the Great Garuda, the environmental and social contradictions of green urban development are glaringly apparent. For one thing, seawalls are a dubious solution to sea level rise. In most cases, they fail to prevent flooding. During the 2011 disaster that led to the meltdown at the

Fukushima Daiichi nuclear reactor, 90 percent of the seawalls along the Japanese coast crumbled when the tsumani hit.[183] As these events suggest, seawalls ironically tend to intensify catastrophes by giving people a false sense of security, leading them to build in unsafe places.

Worse still, the Great Garuda fails to address the basic source of Jakarta's sinking: the tapping of groundwater that is causing subsidence. According to the Dutch architect JanJaap Brinkman, one of the consultants working on the Great Garuda,

> The cheapest and easiest solution is to stop the sinking. The only thing Jakarta needs to do is to stop the deep groundwater usage and the sinking will stop within five to ten years. Then you do not need a closed Jakarta Bay, you do not need a giant seawall.[184]

Jakarta is sinking because groundwater is being tapped by individuals and businesses in Jakarta at an unsustainable rate. If there were a viable alternative source of water, this groundwater use would cease. But there is no such alternative source because of the long-standing pollution of the thirteen rivers that run through the city. At present, the sole wastewater treatment plant in Jakarta, which is unsurprisingly located in the city's business district, purifies only 2 percent of the city's sewage. The rest, along with tons of plastic and other waste, is dumped straight into the city's rivers. Efforts to build a wastewater plant system in Jakarta, estimated to cost $5 billion and to be completed by 2050, have been stymied by disagreements over whether the city or the national government should shoulder the costs.[185] While this political bickering goes on, the city continues to sink at an alarming rate, and proposals for developments such as the Great Garuda have come to seem the only viable option.

But the Great Garuda comes with steep environmental costs. According to a study by the Indonesian Ministry of Marine Affairs and Fisheries, the project will seriously damage Jakarta Bay, into which the Ciliwung and the other rivers that bisect the city flow.[186] In the course of constructing the seawall, sediments will be dug up from the bottom of the bay, a process that will decrease the clarity of the water and damage the bay's already-struggling coral reefs, seagrass beds, and populations of fish, sea cucumbers, manatees, and other marine life.[187] The report also states that the construction process will result in the erosion of some of the archipelago to the north of Jakarta known as the Thousand Islands. Muhamad Karim, director of the Center for Ocean Development and Maritime Civilization, argues that the Great Garuda will destroy $376 million in economic and ecological benefits produced by the marine ecosystem in Jakarta Bay.[188] Karim is urging the Indonesian government to undertake coastal restoration by replacing protective mangrove trees, instead of building the destructive seawall.

Clinching these arguments for a less environmentally destructive approach to coastal urban protection, Taslim Arifin, a researcher at the Indonesian Ministry of Maritime Affairs and Fisheries, states that, if construction of the Great Garuda goes ahead as planned, "the water inside the seawall would become a big pond of pollution. It would become worse if the city administration does not start to tackle the pollution in the rivers."[189] Arifin argues that the seawall will trap waste from the thirteen rives that feed into Jakarta Bay, causing eutrophication that will kill marine biota as the oxygen levels in the bay fall. In response to these environmental critiques, the consulting team that drafted the master plan for the Great Garuna acknowledge that the project "does have an environmental impact [as with any large project], but that this is not at an unacceptable level."[190] The primary rationale for the acceptability of the environmental damage to be caused by the seawall is that "the quality of the habitat in Jakarta Bay is already so poor [due to pollution] that losses would be limited." This assessment directly contradicts the report produced by the Ministry of Marine Affairs and Fisheries and certainly cannot be taken as an unbiased assessment of the condition of the marine habitats that surround Jakarta.

It might be argued that the environmental destruction caused by the Great Garuda will be balanced by the greater good of protecting the citizens of Jakarta. But which citizens will be protected? For one, the project will displace thousands of squatters who reside on the current seawall, in addition to destroying the livelihoods of 24,000 traditional fisher folk who depend on marine life in and around Jakarta Bay.[191] Moreover, it is not clear that the project will significantly ameliorate the threat of flooding faced by the majority of Jakarta's citizens, since a significant portion of this derives from the waste-choked rivers that flow through the city. Indeed, the floods of 2007 were caused not by a storm surge coming in off the ocean but by the rivers and canals that traverse the city, which burst their banks following days of torrential rain.[192] Finally, it is unclear whether the Great Garuda will succeed in attracting elite investors to buy luxury condos situated next to a toxic bay filled with feces and dead fish, despite the best efforts of developers to hype the project.

Who then really stands to gain from the Great Garuda? An answer to this question was suggested by the announcement early in 2016 that work on the project would be suspended for six months pending an investigation by Indonesia's Corruption Eradication Commission of bribery allegations relating to payments received by a city council member from a developer planning to build a residential and commercial complex on the project's artificial islands.[193] These bribes were delivered as the developer sought to clear Jakarta's zoning and reclamation requirements, including city requirements that 15 percent of the development be set aside for low-cost housing.[194] As this rampant corruption underlines, coastal protection efforts such as the Great Garuda effectively constitute a new form of disaster capitalism, one in which highly remunerative real estate development overlaps with engineering megaprojects whose spectacular character is clearly designed to attract speculative capital investment.

This reengineering of coastal cities threatened by sea level rise is one of the most unsavory windfalls of climate change.[195] Undertaken through virtuous-sounding collaborations between local governments, private developers, and apparently philanthropic entities such as the Dutch consulting firm Deltares, with full support of various Dutch ministries, these megaprojects generate plans that are totally inadequate for their environmental context. As Dutch architect Joep Janssen observes, water engineers involved in the projects supported by the Dutch government in Indonesia (as is true in many other places) are of an older generation that was focused solely on defending threatened coastlines rather than taking an integrated approach to complex situations as in Jakarta, where coastal and river flooding generate a combined threat.[196] The resulting megaprojects are doomed to fail given their atomistic approach to the environment. As Janssen puts it, "When we Dutch go abroad, we export our solutions to other countries without exploring the local conditions. We fly in, go there for some weeks without investigating the context, including environmental context and history. We are not really interested in the country, we just want to sell our product."[197]

Mega-engineering projects like the Great Garuda may be legitimated through accounts of rising seas and other perils linked to climate change. But they are environmental and social calamities in their own right, pursued by consortiums of global experts and local developers who use the extreme plight of sinking cities like Jakarta to justify violent land grabs, further displacing the poor majority of urban citizens. If, according to David Harvey, "accumulation by dispossession" constitutes the leading edge of contemporary imperialism, megaprojects such as the Great Garuda are examples of what might be called "accumulation by adaptation."[198] In the name of adapting to the various forms of risk and damage being catalyzed by climate change, which are particularly grave in extreme cities like Jakarta, a new wave of highly lucrative land dispossession is being carried out. Indeed, in cities throughout the global South, the language of climate change–induced danger is used to justify evictions of squatter communities living on land that has become attractive to developers.[199] This is the lexicon of what Amita Baviskar, writing of urban struggles in India, calls "bourgeois environmentalism," which mobilizes notions of cleanliness and order, hygiene and safety, ecological conservation and the public good in order to marginalize and displace the poor.[200] This language of cleanliness, order, and the restoration of ecological integrity sanctions what amount to acts of urban ethnic cleansing.[201] Trumpeting the urban risks constituted by climate change, bourgeois environmentalism plays a key role in sustaining planetary urbanization.

The human toll of bourgeois environmentalism is all too apparent in Jakarta, where squatter communities live not simply on the seawall but also on the banks of flood-prone rivers such as the Ciliwung. Writing of the benefits of redevelopment of the banks of Ciliwung, landscape architects Christophe Girot, Paolo Burlando, and Senthil Gurusamy suggest:

> Many Asian cities, such as Seoul and Singapore, have improved their urban river landscapes considerably in recent decades. This has boosted their global image and enabled them to reap economic benefits that far surpass the investment in river rehabilitation. The Ciliwung River park could become the bearer of such a strong landscape vision for Jakarta.[202]

Turning Ciliwung into what they call the "Central Park of the East" would, according to these architects, not simply be an environmental boon but would also help promote Jakarta's efforts to market itself. At no point in their account of this transformation of the Ciliwung into a park do the architects mention the communities who live along the banks of the river, although their reference to Central Park may be taken as an ironically unaware reference to displacement since the park's construction in the mid-nineteenth century necessitated the liquidation of squatter communities that occupied the land.[203] Similarly, there appears to be no consideration given to the future of the communities that dwell on the banks of the Ciliwung.

Although plans for "restoring the ecosystem services" of the Ciliwung may help address the crises of flooding and subsidence that plague Jakarta in a more holistic manner than building a mammoth seawall, both projects dispossess poor communities while advancing elite interests. Recent news reports from Jakarta state that ruthless evictions of the poor communities inhabiting areas along the city's coastline and waterways did not cease despite the arrest of the Jakarta city council member involved in graft connected to the Great Garuda.[204] According to Joep Janssen, there is no resettlement plan for these displaced people, either by local authorities or within the Dutch master plan for the Great Garuda.[205] The story is the same in Ho Chi Minh City, Lagos, Miami, and New York.[206] Everywhere the juggernaut of planetary urbanization rolls, capital creates new sinks on land that is sinking. In the face of "accumulation by adaptation," it is fitting to remember the violent dispossession that animates planetary urbanization, a violence that the language of bourgeois environmentalism all too often obscures. This threat of dispossession is all too real to the poor, as is their defiance in the face of such threats. "I will never move, not even to a place that has a nice new television," said Madam Arimawati, a resident of one of the squatter communities that line the banks of the Ciliwung River in Jakarta, "because this is my *tanah air* (homeland)."[207]

A view of the Manhattan skyline from the Jamaica Bay
Wildlife Refuge in Queens. Photo by Jeffrey Bary, 2008.

2

Environmental Blowback

Jamaica Bay is dying, and no one knows exactly why. Most New Yorkers probably don't even know that it is sick or that it is part of their city. This in itself is a tragedy. Jamaica Bay is the largest intact tidal wetland complex in New York City. Rivalled in the region only by the New Jersey Meadowlands, Jamaica Bay's watery maze of islands, beaches, waterways, and meadowlands is one of the largest and most productive coastal ecosystems in the northeastern United States. It is home to thousands of different species, including Gossamer Winged Harvester and Painted Lady butterflies, plants like eelgrass and sea-rocket, finfish like striped bass and weakfish, visiting seals, black cherry and pitch pine trees, and hundreds of different kinds of birds who land there during their annual migration from regions as far-flung as the Arctic and South America. The forty-two square mile wetland is the biggest remaining patch of the estuarine ecosystems that dominated the New York region until relatively recently. In 1935, it was estimated that the city's already densely populated boroughs were surrounded by 29,000 acres of salt-marsh similar to those found in Jamaica Bay, an area roughly twice the size of Manhattan.[1] A century earlier, the city's tidal marshlands had been twice as big.

Such ecological riches should come as no surprise. New York City, after all, is situated in the estuary of the Hudson River. Formed when fresh water and salt water intermix, estuaries are uniquely productive ecosystems, generating remarkably fertile environments that provide nurseries to fish, waterfowl, oysters, grasses and trees, and many different mammals, including humans. The immense ribbons of undulating marshlands formed where the low-lying islands of New York met bodies of water like the Hudson River, Long Island Sound, and the Atlantic Ocean, and were fundamental to human habitation in the area thousands of years ago. Along with the area's unrivaled natural harbor, this was one of the prime reasons for European colonial settlement. Yet over the last century, New Yorkers have largely perceived the city's tidal marshlands as barren waste; as a result, they have drained, filled in, paved over, and clogged places like Jamaica Bay with pollution. Worse still, the bay's salt marsh islands have decreased in size by 63 percent since the early 1950s, and the pace of this disappearance has accelerated in recent decades. Sea level rise linked to climate change threatens to level the *coup de grâce* to this imperiled ecosystem. As a recent study of marsh degradation put it, in typically dry scientific language, "projections of future sea level rise ... suggest that under current stresses, marshes are unlikely to keep pace with accelerated rates of sea level rise in the future."[2]

New York has strong reasons to be concerned about the potential demise of Jamaica Bay. If the intrinsic value of the many wild plant and animal species for which the bay provides harbor were not sufficient reason to treasure this rich ecosystem, Jamaica Bay (and wetlands similar to it) play a vital role in diminishing the impact of storm surges, like those that devastated New York during Hurricane Sandy. When Sandy roared in off the Atlantic toward New York City, its winds pushed massive waves into the city's oceanfront communities. While the flooding of the Financial District may have received the most media attention, the storm's onslaught was worst in coastal communities in South Brooklyn, Queens, and Staten Island. Huge, twelve-foot waves stirred up by Sandy pounded the Rockaway

Peninsula, Coney Island, and neighborhoods like Midland Beach in Staten Island.[3] At the same time, New York's distinctive topography pushed the raging ocean northward into New York Harbor and simultaneously elevated water levels in the Jamaica, Sheepshead, Gravesend, and Gowanus Bays, as well as in the East and Hudson Rivers. Long Island and Brooklyn act like funnels for incoming surges, and the right-angle shaped bight or coastal curve at the intersection of the New Jersey and Staten Island coast concentrates surges even more as they steam through the Verrazzano Narrows. At the same time, surge waters were also flooding into the Long Island Sound and rushing south from there toward the city. In other words, the interconnected waterways that are threaded around and through New York City provided perfect conduits for the surge's ferocious onslaught.

These waterways were once lined with tidal wetlands that, had they not been largely demolished over the course of the last century, might have played a key role in absorbing these angry storm waters. Debate among scientists about the extent of wetlands' impact in absorbing storm surges is ongoing, but it seems clear that they can play an extremely important role and that their eradication leaves coastal cities particularly vulnerable to storm surge.[4] As the environmental historian Ted Steinberg puts it, "In trading its tidal wetlands for land development, the city had denied itself a frontline defense against storm surge that, if the sedimentary record is any guide, kept all but the most vicious flooding at bay."[5] Absent these absorbent wetlands, the city suffered massive flood damage. Sandy inundated fifty-one square miles of New York City—a staggering 17 percent of the city's landmass. In many ocean-facing communities in Brooklyn and Queens, the flooded areas were several times the size of the 100-year floodplains on Federal Emergency Management Agency (FEMA) maps. Over 88,000 buildings were in this flood zone, as was much of the city's critical infrastructure, including many hospitals and nursing homes, key power facilities, important parts of the city's transportation network, and all of the city's wastewater treatment plants. Without the significant buffers once provided by marshlands, all of the critical infra-structure was swiftly inundated.

Jamaica Bay has become a laboratory for exploring new approaches to urban ecology. These efforts seek to weave syner-gistic webs between the city and its natural environment, rather than seeing nature as an enemy the city must subdue or conquer. Writing of the bay's Gateway National Recreational Area, land-scape architect Kate Orff says, "Rather than icons of sublime rocky wilderness that affirm the country's past mythology, nature at the edges of towns and cities offers direct experience of natural processes and their reciprocal role in sustaining urban life."[6] The landscape of a place such as Jamaica Bay, all too often still seen as a wasteland on the urban margin, is thus ironically central to the sustainability of the city in the Anthropocene Age, our present geologic era when advanced capitalist nations are shaping the planetary environment. How we handle the complex interrelations of human habitation and vulnerable ecosystems in such a place will be crucial to the future of cities around the planet. "Just as Yosemite symbolized the land of promise and destiny, the muddy ecologies at Gateway have the potential to inspire a new ideology of global sustainability and collaborative stewardship for the twenty-first century," writes Orff.[7]

New York is not uniquely vulnerable as a megacity built in a coastal estuary. All around the world, deltas and coastal zones are urbanizing rapidly. More than half of the world's population currently lives in large cities located on or near rivers, deltas, and coastal zones.[8] Perhaps because of their immense natural wealth, estuaries and the deltas they contain (formed as rivers deposit sediment in their still waters) have always been popular places to live: deltas built by the Tigris and Euphrates, the Nile, and the Yangtze rivers served as the cradles of great human civi-lizations. But the history of habitation in most of the world's deltas can be traced to the rise of capitalism over the last 500 years. As European maritime colonial powers expanded during this period, they established settlements on the mouths of rivers from which commercial and military ventures could penetrate into the hinterland. Kolkatta, Mumbai, Singapore, Hong Kong,

Shanghai, and, of course, New York and New Orleans: these and many other formerly colonial cities are located in some of the most complex, rich, and fragile ecosystems on the planet. Globalization over the last several decades has only magnified the importance of such key nodes in the circulation of people, culture, commodities, and organisms. Indeed, most megacities happen to be port cities, a fact that has been almost totally ignored in the literature on the global city.[9] As a consequence, most of the world's megacities are located in coastal zones, often on deltas and in agglomerations that concentrate truly astonishing numbers of people. Home to close to half a billion people around the globe, these urban coastal cultures share significant traits, including unparalleled cultural cosmopolitanism and exceptional vulnerability to climate change.

As Hurricane Sandy laid bare, storm surges linked to increasingly intense hurricanes and typhoons are of mounting concern to coastal megacities around the world. Even though many of these cities are relatively young, they were all built during the 2,000-year-long period of relative environmental stability that came to a close over the last century. Yet storm surges and the sea level rise that dramatically worsens their impact are not the only threats that these cities face. Inhabitants of delta cities are also living on land that is sinking while the oceans around them rise. This sinking is caused by a variety of factors, including the soil becoming compacted through the removal of water, gas, and oil from the underlying sediments.[10] Equally important are the dams and other diversions in the rivers that trap sediments, which would otherwise replenish the deltas. And, compounding the impact of the sinking of deltas is the erosion of coastal wetlands that form a key shield for cities. In some regions, other factors are at play, but the outcome is similar; much of the Eastern Seaboard of the United States, for example, including cities from Boston to Charleston, is sinking as land pushed up by the weight of ice sheets during the last ice age gradually subsides.[11] As a result of these various changes, 85 percent of the world's deltas suffered severe flooding over the last decade, resulting in the temporary submergence of a shocking 260,000 square kilometers of land globally.[12] And the situation is only going to get worse. Conservative estimates suggest that the flooding will increase by 50 percent in deltas under projected rates of sea level rise over the course of this century. Moreover, this vulnerability could escalate significantly if the capture of sediments upstream persists or accelerates, as it seems likely to do given the current global spate of dam building on rivers such as the Amazon, the Ganges, and the Mekong. In sum, coastal cities around the world face a perfect storm as the land they are built upon sinks, the oceans rise, and increasingly violent storms drive walls of water down upon their vulnerable citizens.

Given that cities have been beset by environmental disasters with increasing frequency, one might expect debates about the future of the city to project a lively awareness of how they are inextricably interwoven with the natural world. One might also expect environmentalists to place cities at the center of their efforts to build ecologically sustainable cultures. But most environmental discussions today neglect or entirely ignore the urban environment, focusing instead on "global" problems such as climate change, deforestation, and desertification. The problem is not simply one of scale: environmental campaigns around issues like the destruction of biodiversity in tropical "hotspots" are simply the latest episode in a long colonial history of regulating nature to better secure profits for the imperial metropoles.[13] This long history continues today: climate negotiations have been characterized by repeated efforts by the world's developed nations to weasel out of their collective responsibility for carbon emissions.[14] Compounding these injustices, few environmental historians fully acknowledge the role of working-class people and communities of color in producing urban nature—or how they are impacted by it[15]—while the field of urban studies gives short shrift to the environmental foundations on which the urbanization process depends.[16]

These oversights have dramatic impacts today. Since the nineteenth century, cities have become home to increasingly massive feats of engineering—sewer systems, public parks, electric grids—that helped engender the forms of social life that city residents largely take for granted.[17] When you drink a glass of water, eat a banana, or ride in an elevator in a city, you are immersing yourself in this "second nature," which is fabricated by complex networks of infrastructure and exchange, stretching from your immediate surroundings to the furthest corners of the globe. This makes cities the key sites where nature is metabolized—where natural resources are consumed and waste is produced. And yet most of the politicians and international organizations attempting to address the impending climate emergency continue to view the planet as a total system to be engineered and optimized.[18] Such views completely gloss over the complex ways that humans interact with our surroundings, either natural or built up. Some scientists fantasize about geoengineering projects like pumping metallic microparticles into the stratosphere in order to deflect solar radiation, but such schemes remain largely impractical and tend to generate legitimate public alarm.[19] By contrast, how cities are structured already has a dramatic impact on the global environment.

This chapter discusses the production of urban nature in two key contemporary sites: the threatened wetlands of New York's Jamaica Bay and the retreating coastal marshes that surround New Orleans. Each of these cities is strategically situated as a key node in the global flow of commodities, people, and capital, which helps to sustain their power in the age of the global city. Each city has also faced significant environmental challenges in the past. In response, mighty feats of engineering were constructed that often enriched the cities and some of their citizens. But in shaping the surrounding natural world to their ends, and in subjecting the environment to the relentless dictates of growth, dominant interests in these powerful cities often laid the groundwork for the dramatic environmental contradictions that would come back to haunt them and their fellow citizens, a phenomenon which I call "environmental blowback." Natural disasters like Hurricanes Katrina and Sandy that battered these cities are often seen as unexpected cataclysms, although a general awareness does seem to exist today about how our efforts to control nature can have side effects. It's true that specific cataclysms can't always be predicted in an increasingly risk-filled world. But it's also clear that these natural disasters were often the product of a knowing and willful negligence on the part of urban elites, who are propelled by the need to accumulate profits irrespective of the social impact.[20] Their callous calculus has seen them choosing short-term profits over the future of their cities and the lives of their fellow citizens.

Jamaica Bay: Urban Wasteland

Marshlands are some of the most productive ecosystems on the planet, the muddy coastal equivalent of a tropical rainforest. They provide habitat for myriad waterfowl and fish species, filter nitrogen and phosphorus from the water, and (not incidentally in this age of climate change) store carbon and protect against storm surges. Hurricane Sandy made this latter feature of Jamaica Bay particularly apparent, pushing a wall of water in through the inlet at the bay's western entrance to flood back bay communities like Bergen Beach and Canarsie. These communities, once protected by marshes, were highly vulnerable to the storm surge even though none of them were supposed to be at risk of inundation according to FEMA flood maps. City authorities had been made aware of the inexorable disappearance of the marshlands by the local environmental group Jamaica Bay Ecowatchers in the mid-1990s, which fought to draw attention to the problem in the face of an unresponsive federal government.[21] In subsequent years, the city's Department of Environmental Protection spent $20 million to restore marsh islands bearing evocative names like Big Egg, Rulers Bar, and Black Wall.[22] Still, the remorseless action of the waves continues their erosion. Oyster beds, which also slow erosion and surges, were built, but the oyster larvae did not survive and the beds died after five or six years. Most recently, the city installed a series of artificial floating wetlands to protect a quarter-mile ribbon of marshland along the bay side of the Rockaways peninsula.[23] These experimental wave attenuators cost $500,000, a steep price to protect such a small patch of land.

The story of Jamaica Bay's disappearing marshes seems at first glance to be a saga of the inexorable power of the tides and a warning about the limits of humanity's efforts to control nature. Yet the crisis of Jamaica Bay is not simply a cautionary tale about the fragility of the city's margins. In fact, the estuary's marshlands have been the target of a century-long campaign of feckless development and real estate speculation—in other words, extirpation—by urban elites.

Long ago, Native American communities and some early European settlers found rich hunting grounds for waterfowl and shellfish in the chain of marshlands threaded through the New York region like a silver necklace. But Europeans had long associated swamps with foul odors that threatened to contaminate both the bodies and the souls of those exposed.[24] The protagonist of John Bunyan's seventeenth century allegory *Pilgrim's Progress* reaches the nadir of his earthly tribulations in the Slough of Despond, a bog in which sinners are mired in the "scum and filth" of their own sinful conditions. These associations were augmented in the following centuries by fears of the degenerative impact of swamps on human health. During the nineteenth century, the aversion of New Yorkers to the marshes that surrounded the city was largely based on "hygienist" fears of the disease-carrying miasmas that were thought to emanate from such places. By the 1890s, medical research had decisively linked swamp-dwelling mosquitos to malaria transmission.[25] As a vector for diseases like malaria and yellow fever, the mosquito had an outsize but unacknowledged impact on European empire-building efforts in the Americas.[26] Wealthy property owners joined ranks behind Henry Clay Weeks, sanitary inspector for the New York's Department of Health, to launch a "war on mosquitos" along the Gold Coast of Long Island, where many of the city's tycoons had their summer homes.[27] Their crusade sought to destroy the region's swamplands, thereby denying the "winged pests" a breeding ground, but experiments in the Newark Meadows showed that digging drainage ditches often sufficed to extirpate significant numbers of mosquitoes. Jamaica Bay became the center of a massive ditch-digging campaign, with over 1.7 million feet of trenches cut through the boggy landscape.[28] In short order, similar techniques were extended to the marshland throughout the rest of the city; ultimately, 30,000 acres of freshwater and saltwater marsh were drained across the city's five boroughs.

Once the mosquitos had been eradicated, areas such as Jamaica Bay seemed primed to enter the city's booming real estate market. In the spring of 1910, *The New York Times* published a lengthy article with the breathless title, "Jamaica Bay To Be a Great World Harbor."[29] "Modern engineering," the article proclaimed, "is about to undertake another of its gigantic tasks. Work is soon to be begun which will ultimately lead to the conversion of the shallows and marshlands of Jamaica Bay into a sheltered harbor. That vast tract, half land and half water, just back of Rockaway Beach, which is currently given over exclusively to the oysterman and the holiday fisherman, is to be dredged into a harbor where a great fleet of future Mauretanias may comfortably dock." The reverent awe with which engineering was regarded in the United States at this time permeates the *Times* article, which describes plans to create a harbor with hundreds of miles of wharves to add to Manhattan's dwindling supply of waterfront. Behind this awe lay a fierce commitment to the ideology of improvement, or what is now known as development. The marshland of Jamaica Bay is described as a "great stretch of territory now lying waste and useless," a space whose exclusive use by the "oysterman and holiday fisherman" is clearly perceived as the squandering of valuable waterfront. For members of the Jamaica Bay Improvement Society, to leave such resources lying fallow would not simply be a lost opportunity for windfall economic profits.[30] It would also threaten New York's place in the competitive global capitalist order.

The Jamaica Bay harbor plan sought to solidify the city's preeminence in the global shipping routes of the early twentieth century by creating not just new harbor facilities, where luxurious ocean liners such as the Mauretania—the largest and fastest ship in the world at the time—would dock, but also by knitting New York's new harbor into a series of continent- and even world-straddling commercial networks. Jamaica Bay, the *Times* article proclaims, would become the "terminal of the $101,000,000 barge canal which is now being dug across the state to link up the Hudson River to the great lakes." The replacement of the Erie Canal by the New York State Barge Canal, completed in 1918, was part of an attempt by shipping interests based in the city to fight off the growing use of railways for freight transportation. It was a project doomed to failure from the moment the canal opened: the shift from water to rail and, ultimately, road transportation was already well underway. Yet, drafted as part of an apparent plan to forestall this displacement of water-based transportation, the World Harbor project imagined a glorious future for Jamaica Bay, one that would also confer benefits to New York's booming real estate interests. Thus, the marshland behind the bulkhead, which would be constructed around the bay to separate land and water, was to be filled in with "sand scooped up from the deepened channels and inlets." By this means, "a great stretch of territory now lying waste and useless will become valuable building sites." A new frontier would thus be created on former wastelands for real estate–based speculation.

This growth was not just an economic imperative; it was also a moral obligation. More than any other nation, the United States could be said to be the republic of growth. The ideology of improvement was key to colonial claims on territory since the earliest days of European settlement. From John Locke's *Second Treatise of Government* (which held that title to land was earned through labor upon and "improvement" of that land, squeezing out Native Americans in the scramble for the "uncultivated waste of America"[31]) to George Washington's declaration that the nation's westward expansion realized the plans of "Providence for the display of human greatness and felicity"[32]—the United States was as much an empire of development as it was an "empire for liberty." Indeed, the two were inextricably linked in the minds of the nation's founders, who believed that nations resembled natural organisms and were consequently characterized by a natural life cycle of birth, growth, maturation, and decay.[33] In order to retain the nation's youth and vigor, to fore-stall decay and degeneration, the citizenry was to be kept active, industrious, and honest by colonizing and developing new land, thereby upholding the republic's democratic institutions. In the process, the republic would bring the moral benefits of "civiliza-tion" to the Native Americans who already inhabited—but did not develop—the land.

With the supposed closure of the western frontier in 1890, this drive to expand and develop took on hemispheric and even global dimensions, making nodal points of American power such as the New York harbor even more key. Speaking before Congress a decade before the Jamaica Bay harbor was proposed, leading Progressive Senator Albert Beveridge sought to justify the increas-ingly bloody suppression of the independence movement in the Philippines by arguing that the "English-speaking and Teutonic peoples" had been endowed with the "spirit of progress" in order to "overwhelm the forces of reaction throughout the earth" and to "administer government among savage and senile peoples."[34] For Progressives such as Beveridge and Gifford Pinchot, Teddy Roosevelt's chief forester, the state's claim to legitimacy lay in its efficient management and conservation of resources, a task to be carried out by scientifically educated elites.[35] Though it was presented as an innate characteristic of Anglo elites, this racial-ized rhetoric of technological mastery developed as a response to environmental crises. In the United States, Progressive conserva-tion laws such as the Forest Services Organic Administration Act of 1897 owed a great deal to George Perkins Marsh's *Man and Nature* (1846), which described the nation's westward develop-ment as a bout of unrestrained destruction, the product of igno-rance and the lack of a strong restraining state.[36] Development and careful control of nature, progressives argued, went hand in hand. This helps explain why the Jamaica Bay World Harbor project was seen as combatting waste: not only were the marsh-lands traditionally seen as barren, but the failure to employ such land productively was regarded as an example of bad manage-ment of the environment. It is deeply ironic that these principles of wise management and conservation of natural resources were being articulated in tandem with plans to foster a culture of luxury living that the cultural theorist Thorstein Veblen famously called "conspicuous consumption."[37]

Proponents of the Jamaica Bay World Harbor scheme fretted that the bay's ever-changing conditions would make the project unsustainable. The laudatory *Times* article mentions that army engineers worried that Rockaway Inlet would not remain open after being dredged as a result of the "suction of the tides and the pounding of the surf," which made the sandy bottom shift about "in a most treacherous manner." But in the end, it was not the protean nature of the coastal environment that led to the project's demise. When former Supreme Court Justice Augustus Van Wyck alluded in an article of 1920 to "some unseen force that is at work to kill" the Jamaica Bay harbor scheme, he was talking about political rather than natural forces. As the project languished for a decade, despite the federal government's offer of matching funds, newspapers began speaking in menacing terms of foreign interests seeking to gain control of the city's port facilities during the era of World War I. But the obscure power undoing the development scheme, Van Wyck argued, was really "a selfish combination of New Jersey with the railroads terminating there to take trade from the City of New York and divert it to New Jersey."[38] Capitalism, it seemed, did not simply produce interimperial competition between rival nation-states (as Lenin had argued) but also stoked antagonism between neighboring states and cities in the United States. Despite strong opposition from figures like Van Wyck and New York Mayor John Francis Hylan, plans for the establishment of a joint New Jersey–New York port authority went forward, laying the foundation for the creation of a port on 500 acres of reclaimed marsh and swamp forest in Newark.[39] Van Wyck's warning that Port Newark Terminal would kill the Jamaica Bay harbor scheme was well founded. Indeed, Port Newark ultimately did just that. It took another forty years and the invention of the shipping container, but the reclamation of the Jersey Meadows and the creation of Port Newark ultimately led to the dismantling of the port of New York.[40]

But by this time, Jamaica Bay had run into another problem. One year after the collapse of the World Harbor scheme, the bay's remarkably productive oyster beds—which supplied 300,000 bushels to New York fish markets every year, one third of the city's entire supply of shellfish—were closed by the city's health department.[41] "Jamaica Bay, Foul With Sewage, Closed To Oyster Beds," the headline read.[42] By the early 1920s, the once pristine waters of the bay had become the terminal point of forty trunk sewers, which disgorged a significant percentage of the raw sewage from Queens and Brooklyn directly into the bay. Levels of contamination had grown so bad that the president of the New York Board of Health, Dr. Royal Copeland, alluded to "several known typhoid carriers near the confines of the bay," a threat whose gravity he underlined by referring to "Typhoid" Mary, the asymptomatic Irish cook whose infection of an uncertain number of people had sparked a panic among wealthy New York families highly dependent on immigrant labor.[43] The reference was calculated: diseases linked to bodily excretions, like typhoid and cholera, provoked disgust among US elites, who feared the spread of contagion from the unwashed immigrant masses.[44] In particular, elites associated these diseases with particular urban sites, like slum tenements in the Lower East Side, where people of all races and classes were thought to mingle indiscriminately, spreading contagion among themselves and, ultimately, to the wealthy families who employed them.[45] To suggest, as Dr. Copeland did in 1921, that the sewage-filled waters of Jamaica Bay might contain typhoid was to dramatically amplify these fears of contagion, placing a moral and physical quarantine around the entire area—and laying to rest dreams of glamorous ocean liners docking in the pestilential site.

Jamaica Bay had long served as the bowels of the city. Although it was located on the margins of New York, as the burial ground for much of the city's industrial effluvia, the bay was surprisingly central to the developing metabolism of the city. Sites such as Barren Island near the bay's inlet provided a dumping ground, for instance, for waste from the construction of Central Park.[46] Jamaica Bay, a place deemed of little aesthetic and social value, unlovely and unloved, could be said to be the antithesis of Central Park. Central Park was a spectacular vision of urban capitalism, an elaborate artifice in which nature was presented in various guises, including the picturesque pastoral space of Sheep Meadow, the semi-wild landscape of the Ramble, and the neoclassical boulevards, fountains, and lakes of the Mall, the Promenade, and Bethesda Terrace.[47] The construction of these landscapes involved 20,000 workers, who moved 3 million cubic yards of soil, planted 270,000 trees and shrubs, built a new reservoir linked to the city's upstate water supply, and dismantled a number of squatter communities who lived on the land that became the park. Yet so successful was the artifice of the "Greensward Plan" laid out by the park's architects, Frederick Law Olmsted and Calvert Vaux, that the massive amount of labor and planning that went into the park's construction was rendered invisible to many observers, who felt that the designers had simply preserved pieces of Manhattan's "first nature." The park helped generate an image of a depopulated wilderness, located in the heart of the nation's greatest metropolis, at a moment when industrialization was radically transforming the settler colonial agricultural order, which had remade the natural world of precolonial America. The simulacrum of a wilderness in the heart of the city, Central Park cemented the idea that nature was somehow the negative image of, and therefore external to, the city and to the processes of capital accumulation that generated urbanization.[48]

The year after the opening of Central Park, two horse-rendering factories were opened on Barren Island near the mouth of Jamaica Bay, an area that became known as Dead Horse Bay, to turn the carcasses of the hundreds of thousands of horses that worked and died in Manhattan into industrial oil and fertilizer.[49] A community of scavengers grew up on Barren Island, composed mostly of Irish immigrants but also of African Americans, who subsisted by working in the island's five carcass and garbage-boiling factories and by picking through the urban waste that was dumped on the island from the rest of the city. These scavenging communities were engaged in exactly the same kinds of urban recycling as the razed squatter communities that had occupied the land that became Central Park. Their work was crucial to the city's metabolism of nature. Jamaica Bay was the final resting place for the city's detritus, including the animal and human workers whose labor allowed the city to grow and prosper, ultimately creating the frictionless spectacle of pristine nature embodied in Central Park.[50]

The problem of waste is a dramatic instance of environmental blowback. Before the large-scale waves of urbanization in the capitalist cultures of Europe and North America, human and animal excrement was not seen as waste but was recycled onto the crops grown by farmers. With the growth of cities, however, a dramatic shift took place that Marx called the *metabolic rift*: excrement that was once turned into fertilizer for agriculture now became simply pollution, waste that had to be disposed of in order to maintain sanitary levels of urban life.[51] At the time that Marx analyzed this rift, the split between cities and the surrounding countryside had produced a crisis of what was called "soil exhaustion" or depleted fertility throughout Europe. In the search for sources of agricultural nutrients, farmers turned to digging up bones in the battlefields of the Napoleonic era, and imperial powers like Britain sought to monopolize Peruvian guano supplies.[52] The invention of synthetic fertilizer from natural gas ended this crisis of nutrient supply. But it did not solve the problem of environmental blowback: the more the city and the capitalist economy developed, the more unusable waste it generated. Some of the most important infrastructures of the modern city were developed to deal with this problem by transporting human waste away from cities, into surrounding bodies of water.[53] This move seemed to solve the problem, but it did so only for a time. Industrial agriculture has seriously disrupted the nitrogen and phosphorus cycles, transferring immense quantities of these two elements from the earth and air onto crops in the form of synthetic fertilizer, food which is then consumed by city dwellers and excreted into nearby bodies of water in a linear rather than circular process that is ultimately unsustainable.[54]

In the case of New York, the sanitary infrastructures of modernity were slow in coming. Despite the construction of the Croton Aqueduct, which brought fresh water supplies to all New Yorkers in the 1830s and 1840s, a citywide sewage system to carry human waste away from homes was not constructed until the late nineteenth century.[55] Before then, sewage infrastructure reflected the class fragmentation of the city, meaning that poor neighborhoods were in general more polluted by human and animal excrement than rich ones. The eventual construction of a citywide sewage system alleviated this unevenness, but did so only by fouling the city's waterways with excrement. For city managers, the solution to the contamination of Jamaica Bay, where water pollution was particularly bad, was the application of new hygienic technologies, which would in turn facilitate further rounds of marsh-leveling development around the bay's periphery. When, in 1927, a significant number of the city's beaches were closed because their waters contained dangerously high counts of colon bacilli, the city's commissioner of health recommended that "every gallon of sewage" should be treated and that the city should set aside the land necessary to build state-of-the-art wastewater treatment plants.[56] Over the course of the next twenty years, four sewage treatment plants were built on Jamaica Bay, the highest concentration of such plants on any body of water in the city, disgorging a total of 300 million gallons of nitrogen-laden effluent into the bay every day. High levels of nitrogen produced by sewage tend to stimulate growth of algae, which, once they die, deplete oxygen levels, in a process known as eutrophication. Over time, eutrophication has a devastating impact on marine biodiversity, leading ultimately to the death of most marine life. Such algal blooms have been a continuing source of concern in Jamaica Bay.

Worsening these problems, the city's system of 6,200 miles of sewers mix household waste with rainwater, treating both together in plants like those in Jamaica Bay. Anytime it rains more than three quarters of an inch in New York, the city's waste treatment plants are quickly overwhelmed, and sewer pipes carry 500 million gallons of raw sewage directly into the

bodies of water on which the plants are located, leading to notorious images of syringes and human waste washing up on New
York beaches. These images led to a ban on dumping sewage
sludge in the ocean following a particularly notorious episode in
1988.[57] Unfortunately it was the city's system of combined
sewers rather than sea-dumping of sewage sludge that was
responsible for this pollution. To deal with this problem, the city
would need to build large reservoirs where storm waters could
be stored and then slowly discharged, but municipal authorities
have thus far been unwilling to shoulder the costs of such a
measure.[58] Many of the city's sewage plants are on rivers, where
tidal action helps to carry the sewage out to sea. But tidal flows
have decreased significantly in Jamaica Bay, leaving much of the
sewage trapped in the bay. Water quality in Jamaica Bay deterio-
rated gradually following the construction of the four waste
treatment plants on the bay. Almost 40,000 pounds of nitrogen
pour into the bay each day, making it one of the most nitrogen-
polluted water bodies in the world.[59] In 2004, local activists
discovered that the city was clandestinely dumping sewage
sludge in Jamaica Bay, causing a sharp increase in levels of
eutrophication.[60] A Clean Water Act lawsuit filed by activists in
2009 resulted in an agreement with the Bloomberg administration to cease such dumping and to spend over $100 million on
upgrades to the four sewage treatment plants. Although
improvements have diminished nitrogen levels in the bay's
waters, according to biologists it is still unclear exactly how the
bay will respond to decreasing nitrogen levels.[61] But the problem of combined sewer outflows—into Jamaica Bay and other
bodies of water in the region—has still not been addressed.

As the bay was transformed into one of the city's major dumping grounds for waste, fresh plans for urban growth in Jamaica
Bay and other outlying areas of the city were laid out and quickly
realized. In 1929, the Regional Plan Association published its
first Master Plan, which sought to provide a typical Progressive
Era antidote to the dysfunctions of laissez-faire urban growth.
Driven by the fear that New York would be left behind by
competitor cities, the master plan advocated distributing urban

growth throughout the New Jersey, New York, and Connecticut region, linking cities like Newark, New York, and New Haven with a coordinated system of road and rail transportation. The plan also called for a regional park system to deal with fast-dwindling open space.[62] But the park system scarcely mitigated the unbridled growth, irrational suburban sprawl, and environmental destruction that the plan helped fuel.[63] Destruction of what was still seen as wasteland was key to the Regional Plan Association's development goals: indeed, the 1929 plan called for "vast schemes of reclamation" in the region's marshlands.[64] In the following decades, this plan for regional development was largely realized, resulting in the destruction of thousands of acres of tidal wetlands. Such development placed human habitation in increasing proximity to a sea whose stability and placidity people had come to take for granted, an assumption evident in the destruction of the wetlands that once acted as a buffer against the rising sea.[65]

Despite the failure of the Jamaica Bay World Harbor scheme, boosters refused to abandon the dream of a global port facility on the bay. In the late 1920s, six million cubic yards of sand were pumped from the bottom of the bay onto Barren Island, connecting it to Brooklyn and raising the level of the island sixteen feet above the high-tide mark. Floyd Bennett Field, a state-of-the-art airport within New York City limits, was dedicated in 1931. Although many famous aviators used the airport, Mayor La Guardia could not convince major airlines to relocate from Newark to Jamaica Bay, and within a couple of years, the city began building a new facility, eventually to be named LaGuardia Airport, on the northern edge of Queens. At the same time, city authorities began exploring the creation of another new airport in the marshlands on the eastern fringe of Jamaica Bay. In 1941, the LaGuardia administration purchased 4,500 acres of marshland surrounding what was then the Idlewild golf course. Repeating the process that led to the transformation of Barren Island, huge intake tubes sucked sand out of Jamaica Bay and dumped it into the marsh to form the land on which the future John F. Kennedy International Airport would be built. The impact on the bay was dramatic: by 1971, Jamaica Bay's vast expanse of 16,000 acres of marshland had shrunk to 4,000 acres.[66] A wetland ecosystem the size of Manhattan had been destroyed, although the process was described in Orwellian terms as land "reclamation."

The "improvement" of Jamaica Bay was met with increasing resistance, with efforts to protect the fragile ecosystems of Jamaica Bay dating back to the mid-twentieth century. Surprisingly, Robert Moses, the much-vilified master builder who implemented so many of the environmentally destructive plans of the Regional Plan Association, was a protagonist in efforts to conserve the bay. When New York City Sanitation Commissioner William Carey revived plans for a deepwater port in Jamaica Bay during the 1930s, a development whose evil twin was to be a garbage incinerator and ash dump to replace the recently closed dump on Rikers Island, Moses lobbied hard against the plan, arguing for a "place within the limits of the city where the strain of our city life can be relieved . . . where the old may rest and the young can play."[67] Under pressure from Moses, jurisdiction over the bay was transferred from the Department of Docks to the city Parks Department, and a series of bird feeding and nesting areas were designated as part of a plan to open the park to swimming, fishing, and other outdoor activities. Jamaica Bay was thus not to be preserved in its raw state, but rather transformed into a space where urbanites could find a modicum of relief from the social stresses generated by a metropolis bent on breakneck, unlimited growth, and where a culture of virile athleticism (perceived as integral to national character) could be cultivated. Recreation zones such as those created by Moses in Jamaica Bay were conceived as the necessary complement to the spaces of dutiful toil that dominated the modern city.[68]

Jamaica Bay was also integrated into the vast network of roads that Moses was so instrumental in constructing. Moses's "Marginal Boulevard," later renamed the Belt Parkway, was touted as the "greatest municipal highway venture ever attempted."[69] Ringing the coastal fringe of Brooklyn and circling around Jamaica Bay, the Belt Parkway opened Long Island up to urbanites with cars, vastly expanding the suburban expansion of New York. As with so many of Moses's other highway projects, it also cut off the waterfront and concentrated massive amounts of polluting cars on the edge of fragile marshland. Armed with both federal housing and highway funds, Moses then pushed public housing projects out to the farthest reaches of the city, to decrepit oceanfront communities in Coney Island and Far Rockaways. In these communities, as in the former dockside communities that lined the New York harbor, land was cheap or could be seized by the city using powers of eminent domain, a legal arrangement that allowed the government to take over private property for public use. What resulted was the "Rockaways Improvement Plan," a Le Corbusier–inspired city of the future, composed of tall apartment blocks with no organic links to the surrounding community or the rest of the city.[70] The Arverne and Edgemere developments in the Rockaways, for example, consisted of twenty-four buildings, each seven to nine stories tall. Although only a tiny fraction of the population of Queens lives in the Far Rockaways, under Moses's tenure it became home to more than half the borough's public housing. Conveniently separated from the rest of the city by Jamaica Bay, the projects in Far Rockaways were increasingly used to warehouse people on public assistance. Although Moses's vicelike grip on power in New York loosened by the 1960s, the city continued to build public housing in the Rockaways. The projects that lined the seven-mile-long peninsula were soon also interspersed with high-rise nursing homes and facilities for recently deinstitutionalized mental patients. These public housing projects would be some of the areas worst hit when Hurricane Sandy bore down on the city.

By the early 1970s, Jamaica Bay was at an environmental crossroads. The Port Authority, which controlled Kennedy Airport, was proposing to deal with congestion at the country's busiest international airport by adding runways. This entailed more dredging and filling of the bay. At the same time, reacting to calls for help after two strong storms that were accompanied by high winds and high tides caused flooding around the periphery of Jamaica Bay, the Army Corps of Engineers proposed the building of a hurricane barrier across Rockaway Inlet. The barrier and accompanying dikes and seawalls would have cost an estimated $65 million, with a significant portion of the tab to be picked up by the city.[71] A national study group rejected both of these proposals on environmental grounds, arguing that the storm barrier would interfere seriously with the tidal flows necessary to maintain the health of the bay, despite the Army Corps' assurances to the contrary. In addition, the group opined that the barrier was unnecessary since hurricanes are "rather rare in the New York area."[72] At the forefront of the study group report was the need for recreational space for the people of New York. Noting that over 1 million people were using Coney Island for bathing on hot summer days at that time, a member of the study group, testifying before Congress about the potential designation of the area as a national park, argued that "a person [at Coney Island] has only about three times as much room as they used to have on slave ships in the seventeenth and eighteenth centuries."[73] Plans to create what came to be called Gateway National Recreation Area went forward, despite the National Park Service's lack of "awareness of the needs of central city people for recreational facilities."[74]

Jamaica Bay is the largest segment of Gateway National Recreation Area, a chain of geographically discontinuous beaches, marshes, piers, and disused urban infrastructure that spans the New York City harbor from northern New Jersey to western Long Island. Although Gateway is managed by the National Park Service, it has little in common with most of the other parks in North America. Indeed, Gateway and Jamaica Bay might be seen as the antithesis of the sites of rugged natural beauty made famous by photographers of the West such as Ansel Adams. Jamaica Bay has none of the sublime qualities of iconic wilderness sites such as Cathedral Rock in Arizona's Coconino National Forest or Yosemite Valley's El Capitan, places that have become defining icons of US national identity.[75] Indeed, Gateway's designation as a "recreation area" underlines its place far down the pecking order of spaces that the Park Service is charged with protecting, a site that is culturally and legally constructed as far less natural, and consequently less valuable in terms of national aesthetic heritage, than a "wild" river or a "scenic" trail.[76] Yet the implied culture–nature binary in these designations is deceptive. The great majority of national parks in North America were founded on mixed motives that included elite desires to maintain these sites as sport hunting grounds for well-heeled residents of the cities of the Atlantic seaboard and Europe, as well as national pride in the country's picturesque vistas. In addition, during the period in the mid- to late-nineteenth century when famous parks such as Yosemite were established, the conservation movement viewed most parks not as sacrosanct preserves, but as sites for scientific management of "natural resources."[77] Parks have thus always been subject to intense commodification, whether by the tourism industry or by resource extraction interests such as forestry, mining, and ranching.[78] The notion that these places constitute "wilderness" hinges on conveniently forgetting that Native Americans inhabited these lands and on city people's distaste for the densely populated places where they spend their lives. But Gateway never seemed "wild" enough.[79] Just as the Jamaica Bay Environmental Study Group had predicted, the National Park Service failed to invest in adequate transportation service to the park.[80] Today, Gateway remains relatively inaccessible, unacknowledged and unvisited by most New Yorkers.

Meanwhile, Jamaica Bay's wetlands continued to decline. In the mid-1990s, local activists informed National Park Service officials that the marsh islands of the bay were disappearing at an increasing rate.[81] Although activist claims were ignored initially, when they backed up their arguments by submitting historical photographs of the bay and comparing them to contemporary satellite images, the Park Service assembled a task force that eventually validated their claims. It was discovered that the development of the bay, and above all its treatment as a sink for the toxic byproducts of urbanization, had helped catalyze an alarming loss of the salt marsh islands that remained in Jamaica Bay. Comparison of aerial photographs of salt marsh islands in the bay showed a loss of 12 percent in land area from 1959 to 1998, but subsequent measurements showed a rate of decline so precipitous that the Jamaica Bay Watershed Protection Plan Advisory Committee, established in 2005, predicted that the bay's marshes were likely to disappear within a decade or so.[82] What explained this lightning decline? To start with, all the sand dredged out of the bay and pumped into the wetlands increased the average depth of the bay from 3,000 to 6,000 feet.[83] This means that it takes three times as long for tides to flush out the toxins discharged into the bay, worsening eutrophication and marsh erosion. But pollution of the bay waters was not the only problem generated by reclamation. As the marshland was filled in, tributary streams flowing into Jamaica Bay were covered over by roads, housing, and factories. This not only blocked significant infusions of fresh water—treated water from the four sewage plants is essentially the only source of water flowing into the bay—but also sediment flows that might have been carried by such streams. With no sediment flowing into the bay, there was no source to replenish the sand that was pumped out of the bay for reclamation projects such as airports, and no means to fill in the channels that had been dredged through the bay over the decades for shipping.[84]

Restoration work on the marsh islands began in the early 2000s, with sediment scooped up off the bay's floor and sprayed first onto Big Egg Marsh, resulting in the recreation of 2 acres of marshland, followed a decade later by work on two other islands, Elders West and Elders East, an area totaling 60 acres.[85] As a result of these efforts, marsh loss has been slowed to 15–20 acres annually.

But the Jamaica Bay ecosystem will never be restored to pristine condition: it's been transformed to the point where architects and biologists talk about it as a "sewershed" rather than a watershed. So the idea of marshland restoration is based on a kind of fantasy of returning to a wilderness condition, one in which nature was not impacted by human activity.[86] In addition, notwithstanding the increasing awareness of Jamaica Bay's fragile condition, and the millions of dollars being spent on marsh restoration, the bay continues to face escalating threats. In 2011, for example, the Regional Plan Association, which had resisted plans for the expansion of Kennedy Airport in the 1970s, proposed building one or more additional runways at JFK on landfill built into the bay, which the association characterized as a "dead zone" in their report.[87] It might have been more apt to call the area near JFK a kill zone, since airport authorities employed first a falconry program and ultimately marksmen to kill thousands of laughing gulls each year to try to stave off bird-aircraft collisions, an ironic result of the successful restoration of Jamaica Bay to a state that has attracted tens of thousands of migratory birds.[88] Indeed, one of the huge contradictions of marsh island restoration efforts is that no such endeavors can take place within one mile of Kennedy Airport because of the danger that such restoration will attract larger bird colonies, further imperiling aircraft.

Flooding in communities around Jamaica Bay has focused attention on whether ecological restoration of the bay can be an integral feature of the flood protection that coastal communities so desperately need. Implicit in this question is the thorny issue of whether the bay's natural systems and human communities can be adapted to avoid calamitous flooding, or whether grand works of engineering should be attempted to stop waters surging into the bay in the first place. In other words, should we attempt to control nature or adapt to it? The public authority that has largely set the terms of this debate, the Army Corps of Engineers, has historically evinced an overweening desire to dominate nature, one that has repeatedly failed to anticipate the environmental blowback caused by its interventions in natural systems. That hubristic approach has begun to shift in recent years. In the wake of Hurricane Sandy, USACE published a $19.5 million study entitled *North Atlantic Coast Comprehensive Study Report* that shifted the organization's philosophy from "flood control" to "coastal risk management."[89] But if they've muted the macho language of dominating nature in recent official pronouncements, the appeal of muscular engineering projects has not diminished. In Jamaica Bay, USACE is considering two projects to cope with the threat of future storm surges: a series of levees, grassy berms, and sea walls that would ring the interior perimeter of the bay, or a giant hurricane barrier that would span the Rockaway Inlet.[90] The latter project is a revival of the proposal that Congress rejected in 1964, although the price tag has now gone up to somewhere between $2–4 billion, and the location of the gate has moved further west than originally proposed, stretching from Breezy Point in the Rockaways to Manhattan Beach in order to protect significant sections of Brooklyn. This barrier would have to tie into upland high ground, which would entail the building of a giant sea wall in the Rockaways.[91] Stretching for over a mile across the inlet, the barrier would be open most of the time but would close when a hurricane approached in order to fend off the storm surge. It is a solution similar to the Thames Barrier that protects London from storms blowing off the North Sea, the massive 5.5-mile long Oosterscheldekering in Holland, and Venice's perpetually delayed MOSE floodgate project.[92]

The challenges to the Rockaway Barrier are exactly the same as those faced by the proposed storm gate half a century ago. Foremost among these is the potentially damaging impact of the barrier on Jamaica Bay's already polluted waters. If the barrier impedes tidal flows, it will worsen water quality in the bay, leading to intensifying eutrophication and marsh island loss. It is absolutely clear that there is no element of ecosystem restoration to this plan: it is purely about protecting vulnerable communities and expensive infrastructure, Kennedy Airport first and foremost. Consequently, the barrier plan is opposed by both marine biologists and landscape architects, for whom Jamaica Bay has become a key proving ground for diametrically opposed approaches to coping with coastal vulnerability and sea level rise.[93] Hoping to nurture alternatives to USACE's proposed Rockaway Barrier, architect Catherine Seavitt has proposed a series of interventions around the perimeter of the bay as part of her Structures of Coastal Resilience project.[94] Seavitt's design team imagines three key measures for Jamaica Bay, mixing novel techniques of ecosystem restoration with nature-based storm protection infrastructures.[95] First, the team aims to amplify the flow and circulation of tidal currents through the construction of overwash plans, tidal inlets, and flushing tunnels on the Rockaway Peninsula that would transfer water and sediment across the barrier island and into the bay during times of high water. This would help circulate the increasingly stagnant waters of the bay and replace scarce sediment.[96] Second, the team proposes to build up the verges of the Belt Parkway and other back-bay areas using marsh terraces, earthen berms, and sunken attenuation forests. The aim here would be to protect communities that line the perimeter of the bay from storm surges while improving their quality of life with attractive but functional landscaping on the edge of the water. Finally, Seavitt and her colleagues have developed models for what they call an *atoll terrace and island motor*—minimal, carefully placed quantities of dredged material that would catch sediment being carried by existing tidal flows. Trapped by the atoll terrace, sediment would naturally build marsh islands with minimal human intervention in an adapted version of the "sand engine" developed by Dutch architects to replenish coastal beaches.[97] This approach would require much less sediment than the marsh island restoration efforts currently underway, and consequently, it is projected, would also be much less capital intensive. The hope is that these natural processes of accretion would allow marsh islands to grow upwards in tandem with sea level rise.

Despite the environmental benefits of Seavitt's proposed Structures of Coastal Resilience project, the plan would still require placement of berms and levees on present-day wetlands, an approach that is sure to prove controversial with local environmentalists who have fought for generations against the destruction of the marshlands. The USACE perimeter plan, although it speaks in the nature-friendly lexicon of landscape architecture, would likely feature even more invasive barriers on coastal edges around the bay's perimeter. But probably the greatest challenge to Seavitt's urban ecological vision for Jamaica Bay lies in the question of how Kennedy Airport will be protected. As USACE engineer Dan Falt puts it, "I don't know if you want to build tall walls near airports, so there may be increased benefits from a hurricane barrier."[98] The capital fixed in Kennedy Airport, and its importance as a key element of the city's transportation infrastructure, mean that it is likely to have a strong role in deciding what form of protection will be constructed in the bay, despite the failure of its repeated efforts to build more runways into the bay. Finally, it should be noted that funding is likely to impede the realization of ecologically benign flood protection features. At present, USACE has received $4 billion from the federal Sandy aid bill to fortify the Rockaways, but Congress is not expected to fully fund the bayside protections. Additional federal funding, as well as money from New York City and State would be necessary to realize any of the ambitious plans for structures of coastal resilience. As Hurricane Sandy becomes more of a distant memory for the many people who were not directly and enduringly affected by the storm, the chance of these funds dwindles. Grand engineering projects of any kind thus may not be in the cards, and individual citizens and communities are likely to find that they have only themselves to rely on when the next fearsome squall comes racing in off the Atlantic.

The history of Jamaica Bay demonstrates the ways in which "reclamation"—really a wholesale transformation—of a landscape that was represented as a wasteland generated a series of unexpected environmental blowbacks. Across the twentieth century, such crises were most often coped with through technological innovation, generating increasingly complex and intricate urban infrastructure. Some of these constructions have made urban life feasible and maybe even pleasant for masses of people, but the transformation of devalued landscapes like Jamaica Bay's marshes has also exposed nearby residents to ever greater risk. Utilizing the landscape itself as a kind of living infrastructure, architects like Catherine Seavitt seek to restore some of the buffering natural processes that characterized the ecosystems in New York's estuarial waters. Such important efforts come in a context of cascading environmental blowbacks that render urban life increasingly fragile. New York is but one site where such precariousness is evident.

In riverine deltas across the globe, for instance, people are drilling into the sedimented soil beneath their communities in search of drinking water that the city does not otherwise provide. In doing so, they collectively contribute to processes of land subsidence that leave them more vulnerable to rising seas and extreme storms. Moreover, as nations scramble to develop themselves into industrial powerhouses, they generate new forms of environmental blowback for their own citizens and for those downstream. Like many other developing nations, for instance, India wants to expand its hydroelectric capacity and has launched plans to build more than 150 dams in northeastern states such as Arunachal Pradesh and Assam on rivers that eventually find their way to Bangladesh and the vast archipelago of marsh islands called the Sundarbans. The dams threaten fragile ecosystems and indigenous communities in the Himalayan foothills in the name of stoking high growth rates that do little to help the majority of Indian citizens.[99] At the same time, by diverting rivers such as the Brahmaputra and Subansiri, the projects are likely to have serious impacts downstream in the floodplains of Assam and Bangladesh. When less water flows downriver and out into the ocean, salty ocean water is able to penetrate further into the fragile estuarial lands of the region. Increasing salinity levels are largely invisible but are nonetheless deadly, killing the namesake Sundari trees of the region and increasing damaged cropland from less than 4 million acres in 1973 to a projected 8 million today.[100] Compounding the relatively invisible scourge of salinity in the delta are three other key impacts of climate change: increasingly wide and damaging seasonal flooding; sea level rise, which, at the lowest UN estimate of three feet, will submerge a fifth of Bangladesh by 2100; and, finally, cyclones, which are increasing in strength as the ocean heats up. But if Bangladesh is ground zero for the climate crisis, getting hit from both ends of the fragile ecosystem it is built on, there are many other cities built on riverine deltas that face similar constellations of problems, including places as diverse as Buenos Aires, Casablanca,

Kolkata, Manila, Rotterdam, and Shanghai. In such places, development—nature's metabolization by capital—brings riches to a few, but ultimately generates environmental blowback that affects many. Who benefits from such development and who is harmed when nature bites back has always been a product of a skewed social calculus, but as the environmental blowback intensifies, these disparities become ever more apparent.

New Orleans: The New Atlantis

Early in 2016, Julián Castro, secretary of the U.S Department of Housing and Urban Development (HUD), announced the winners of a $1 billion nationwide competition for disaster-affected communities. The state of Louisiana was awarded $92 million in the federal disaster resilience competition. More than half of this sum ($52 million) is directed to helping members of the Isle de Jean Charles Band of Biloxi-Chitimacha-Choctaw Indians relocated from their island home to a "resilient and historically contextual community."[101] In 1955, the Isle de Jean Charles comprised more than 22,000 acres, enough land for community members to farm, trap, and shelter from storms sweeping in off the Gulf of Mexico. Today, only 320 acres remain. More than 98 percent of Isle de Jean Charles has been lost to the seas, making the island's residents one of the most threatened coastal populations of Native Americans in the continental United States.[102] The HUD grant is the fruit of nearly two decades of work by tribal leaders to resettle the island residents. In dedicating these funds to the Isle de Jean Charles Band, the federal government has offered the first government recognition of and assistance to internally displaced climate refugees. This is a momentous decision, one with potentially sweeping implications. If the residents of Isle de Jean Charles are to be resettled, what about other neighboring communities in coastal Louisiana, not to mention coastal communities threatened by sea level rise in other parts of the country, and, indeed, the world?

Over 75 percent of the ocean shoreline of the United States is disappearing, with much of the erosion due to human interventions of various kinds.[103] But conditions confronting communities in coastal Louisiana are undeniably extreme. The state is losing land to the sea faster than almost anywhere else in the world. A football-besotted state, Louisiana is notoriously losing a football field's worth of land every hour. If New York were losing land this quickly, Central Park would disappear in a month, and Manhattan would sink into the sea in a year and a half.[104] Since the 1930s, Louisiana has lost about 2,000 square miles of coastal wetlands, roughly one third of the deltaic plain.[105] The vast majority of this land loss is the result of human intervention. Coastal Louisiana could thus be said to be ground zero for environmental blowback. Yet this is not a case of unintended environmental consequences. Louisiana's environment was systematically reengineered with surprisingly detailed knowledge of the ultimate destructive consequences. When these changes were made, however, environmental blowback seemed a distant prospect, far outweighed by the short-term gains to be made through environmental reengineering. Coastal Louisiana thus needs to be seen as a tragedy of capitalist culture's lack of foresight, as well as a clear case of environmental blowback.[106] It is also, crucially, a tale of profound corruption, of deep and enduring complicity between political elites, state regulators, and the fossil fuel industry in a quest for private profits that, while it may have trickled down to the rest of Louisiana to a certain extent, ultimately has washed away a significant portion of the very ground on which the state stands.

When French settlers arrived in Louisiana in the seventeenth century, they found one of the most dynamic environments on the continent. The Mississippi River drains 41 percent of the continental United States, including thirty-one states and two Canadian provinces.[107] This mighty river brought vast quantities of sediment-laden waters down a wide alluvial valley into the slack waters of the Gulf of Mexico, where the water dumped its sediment load. Over the course of the last seven millennia, this deposition formed a series of deltaic lobes that extended out into the Gulf of Mexico, creating freshwater swamps with ridges of land built up along the banks of the river. This landscape was constantly in motion: seasonal floods would push muddy water over the river banks, depositing sediment in the surrounding marshes; crevasses periodically opened in the banks of the river, spilling sediment out into the wetlands; and, every once in a while, seeking a more direct route to the gulf, the river would jump its banks and begin forming a new lobe.[108] Native Americans had lived with this fluid environment for thousands of years, setting up camp along the raised edges of the roving river, but European settlers brought expectations about landscape and urbanization that were far more static and that required a relatively firm delineation between land and water.[109] Following the founding of the strategic city of New Orleans on a convenient portage route connecting the Gulf Coast with the Mississippi River in the early eighteenth century, French settlers in the city and in the plantations that were established along the adjacent banks of the Mississippi began to build riverfront levees to protect their property from annual floods. In doing so, they began a process that the oceanographer Richard Condrey describes through the analogy of applying a tourniquet to a bicep: by constricting the river to a single channel, the levees gradually starved the land around New Orleans of its lifeblood, the critical sediment and fresh water that had built one of the world's greatest deltas.[110]

Modern engineering vastly compounded this process of sediment starvation. In the early colonial period, levee construction was the responsibility of individual landowners, which meant that the constriction of the river was relatively haphazard. Individually built levees were often inadequate to repel floods, and when one person's levees were breached, surrounding lands were inundated. In 1879, following the defeat of the Confederacy, the US federal government created the Mississippi River Commission, centralizing flood and navigation control over the river. Subordinated to a central authority, the tourniquet binding the Mississippi was remorselessly tightened. Each brilliant solution to an immediate problem in the problematically fluid landscape intensified the ultimate environmental blowback. For instance, in 1875, the self-taught engineer James Eads came up with a scheme to clear away sediment shoals that were preventing ships from entering the Mississippi using a series of parallel jetties built just north of the river's mouth. The jetties constricted the river's flow, causing it to speed up, deepening the channel and scouring out the entrance to the river. This permitted ocean-going vessels to enter the Mississippi and head upriver to the port of New Orleans, generating a massive boom in the city's economy. However, the jetties also ensured that the river's sediments would be shot off the edge of the continental shelf into the deep waters of the gulf instead of continuing to build up the marshes of the delta.

In 1885, the Army Corps of Engineers, given authority over the entire Mississippi system, adopted a levees-only policy to deal with periodic flooding, in the mistaken belief that Eads's solution would deepen the entire bed of the river by increasing the abrasion of the river bottom.[111] But instead of digging deeper, the waters of the Mississippi, given no natural outlets, swelled higher. Higher levees had to be built periodically, which inevitably generated higher waters in a vicious spiral. The river and its levees rose higher and higher above the surrounding countryside, until, eventually, a particularly high flood would cause catastrophic breaches all along the line of levees. The worst such episode occurred in 1927, when a series of 145 breaches flooded 27,000 square miles of land in the Mississippi Delta and contiguous states to a depth of thirty feet.[112] It was and remains the United States's greatest environmental disaster. Nearly a million people, many of them the still-impoverished descendants of slaves who had worked the plantations along the banks of the Mississippi, were displaced, helping to trigger the Great Migration of African Americans to the cities of the industrialized north.

In his brilliant book *The Control of Nature* (which, as its ironic title suggests, catalogues the history of environmental blowback in the delta), John McPhee describes the orientation that undergirded these feats of engineering: nature was viewed as the enemy of the state, a large and powerful adversary that had to be fought systematically and ultimately dominated to ensure the country's status as "first among trading nations."[113] Many of the engineers whom McPhee interviews in his book, which was published in 1989, describe the increasingly baroque and hubristic plans of the Army Corps of Engineers to control the Mississippi as a departure from conditions in the past, when the perpetual flux of the river was accepted. McPhee describes a conversation with LeRoy Dugas, manager of the Old River control structure that prevents the Mississippi from switching into the Atchafalaya River, and thereby finding a far quicker outlet to the gulf. Dugas says that in his youth, "he took the vagaries of the river for granted, not to mention the supremacy of their force in flood."[114] Such quotations suggest a phenomenon whereby each new generation finds itself surprised by environmental blowback.[115] Yet there is ample historical evidence to suggest that the impact of the levees and other engineering interventions on the Mississippi were well known long ago. An 1897 article in *National Geographic*, for example, evinces clear awareness of the problem of sediment starvation but concludes that "no doubt the great benefit to the present and two or three following generations accruing from a complete system of absolutely protective levees [. . .] far outweighs the disadvantages to future generations from the subsidence of the Gulf delta lands below the level of the sea and their gradual abandonment due to this cause."[116] Notwithstanding this sobering conclusion, the article's author argues that this environmental blowback can always be coped with through the more ambitious engineering schemes of the future.

As this *National Geographic* article suggests, the cosseting of the Mississippi by ever-higher levees not only denied the delta new sources of sediment: it also spurred subsidence of the land on which the levees, as well as the city of New Orleans, was built. Without fresh water, the fine sand, silt, and clay particles that made up the soils of the delta began to settle, and organic matter spread throughout the soil to decompose, leading to a process of subsidence. Although the Army Corps of Engineers developed a system of spillways after 1927 that effectively ended the threat of flooding from the river, subsidence has turned the delta into what McPhee calls an exaggerated Venice, a 200-mile wide trelliswork of rivers, canals, and bayous pulsing like elevated veins through the increasingly ebbing marshes of the delta. Subsidence is particularly threatening for New Orleans, over half of which is below sea level. An urban drainage system built during the Progressive Era encouraged what the geographer Richard Campanella calls the "levee effect," in which flood-control structures paradoxically increase flood damage by encouraging floodplain development.[117] In the case of New Orleans, the new drainage system led to the development of low-lying "backswamp" areas of the city, where land that was once frequently flooded was suddenly available to those who could not afford to live on the high ground formed by the river's natural levees. Subsequent interventions would increase this trend to colonize risky terrain, placing relatively poor people looking for affordable real estate in harm's way. But the engineers who built this system made a fatal mistake: they placed the pumps designed to move water out of the city through canals to nearby lakes at the bottom of sub-basins in the middle of the city. This meant that, as the drained land began to subside, New Orleans ended up seamed through with a series of outfall canals that, like the levees on the Mississippi, grew higher and higher while the land sank.[118] The drainage system now hangs over the rooftops of the city like a watery sword of Damocles.

It was the collapse of levees built along these outfall canals (and along shipping corridors like the Industrial Canal and the Mississippi River-Gulf Outlet) that led to the disaster following Hurricane Katrina.[119] The levees were not overtopped, as the Army Corps of Engineers initially claimed, but rather caved in as massed water penetrated below their concrete pilings.[120] Yet if Hurricane Katrina drove a storm surge down on New Orleans, that surge was able to hit the city with such devastating impact because of a series of man-made canals that allowed it to penetrate far inland. These canals included not just shipping channels like the Mississippi River-Gulf Outlet, but also a spidery web of many thousands of miles of canals built by the fossil fuel industry to facilitate drilling for oil and gas in Louisiana's wetlands. In addition, 191 separate pipeline systems cut through coastal marshes from offshore drilling rigs to inland transfer stations.[121] The pipelines and canals cut up the barrier islands that protected coastal marshes into shrinking chunks, eroded by wave action and by the gulf's frequent storms.[122] Canals dredged through the interior marshes allowed saline water from the gulf to penetrate into freshwater environments, killing the delicate marsh plants that held coastal land together in the face of even the most ferocious hurricanes. The spoil banks, piles of debris left over from dredging operations, cut off the exchange of nutrients in interlinked coastal ecosystems, hastening the death of wetlands surrounding the canals. As a result, canals through-out the delta gradually widened, dissolving the surrounding marshes like veins of acid. In tandem with this surface erosion, the oil and gas industry was also extracting massive volumes of hydrocarbons and water from below the coastal wetlands, generating dramatic rates of subsidence that significantly exac-erbated the destruction of the marshes.[123]

When, following the explosion of the Deepwater Horizon drilling rig off the Gulf coast in 2010, federal agency heads and scientists were flown out from New Orleans on helicopters to look for the oil plume, they expected to see miles of blackened marsh. What they saw instead was a landscape like Swiss cheese, the tattered remains of coastal marshes torn apart by the oil industry's infrastructure of canals and pipelines.[124] Dramatic photographs of the gaping holes in the marshes south of New Orleans, a space now more water than land, alerted the public to the destruction of the coast, as well as to the heightened peril faced by a city increasingly exposed to storm surges. New Orleans was becoming a New Atlantis, an island protected from the menacing sea by nothing except its rebuilt levees.[125] Yet despite the shock with which visiting scientists and dignitaries reacted to their flights over this blasted landscape, knowledge of the fossil fuel industry's impact on the coastal environment was decades old. As far back as the 1950s, for instance, oystermen warned that the oil industry was destroying the offshore oyster reefs, and a trade journal for the oil company Esso (now ExxonMobil) cautioned that the canals were causing erosion.[126] Employees of Louisiana's Wildlife and Fisheries Commission stated that valuable game and fish populations in these areas "may be totally destroyed or drastically reduced."[127] By the 1970s, even the Army Corps of Engineers had concluded that "onshore pipeline construction may cause irretrievable marshland loss."[128] But if knowledge of the decimation of the coastal environment was widespread, why was nothing done to halt this destruction?

In a word: corruption. As John Barry, a member of the New Orleans levee board that sued nearly 100 fossil fuel companies for their role in destroying Louisiana's coast, stated, "the oil industry realized that it was much cheaper to buy politicians than to adhere to regulations."[129] Since the days of populist Louisiana governor Huey Long, the notorious Kingfish, oil and gas companies were given relatively free rein to exploit the state's coastal resources in exchange for providing jobs, a modicum of economic redistribution to the state's citizenry, and, of course, handsome contributions to individual politicians.[130] So intimate was this relationship between the state and fossil fuel companies that the ironically named Office of Conservation within Louisiana's Department of Natural Resources, which was tasked with managing oil and gas development, derived its budget from the granting of leases for the exploitation of minerals on state land.[131] Where the wetlands were not leased out, they were bought up: by the 1980s, five corporations, two of them subsidiaries of General Motors, owned 25 percent of coastal Louisiana.[132] These entities fought efforts at environmental regulation fiercely, not only buying up the votes of local politicians but also packing the state legislature with bosses of the very oil and gas companies that were tearing up the coast. Any effort at legal regulation inevitably ended up dying in the state legislature's committees on natural resources, which were controlled by industry players.[133] In Louisiana, it was not so much that corporate power influenced the state: corporations essentially *were* the state.[134]

If there were any doubt about the fact that Louisiana was a petro-state, it was banished by the reaction to the New Orleans levee board's suit against Big Oil. This suit was a clear recognition that the obliteration of the coastal wetlands represented a grave threat to the city: without these natural barriers, even a weak storm could inundate New Orleans. Since studies conducted by the oil industry itself had recognized culpability for up to 36 percent of this land loss—a lowball figure, for sure, but an admission of responsibility nonetheless—John Barry and his colleagues on the levee board thought that Big Oil should shoulder its responsibility for coastal restoration efforts. Known as the Coastal Master Plan, the state restoration project proposed to work on over one hundred separate flood-risk-reduction and land-building efforts, with a slated price tag of at least $50 billion. The only hitch: there was no funding for the project. Since the operating permits that allowed the oil and gas industry to work in sensitive coastal wetlands specified responsibility for repair of any environmental damage, Barry and the other members of the levee board thought they had a good case against the ninety-seven companies named in their suit. But within a few hours of the suit's announcement in the summer of 2013, Louisiana governor Bobby Jindal issued a press release denouncing the suit as a "windfall for a handful of trial lawyers," whose personal gain would come "at the expense of our coast and thousands of hardworking Louisianians who help fuel America by working in the energy industry."[135] Jindal began to purge the levee board of anyone who supported the suit, including Barry. Nearly twenty separate bills to kill the case were proposed in the state legislature, aiming to terminate the suit before the courts could even consider it. Despite surprising public support for the suit—surprising given the long history of public acceptance of the argument that what's good for Big Oil is good for Louisiana—one of these bills eventually passed and was signed by Jindal. Although a couple of the most adversely affected parishes have followed the levee board's example in suing Big Oil for damage to the coastal wetlands, the Louisiana Attorney General has announced that the state is going to take over these suits, which means that they're going to be quashed.[136]

The irony here is that the oil and natural gas companies need coastal restoration just as much if not more than the citizens of the delta. Big Oil has billions of dollars worth of infrastructure sunk in the Gulf Coast, including pipelines, terminals, oil tanks, and 15 percent of the nation's refineries, all of which is massively exposed to the next major hurricane to hit Louisiana. This is why the industry supported the state's Coastal Master Plan. It just doesn't want to help pay for it. To avert this responsibility, Big Oil not only flexed its political muscle, but also engaged in a sophisticated ideological campaign. In 1989, lobbyists working for the industry formed an organization called the National Wetlands Coalition, which played a key role in crafting the Comprehensive Wetlands Conservation and Management Act, which, despite its beneficent name, removed the federal Environmental Protection Agency's authority over wetlands protection and required cash payment to Louisiana by the federal government for any coastal protection the Army Corps of Engineers might undertake.[137] In subsequent years, the National Wetlands Coalition developed this strategy further, calling actively for restoration of coastal wetlands but blaming coastal collapse solely on the Corps' levee-building projects and insisting that restoration efforts be funded exclusively by US taxpayers. This dodge has been highly successful. The Wetland Coalition has been joined in its efforts to secure federal funding for coastal restoration by major national environmental groups like the Environmental Defense Fund, the National Wildlife Federation, and the Audubon Society, who apparently do not understand local politics or historical responsibility for the destruction of coastal wetlands.[138] Moreover, the responsibility of Big Oil for the obliteration of Louisiana's coastline was mentioned in neither of the state's restoration plans. While it is certainly true that environmental blowback from the construction of levees played a role in the loss of Louisiana's coastal wetlands, it is, as John Barry put it, in typically colorful language, a "stone cold lie" to suggest that this is the sole factor.[139] To

clarify the degrees of responsibility, Barry offers a potent analogy: think of the levees as the equivalent of taking a block of ice
out of a freezer on a hot summer day. It will of course begin to
melt gradually. Now think of Big Oil's canal dredging as the
equivalent of taking an ice pick to that melting block and smash-
ing it into small chunks of ice that disappear before your eyes.

The explosion of the Deepwater Horizon in 2010 significantly changed the debate. Suddenly, a large—if inevitably not
adequate—windfall would rain down on Louisiana. In 2012,
President Barack Obama signed the RESTORE Act, which
directs 80 percent of the $18 billion worth of penalty money to
be paid by BP for its damage to the Gulf Coast to a restoration
trust fund.[140] In its 2012 plan, one of the major beneficiaries of
this funding, Louisiana's Coastal Protection and Restoration
Authority (CPRA), promised to halt the loss of wetlands in
twenty years and to build up to 800 square miles of wetlands
and barrier islands over the next fifty.[141] CPRA also proposed to
use $20 billion to dredge the Mississippi riverbed to allow huge
freighter ships to transit up to port facilities in New Orleans and
then to pump that material to areas in danger of being submerged.
"There are strategic pieces of marsh, strategic barrier islands,
that help maintain a larger portion of wetlands than others,"
Kyle Graham, CPRA's executive director argues.[142] This language
of "strategic" restoration is a thin mask for the piecemeal nature
of restoration efforts. It may be politically expedient to be able
to point to a restored barrier island built with dredged sediment
that conveniently helps the shipping industry, but even CPRA
admits that such isolated islands are likely to be carried away all
too quickly by the tides.[143] So far, the agency has spent $77
million to restore Pelican Island, a 2.5-mile-long strip in the
Barataria Bay, but CPRA admits that it will be devoured by the
sea within twenty years.[144]

Recognizing the insufficiency of such dredging schemes,
CPRA also proposes a series of "sediment diversion" schemes,
in which state authorities would breach levees along the
Mississippi in strategic places, allowing the river to flood into
and deposit silt around sediment starved land. According to

Virginia Burkett, chief scientist for climate and land use change at the US Geological Survey, CPRA's plan diverges from earlier, failed restoration plans in that it aims to mimic the natural processes of deposition that existed before the river was constricted by levees.[145] There is, however, one big problem with this plan to harness natural processes: according to an article published in 2009 in *Nature Geoscience*, even if such processes are effectively mimicked, the Mississippi River now lacks sufficient sediment load to counter a predicted one meter of sea level rise. In chillingly plain language, the authors of the article conclude, "significant drowning of the Mississippi Delta is inevitable because sea level is now rising at least three times faster than during delta-plain construction."[146]

According to Richard Condrey, a professor emeritus of oceanography at Louisiana State University, the state's own data on land loss show that, even with BP's huge infusion of capital, the coastal restoration plan is not working.[147] Rates of land loss have been continuous for decades, and the state's restoration efforts have not significantly slowed this trend. In addition, Condrey suggests that even the most ambitious sediment diversion schemes are fatally flawed because they are based on the assumption that the delta is dying simply because it lacks new soil. Contrary to this, Condrey argues that the wandering Mississippi River once played a vital role in recharging the aquifer that lies below the delta. Condrey's research suggests that, up until the 1930s, the Mississippi continued to feed the lobes of the delta with these underflows and overflows through the aquifer. When the river was constrained by levees, these revitalizing flows of water into the aquifer were gradually removed. Moreover, the outflows from the aquifer that had once kept the waters of the gulf at bay gradually dwindled, leaving the vegetation of coastal wetlands and the large oyster shoals that once protected barrier islands exposed to increasingly high levels of salinity. Without this animal and plant life to anchor it, "restored" coastal barrier islands and wetlands will gradually wash away, even assuming that enough sediment could be dredged to replace the reduced quantities currently carried down the Mississippi.[148]

If even the most ambitious, well-funded restoration plans are not working, what alternative remains to the people of coastal Louisiana? This vexing question inevitably prompts a return to HUD's grant to the Isle de Jean Charles Band of Biloxi-Chitimacha-Choctaw Indians. Although very few politicians in Louisiana are yet willing to talk about it, the residents of Isle de Jean Charles are pioneering what is increasingly seeming like an inevitable fate for many communities in coastal Louisiana: retreat. At present, however, they are the only community to whom financial support is being given for resettlement. And, since it is still politically anathema to discuss the idea of abandoning the coast, theirs is also the only planned retreat.[149]

There has, however, been a relatively high-profile competition to cope with the slow death of the delta in which community relocation figures: Changing Course.[150] Funded by the Rockefeller Foundation and Shell Oil, among others, Changing Course engaged a series of teams—composed, like the Structures of Coastal Resilience project, of an interdisciplinary group of renowned engineers, scientists, planners, and designers—to come up with plans to establish a self-sustaining delta ecosystem. These teams were tasked with using the state's Master Plan for coastal restoration as a basis for proposals for "protection and restoration of the Delta landscape while addressing the needs and goals of the industries—especially the navigation industry, communities and economies of the Delta."[151] The flawed grammar in this mission statement is inadvertently revealing: the communities of the delta are collapsed grammatically into the industries that have historically dominated the region, including the shipping industry and the ubiquitous but not-to-be-named fossil fuel industry. As we will see, this carefully elided link to Big Oil has serious implications.

Nonetheless, the three winning proposals in Changing Course each call for a change of truly epochal significance: the abandonment of all of the delta land south of the city of New Orleans. Each of the three teams proposes some variation of "taking the river out of the channel" by establishing controlled breaches or crevasses in the levee system that constrains the Mississippi in order to build land up through sediment deposition and fresh-water inflows. All of the teams plan for these land-building processes to be deployed at key points upriver from English Turn, a sharp bend in the Mississippi just downriver from New Orleans. The proposals suggest cycling through these newly created "mouths" of the river in order to ensure even deposition and growth in the radically diminished but "self-sustaining" delta. Each of the three proposals recognizes the human impact of land abandonment and attempts to offer a solution to the resulting mass displacement of human communities. The plan created by Baird and Associates, for example, proposes a "Two Home Program," which would use a land bank in protected upriver locations to establish second homes for members of threatened coastal communities.[152] The land trust program would provide lots to groups, such as the Isle de Jean Charles Band of Biloxi-Chitimacha-Choctaw Indians, wishing to move together in order to preserve their community integrity. The plan would address fears about displacement and dispossession by guaranteeing that residents could retain their current homes, with the new second homes functioning as "a temporary home / refuge from storm," although it is envisaged that "over time the inland lot could shift to be a more permanent home."[153] Adding to these efforts at community relocation, the proposal created by the MISI-ZIIBI team, the Living Delta project, calls for incentivizing resettlement through the creation of new communities characterized by the highest possible levels of storm-surge protection and by attractive civic features and amenities such as schools, hospitals, and parks.[154] The MISI-ZIIBI proposal recognizes that migration will inevitably entail training in new vocations and technical skills for the predominantly rural population of the delta, most of whom are presently engaged in some form of employment tied directly to the land and water of the delta.

The Changing Course project is impressive first and foremost in its forthright admission that the combination of sediment starvation and canalization has doomed the lower delta. The project proposals to use the Mississippi's natural land-building capacity to establish a sustainable—if foreshortened—delta are also notable, as is their commitment to social justice to displaced denizens of the delta. But the proposals raise a number of vexing questions in each of these domains. First of all, although the engineers and natural scientists engaged by each team clearly know their stuff, their plans to use the Mississippi's natural land-building capacity are based on projections derived from current sediment flow rates and accepted projections of sea level rise. Yet both of these sets of projections are extremely uncertain and likely to be low-balled. Studies by scientists at Louisiana State University suggest, for example, that "even with modest estimates of soil subsidence and sea level rise and generous approximations of future sediment supply, the delta will run a nearly insurmountable sediment deficit of 1 to 5 billion tons, *possibly up to 17 billion tons*, by the year 2100."[155] A smaller delta may require less sediment to maintain, but the wide spectrum in these projections of sediment starvation suggest that even a reduced delta may still struggle with sediment deprivation. In addition, scientists such as James Hansen have released studies suggesting that existing projections of sea level rise are fatally flawed by their failure to consider feedback mechanisms in melting ice sheets in Greenland and Antarctica. Tides, and storm surges, are likely to rise far faster than the Changing Course teams project. Finally, time is of the essence here. More land disappears into the sea not just every year and every month but every day and every hour. The longer authorities wait to inaugurate these coastal rebuilding processes, the more diminished the existing delta will become and the less sediment will be available for replenishment.

Another major technical obstacle that the Changing Course projects fail to consider is linked to the competition's framing insistence that New Orleans's port facilities are integral to a future reduced but sustainable delta. This insistence on not just maintaining but expanding shipping is not particularly surprising: the Mississippi River is one of the country's most important economic transport arteries, carrying, for example, 60 percent of all grain exported from the country.[156] US waterborne trade along the river constitutes a relatively small portion of the Gulf Coast economy, but it is nonetheless often valued in the hundreds of billions of dollars.[157] Yet, as Richard Condrey emphasizes, continued dredging of the river to facilitate entrance of the massive post-Panamax container ships, which require a depth of at least fifty feet for maneuver, is likely to significantly exacerbate the negative environmental blowback of the destruction of shallow submerged sand bars at the river's mouth, destruction begun over a century ago with the construction of Eads's jetties.[158] These jetties hastened the flow of the Mississippi, shooting sediment away from the delta and into the deep waters off the coastal shelf. These jetties, Richard Condrey adds, also have a negative impact on the river's ability to recharge its aquifer. Dredging the channel deeper near New Orleans in order to maintain the port's place in global shipping would likely intensify this disruption of the aquifer, even as the rapidly eroding remaining wetlands expose the city to increasingly strong storm surges. (Currently, every 2.7 miles of wetlands are estimated to absorb a foot of storm surge.)[159] The insistence on freeing the mouth of the Mississippi would, in other words, place New Orleans in ever greater peril. The city will be a New Atlantis surrounded by ever-higher levees and with no natural barriers to hold back the slow violence of sea level rise and the more ferocious storms that surge in off the Gulf with increasing frequency.

Perhaps the most impressive element of Changing Course is its insistence on social justice for coastal communities. But, as attractive as plans to provide for community relocation and vocational retraining are, this element of the plan is likely to run into some key snags. First, there are the logistical questions. The examples of successful relocation to which Changing Course teams point involve exclusively small, tightly knit communities numbering only in the hundreds. It is costing the federal government over $50 million to resettle the Isle de Jean Charles Band of Biloxi-Chitimacha-Choctaw Indians. But the Gulf Coast is currently occupied by tens of thousands of people. Where will the funds come from to move such large numbers? Where will they be settled? How much choice will they have about their destinations? And how will community and family ties be preserved in the face of this mass resettlement?

These thorny logistical questions are likely to provoke an outcry from coastal communities, with many residents adamantly unwilling to contemplate moving away from their current homes.[160] At first glance, this opposition may seem surprising given the fact that coastal communities have historically been mobile: coastal people traditionally lived in extended families and would simply move up the bayou to stay with relatives when a particularly bad storm hit.[161] Coastal communities have an intensely strong pride in place, with many families tracing residence on the coast back at least six generations, but this did not preclude significant mobility. But now, communities are increasingly resistant to any talk of relocation. This resistance is connected to a broader distrust of the federal government and outsiders to the coast in general, distrust that Republican legislators have done much to stoke with their vitriolic attacks on "Washington."[162] The hypocrisy of legislators' antigovernment stance is quite transparent given the rush to accept federal money after the Katrina disaster, as well as the intense lobbying for federal coastal restoration aid. Nonetheless, given the many glaring injustices of the Road Home program and the post-Katrina redevelopment of New Orleans and the rest of the Gulf Coast in general, it should not be surprising that there is significant apprehension among residents about relocation programs.[163] Whatever the cause, the upshot is that inaction gets locked in, at least until the next massive disaster engulfs the coast, forcing people to relocate under the most extreme conditions.

Last but not least, there is the question of Big Oil. Proposals such as Living Delta imagine the creation of "navigable waterway corridors designed to consolidate energy transmission pipelines and improve access to resources (for example, petroleum refineries, inland and offshore oil platforms, inland waterways and ports)" that "will reduce the number of access canals in the wetlands."[164] But will the fossil fuel industry be willing to abandon significant portions of its existing infrastructure, not to mention the practice of aggressively prospecting for new wells and cutting fresh canals through the wetlands? There is little support for such a supposition in the historical record. And even if Big Oil is willing to become a responsible citizen of the new, redesigned delta, can the fossil fuel industry be part of a sustainable delta? The Changing Course teams seem to think so. The Living Delta proposal, for instance, argues that "the energy sector in southern Louisiana will continue to be a large economic driver for the region and the nation. The Living Delta concept supports this industry through a series of strategies that allow the energy sector to expand in an ecologically sound manner using cutting-edge technological advances."[165] But how can the expansion of the energy sector be consistent with ecologically sound practices? As we have seen, the historical expansion of the industry has been responsible for a good part of the destruction of coastal wetlands. In addition, even if the dredging of canals were to cease tomorrow, plans for continued expansion of the fossil fuel industry necessarily mean heightened greenhouse gas emissions. These would accelerate the rates of sea level rise, dooming the Changing Course projections for a sustainable delta to irrelevance.

Any truly credible plan for a "self-sustaining delta" must include an extremely rapid transition away from fossil fuels. Such a plan is not contemplated in Changing Course or in any other plans for the future of coastal Louisiana. The reasons for this are patently apparent. Petro-governance makes any such plans politically suicidal at present. But there's a catch-22 here, since any plans that are not centered on a rapid and just transition away from fossil fuels are inevitably hollow exercises when viewed on a more holistic and long-term scale. Individual components of plans such as Changing Course may be appealing, and their ideas about community relocation through entities such as community land trusts are suggestive of steps for the future, but unless such plans wrestle with the task of imagining and planning for a post–fossil fuel future, they inevitably prepare the way for future rounds of environmental blowback.

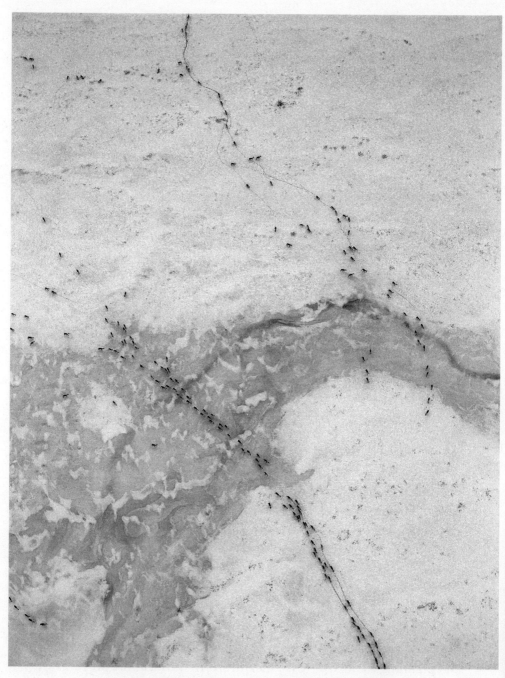

Caribou Migration I, from *Oil and the Caribou*
(Arctic National Wildlife Refuge), 2002.
Photograph by Subhankar Banerjee.

3

Sea Change

Sinking Feelings: Of Glaciers, Zombies, and Catastrophic Affect

Milestones on the road toward climate chaos are all too frequent these days: in 2015, the Manua Loa Observatory in Hawaii reported that the daily mean concentration of CO_2 in the atmosphere had surpassed 400 parts per million (ppm) for the first time; each year Arctic sea ice levels grow lower and lower; permafrost in areas like Siberia and Alaska is melting, releasing dangerous quantities of methane into the atmosphere; and each year brings more violent storms and more severe droughts to different parts of the world. Indeed, news of apocalyptic climate-related events is so manifold that it can feel overwhelming, producing a kind of disaster fatigue.[1] One recent announcement merits particular attention, however: in the summer of 2014, a team of NASA scientists announced conclusive evidence that the retreat of ice in the Amundsen Sea sector of West Antarctica had become unstoppable.[2] This melting alone, they concluded, will drive global sea levels up by over 1 meter (3 feet). As the Pine Island, Thwaites, and other glaciers of the Amundsen Sea sector collapse into the ocean, the effect is expected to be like a cork removed from a bottle of champagne: the ice the glaciers held back will rush rapidly into the sea, and the entire West Antarctic ice sheet will collapse. Sea levels will consequently rise 3 to 5 meters (10–16 feet). In addition, it was recently discovered that the same process that is driving this collapse, the intrusion of warmer ocean water beneath the glaciers in West Antarctica, is also eroding key glaciers in East Antarctica.[3] The East Antarctic ice sheet contains even more ice than the western sheet: the Totten glacier alone would account for 7 meters (23 feet) of sea level rise.[4] As if this weren't bad enough news, a similar process of melting is also taking place in Greenland, where fjords that penetrate far inland are carrying warm water deep underneath the ice sheet.[5]

These reports overturn long-held assumptions about the stability of Greenland's glaciers: until recently, scientists had predicted that Greenland's ice sheet would stabilize once the glaciers close to the warming ocean had melted. The discovery of ice-bound fjords reaching almost sixty-five miles inland has major implications since the glacier melt will be much more substantial than anticipated. The Antarctic and Greenland ice sheets combined contain over 99 percent of the Earth's glacial ice. If they were to melt completely, they would raise global sea levels a virtually inconceivable 65 meters (200 feet).[6] Although it remains unclear exactly how long the disintegration of these ice sheets will take, the implications of such melting for the world's coastal cities are stark, and still almost totally unacknowledged by the general public. As Robert DeConto, co-author of a recent study that predicts significantly faster melt rates in the world's largest glaciers, points out, we're already struggling with 3 millimeters per year of sea level rise, but if the polar ice sheets collapse, "We're talking about centimeters per year. That's really tough. At that point your engineering can't keep up; you're down to demolition and rebuilding."[7]

Shockingly, few orthodox scientific predictions of sea level rise have taken the disintegration of the Antarctic and Greenland ice sheets into consideration. The latest report by the Intergovernmental Panel on Climate Change (IPCC), for example, projects a high of three feet of sea level rise by 2100, but this prediction does not include a significant contribution from the West Antarctic ice sheet.[8] Like the IPCC's projection for Arctic sea ice collapse, which has moved up from 2100 to 2050 in the latest report, this prediction is clearly far too low. What explains such gross miscalculations? The protocols of scientific verifiability provide a partial explanation. The general public has urgently wanted to know, after city-wrecking hurricanes like Katrina and Sandy, whether the devastation was caused by climate change. But unfortunately scientists have until quite recently been unable to make direct links between particular extreme weather events and climate change in general. This, as environmental philosopher Dale Jamieson puts it in *Reason in a Dark Time*, would be like saying that a specific home run is "caused" by a baseball player's batting average.[9] If scientists are becoming less reticent to make these links, as the science of attribution grows more sophisticated and able to track the causes of weather extremes, the change is still occurring slowly.[10]

Nevertheless, the IPCC's failure to account for the destruction of the Antarctic and Greenland ice sheets can only add to skepticism toward their predictions, especially after they were widely attacked for their 2007 calculations about the speed of Himalayan glacial melting. Further fueled by the climate change denial industry, the IPCC's own excessively rosy predictions for the future will only increase skepticism. In their 2000 report, for example, the body assumes that nearly 60 percent of hoped-for emissions reductions will occur independently of explicit mitigation measures. As the urban theorist Mike Davis has pointed out, the IPCC's mitigation targets assume that profits from fossil capitalism will be recycled into green technology rather than penthouse suites in soaring skyscrapers.[11] The IPCC projects a market-driven evolution toward a post-carbon economy, a set of assumptions that, as spiraling levels of greenhouse gas emissions since 2000 demonstrate all too clearly, are dead wrong. These projections concerning sea level rise and the vulnerability of coastal cities will have to be radically revised, especially after spectacular urban disasters hammer home the inadequacy of current projections. But these world-changing transformations will not take place in the distant future. Citing evidence drawn from the last major ice melt during the Eemian period, an interglacial phase about 120,000 years ago that was less than 1°C warmer than it is today, climatologist James Hansen predicts that, absent a sharp and enduring reduction in greenhouse gas emissions, global sea levels are "likely to increase several meters over a timescale of 50 to 150 years."[12] Should they prove accurate, Hansen's forecasts spell an utter transformation of human habitation across the globe within one generation.

The IPCC's lowball predictions are of a piece with one of the key ethical dilemmas of the Anthropocene Age, the era of human dominance over the planetary environment. Despite the increasingly destructive impacts of climate change around the planet, both cause and effect, and perpetrator and victim, are extremely difficult to pinpoint, either in time or space. Climate change is the ultimate form of slow violence.[13] This has made it difficult to identify who should be responsible, and has led to political paralysis. As the philosopher Stephen Gardiner argues in *A Perfect Moral Storm,* three structural asymmetries create the present cul-de-sac.[14] Around the globe, the hyperwealthy 1 percent are engaged in a feckless, hedonistic binge to end all binges, their systematic consumption obliterating the prospects of the poor, nature, and future generations. While they loot the planet, the rich live in well-protected penthouses and suburban garrisons, assiduously averting their eyes from the global majority, the swiftly deteriorating natural world, and the future they are so heedlessly obliterating. At present there is no way for future generations to interrupt the orgies of the rich, no way for the natural world to assert its rights, and slender chance for the victims of climate chaos to overthrow the tyranny of the 1 percent.

Disasters like Hurricane Sandy make us realize that we are victims of modernity's technological accomplishments, but we find ourselves unable to halt the headlong rush toward disaster that our cities catalyze. Theorists of disaster have come up with various ways of making sense of this condition. Writing of Americans' reactions during the Cold War to the possibility of total annihilation in nuclear warfare, the psychiatrist Robert J. Lifton describes a condition of psychic numbing into which people retreat when confronted with the threat of extinction, a psychological state of disavowal that helps make sense of contemporary reactions to a future of anthropogenic climate disruption.[15] Building on this analysis, sociologist Kari Marie Norgaard has written of the social organization of denial that takes place in affluent countries such as Norway and the United States, where the majority of the population not only are not yet adversely affected by climate change but may be said to benefit from the continuing consumption of fossil fuels that imperils not just the future but increasingly wide portions of the planet at present.[16] Similarly, the critical theorist and professional provocateur Slavoj Žižek argues that our responses to looming Armageddon are shaped by forms of collective denial, despair, and withdrawal.[17]

Both pop culture and everyday life have become saturated by what might be called "catastrophic affect"—a visceral feeling that we are not just headed toward civilizational collapse but are already in the midst of it.[18] The result has been a fascination with apocalypse, sometimes related to the overarching crisis of climate change, and sometimes of a more imaginative variety: ubiquitous zombies, global pandemics, tidal waves, flash freezes, famines.[19] These provide people with an experience of climate catharsis, an ability to live out fearful fantasies of apocalyptic environmental and social breakdown, while also being soothed by what frequently double as thinly disguised settler-colonial jeremiads where strong white male protagonists lead a rag-tag group of survivors as they seek to reconstruct a purged social order. Contrasting with these sensational and utterly reaction-ary stories, photographers such as Subhankar Banerjee create ghostly aerial images of the shifting migration routes taken by caribou in the Arctic National Wildlife Refuge as the tundra melts under them, while James Balog documents the hasty retreat of the globe's glaciers in sublime but unnerving time-lapse images.[20] Yet all create images that challenge any notion that history progresses linearly, suggesting instead a present and future that is fragmented, incoherent, punctuated by disaster and, increasingly, apocalyptic.

The Urban Climax: The Collision of Planetary Urbanization and Climate Change

Christian Parenti begins his book *Tropic of Chaos* with a description of the body of a man named Ekaru Loruman.[21] Loruman was a pastoralist from the Turkana tribe of north-western Kenya, a man who tended cattle in the arid savannas of the Rift Valley. According to Parenti, he was killed during a cattle raid launched by members of the neighboring Pokot tribe, into whose territory the Turkana had ventured as their traditional grazing grounds were decimated by severe drought. Parenti uses Loruman's death to engage in what he calls "climate war forensics," an inquiry into the large geopolitical and climatological forces that lie behind the proximate causes of Loruman's killing. For Parenti, the formerly colonial countries that lie within the global-spanning tropical zone are increasingly subject to a convergence of three factors: enduring civil strife that is the legacy of the proxy wars of the Cold War era; hollowed out and largely powerless state apparatuses produced by decades of neoliberal austerity programs in the global South; and anthropogenic climate change, which places increased stress on already over-taxed environmental resources such as the grazing grounds of the Turkana and Pokot peoples in the Rift Valley.[22] The World Health Organization calls such overlapping crises "complex emergencies." Climate change causes extreme weather conditions such as droughts that accelerate complex emergencies throughout the zone that Parenti calls the "tropics of chaos."

Parenti tells us that Ekaru Loruman had three wives and eight children. He does not explain what happened to these women and children after Loruman's death. Perhaps they struggled to keep Loruman's remaining cattle alive in the face of hostile environmental and social conditions. Certainly they would have turned to fellow tribesmen and women for help, but given the conditions described by Parenti it seems unlikely that they would find easy sanctuary in a stable family of kinsmen and women. Perhaps Loruman's wives and children would eventually have followed the footsteps of the millions driven off the land every year around the world. Abandoning Loruman's bitterly contested and arid land, his wives and children might have sought refuge in a nearby town or city. There they would have expected to find higher standards of living and more peaceful existence, but they would also face yet another convergence, equally fearsome as the one Parenti described, a conjuncture with even greater significance for the future of humanity and life on Earth in general: the collision of an urbanizing humanity and the increasingly extreme forms of weather unleashed by climate change.

Two great tides are converging on the world's cities, generating an unprecedented urban climax. The first of these is a human tide. In 2007, humanity became a predominantly city-dwelling species. Of the approximately 7 billion humans current living, 3.3 billion live in cities. But if the human condition is now an urban one, this urban humanity is not spread evenly across the world's cities. Although urbanists in the global North often regard urbanization through the lens of city-building processes in Europe and North America over the last two centuries, most of today's urban population lives in the developing world, where the vast majority of urban population growth will take place. These city-dwellers are to a significant extent refugees from policies of agricultural deregulation and financial liberalization.[23] Enforced by tools of the developed world's financial hegemony such as the World Bank and the International Monetary Fund, these policies of economic austerity pushed millions of peasants off the land and into slums in the rapidly growing but largely deindustrialized urban conglomerations of the global South during the last half-century. This bitter harvest of the worldwide agrarian crisis has been one of the largest transformations in human history.[24] The neoliberal world order has essentially been a machine generating forms of extreme urbanization rooted in inequality. In the cities of the global South, one third to a half of the urban population lives in informal settlements.[25] Residents of these unplanned zones face highly difficult conditions in their struggle to survive. As Mike Davis puts it, "Instead of cities of light soaring toward heaven, much of the twenty-first century urban world squats in squalor, surrounded by pollution, excrement, and decay."[26] Davis has been criticized for the hyperbolic tenor of his description of the neoliberal "planet of slums," and somewhat unjustly has been charged with ignoring the everyday forms of human solidarity that knit together even the poorest informal settlements.[27] Nonetheless, his account captures the radical challenges occasioned by this fundamental transformation in the human condition (even if he fails to discuss climate change at length).

The hazardous nature of what Davis calls slum ecology is a key element of contemporary urbanization. The only land available to the poor tends to be located in the most disaster-prone precincts of cities, on terrain that has not been developed because of the natural perils—from landslides to floods—that make it unsuitable for elite habitation.[28] Often urban squatters live in the midst of toxic landfills or industrial waste dumps, on the verges of railways and electricity lines, or in low-lying, flood-prone land. Their vulnerability to environmental disasters is an extension of the harsh social calculus that drives them to live in dangerous sites. In addition, simply by living in these places, the poor generate conditions that threaten their own lives, including what Davis calls an "excremental surplus."[29] Since few slums have functional sanitary infrastructure, illnesses related to water supply, waste disposal, and garbage kill thousands of people around the world every day.[30] This lack of infrastructure is, in many cases, a legacy of colonialism, when European settlers viewed the colonized as inherently unworthy of living in cities, and consequently systematically denied the amenities of modernity to urban neighborhoods where the indigenous lived.[31] The

wretched legacy of this colonial infrastructural has been intensified rather than ameliorated in recent decades by the moves of
international financial institutions such as the World Bank to
privatize sewage systems and water treatment plants in the cities
of the global South.

Exacerbating this hazardous slum ecology, the vast majority
of the world's city dwellers lie directly in the path of increasingly extreme forms of weather. Exiled by austerity, concomitant civil conflicts, and climatic turbulence into the world's
megacities, an increasingly large proportion of humanity finds
itself especially vulnerable to the second great transforming
force of our age: anthropogenic climate disruption. Close to
70 percent of the world's population today lives in drought-
prone areas; in cities, the heat-island effect can intensify the
impact of heat waves and bring deadly infectious diseases such
as meningitis, malaria, dengue, and the West Nile Virus. In
addition, nearly two thirds of the world's cities with more than
5 million inhabitants are partially located in low-elevation
coastal zones, where they are subject to ever more frequent
and intense cyclones and coastal storms catalyzed by climate
change.[32] Close to 2 billion people, 38 percent of humanity,
currently live in densely populated coastal areas that are highly
prone to devastating floods.[33] Tropical storms and cyclones
currently affect 1.4 billion people each year, 24 percent of the
world's contemporary urbanized population. The number of
people exposed to cyclones alone is projected to more than
double to 680 million by 2050.[34] The areas most prone to such
disasters extend in a band across the planet's tropics, including
urban regions in Central America, the Caribbean, the Bay of
Bengal, China, and the Philippines. In this urban "tropics of
chaos," the calamities that befall slum dwellers must be seen
not as "natural" disasters, but as anthropogenic climate disruptions in which uneven development and social inequality play
a key role.

But the catastrophic climax is not unfolding in the global
South alone. The threat posed by climate change to wealthy
nations is real, present, and escalating. Perhaps the starkest

warning of the mayhem to come was the European heat wave of 2003, which killed an estimated 70,000 European city-dwellers, a figure that dwarfs the 1,800 deaths from Hurricane Katrina in New Orleans.[35] In addition, rising sea levels will affect many of the world's powerful global cities, the key command-and-control nodes of the global capitalist economy. Most of these metropoles happen to be port cities, a fact largely ignored in the literature on the global city.[36] The United States for example has eight key global cities: New York, Los Angeles, Chicago, Boston, San Francisco-Oakland, Washington, DC, Miami, and Philadelphia, all lying in coastal zones. (Chicago is located on the inland coast of Lake Michigan.) Rising sea levels and intensifying storms threaten almost all of them. In global terms, the top ten cities whose populations are exposed to natural disasters today are almost evenly split between developed and developing countries: Mumbai, Guangzhou, Shanghai, Miami, Ho Chi Minh City, Kolkata, Greater New York, Osaka-Kobe, Alexandria, and New Orleans.[37] In terms of imperiled economic assets, however, the list tilts heavily toward the developed world, with Miami, Greater New York, New Orleans, Osaka-Kobe, Tokyo, Amsterdam, Rotterdam, Nagoya, Tampa-St. Petersburg, and Virginia Beach topping the list. Although these cities contain 60 percent of threatened economic assets, they are located in only four countries: the United States, Japan, the Netherlands, and China. Each of these cities is a key node in global circuits of transportation and exchange. There will be extremely grave ramifications for the global economy if any of them are seriously damaged by the storms to come. It is projected that the threat to these cities' wealth will multiply tenfold by 2070, while the total population exposed to natural disasters could triple to around 150 million people.[38] These statistics highlight the fact that vulnerability to extreme weather is not simply a result of the exposure of masses of people to hurricanes, cyclones, and droughts, but a product of the complex interplay of populations, infrastructures, economic and political institutions, and anthropogenic climate change.[39]

Coastal cities face a future of ongoing systemic crisis as a result of climate change. These crises are likely to unfold as a slow cascade of rising mortality rates punctuated by spectacular disasters. As population numbers soar in these cities, increasing numbers of people are likely to be abandoned to their own devices, left exposed by the nonexistent or fraying infrastructures that buffer people from disasters. Compounding the threat of rising sea levels, the land on which most coastal cities are built is simultaneously sinking in a process known as subsidence. This process was directly responsible for the devastating impact of Hurricane Katrina on New Orleans, but it is a process unfolding around the world in fast-urbanizing river deltas, including the Po delta in Italy, Egypt's Nile delta, the Ganges-Brahmaputra in India and Bangladesh, Vietnam's Mekong, and China's Yellow River delta. More than 500 million people currently live in the world's river deltas, incredibly rich but ecologically sensitive regions that are subsiding at an alarming rate of 10 centimeters or so a year, causing the sea to swallow up dozens of meters of land in these regions each year. Over the past decade, 85 percent of the world's major river deltas experienced flooding, killing hundreds of thousands of people.[40] In tandem with this process of subsidence, coastal erosion is destroying the natural barriers that protect deltaic cities from increasingly severe storms and their surge waters. As mountain glaciers melt, hundreds of trillions of gallons of meltwater rush into surrounding seas that are themselves warming and, consequently, growing in volume. This convergence means that increasing numbers of the world's coastal cities will soon fall below sea level, and will be exposed to the increasingly severe storms and surges born of an overheated planet.

While residents of coastal cities around the world will face increasingly extreme conditions in the coming years and decades, it is the poor who are the most vulnerable to cascading climate disruptions in cities. In the cities of the global South, already life-threatening conditions in informal settlements are being exacerbated by climate change. When disasters do not directly take people's lives by collapsing hastily fabricated buildings and unstable land, the lack of storm drainage and solid-waste disposal can magnify the impact of floods. Infectious diseases can be rapidly transmitted through floodwaters, leading to outbreaks of cholera, typhoid, leptospirosis, and meningitis that destroy the lives of the poor even after the floodwaters recede. Increasingly fragile, global-spanning food supplies are disrupted. For people living in informal settlements, infrastructure is a constantly improvised and negotiated collective achievement rather than an invisible and taken-for-granted aspect of urban life.[41] As a consequence, everyday hazards can often turn into disasters for the urban poor in the global South. But when extreme weather events cause infrastructure to break down, vulnerable denizens of even the world's most wealthy cities can find their lives imperiled, as the hurricanes in New Orleans and New York and the heat waves in Chicago and Europe demonstrated. In such circumstances, the catastrophic climax of urbanization and climate change affects vulnerable people such as the elderly and the poor above all, but it also threatens massive amounts of capitalist assets. Why, given these dramatic present-day and future threats, is there not more public alarm?

Invisible Cities: How Contemporary Cities Are Both Hypervisible and Totally Ignored

On 30 July 2012, sweltering heat in India's capital city New Delhi led to record power use, as people set electrical pumps to work drawing water from wells and the affluent cranked up their air conditioners. In tandem, farmers in the northern states of Punjab and Haryana, struggling to keep their crops growing in the face of a delayed monsoon season, drew increased power from the grid to run pumps irrigating paddy fields. The failure of the monsoon rains to arrive ironically also meant that hydropower plants were generating less electricity. While Indian citizens are used to rolling blackouts, the cascading collapse that knocked power out in most of northern India that day set records. Over 300 million people were without electricity. Phones and traffic signals stopped working.[42] Railways were shut down for hours, trapping many people in the middle of their morning commute. Many hospitals had to suspend operations. Water supplies broke down as treatment plants and pumping stations stopped functioning. It became impossible to draw water from wells powered with electrical pumps. Although power was restored relatively quickly, the following day, 31 July, an even broader power outage knocked out power for 620 million people.

India faces unique challenges relating to its electrical infrastructure: an estimated 27 percent of energy generated is lost in transmission or stolen, according to India's Central Electricity Authority, and 25 percent of the country's population, about 300 million people, have no access to electricity at all.[43] But lest the denizens of developed countries feel smug about power failures in the developing world, it's worth recalling that the northeastern United States suffered a similar cascading power outage during the summer of 2003, an event that shut off electricity for 55 million people in the midst of an intense summer heat wave.[44] Subways in New York stopped running. Air conditioners no longer worked. Water stopped flowing out of faucets. Hundreds of thousands of people had to walk back to their homes in the outer boroughs in the blistering sun.

Heat waves and the cascading power outages that they often occasion are becoming increasingly frequent in cities across the global North and South. Extreme heat already accounts for more weather-related deaths per year than any other form of extreme weather.[45] What would happen if a prolonged heat wave were to plunge a major city such as New York or São Paulo into a multiday blackout? What emergency systems are in place to support an urban population of tens of millions when electrical pumps are no longer working to deliver water, and when transport systems that might move people out of a blackout zone are crippled? If the deadly heat waves of 2003 in Europe and of 1995 in Chicago demonstrate the potentially catastrophic impact of heat extremes, surprisingly little attention has focused on what scientists call the urban heat island effect and on the vulnerability of urban populations. The heat island effect means that cities are, on average, 30 percent hotter than the countryside. Yet climate science measures climate change on the scale of the planet as a whole, rather than on the urban scale, where the impact of warming is demonstrably far more extreme. In fact, scientists statistically adjust data collected from urban weather stations when they seek to measure global temperature fluctuations.[46] As a result, the extreme forms of warming occurring in cities—the places where the majority of humanity now lives—are edited out of scientific assessments of climate change. This effectively means that official assessments radically underestimate the magnitude of warming experienced by city dwellers around the globe today. As Brian Stone puts it, "For many, to live in a large city today is to live on the leading edge of the most rapidly changing environmental conditions ever experienced by humans—and to not even know it."[47]

If climate science has effectively made cities invisible, it builds on a long-standing refusal within Western environmentalism to think of the city as a site forged in the crucible of nature. Western thought, in fact, has long represented the city and the country, society and nature, as radical antitheses.[48] Environmental theory has consequently largely ignored the urbanization process as one of the driving forces behind environmental issues and neglected to discuss the city as the site where social and environmental problems are experienced most dramatically.[49] However, cities are where humans metabolize nature (see Chapter 1), and the record blackouts in India and the United States highlight just how complex and precarious these metabolic processes can be: a storm in the Midwest, a delayed monsoon, higher temperatures in cities like Delhi and New York lead to unpredictable, cascading power outages that make the most basic amenities of contemporary life—access to clean drinking water, for instance—impossible. Yet notwithstanding the centrality of cities as sites for the production of nature, the intellectual legacy of environmental thought leads contemporary scientists to frame climate change in global terms, a scale that ignores what is happening in the specific places where most people now live.

Despite this unfortunate intellectual tradition, the city is the terrain where the catastrophes of climate change are felt most intensely. Hurricane Katrina generated some of the most powerful representations of what the sociologist Ulrich Beck calls "the world at risk," as the media was saturated with images of New Orleans's poor and predominantly African-American residents abandoned by their country, standing on rooftops begging for help, huddled in unsanitary conditions in the Superdome, lying face down in the toxic floodwaters.[50] Images of New York following Hurricane Sandy did not convey the same visceral sense of social injustice, but they did dramatize the fragility of the modernity that residents of global cities such as New York take for granted. As the power grid went down, the subways and roadways flooded, cell phone service was interrupted, and, in some parts of the city, residents were trapped by broken elevators in unheated buildings. Hurricane Sandy made it clear that contemporary urban life is increasingly fragile and risky, dependent on a huge range of interwoven, surprisingly vulnerable infrastructure networks.

Cities are the hubs of the vast, globe-spanning infrastructures of energy, water, waste, material goods, communication, and capital.[51] If cities embody the Enlightenment dream of controlling nature through science and technology, this dream is facilitated by all-too-tangible infrastructure. While this infrastructure is sometimes elevated as a symbol of collective achievement, providing powerful ideological legitimation for states and nations, it is frequently taken for granted, its success measured by ubiquity and invisibility. This is not the case everywhere. In much of the global South, infrastructure such as the pipes that bring life-sustaining fresh water and take sewage away remains inaccessible, and access to electricity is provisional and precarious. Improvisation and overlapping backup systems play key roles in such situations. Rather than disappearing, these conditions of precarious infrastructure have been dramatically extended during the neoliberal age; indeed, many residents of cities in the global North now find access to water curtailed by neoliberal schemes of privatization and fee-paying. As these elements of urban modernity, formerly considered universal and mundane, are stripped away, their political character is made apparent.

New York has long been an epicenter for fears about the fragility of urban life.[52] The destruction of the World Trade Center on 9/11 revived a long-standing pop culture genre of New York being hit by disaster. For over two centuries, New York has been flattened by monsters, blown up, and swallowed by the sea in novels and films. Alexis Rockman's mural depicting Brooklyn as a vast floodplain, with familiar landmarks such as the Brooklyn Bridge metamorphosed into tropical plant-covered ruins, is but the latest example. These representations, which stretch all the way back to the Italian painter Nicolino Calyo's portrayal of the calamitous fire of 1835 in Manhattan, give form to the everyday processes of demolition and construction that are endemic to city building.[53] Yet if each generation has produced images of destruction that reflect and seek to resolve its own fears, perhaps the central theme running throughout the disaster genre has been the city's destruction at the hands of angry working-class mobs and revolting immigrants. From Joaquin Miller's *The Destruction of Gotham* (1886) to films made during the city's financial crisis such as 1981's *Fort Apache, the Bronx* and *Escape from New York,* fears of a city consumed by racial and ethnic violence have loomed large in the imagination of New York. The city's diversity and stark inequalities make it a fitting setting for the genre, but so do the particular architectural and urban qualities of the city: its density and the verticality of its buildings make it a peculiarly spectacular site to destroy on screen. Ultimately, however, it is the reactionary class- and race-based fears of the city's elites that provide the foundation for such apocalyptic fantasies.

The attacks of 9/11 made these fears a reality, turning one of the city's primary connections to the world, the commercial airliner, into a weapon. To the extent that financial decisions made in New York, the capital of capital, now affect the life chances of millions of people around the world, the al-Qaeda attacks were an instance of the racialized urban destruction genre, played out on a global stage. The performances of grief and defiance at Ground Zero by public figures such as President George W. Bush and Mayor Rudolph Giuliani focused on demonic attacks by foreign terrorists, heroic response by brave New Yorkers such as firefighters and paramedics, patriotic rebirth, and urban resiliency. Ongoing issues related to 9/11, from the struggles of many first responders to receive adequate health coverage to the yawning elite bias of financial incentives to repopulate downtown Manhattan, were conveniently brushed over by this anodyne elite narrative.

Hurricane Sandy took some of the air out of the prevailing accounts. It suddenly seemed to many New Yorkers that we had spent the last decade preparing for the wrong threats. Billions of dollars spent to insulate the city during the War on Terror could do nothing to turn back the rising tides of climate change. Instead of locking down public space and shredding civil liberties in preparation for terrorist attacks that never materialized, the city might have devoted its substantial energies to preparing for storm surges and sea level rise. Sandy made it plain that New York faces not just the fire but also the flood next time.

Hurricane Sandy confirmed new understandings of risk that began to emerge in environmental politics, insurance institutions, and financial markets in the late 1980s. In these interconnected realms, catastrophic risk came to designate "a technological accident of biospheric proportions, operating simultaneously at the microscopic and pandemic levels," or in other words, accidents that span many nations and that also unfold on an invisibly small scale.[54] From emerging epidemics like Ebola to global warming, ozone depletion, and "complex humanitarian disasters," the concept of catastrophic risk introduces a fundamentally new calculus of the accident. Unlike car accidents or heart attacks, the occurrence of which can be calculated in statistical terms with great accuracy, catastrophic risks are so unpredictable and so vast in scale that they cannot be

insured against. And because of the global networks that undergird contemporary cities, that risk is spread across much larger
swaths of land, with local crises increasingly more likely to
produce systemic collapse. The financial crisis of 2008, for
example, showed how a relatively localized event could threaten
to destroy the entire world's economic infrastructure.[55]

Yet experts in urban planning had been issuing warnings
concerning the vulnerability of New York's infrastructure to
extreme weather long before Hurricane Sandy arrived. In 2009,
for example, the New York City Panel on Climate Change issued
a prophetic report. Speaking of the dangers faced by the city,
panel member William Solecki, a geographer at Hunter College,
wrote, "In the coming decades, our coastal city will most likely
face more rapidly rising sea levels and warmer temperatures, as
well as potentially more droughts and floods, which will all
have impacts on New York City's critical infrastructure."[56]
While remarkably prescient, Solecki's warnings echoed the char-
acteristically muted and distant future-oriented frame of established climate science, an ironic frame given the fact that his
predictions came true only three years later. Conversely,
Hollywood blockbuster films like *The Day After Tomorrow*
(2004), which focused on the destruction of New York by a wall
of water and a subsequent flash freeze, usually seem so hyperbolic as to be utterly fanciful. Such alarmism and spectacle paradoxically underplay the real threats to the city's infrastructure.
In the face of such manipulative eco-catastrophism, the
Bloomberg administration could only respond to climate change
by intrepidly building bike lanes, as if this was enough to save
the city. No efforts were made to implement even the simplest
defenses against rising tides, such as elevating subway entrances
in vulnerable parts of the city. Representations of spectacular
disaster tend to ignore the attenuated, attritional catastrophes
that wear away at urban infrastructures, material and social,
from increasing rates of asthma to aging power grids, preparing
the way for more swift and spectacular disasters such as Sandy.

But perhaps the greatest reason for the city's failure to prepare
for Hurricane Sandy lies in the monomaniacal focus of urban

and national elites on antiterrorist infrastructure and unrestrained urban development. As the architect and urban theorist Michael Sorkin and his colleagues have shown, the architecture of the national security state paradoxically spawned widespread feelings of insecurity,[57] with defensive measures such as concrete barriers in front of public buildings throughout the city to less tangible forms of surveillance in public spaces, such as airports and the Internet, drumming home the message that we are imperiled. Such fear was of great utility to the elites who controlled the state after 9/11, as it legitimated unprecedented levels of policing and militarism both domestically and abroad. Media depictions of the attacks made the public even more acquiescent to an expansive regime of capitalist imperialism, just as they had during the Cold War.[58] This had profound social and material effects. By focusing public attention on particular threats, such as the foreign terrorist, this regime of fear rendered other threats invisible, deflecting New Yorkers' attention from the ones posed by climate disruption.

Hurricane Sandy unmasked the contradictions and injustices of these narratives of security and resilience. Urban elites and officials had assured the public that they were strengthening the resilience of "critical infrastructures" after 9/11, yet when Sandy struck the city, infrastructural collapse cascaded through the urban system. As in New Orleans following Hurricane Katrina, the differences in how the storm impacted different parts of the city were dramatic. While it flooded the wealthy downtown area and the financial district first, the distribution of power in the city was nevertheless made apparent both in terms of who had access to clean water, to food, to power, and to transportation in the city and in how and where resources were allocated in reconstruction. Most of all, it became clear that the defense of critical infrastructure which the city had engaged in for over a decade had little to do with protecting ordinary people from the risk of violent death. Instead, the post-9/11 state of terror was really focused on protecting the infrastructures that allowed elites to continue accumulating capital.

Cities Will Make You Happy: The New Urban Boosterism and the Limits of Market Environmentalism

Not everyone holds such gloomy attitudes toward urban life. As humanity has transformed into a predominantly urban species, a bevy of analysts has emerged, publishing books with relentlessly optimistic titles like *Happy City, Smart Cities,* and *Welcome to the Urban Revolution.* These new city boosters, who might be called the *citerati,* frame planetary urbanization as a relatively unmitigated good.[59] The *citerati* are late arrivals to the urban party, setting up shop decades after elites discovered the city as a site for highly profitable real estate speculation, but their adoration of urban life reflects the continuing significance of urban redevelopment to global capitalism.[60] Most of these commentators are based in the United States and are economists by training. Many are also "urban strategy consultants," "social entrepreneurs," and fellows at prominent conservative think tanks such as the Manhattan Institute.[61] All have failed to address, in any significant way, the most crucial characteristic of extreme cities.

Edward Glaeser, an endowed chair in economics at Harvard, is the highest profile member of the *citerati,* and his views are also representative of the group as a whole. "Cities," he writes in *The Triumph of the City,* "have been engines of innovation since Plato and Socrates bickered in an Athenian marketplace,"[62] places where "proximity, denseness, closeness" have unleashed human creative potential, and especially that most-loved buzzword of neoliberalism: innovation. In other words, the density of talent in cities constantly generates new ideas and technologies that drive humanity forward, from startups to intellectual life. This argument is founded on astonishing historical ignorance. The idea that global centers of capital accumulation such as London and Tokyo have risen to prominence through innovation ignores their role in the transatlantic slave trade, in a hierarchical imperial world order, or as nodes of command and control over financial flows. Cities across the ages have certainly been crucibles of immense creativity, but their growth over the last 500 years was produced through a capitalist system of yawning inequalities. The prosperity of some cities, alongside the poverty of others, is a direct product of this system, in much the same way as the wealth of a few relies on the misery of the many. This oversight allows Glaeser to attribute the poverty of some cities to the lack of imagination of their inhabitants. "The failure of Detroit and so many other industrial towns doesn't reflect any weakness of cities as a whole, but rather the sterility of those cities that lost touch with the essential ingredients of urban reinvention,"[63] he writes. Glaeser conveniently ignores Detroit's sordid history of racism, corporate flight, and neoliberal abandonment.[64] In addition, he views slums around the world in a positive light. "There is a lot to like about urban poverty," he writes.[65] "The flow of less advantaged people into cities from Rio to Rotterdam demonstrates urban strength, not weakness.[66] In other words, urban poverty should not be judged by comparison with urban wealth but in relation to rural poverty. Urban slums "often serve as springboards to middle-class prosperity."[67]

There are a number of glaring omissions in Glaeser's blithe account of life in the world's shantytowns. For one thing, it is not clear how often the hundreds of millions of people living tenuously in informal settlements manage to bootstrap themselves into "middle-class prosperity." Nor is it clear what Glaeser means by the term, basing his argument on the example of "Jews who settled in the Lower East Side [of New York]"—hardly an example of great relevance for people living in a shantytown in Karachi or Harare today—and on the story of a Brazilian beauty salon owner who grew up in a Rio favela. Such carefully selected anecdotal rags-to-riches success stories reflect a threadbare trickle-down theory, in which the growing wealth of a city will ultimately enrich all of its occupants.[68] This view might have resonated with some in New York during the 1890s, but in today's world of vertiginously increasing inequality it is credible neither in Bangalore nor in New York.

Worse yet, Glaeser gives a totally distorted view of the factors that drive people to migrate to cities. For Glaeser, it is the inexorable improvement of agricultural productivity that pushes people out of the countryside, a take that conveniently ignores the impact of decades of neoliberal structural adjustment programs on the agricultural sector in the global South.[69] As Mike Davis has documented at great length in *Planet of Slums*, these programs have pried open the tariff systems protecting agriculture in postcolonial nations, subjecting them to an onslaught of subsidized agricultural goods from wealthy capitalist nations that has contributed to a wholesale dispossession of the global peasantry.[70] These neoliberal policies have been an unacknowledged instrument for the mass production of slums, while concomitantly drastically undercutting the urban antipoverty programs of the development era. By ignoring these structural push factors, Glaeser is conveniently able to elide the immense misery they generate, the economic actors responsible for that misery, and, most importantly, the structural contradictions of the capitalist world system that are producing a planet of slums without generating the well-paying urban jobs and infrastructure that made the cities of the industrial era into economic springboards.

And nowhere in *The Triumph of the City* is there any serious acknowledgement of the threat that climate change poses to cities in either poor or rich countries. Perhaps the most blatant omission in Glaeser's discussion of global cities is any consideration of what Mike Davis calls "slum ecologies," the forms of inequality that push urban squatter communities to live in the most marginal and often dangerous portions of the city. Slum ecologies place squatter communities living in the burgeoning cities of the global South in the frontlines of the climate crisis. When Glaeser does write about cities and climate change, it is to warn about the threat of urban sprawl and to extol the ecological benefits of living in high-density cities like New York. The argument, advanced in more detail in David Owen's *Green Metropolis: Why Living Smaller, Living Closer, and Driving Less Are the Keys to Sustainability,* is that the United States's sky-high contemporary greenhouse gas emissions is primarily caused by white middle-class flight to the suburbs after 1945.[71] The peculiarly American nexus of oil, highways, automobiles, and suburban housing tracts and their "grotesquely oversized environmental footprints," as Mike Davis writes,[72] means that American cities cannot be an example to the rest of the world. But density does not automatically diminish emissions. That requires other measures to hold consumption and pollution in check. In fact, luxury housing developments in high-density global cities are one of the leading components of carbon emissions. In New York, for example, 2 percent of the city's buildings—the luxurious condos and corporate skyscrapers of the city's elite—use 45 percent of the city's energy.[73] The promotion of density by Glaeser and other *citerati* utterly ignores the unsustainable character of an urban regime that, like the broader capitalist system, is dedicated to unchecked, senseless growth.

Among the *citerati*, Matthew Kahn, a sometime collaborator of Glaeser's and author of *Climatopolis: How Our Cities Will Thrive in the Hotter Future*, is exceptional in the attention he devotes to climate change and the city.[74] Kahn is not only willing to critique how wealthy urbanites insulate themselves from climate change-related risks.[75] He also acknowledges the significant threats posed to megacities in the global South. "I am willing to name some cities that I would not advise buying property in: Dhaka, Jakarta, Manila, and Calcutta. These cities are precariously located in coastal at-risk areas. Their population density is high. It is already hot in these cities, and at least up to this point, their governments do not appear to be up to the job of protecting them," he writes.[76] The problem with Kahn is that he believes the market will solve all such problems. "We're not all on board one big ship that we can save through one collective decision," he writes. "Instead, we'll be 'saved' by a multitude of self-interested people armed only with their wits and access to capitalist markets. Capitalist growth created the problem of mass greenhouse gases, but now capitalism's dynamism and its ability to reinvent itself will help us adapt to the climate changes we have created."[77] It is no accident that the United Nations, the primary locus for global negotiations to curtail carbon emissions, is mentioned only once in *Climatopolis*, and not in connection with climate change negotiations.[78] Kahn may be willing to admit that capitalism is responsible for climate change, but, as a proponent of the dismal science of neoliberal economics, he cannot abide the idea that humanity should respond to this disaster through collective means.

"As climate change heats up our cities, it will create enormous demand for new products to protect people," he writes, celebrating the magic hand of capitalist markets. "Households that continue to live in a hotter Phoenix will seek out new architectural designs for homes, windows, and more energy-efficient air conditioning to protect them from summer heat. This is just the tip of the iceberg. Such anticipated demand creates opportunities for green entrepreneurs to step in and innovate, as well as serious competition as they fight with one another for market share."[79]

Amphibious Cities: The Vicissitudes of Adaptation and Urban Greening in Holland

If any cities can be seen as a test case for Kahn's argument, it would be those of the Dutch megalopolis known as the Randstad, which includes the cities of Amsterdam, Rotterdam, The Hague, and Utrecht. One quarter of the Netherlands lies below sea level, and half of the country is threatened by storm surges and flooding rivers. The Dutch people's world-renowned fight against flooding is not only on display in the low-lying *polders*, tracts of land from which water has been pumped (originally by windmills and today by diesel engines), but also in Dutch cities. These cities are seen by urban planners as exemplary for their balanced economies, their integrated land-use and transport planning, and their dedication to living with finite resources.[80] They are also increasingly touted as paradigm setters for adaptation to climate change. Rotterdam, for instance, is surrounded on all four sides by water, meaning that it can't simply flush the water away. The city has won plaudits from designers and environmentalists for its urban climate change adaptation projects. Examples include *Benthemplein* park, a space that functions both as a public square during normal times and as a giant water-absorbing cistern during periods of strong rainfall. Other celebrated examples in Rotterdam include large underground car parks built by the city that can double as water storage facilities, a city-subsidized green roof scheme, and an amphibious solar-powered pavilion that floats in the city's old harbor. These experiments with urban adaptation have brought global fame and lucrative consultation contracts to Dutch engineering and design companies. "The world makes its money in big cities, so they have to be operational, which means they'll need climate change protection and infrastructure," remarks Piet Dircke, global water management director for the Netherlands-based company Arcadis, which advises cities from Jakarta to New York on climate change adaptation.[81] The success of companies such as Arcadis, and of individuals like Henk Ovink, a Dutchman who moved from being director of his country's Office of Spatial Planning and Water Management to working as senior advisor to Shaun Donovan, US Secretary of Housing and Urban Development under President Obama, seems to support Matthew Kahn's arguments about how urban climate change adaptation efforts will be driven by innovative entrepreneurs.[82]

The extreme conditions faced by the Dutch may have made their fight against water famous, but they also make it relatively distinctive and probably not applicable to many other contexts. For one thing, the Dutch coastline, at 1,139 miles in total, is relatively short.[83] The coastline of Florida alone is 200 miles longer. In addition, Holland is both rich and relatively homogeneous culturally, which means that the economic and political capital for large-scale engineering feats is not as difficult to mobilize as it would be in many other parts of the world. These specificities should prompt questions about the translatability of the Dutch experience with water. Are the solutions pioneered by Dutch cities to cope with rising seas really viable in other contexts? How truly sustainable are Dutch cities such as Rotterdam? And to what extent are these Dutch innovations really driven by the free markets celebrated by the *citerati*?

Holland was one of the first modern capitalist economies, an empire based on the mercantile prowess of its globe-straddling fleets.[84] But the Dutch relationship with water has been determined more by structures of democratic govern-ance than purely capitalist exploitation. The creation of the polder system and the reclamation of large tracts of land from the North Sea was overseen by the Dutch water boards, locally based and collectively run institutions responsible for main-taining dikes and dams and for ensuring the adequate func-tioning of the extensive hydraulic engineering systems that kept the country dry from the Golden Age in the seventeenth century to the present.[85] As their names suggest, trading cities like Amsterdam and Rotterdam evolved around coastal dams and dikes, which offered a winning combination of flood protection, well-placed harbors, and urban water systems that were frequently cleansed by river water flowing through the cities' extensive canals out to the sea. But their success in taming the sea and rivers generated a control paradox: as the land dried out, it also subsided, meaning that the country's protective barriers needed to be raised constantly. Stronger protection against water ironically served at times simply to intensify the power of the waters that raged against those barriers. The Dutch have consequently grown used to frequent but relatively inconsequential floods.

It was in the twentieth century that Dutch ambitions to tame the water led to a series of massive engineering projects, which necessitated shifting Dutch water planning traditions from a local to a national scale. The first of these projects, largely built in the interwar period, dammed off the Zuiderzee, a large, shal-low inlet of the North Sea to the northeast of Amsterdam. Thousands of kilometers of land in the newly enclosed waters were then reclaimed using the traditional system of polders. The Zuiderzee Works protected the country's northwest flank from catastrophic flooding but in 1953 a huge storm surge pushed water from the North Sea into the network of estuaries surrounding Rotterdam in the country's southwest, inundating 165,000 hectares of land and drowning 1,835 people and 30,000 animals. Dutch officials vowed that such deadly flooding would never again strike their country. They set about constructing the Delta Works, a massive system of dams, sluices, dikes, levees, and storm-surge barriers that effectively shortened and armored the coastline of the southeast against future storms.[86] But the Delta Works do not form a totally impervious barrier; if they did, the region's rich tidal estuaries, with all of their abundant wildlife, would be condemned to death. To prevent this, Dutch engineers built a series of retractable sluice-gate-style doors into the nine-kilometer-long *Oosterscheldekering* or Eastern Scheld storm-surge barrier. The doors remain open most of the time, preserving the rich but fragile local ecosystem, but can be lowered when storms on the North Sea threaten to drive storm-surge waters into the delta region. Once this barrier was completed in 1986, only one opening to the North Sea remained: the channel leading up the Rhine river to Rotterdam, the busiest seaport in the world and the entrance point for cargo to the European heartland. The river had to be kept open for shipping, but as long as it remained so the city of Rotterdam was threatened with potentially catastrophic flooding. To beat this apparent catch-22, Dutch water engineers designed the *Maeslantkering*, a pair of storm-surge barriers that pivot on massive robotic arms to seal off the waterway when storm surges threaten the city. Construction on the *Maeslantkering* began in 1991, and, once completed six years later, finished the complex of Delta Works, apparently realizing the vision of totally protecting Holland from stormy seas once and for all.

Holland's Delta Works warrant three principal observations, each of which sheds critical light on the arguments of the *citerati*. First, these massive projects—some of the greatest feats of engineering in the world—were possible only through the combined political and economic support of the Dutch state. The tradition of democratic control of flooding that emerged from Holland's water boards and the recognition that risk is distributed widely across Dutch society meant that there was negligible political opposition to hefty state spending to fund the megaprojects. The political calculus behind the Delta Works was a world away from the free market ideology that is so dominant in the United States and that animates the vision of *citerati* like Matthew Kahn. While individual engineering firms were involved in the Delta Works and often displayed immense ingenuity in response to the ecological challenges of the delta, the massive infrastructure projects constructed in Holland over the course of the twentieth century could only have been undertaken by a strong central state. One has to reach back in the United States historical record to the dam- and highway-building efforts of the New Deal to find an equivalently ambitious nation-spanning dedication to public infrastructure. To imagine that a Twitter or a Tesla would be capable of such extensive public works—that capitalist corporations, in other words, would address the threat of flooding on such a massive and systematic scale—is to fundamentally misunderstand the task of building infrastructure, which, in a case such as Holland where a breach in one dike threatens vast swaths of the country, must be holistic or must fail utterly. The fragmentation and advanced decline of public infrastructure in the United States— our collapsing bridges, mass evacuations from unstable dams, and highways that are more potholes than roads—is a symptom of the neoliberal doctrines of private affluence and public penury.[87]

The second thing to observe about the Delta Works is that the sluice gates and robotic arms of the *Oosterscheldekering* and the *Maeslantkering*—what makes them truly distinctive—derive not simply from the ingenuity of Dutch engineers but also from the political mobilization of Dutch environmentalists and maritime laborers, who fought to save the tidal estuaries around Rotterdam. In other words, the renowned Delta Works were not solely innovations in design; they were significant cultural shifts. If the Dutch struggle against floods gave birth to typically modern attitudes that celebrated humanity's Promethean power to mold and subdue the natural world, the environmental struggles around the Delta Works helped catalyze a cultural shift that challenged such hidebound ideas of mastery over nature. The Dutch began to ask how it might be possible to live alongside nature, to use natural formations as a protective force rather than to simply armor themselves off from the watery world that surrounds them. This shift in attitudes toward the natural world also sparked a change in the people engaging with water, adding ecologists and landscape architects to the ranks of engineers and water managers charged with protecting Dutch cities and countryside from floods.

Yet despite their Pharaonic scale, the Delta Works didn't solve the control paradox that plagued the Dutch. Indeed, in some ways they exacerbated this paradox. The Dutch had long looked to their coasts as the frontlines in their fight with rising tides, and in many ways the Delta Works constituted the capstone in their battle on this front. But by looking to the sea, the Dutch gave relatively short shrift to the dangers posed by riverine flooding. This fact was made clear in the mid-1990s, when strong rains swelled rivers in the delta to bursting point. The resulting flooding was the worst to strike the country since 1953, occurring despite the monumental Delta and Zuiderzee Works. Although the rivers ultimately receded without causing catastrophic damage, the threat of flooding from the rivers that traverse the country had been hammered home. Dutch scientists by this time understood that climate change would bring increasingly strong precipitation, creating an intense control paradox: sealing off the coastline to potential storm surges could mean bottling in floodwaters coming down rivers like the Rhine and Meuse. While heavy precipitation linked to climate change threatened intense disaster, climate change also brought the potential for more slow-moving and invisible risk, as increasingly dry summers diminish freshwater flows through the aquifers in Holland, allowing growing penetration of both freshwater and soils by salt water that threatens the country's agriculture.[88]

When New Orleans was decimated by Hurricane Katrina in 2005, the Dutch saw a premonition of the potential fate of their own cities. They reacted by appointing a second Delta Commission that was charged with drafting a series of proposals to climate proof the country for the coming age of climate chaos. This commission proposed a suit of relatively traditional but nonetheless forward-thinking steps, including raising flood protection levels in all diked areas by a factor of ten and creating a special fund to pay for such changes through a levy on natural gas revenues totaling roughly 1 percent of the Dutch gross national product.[89] The commission also helped spawn the national Room for the River program, which further shifted Dutch attitudes toward the natural world. Recognizing that efforts to exclude water completely would not necessarily increase safety, Room for the River proposed to improve the discharge capacity of rivers such as the Rhine, Meuse, Waal, and IJssel through a variety of engineering measures. It also proposed to prepare for periods of potential riverine flooding by buying up plots of farmland to be used as strategic zones of controlled flooding in times of need.[90]

Similar plans for dealing with the threat of urban flooding such as *Rotterdam Water City 2035* (2005) also emerged to deal with the inadequacies of urban drainage infrastructure. (This was a problem generated to a certain extent when many of Rotterdam's historical canals were covered over by "modern" waterworks introduced in the twentieth century.) *Rotterdam Water City* sought ways to increase the amount of space for water catchment in the city, generating design initiatives such as *Benthemplein* water square that have turned the city into an icon of adaptation to rising seas. In both Rotterdam and Amsterdam, these experiments with urban water management have been linked to urban revitalization efforts, as disused former harbor areas have been transformed into new residential districts with the help of urban ecologists, not simply to minimize the impact of the city on the natural world but to make a positive contribution to local ecosystems. In IJburg, a new residential zone built to the east of Amsterdam in the 2000s, an archipelago of seven small man-made islands helped accelerate water flows in a section of the Zuiderzee, an area that had grown increasingly stagnant as a result of the damming of the area in the twentieth century.[91] Environmental groups initially hostile to this planned development were won over when city planners and developers employed urban ecologists to come up with such forms of bioremediation. The increasing health of aquatic ecosystems and waterfowl abundance in the area, which had been recognized as a wetlands habitat of international importance, contributed to what has been called the greening of urban water: the recognition that urban water systems such as canals can be important sites for habitat restoration.[92]

But the well-publicized environmental successes of IJburg have not mollified critics. Ecologists remain uncertain about the impact of these developments on the Lake District as a whole over an extended period of time.[93] Biodiversity, they worry, may have been heightened in only a relatively small area. In addition, the broader, long-term impact of urban expansion, which brings more roads and cars, adding to stormwater runoff and, ultimately, to climate change, remain unresolved. Nevertheless, the IJburg project's purported stimulation of biodiversity has become a key marketing tool for real estate developers, turning the area into one of the fastest developing and most expensive zones of Amsterdam. Urban water has been greened in more ways than one. Above all, IJburg has done little to address issues of urban inequality, and as Hurricanes Katrina and Sandy demonstrated all too clearly, it makes little sense to talk about urban resilience in the face of climate change without considering how social inequality renders particular neighborhoods dramatically more vulnerable than their more well-heeled neighbors.

If the risks of city life are amplified by combined and uneven development in places such as Amsterdam, they are also increasingly apparent on a national scale in Holland. One of the biggest controversies in Holland around the Room for the River program was its plan to allow water to inundate agricultural land periodically, which seemed to devalue rural life.[94] Much of this land had been in families for many generations, and deep cultural memories were woven into the rural landscape. While the Dutch possess a strong orientation toward the collective good, the policy's uneven way of distributing benefits and losses became particularly apparent as urban developments such as IJburg steamed forward at the same time as agricultural land was being sacrificed. For rural people, the idea that climate change made the evacuation of their ancestral lands inevitable was seen as opportunistic. Why should only farmers be asked to make sacrifices, they asked? The Dutch government mobilized significant economic resources to remunerate and resettle these displaced people, but money could not buy back the lost attachment to revered places and homes. This controversy holds important lessons for efforts to retreat from threatened shores in other parts of the world. All too often, community resettlement is at best an afterthought as engineers and architects go about refashioning the landscape.[95] The maintenance of community integrity during the resettlement process must be paramount if people are not to become embittered and even incapacitated by loss.

Once we admit that adaptation is not always a win-win situation, the thorny question of who pays for these efforts inevitably rears its head. Schisms between cities and the countryside that manifested through the Room for the River program are testing Holland's relatively egalitarian arrangements for dealing with rising seas. As climate change places additional strains on hydrological systems already coping with huge demands, it grows more expensive to please everyone. Increasingly, the eastern portions of the country are expressing skepticism about paying for expensive solutions to save industries located in the west such as agriculture threatened by increasing salinity.[96] In tandem with the penetration of salt water, corrosive neoliberal ideologies have also made inroads into Dutch systems of governance. Recent decades have seen the gradual erosion of the Dutch welfare state, national hydraulic engineering, and the comprehensive, rationalized town planning that gave birth to the *Randstad*.[97] In their place, emphasis has increasingly been placed on regional planning. The problem is that it is not clear exactly who should be responsible for planning at such a scale, nor how divergent policies articulated at this scale in different parts of the country should be integrated. Indeed, Dutch cities are increasingly competing with rather than collaborating with one another, rather as cities in the United States do. In a low-lying country like the Netherlands, such a lack of coordinated collaboration holds significant perils as climate change intensifies.

Then there are the questions of scale, and of the relation between specific regions, cities, neighborhoods, and even individual buildings and the whole. Can relatively isolated urban experiments like the IJburg neighborhood in Amsterdam and *Benthemplein* water square in Rotterdam be scaled up to ensure the sustainability of the entire city? For the Dutch architect Koen Olthuis, the Dutch design innovations that have attracted international renown "are often isolated showpieces that hardly contribute to the overall transformation of the urban water system. Neither does replication of demonstration projects take place on a large scale. Therefore, they remain isolated and fail to influence mainstream day-to-day urban water management practice."[98] There are a variety of reasons why such experimental projects are not scaled up to a neighborhood or citywide level. Perhaps the most prominent is cost: it would simply be prohibitively expensive to demolish properties and build water squares throughout a city like Rotterdam.[99] *Benthemplein* consequently remains more of an attractive—and publicity grabbing—demonstration project than a genuine solution to the problem of water and the city. Municipal authorities in places like Rotterdam have in fact recognized that large-scale innovation will ultimately be insufficient to address the problem of flooding, particularly as climate change brings increasingly strong storms. Daniel Goedbloed, Rotterdam's senior advisor on water management, stresses that individual homeowners must accept responsibility for defending against flooding on a home-by-home basis.[100] This recognition is the driving factor behind the city's program of tax incentives for the installation of green roofs, water-absorbing gardens, and other small-scale adaptation schemes. Despite the significant progress catalyzed by such programs, Goedbloed admits that certain neighbor-hoods will inevitably face more frequent inundation. What is needed is an integration of planning for everyday life in Holland, from housing to infrastructure provision, with water manage-ment plans, but ironically the fragmentation of the political sphere is making such holistic planning more difficult just when it is most necessary.

Meanwhile, the storm-surge barrier in the Eastern Scheldt, the *Oosterscheldekering*, has significantly interrupted inter-tidal zones.[101] This has in turn reduced accretion of sand in the area around the protective barrier, leading to an erosion of the area's protective tidal flats. Dutch water authorities plan to replenish the lost sand in the short term while simultaneously increasing flood protection in adjacent areas. But even they know that massive works of engineering such as the *Oosterscheldekering* will eventually become obsolete. The measured withdrawal envisioned in the Room for the River program thus may ultimately be succeeded by more sweeping forms of retreat. As the disaster-risk expert and climate scien-tist Klaus Jacob remarks, he always tells his Dutch colleagues that they had better stay good friends with their neighbors, the French and the Belgians.[102]

Above all, the control paradox experienced by the Dutch is intimately tied to the contradictions of the capitalist economy. As the Dutch geographers Jochem de Vries and Maarten Wolsink argue, "flood defense measures decrease the likelihood of a flooding event and then an area subsequently becomes more attractive for development. This development leads to more disastrous consequences in the case of flooding."[103] The paradoxical result is that "despite all the investments in flood defense, the overall risk has probably increased in the last decades."[104] As real estate development becomes an increas-ingly central engine for Holland's economy, the Dutch are driven to build in places that should be abandoned even while they abandon areas that may have remained habitable. And even as flexibility is added to Dutch water systems, the underly-ing dynamic of the global economy is driving planetary ecosystems to the brink. Absent collective and egalitarian efforts toward massive decarbonization and resource restraint, the Dutch, despite their great ingenuity and grit, will remain prisoners lashed to a sinking ship. As long as the present capitalist system endures there can be no completely safe harbor from the gathering storms.

Image by Rebuild by Design / the BIG team.

4

The Jargon of Resilience

Designing urban spaces to deal with climate change can make cities live up to the utopian hopes of modern architects and urban planners, who dreamed of building metropolises that would weave people and their living spaces into organic relationships. In place of urban alienation and the rule of giant bureaucracies and finance capitalism, urban critics like Lewis Mumford and Jane Jacobs fought to make cities crucibles of community and civic culture. Bjarke Ingels, principal of the immodestly named architectural firm BIG, sees himself as an inheritor of this project and argues that adapting cities to climate change can make them better places to live in both the short and long term. Along with a clutch of other architectural and engineering firms, BIG's design for a ten-mile-long, fifteen-foot-high storm-surge barrier around the southern tip of Manhattan won the top prize in the federally funded Rebuild by Design competition. Ingels conceives of the protective barrier, which he dubs the Dry Line, as a new waterfront park for the city, an attractive public amenity along the lines of the High Line park (repurposed from an elevated train track which once brought cattle to the Meatpacking District). For Ingels, the Dry Line is to be "the love-child of Robert Moses and Jane Jacobs," a project with Moses's scale of ambition that is simultaneously attentive to "the fine-grain scale of the neighborhoods. It shouldn't be about the city turning its back on the water, but embracing it and encouraging access."[1]

The engagement of a high-profile firm such as BIG in Rebuild by Design suggests that an important transformation has taken place in the field of architecture. As the architect and critic Mohsen Mostafavi observes in *Ecological Urbanism*, the proportion of architects committed to sustainable and ecological practices has been small until relatively recently, despite the work of ecologically minded predecessors like Buckminster Fuller and Ian McHarg in the 1960s and 1970s.[2] Mostafavi and other commentators maintain that two key dilemmas have impeded environmentally sensitive architecture: first, a commitment to sustainable building has often been accompanied by poor design; and, second, environmentally oriented architecture has mostly been applied at the level of the building rather than at the scale of the city.[3] Mostafavi argues that increasing awareness of Earth's fragility can push architects and urban designers to develop high-quality "speculative design innovations" for the larger scale of cities and even urban regions.[4] The climate crisis can thus be said to constitute an urgent new imperative for architecture: the necessity to think about environmental design in relation to the ecological life and death of contemporary cities.

The horizon of urban survival is transforming the field of architecture, pushing it, as Mostafavi and Ingels suggest, to jump scale from isolated architectural objects such as buildings to thinking on far broader planes. What, after all, is the point of designing a LEED-certified green building if it's located in a flood zone? Engaged architects and urban designers have begun to take a broader, more holistic approach, viewing neighborhoods alongside surrounding cities and regions, and focusing on the far-flung infrastructure networks that bind together cities, their rural hinterlands, and global sites. As a consequence, landscape design has to a certain extent superseded traditional architecture as the fundamental way of approaching cities.[5] Cutting-edge designers now tend to work in interdisciplinary teams, alongside landscape architects, engineers, biologists, and even anthropologists and sociologists.

At the same time, increasing attention is being paid to the value of participatory and activist planning by citizens[6]—an acknowledgment of sorts of how informal settlements the world over have improvised solutions to the intractable problems of urban life from the ground up. Some architects have responded with what they call "tactical urbanism,[7] abandoning the traditional modernist master plan, with its brazen disregard for the established bonds of communities. Instead, tactical urbanism seeks to support the existing social fabric while engaging in what the renowned Brazilian urbanist Jaime Lerner calls "urban acupuncture": carefully targeted interventions like well-designed and ecologically sustainable public spaces that can transform surrounding settlements.[8] While not entirely eschewing the insights of urban planning, tactical urbanism focuses on the people of a community in planning development using limited resources and flexible thinking.[9]

In these ways, new paradigms of urban design have become key for responding to the catastrophic convergence of climate change and urbanization. Indeed, urban design innovations may offer the greatest hope in a global culture that otherwise regards climate change with dread, enervation, and despair. As politicians continue to stall on capping carbon emissions, the notion of "adaptation" has become increasingly prominent. Since we can no longer maintain the relatively stable environment humanity has enjoyed since the Neolithic Revolution, popular attention and aspiration have turned toward imaginative forms of adaptation to the unfolding climate chaos. Architecture is at the center of such adaptive measures, supported by an array of cultural institutions.[10] Through exhibitions such as the Museum of Modern Art's (MoMA) *Rising Currents: Projects for New York's Waterfront,* the BMW-Guggenheim *Urban Lab,* and the Whitney Museum's *Undercurrents* exhibition, cultural institutions have laid bare the hubris of twentieth century dreams of the city as the epitome of absolute human control over nature. Visitors to these exhibits were invited to contemplate an urban environment in which fossil capitalism has broken down the neat borders between nature and society, showing how they are entangled. In the increasingly disaster-prone context of the extreme city, survival becomes the keyword, with architecture blazing a trail into the urban future through investigations of tactical adaptation measures. MoMA's *Rising Currents* responded to this imperative, for example, by bringing together five teams of architects, landscape architects, engineers, ecologists, and artists to reenvision areas of New York City's coastline in light of sea level rise and more frequent extreme weather events.

At the center of these experiments has been the concept of "resilience." The National Academy of Sciences defines *resilience* as "the ability to prepare and plan for, absorb, recover from, and more successfully adapt to adverse events."[11] Unlike sustainability, which is a static, defensive mode, resilience is fluid, adopting a nimble, dynamic pose. Predicated on the ability of complex systems (such as cities) to organize themselves at multiple scales and to bounce back from various forms of stress, resilience connotes an ability to withstand the various, unpredictable shocks of the catastrophic convergence of urbanization and climate change. In recent years, the concept of resilience has become a key buzzword across a wide variety of sectors, including disaster preparedness, high finance, national defense, and efforts to fight terrorism.[12]

But it is on the question of cities that resilience has found its most fertile ground, readily apparent in the field of architecture and urban planning in the wake of Hurricanes Katrina and Sandy. As Rockefeller Foundation President Judith Rodin wrote in her introduction to *Rising Currents,* we need to confront "the threat of climate change head on, turning the risks into incentives to create a more inviting, livable, and resilient world."[13] As Rodin, who is also the author of *The Resilience Dividend*, suggests, efforts to build urban resilience attempt to enhance the capacity of the city to endure shocks. The city is consequently regarded as a complex system where tidal currents, sewage flows, and the global circuits of container ships (to name but a few) are inextricably intertwined with the vagaries of human affairs.[14]

This holistic approach is a welcome departure from the binaries between human beings and the natural world that have dominated capitalist modernity in the past, but all too often, it also fails to question the political conditions that give rise to the shocks cities must now adapt to, as if they were natural. Resilience is consequently an opportune lens for elites to adopt in coping with the extreme city. Instead of questioning and contesting the manufactured insecurities of the extreme city, resilience discourse tends to shunt the responsibility to adapt to hazard onto individuals. Rather than sparking collective solidarity in the face of extreme risk, in other words, the idea of resilience tends to disaggregate society into a group of isolated survivalists, who must struggle, rather like contestants on a reality TV show, against increasing odds or be purged from the body politic.[15] Resilience has become the dominant jargon for addressing the manifold crises of the extreme city without fundamentally transforming the conditions that give rise to these crises.

This chapter explores discourses of resilience as they are applied to the extreme city. I focus on the Rebuild by Design competition, a post-Hurricane Sandy initiative funded by the Rockefeller Foundation and the US Department of Housing and Urban Development that sought "a new way to connect design, funding, and implementation strategies for a more resilient future."[16] Rebuild by Design offers a particularly telling—and internationally prominent—example of how recovery was conceptualized in New York after Hurricane Sandy, constituting perhaps the most ambitious and engaged experiment in urban adaptation using landscape architecture. It also highlights the enduring challenge of creating more just cities in an era of climate change.

Rebuild by Design and Environmental Justice

One of the primary novelties of Rebuild by Design is its leveraging of Rockefeller Foundation money, funds that were used to kick-start a process of collaborative research, design, and jury-based awards for projects to make the New York region more resilient after Sandy. The US Department of Housing and Urban Development in turn bankrolled the six competition-winning projects. This collaboration between public and private entities was particularly lauded for beginning to shift the federal government's focus from postdisaster emergency aid to disaster prevention. Rebuild by Design thus helped move the federal government from a purely reactive stance, in which funds are typically allocated only after disasters take place to repair damage, to the creation of a future-oriented stormproofing network.[17] As the Rockefeller Foundation website asserts, Rebuild by Design was notable for "innovating how federal dollars are spent—and how US communities rebuild—after disasters."[18]

Rebuild by Design also departed from established practices of disaster management by coordinating a community-engaging, participatory design process emblematic of those advocated by champions of tactical urbanism. The process began with an intensive, three-month program of field research. Led by a Research Advisory Board of experts in various fields, design teams spread out across the Sandy-affected area in order to gain a sense of the region's vulnerabilities to future risks.[19] As part of this fieldwork, Rebuild by Design sent teams of architects, engineers, environmental scientists, and urban planners to communities in places like Tottenville in Staten Island and the Far Rockaways in Queens, neighborhoods that were still reeling from the devastation of Hurricane Sandy. The teams were charged with investigating community needs and future vulnerabilities. Based on this fieldwork and on in-depth research of the morphology of the sites visited, each team produced a comprehensive vulnerability assessment. In all, a jaw-dropping total of 535 community organizations were engaged in this field research. The projects proposed by each team for the Rebuild by Design competition were developed as direct responses to these vulnerability assessments. In its evaluation of the project, the Urban Institute wrote that

"Rebuild by Design broke the mold of traditional design competitions with its approach to teamwork and encouragement of creativity ... Including the public in the early stages of design development and continually incorporating their feedback was vital to creating proposals that represented the needs of large groups of stakeholders and gathered support from a number of different sectors of society.[20]

The Rebuild by Design competition resulted in six award-winning finalists, who received a total of $930 million from the federal Department of Housing and Urban Development. Barke Ingels's firm was, appropriately, the biggest winner for its proposal for the BIG U, a ten-mile-long "bridging berm" to defend low-lying land at the southern tip of Manhattan from storm surges and rising sea levels. BIG's proposal was driven by recognition that flood-protection infrastructure would only actually be used by the city for a tiny percentage of time. The rest of the time, BIG argued, such infrastructure should actively improve New Yorkers' connection to the waterfront, undoing some of the alienating impacts of mega engineering projects of the Robert Moses era such as FDR Drive, which cuts Manhattan off from the East River.[21] Engineered around the perception that "each flood threat needs to be countered by a particular geometry," the BIG U is made up of a series of different units that connect along its ten-mile course from West 57th Street, south to Battery Park, and then back up the east side to East 42nd Street. In the Lower East Side, the BIG U is made up of landscaped bridges that connect the traditionally working class but now heavily gentrifying neighborhood to a new East River Park built atop BIG's protective berm. Further south, east of Chinatown, BIG proposed a series of giant steel panels that would nestle underneath the FDR Drive, creating space for skate parks and tai chi platforms and flipping down to protect against occasional storm surges. In Battery Park, the BIG U morphs into a series of landscaped berms and a "reverse aquarium" through which visitors can view the passing aquatic wildlife of the New York harbor. The BIG U was clearly shaped by the forcefully articulated needs of all-too-often marginalized community groups in areas such as Chinatown and the Lower East Side for accessible urban amenities, but it also taps into the burgeoning tourist industry through its invocation of the wildly successful High Line in an extremely canny manner.

Yet the limits of the BIG U are surprisingly apparent when one looks at its projected extent. Even if the entire BIG U gets constructed as currently proposed, it is built to a fixed height of 16 feet based on projected sea level rise to the year 2050. But what happens after 2050? And what about if sea levels rise faster than currently projected, a very real possibility given the constantly escalating amount of ice melt coming in from measurements in Greenland and Antarctica? As sea levels rise, ever-smaller storms can overtop barriers built for much lower seas. Consequently, climate scientist Klaus Jacob has observed that the BIG U is an example of an intervention that actually *increases* risk rather than diminishes it, at least when looked at on a time-scale beyond the current generation.[22] As is true of New Orleans's levees, such barriers magnify future danger by providing a false sense of security, leading people to build up risk in fundamentally unsustainable sites.

But the BIG U doesn't just displace danger into the future. It also displaces it to other physical locations. Berms such as those that form the backbone of the BIG U are famously problematic in that they keep some communities dry while displacing water to surrounding communities. Where will the water that the BIG U turns aside go? It is likely to end up in adjacent communities with large poor populations such as Red Hook, where Hurricane Sandy hit public housing particularly hard. Interestingly, BIG looked at flood defenses for Red Hook in its research, but this was not part of the final proposal. It should not be particularly surprising that defense of Wall Street garnered more attention and funding than defense of a historically poor (if rapidly gentrifying) neighborhood such as Red Hook. If exposure and vulnerability to anthropogenic climate disruption in global cities is combined but uneven, so-called natural disasters are not catastrophes that strike otherwise intact and egalitarian cities. Cities are heterogeneous and unequal, which is why it makes little sense to talk about building urban resilience in general. Faced with such universalizing discourses, it is wise to ask whose resilience we are talking about. The storms of the future will affect urban communities, some of which may be resilient due to their access to financial and social capital, but many of which are already riven by slow-moving, chronic crises linked to poverty, low and precarious employment, and a lack of access to basic resources such as transportation, health care, and education.[23]

Another problem with the BIG U derives from the fact that the storm surges of the future will certainly not stop in their tracks at 42nd Street, where the berm will end. During Hurricane Sandy, for example, high waters traveled all the way to the town of Beacon, 65 miles up the Hudson River from Manhattan.[24] If the BIG U protects communities in the southern tip of Manhattan, where, not coincidentally, the financial industry is located, what will happen to low-lying communities to the north? Much of the highly valuable real estate of Midtown Manhattan, most notably the Hudson Yards development, lies just south of 42nd Street. A major portion of Hudson Yards's twenty-six-acre footprint is within the 100-year floodplain.[25] Developers claim that the platform over the rail yards, on which many of the buildings will be constructed, puts the first floor of the many luxury high rises being built above the floodplain, but of course this is the floodplain as it is presently constituted; by the time the buildings are completed and occupied, the floodplain—and the storm surges that reach it—is likely to be higher.[26] In addition, some of the first buildings to go up in the project are not built on the platform. While some of the new luxury housing may have essential infrastructure placed on higher floors, these new buildings will push floodwaters toward older, less well-defended buildings, which tend to be occupied by lower income residents. As was true during Hurricane Sandy, the flood defenses of wealthy citizens can actively endanger the lives of their poor neighbors.

Further north, in Harlem, the threat of flooding is even more grave. Harlem has long suffered from environmental injustice. The neighborhood has a long history of neglect in terms of the provision of open spaces and parks that stretches all the way back to the mid-century era of Robert Moses, who devoted his energies to beautifying the predominantly white Upper West Side through initiatives such as the creation of Riverside Park while basically ignoring the needs of African-American residents of Harlem.[27] In subsequent decades, some of the city's most toxic facilities, from bus depots to incinerators, were sited in Harlem. As a result, the area has had some of the highest rates of childhood asthma in the city. In the late 1980s, the residents of Harlem rose up against the noxious fumes emitted by the North River sewage treatment plant, which processes wastewater for most of the west side of Manhattan, from Greenwich Village all the way up to Inwood on the northern tip of the island. Located on the Hudson from 137th to 145th Streets, the North River facility spewed noxious fumes into Harlem, leading to dramatic public protests and a successful lawsuit that forced the city's Department of Environmental Protection to reduce odors from the plant.[28]

If you've ever taken the 1 train up the West Side to 125th Street, you know that Harlem also faces serious flood threats. The train roars out of an underground tunnel around 120th Street and zooms across a rickety steel trestle bridge before stopping at the 125th Street station, located about fifty feet in the air above the Harlem Valley. A few blocks west is the Hudson River. It is in this exact area that Columbia University is building a massive new campus. After winning the right to displace property owners in the area using eminent domain, Columbia plans not just to put up many new tall buildings in the area that it is calling Manhattanville, but also to build the largest underground complex in the city. This eighty-feet-deep basement will stretch for seventeen blocks and will extend to only a few hundred feet from the banks of the Hudson. The Environmental Impact Statement released by Columbia in 2007 dismissed the threat of flooding using Federal Emergency Management Agency flood maps last updated in 1983.[29] According to the General Project Plan that Columbia issued for the Manhattanville development, the basement facility will house "centralized energy plants to provide heating, ventilation, and cooling, and other mechanical facilities," as well as a bus depot for the city.[30] In addition, according to the Coalition to Preserve Community's White Paper on the facility, the underground complex would also house a Biomedical Research Level 3 laboratory that would allow Columbia to snag millions of dollars of federal funding for biodefense and biomedical projects.[31] Columbia already houses the Northeast Regional Center of Excellence for Biodefense & Emerging Infectious Diseases, but stands to earn far more money from the Department of Homeland Security if it can establish a Biosafety Level 3 facility, which would work with toxins such as typhoid fever, West Nile virus, avian flu, the plague, malaria, influenza, and anthrax.[32] Columbia has refused to disclose information about these potential facilities, but it has a poor record in handling toxins; in 2002 the EPA fined the university nearly $800,000 for violations of safety protocols in the disposal of toxic waste.[33] Although Biosafety Level 3 facilities are protected with very tight security, such measures would do nothing to stop the advancing tides in the event of a serious flood in the Harlem Valley.

The Rebuild by Design competition did recognize a site of vulnerability in one of the city's poorest neighborhoods: the South Bronx. But it did so because this neighborhood is home to the city's largest produce, meat, and seafood markets, which together generate over $5 billion in annual revenue. When Hurricane Sandy hit New York, it demonstrated the vulnerability of the Hunts Point Food Distribution Center to flooding as well as to power and fuel outages. Had Sandy hit six hours later, when the Bronx River was at high tide, food supplies for 22 million people around the metropolitan region would have been decimated. Protecting these vital infrastructural resources for the city and the region was of prime importance for the design team, but designers could not simply ignore calls for social and economic justice articulated by community members in the South Bronx. The proposal for redevelopment of Hunts Point by a team led by PennDesign/OLIN, entitled Hunts Point Lifelines, consequently acknowledges the interlinked local and regional significance of the square mile of land that is Hunts

Point. To gain any traction in the South Bronx, resilience had to be broadly defined to include social and economic benefits to a vulnerable local community as well as environmental sustainability that would benefit the entire metropolitan area. The PennDesign/OLIN plan consequently strives to present "a formula for a working waterfront, working community, and working ecology that grows out of long-term community plans."[34] The presentation of Hunts Point Lifelines highlights the fact that the food distribution facility provides over 10,000 direct jobs in what is the poorest congressional district in the country. Investing in the resilience of Hunts Point, the design team reasons, would provide regional food security, protect living-wage jobs, and model authentic community-based action to sustain one of the city's most important working waterfronts.

There are four major components to Hunts Point Lifelines. The first of these is a "Levee Lab," a series of flood protection measures integrated into the South Bronx Greenway, a proposed network of waterfront parks, designated green streets, and bike and pedestrian paths designed to significantly increase access to the Bronx River, improve transportation safety, and reverse environmental degradation. The PennDesign/OLIN plan calls for a series of buoyant floodgates that would accommodate large openings in the levee, permitting the construction of a new pier and restaurants proposed by the Fulton Fish Market.[35] This emphasis on public use is extended in thick sections of the greenway, where the design team proposes habitat and platforms for recreation on the water, such as an extension of the youth sailing program run by Rocking the Boat. The second element of the Hunts Point Lifelines proposal pairs the foregoing design proposals with a promise to engage in local procurement and labor force strategies designed to address high levels of unemployment in the area while also generating a stronger knowledge of waterfront dynamics and popular engagement. The final two elements of the proposal center on major infrastructural transformations. Part three, called *Cleanways*, proposes links to public transportation, including a new train station to be built in Hunts Point, as well as a "clean Tri-Gen Power Generating Station" designed to "turn waste heat into chilled water" in order to cope with the "huge thermal load of a district dependent on refrigeration."[36] According to the design team, this power station would allow "the Hunts Point peninsula to act as a microgrid island when the City grid goes down."[37] The final element of the PennDesign/OLIN plan calls for Hunts Point to be used as a distribution node and supply stockpile site for an emergency maritime supply chain for the entire East Coast. This element of the proposal builds on the fact that maritime access to disaster-affected sites can often be restored before other modes and that 15 million people in the New York metropolitan area live within a few miles of navigable waterways, including New York Harbor; the East River; Long Island Sound; and the Hudson, Passaic, and Raritan rivers.[38]

Hunts Point Lifelines contains many progressive elements, clear evidence of the design team's engagement with local community groups such as THE POINT, Sustainable South Bronx, and the Bronx River Alliance, all of which are nationally recognized leaders in environmental education, action, and green jobs strategies. In order to understand the long-standing struggles of these groups, and some of the shortcomings of the PennDesign/OLIN plan, Hunts Point needs to be seen as part of the broader industrial zone along the waterfront in the South Bronx. This area is one of only six designated Significant Maritime Industrial Areas (SMIAs) in New York City, the others being Sunset Park, Red Hook, Newtown Creek, Brooklyn Navy Yard, and the North Shore of Staten Island. The SMIA designation is intended to encourage the clustering of heavy industrial and polluting infrastructure. It is no coincidence that all of these SMIAs are located in predominantly low-income communities of color. In 2010, the Waterfront Justice Project of the New York City Environmental Justice Alliance (NYC-EJA) discovered not only that all six SMIA's are located in storm-surge zones, but that the city had not analyzed the cumulative contamination exposure risks associated with clusters of heavy industrial use in such vulnerable locations.[39] After sustained pressure from groups such as the NYC-EJA, the city agreed to develop a Waterfront Revitalization Program that requires new businesses to develop risk management plans to prevent the release of hazardous substances during flooding and other extreme weather events. Existing business are, however, exempt from these requirements.

The South Bronx is the largest of New York's SMIAs, and consequently it is one of the most contaminated places in the city. It is home not just to the low-lying sewage treatment plant mentioned in the PennDesign/OLIN plan, but to a fuel depot containing 100 million barrels of home-heating oil, four out of New York State's ten natural gas power plants, and over a dozen waste transfer stations where garbage is placed in long-haul trucks.[40] Facilities in the South Bronx handle not just all of the waste produced in the Bronx but also 23 percent of the entire city's commercial waste. Along with the Hunts Point food distribution center, these facilities bring over 16,000 trucks every day to the streets of the South Bronx. A 2014 study by the state comptroller found that the Bronx has the highest asthma death rate in all of New York state, almost four times the state average.[41] Community organizations such as South Bronx Unite have been fighting against new facilities such as a proposed central depot for the food delivery company FreshDirect, as well as against the extension of the operating permits for the area's natural gas power plants, which were supposed to be temporary installations to cope with peak electricity demand in the city but have been operating continuously for fourteen years.

It should come as no surprise, then, that community organizers should respond with skepticism to the Hunts Point Lifelines plan for an additional "clean" power station. What would be the fuel source for such a power station, Mychal Johnson of South Bronx Unite asked?[42] Would it be fossil fuel? If so, it would contribute to the already massively disproportionate environmental burden borne by residents of the South Bronx, a burden that allows denizens of nearby wealthy neighborhoods such as Manhattan's Upper East Side to enjoy abundant electricity and clean streets without having their pristine riverfront parks and clean air fouled by sewage and air contamination. The co-generation process that the projected power plant would employ is certainly cleaner than traditional power plants because it produces not simply electricity but also useful heating and cooling capacity; nonetheless, such a plant needs a fuel source, and there is no discussion in Hunts Point Lifelines of running the new facility using a renewable energy source such as solar power. While the slated Tri-Gen power station would provide additional power for refrigeration facilities in the Hunts Point market complex, it would exacerbate already chronic pollution in the South Bronx in general. A plan to promote genuine environmental justice would involve shutting down polluting power plants rather than building new ones.

This question of equity figures prominently in community challenges to the Hunts Point Lifelines plan, particularly in relation to the job-creation promises made by Rebuild by Design. Hunts Point Lifelines indicates that job opportunities to be created by the project include "specific construction roles, maintenance, ecological productivity monitoring, as well as private sector growth."[43] In addition, the design team pledges to use "local procurement and labor force strategies." One would expect such prospects to be among the greatest attractions of the redevelopment plan given the fact that the South Bronx has consistently had the highest unemployment rate in the state and the largest percentage of poor residents of any urban county in the nation.[44] But, as Mychal Johnson puts it, "we've heard these [job creation] promises before, but where do the jobs come from and how do they affect local unemployment?"[45] Despite the rosy employment picture painted by Hunts Point Lifelines, Johnson said that he and other community members see no guarantee in the plan that any contract that is funded through the project will add local people to the employment rolls through apprenticeship programs that train them to take whatever skilled jobs may be on offer.

There is a long history of businesses moving into the South Bronx SMIA without establishing such training programs; as a result, the industrial development of the peninsula has not trickled down in the form of decent jobs paying a living wage to local residents, as the enduringly high unemployment rate in the area suggests. In reaction, community organizations have developed their own job training programs; Sustainable South Bronx's Bronx Environmental Stewardship Academy (BEST) is a strong example of such local job-creation efforts.[46] But such efforts need to be scaled up as capital flows into the area if the South Bronx is not to see an intensification of historical inequalities. In response to a wave of real estate speculation that threatens the area with "hyper-gentrification and mass displacement," South Bronx Unite has developed Principles for Private Development,[47] which specify exactly the policies notably lacking in Hunts Point Lifelines. The following demands were articulated by South Bronx Unite: (a) all real estate development construction opportunities should be given to unionized workers, with preference to South Bronx residents and with a significant percentage to be given through apprenticeship programs to South Bronx residents of color in all building trades; (b) a significant percentage of any new residential rental and for-sale development should be set aside for local residents at an affordability rate based on the current average median income of the South Bronx; (c) developers should analyze the health impacts of their projects and use best practices to guide their design process to create spaces that promote health; and (d) all real estate developers must support community-designed and community-driven waterfront redevelopment plans, as well as the *reduction* of the 850-acre South Bronx SMIA.[48] South Bronx Unite's Principles for Private Development offer a series of specific and relatively easy to implement policies that would go some way toward addressing the history of combined and uneven development that marks the South Bronx. It is lamentable that such concrete demands for social and environmental justice were not included in the Hunts Point Lifelines plan.

Finally, South Bronx residents questioned the geographical limits of the Hunts Point Lifelines plan. By focusing exclusively on the Hunts Point peninsula, the PennDesign/OLIN proposal excludes neighboring communities such as Mott Haven and Port

Morris that are part of the South Bronx SMIA, neighborhoods that bear an equal brunt of multiple life-threatening pollutants.[49] In these neighboring areas, 90,000 people are excluded from the Rebuild by Design plan, left with the potential of being inundated and unable to get to the food markets located less than half a mile away. According to South Bronx Unite's Mychal Johnson, many meetings were held with the PennDesign/OLIN team in which community members urged the team to protect the entire peninsula rather than Hunts Point alone. South Bronx Unite even spearheaded the creation of an autonomous sustainability plan, the Mott Haven–Port Morris Waterfront Plan.[50] These demands for inclusion were not incorporated in Hunts Point Lifelines, although the communities of the South Bronx have been promised that there will be a second phase to the redevelopment project that will ultimately extend greening and flood protection measures to the rest of peninsula. For now, however, the profits generated by the Hunts Point food distribution complex clearly are the most important priority. It is not clear when or even whether phase two of the project will be implemented. While Mychal Johnson and other community members say that they understand the need to secure the city's food supply, they see this prioritization of Hunts Point over neighboring communities as part of a longer history of environmental injustice that has affected the South Bronx more than any other area of the city. As Johnson puts it, "history has not shown that capitalism protects poor people."[51]

The Jargon of "Resilience"

The same year that the Department of Housing and Urban Development launched the Rebuild by Design program, the Department of Homeland Security (DHS) announced $20 million dollars of funding for a new center of excellence on critical infrastructure resilience, to be housed at the University of Illinois. A bevvy of resilience-related centers have since been created by DHS, including one devoted to coastal resilience and another focused on "food protection and defense."[52] Subsequently, the Department of Housing and Urban Development established a $1 billion National Disaster Resilience Competition that disaster-affected communities can enter.[53] In tandem with these resilience-related initiatives, the Rockefeller Foundation created a managing director position focused explicitly on resilience and launched its 100 Resilient Cities initiative. In 2014, the foundation's president, Judith Rodin, published a book entitled *The Resilience Dividend: Being Strong in a World Where Things Go Wrong.*[54] Adding to the din of resilience discourse, the World Bank launched its Resilient Cities Program under the aegis of its Global Facility for Disaster Reduction and Recovery, emphasizing the need to fold adaptation in the face of climate change-induced disasters into the bank's global development programs.[55] These developments, which span the US federal government, the philanthropic foundation sector, and international financial institutions, are testimony to the centrality of resilience in global strategies of governance today. Resilience has become a key discursive trope that weaves together a breathtaking variety of areas, including urban infrastructure, disaster preparedness, high finance, national defense, and efforts to check terrorism of all varieties.

Part of the power of the term *resilience* lies in the sheen of hope it offers. Indeed, resilience and related adaptive measures offer a welcome respite for policy makers from the paralysis surrounding international efforts to promote meaningful mitigation measures. In addition, resilience is no doubt attractive because of the many meanings that can be attached to the term, allowing people and institutions with very different agendas to embrace superficially similar ends. But above all, the vogue for resilience has to do with how it dovetails with dominant neoliberal views concerning the role of the state in hazardous times.[56] Deriving from the biological sciences, resilience tends to imply that there are certain inherent properties of an organism, an ecosystem, a society, or any other complex system that strengthen its ability to "bounce back" in response to adverse conditions. While it is clearly in everyone's interest to prepare for climate change, resilience seems to offer adaptive solutions without addressing the political roots of contemporary social risk and disaster.

Resilience emerged as a concept from the work of ecologist C.S. Holling, which critiqued mechanistic models of ecosystem equilibrium that dominated the Cold War era. These models assumed the existence of a "balance of nature" (an equilibrium) to which life returns if left to repair itself following disruption. By contrast, Holling emphasized how nature absorbed and adapted to disruptions, describing resilience as "the capacity of a system to absorb and utilize or even benefit from perturbations and changes that attain it, and so persist without a qualitative change in the system's structure."[57] This concept of resilience has been adapted in a bewildering variety of fields over the last two decades, stretching Holling's basic definition in myriad directions. As Andrew Zolli, author of a popularizing book on resilience, puts it:

> In engineering, resilience means the degree to which a structure like a bridge or building can return to a baseline condition after being disturbed. In emergency response, it suggests the speed with which critical systems can be restored after an earthquake or flood. In ecology, it refers to an ecosystem's ability to keep from being irrevocably degraded. In psychology, it signifies the capacity of an individual to deal effectively with trauma. In business, it often means putting in place backup systems to ensure continuous operation in face of man-made or natural disasters.[58]

Zolli suggests that these disparate definitions are united by an emphasis on the ability of a system, enterprise, or person to endure and recover in the face of change. Yet this idea that resilience is based on the ability to "bounce back" in the face of adversity is a drastic simplification of the concept, one that ignores some of its more radical implications.

Resilience has been defined in ecology with two contrasting connotations. The first of these is consistent with classical

ecology, which presumes that nature possesses a single equilibrium state, with resilience related to the speed that the system
returns to this equilibrium state after a disturbance.[59] The most
well-known example of this is the famous "balance of nature."
Inspired by this paradigm, efforts to engineer resilience focus on
maintaining constancy, predictability and efficiency. These
ecological models undergirded *Our Common Future*, the 1987
report of the United Nation's Brundtland Commission that
made the concept of sustainable development famous. The
report envisaged the possibility of maintaining a planetary
steady state equilibrium (something like a balance of nature), if
economic growth could be appropriately limited by environmental protection and social equity measures. The report defined
sustainable development as "development that meets the needs
of the present without compromising the ability of future generations to meet their own needs."[60] This commission eventually
helped lay the ground for the landmark Rio Earth Summit of
1992, with its efforts to establish an equitable framework for
reducing global carbon emissions.

Yet there were notable problems in *Our Common Future*, not
the least of which was the assertion that the Earth's species and
ecosystems are "resources for development." It also assumed that
economic growth would generate increasing capital that would
be put toward a wide variety of conservation and mitigation
efforts,[61] and it echoed the prevailing approach to coping with
rampant urbanization: "sustainable urban development will
depend on closer work with the urban poor who are the true city
builders," it stated, "by 'site and service' schemes that provide
households with basic services and help them get on with building sounder houses around these."[62] As Mike Davis documented
in devastating detail, this call for grassroots urban development
served as a cover for cuts to housing provision programs in poor
nations, in line with the neoliberal, state-shrinking doctrines
being peddled by financial institutions such as the World Bank.[63]
Moreover, the equilibrium advocated by *Our Common Future*
has overshadowed concern for the well-being of future generations.[64] Since its publication in 1987, carbon emissions have

spiraled. It is manifestly impossible to achieve an equilibrium state in a capitalist system devoted to what Joseph Schumpeter called a "gale of creative destruction."[65]

But resilience can also be defined in far more disruptive terms as "ecosystem resilience," which characterizes systems with multiple states of equilibrium.[66] "Ecosystem resilience" insists on the interconnectedness of networks of nonhuman and human actors such as weather systems, electric grids, and urban dwellers.[67] Such systems tend to be complex, involving multiple entities or layers that, interacting with one another, allow the system as a whole to adapt. Perhaps the most well-known example is the Internet, which was originally designed as a system of interconnected but autonomous networks capable of withstanding the destruction of any single node. Other examples include old-growth forests, with their blend of diverse trees and plants, and the many different creatures that coexist beneficially in coral reefs. But if enough parts of such resilient systems are placed under stress, the systems as a whole can traverse tipping points that produce what are known as "regime shifts," where the entire system may undergo abrupt and dramatic changes in structure and function. The global collapse of coral reefs—which face multiple stressors, including over-fishing, eutrophication, and sedimentation—is an instance of such a tipping point.[68] While regime shifts may be gradual and more continuous, they can also be abrupt and unpredictable. They also tend to exhibit four phases of evolution: growth; conservation or consolidation; release or collapse; and reorganization or renewal.[69] While adaptive cycles of growth, destruction, and renewal are fairly common in natural ecosystems, the human rage for order and continuity tends to militate against such cyclical dynamics. Indeed, Zolli's definitions of resilience all basically derive from notions of "engineered resilience" that assume the goal to be maintaining continuity and basic stability.

While popularizers of "resilience" such as Zolli and Rodin are seeking to promote the capacity of infrastructural networks to bounce back after disasters, they are clearly not allowing for

the possibility of complete reorganization or collapse of particular systems. "As you build resilience, therefore, you become
more able to prevent or mitigate stresses and shocks you can
identify and better able to respond to those you can't predict or
avoid," Rodin writes. "Ideally, as you become more adept at
managing disruption and skilled at resilience building, you are
able to create and take advantage of new opportunities in good
times and bad. That is the resilience dividend."[70] In other words,
she assumes resilience will strengthen systems and even allow
them to profit from catastrophe. She also takes for granted a
sense of continuity within the system that informs models of
"engineering resilience," with no sense that the system might be
utterly transformed by a traumatic disruption. Also, resilience
for her involves not only enduring in the face of adversity but
making money from it. Rodin's reference to the "dividend" to be
gained from tragedy suggests that the not-too-hidden "you" she
addresses is actually the transnational business elite and their
multinational corporations.

It is also notable that Rodin describes these disruptions as
inevitable. Citing factors such as galloping globalization, urbanization, and climate change, Rodin represents disruption in a
manner that suggests that its root causes are simply a given and
that the only reasonable response is to adapt.[71] This reflects a
broader shift by elites away from meaningful forms of carbon
mitigation, while failing to question the conditions that generate
these disruptions. But the last four decades of globalization and
urbanization are not natural; they are the product of an increasingly unrestrained capitalism, involving neoliberal efforts to
abolish public regulation and to throttle the public sector while
empowering private sector forces of various kinds. In addition,
the last major disruptive factor mentioned by Rodin, climate
change, should itself be seen as a planetary disruption inextricably intertwined with carbon-based capitalism.[72] As Naomi Klein
has pointed out, efforts to reduce carbon emissions have failed
so dramatically precisely because of the hegemony of neoliberal
doctrines that skewer all regulatory efforts.[73] The discussion of
"resilience," just like the concepts of sustainable development

that preceded it, obscures these root causes of global instability and suffering, suggesting that those most imperiled by inequality and risk have no recourse but to adapt to the forces bearing down remorselessly upon them.

Given the snug fit between the concept of resilience and contemporary neoliberalism, it is worth asking where it came from. What were its impacts before it became the term of choice across so many sectors? As I mentioned earlier, the ecologist C.S. Holling coined the term during the 1970s as part of his critique of resource management models that assumed that systems should remain in equilibrium over time. Holling felt that such models ignored the complex interdependencies of ecosystems which, when pressed over time by intensive methods of agriculture and resource management, could become increasingly fragile and collapse unexpectedly.[74] Researchers like Holling were interested in finding ways to sustain yield from ecosystems that were experiencing conditions of extreme instability like the collapsing Atlantic northwest cod fishery. As a result, he emphasized the limits of what humans are able to predict in the behavior of ecosystems and sought instead to find ways to magnify the ability of ecosystems to endure unexpected and often extreme forms of turbulence.

Holling's work on resilience unfolded in tandem with that of neoliberal godfather Friedrich von Hayek, who was developing an analysis of economic markets as complex adaptive systems. Paralleling Holling, Hayek argued that it was ultimately impossible for central planners to control or even to predict the gyrations of the market effectively.[75] In his Nobel Prize acceptance speech, "The Pretense of Knowledge" (1974), Hayek argued that public expectations concerning the ability of science to analyze and then mold society were vastly exaggerated, partially as a result of the magnitude of achievement in the natural sciences during the modern period.[76] Deep knowledge of society, Hayek argued, tends to dampen rather than stimulate aspirations for improvement. Yet the public is so hungry for hope that it is willing to believe virtually any flimflam pronounced in the name of "expert knowledge." While this might sound like a resounding challenge to the pretenses of today's neoliberal economic gurus, who prescribe repeated rounds of austerity despite their many catastrophic failures, when Hayek delivered his speech in 1974 he had the efforts of Keynesian state regulators squarely in his sights. Moreover, his animus against any efforts to regulate the market is made quite clear in a glancing reference to the Club of Rome's *Limits to Growth* report, which severely challenged capitalism's growth imperative.[77] In what would become a form of dogma during the coming decades, Hayek derided the idea that capitalism was on a trajectory that would deplete and ultimately destroy vital planetary ecosystems; for Hayek, such a perspective was the product of "men's fatal striving to control society."[78] In other words, free markets are most akin to the state of nature and operate best when left uncontrolled.

Hayek's resistance to regulations derived partially from his impressively polymathic research in neurology and from his encounters with organicist biologists such as the Austrian Ludwig von Bertalanffy. During his student years in Vienna in the 1920s, Hayek studied contemporary psychology and worked with anatomists tracing the path of bundles of nerve fibers in the human brain. In *The Sensory Order* (1952), he returned to and synthesized this early research, arguing that what we term "the mind" — from sensory impressions to beliefs and plans—is an emergent property of the interactions of neurons in the human brain.[79] *Emergence* as it is used by Hayek refers to the idea that interactions between different parts of a system form properties that would not otherwise exist (i.e. the whole is greater than the sum of its parts).[80] Frequently cited examples include ant colonies, which display highly complex forms of social organization despite the simple nature of individual ant behavior, and the human form of social organization known as the city. Similar ideas informed the work of biologists whose work shaped Hayek's thinking such as Bertalanffy. For Bertalanffy, biological organisms and systems consist of nested hierarchies of organized parts, from the organs of individual animals to the diverse organisms that populate particular ecosystems.[81] In a framework that he termed "general system theory," Bertalanffy held that these principles applied to all phenomena exhibiting organized complexity. Applying these insights to economics and society, Hayek argued that free markets function analogously to the structured interactions of brain neurons or ecosystems, developing emergent forms of self-organized complexity without the need for any outside intervention.

By the time he gave his Nobel-prize lecture, Hayek was drawing on the work of biologist C.S. Holling, who by then was arguing that efforts to conserve threatened ecosystems by eliminating competitors and predators could unwittingly weaken the resilience of the ecosystem as a whole.[82] Drawing on these ideas, Hayek insisted that external interventions to markets, such as Keynesian policies to pump money into failing economic sectors (sectors he considered "unhealthy" or "unsustainable"), had a debilitating long-term effect on economic systems. In Hayek's sweeping equation of finance, society, and biology, complex systems tend to move spontaneously through periods of disturbance and emerge with greater levels of complexity. But for Hayek the role of the state is not to step aside, as some of his colleagues argued at the time. It was to radically transform society to better allow for free markets to organize themselves. "If man is to do more harm than good in his efforts to improve social order," he wrote in *The Pretense of Knowledge,* "he will therefore have to use what knowledge he can achieve, not to shape the results as the craftsman shapes his handiwork, but rather to cultivate growth by providing the appropriate environment, in the manner in which the gardener does this for his plants."[83]

Today, these arguments, once considered marginal, are central to neoliberal discussions of resilience, where the role of the state is to create optimal conditions for individuals and companies to operate, rather than trying to achieve centralized control. But in societies, these entities coexist with people, and indeed, in much resilience-oriented work, human populations are an afterthought. Such assumptions undergird the Rockefeller Foundation's programs to build a resilient planetary urbanism.

The 100 Resilient Cities program, which extends Rebuild by Design to a host of global cities, is neoliberal because designation as a "resilient city" is competitive, and hundreds of applicant cities were turned away from the program and its funding schemes (as if only the most competitive cities deserve to be resilient).[84] In addition, the program proposes to build resilience through public–private partnerships leveraged by Rockefeller Foundation funds, which bankroll the establishment of a "Chief Resilience Officer" tasked with drawing up a resilience plan in selected cities.[85] Moreover, most of the "platform partners," who are intended to give these lone resiliency czars access to resources necessary for resilience, are private companies[86] like Microsoft and Cisco. It also includes less well-known corporations like Palantir, a data mining firm with roots in the homeland security and financial sectors; Sandia National Laboratories, an arm of the US military-industrial complex that specializes in nuclear technology; and Veolia, a French transnational company that has played a key role in privatizing urban water supplies in poor nations.[87] Some of the partners involved in the 100 Resilient Cities program have also proposed agendas that shift risk onto the backs of vulnerable communities. The consulting firm ICF International, for example, is notorious for its role operating the Road Home program following Hurricane Katrina. One of the many politically connected firms offered no-bid contracts after the disaster, ICF International had distributed assistance to only 55 percent of applicants five years after Katrina; the remainder were disqualified, denied, or gave up on receiving assistance.[88] The inclusion of ICF International in Rockefeller's 100 Resilient Cities initiative is a reminder of how disaster-relief efforts organized under the brand of resilience actually work. Despite all of the shiny rhetoric concerning competition and effective service provision, such privatized relief and recovery efforts are chiefly effective at developing inventive new forms of corruption, at lining the pockets of corporate executives and shareholders at the expense of the public and suffering disaster victims.[89]

Of course, many well-meaning individuals and organizations are involved in efforts to build community resilience. It is a concept that offers alluring hope at a moment when catastrophes threaten to numb many into a state of complete despair and disregard. Yet the ideological underpinnings of the concept are all too often obscured, creating a depoliticized context in which individual efforts, no matter how altruistic, simply advance destructive forms of neoliberal governance. This is certainly the case with initiatives advanced by the Rebuild by Design competition, which proffer exciting-seeming design initiatives that all too often ignore the broader context of how cities have evolved under neoliberalism. And these contradictions are even more apparent in the 100 Resilient Cities program, as their lineup of "platform partners" makes clear.

Glaringly absent in these discussions is the most resilient aspect of planetary urban life today: the trend toward the accumulation of profit by dispossession. Indeed, resilience may be seen not simply as a discourse that supports austerity but as one that actively promotes dispossession.[90] As geographer Tom Slater argues, there is a long history of city planners and politicians importing concepts derived from the biological sciences into urban affairs, with incredibly destructive effects on poor communities. For example, the influential Chicago School of Human Ecology drew on biological theories to legitimate forms of "urban regeneration" that broke up and scattered residents of "blighted" neighborhoods.[91] The use of the ecosystem science concept of "resilience" is but the latest example, one that obscures the political roots of the global recession and that has led to public expenditure cuts in cities across the globe in the name of restoring community resilience. It should not be surprising that powerful purveyors of urban resilience seldom discuss the ceaseless quest for real estate profits that drive land grabs and forced evictions around the world. After all, windfall profits are also to be made from advising cities how to adapt to these policies, as well as to the impact of anthropogenic climate change. To adapt an Upton Sinclair aphorism, it is extremely difficult to get a consultant to see the roots of a problem when his salary depends on not understanding it.

Rebuild by Design and the Oceanic Commons

In an essay on design in watery terrains like deltas, architect Ila Berman writes, "we need to generate a new culture–nature continuum that moves toward soft dynamic infrastructures, fluid and adaptive spatial strategies."[92] Key to her argument is the sense, explored in more detail in Chapter 2, that the fields of architecture, engineering, and the arts have tended to see *terra firma*—land—as the terrain of human culture.[93] By contrast, water is the antithesis of all that is human, as a disorderly force of chaos and even death. As a result, maps have tended to draw hard lines separating water from land, binary divisions that obscure the fact that watery terrains such as deltas and coastal zones are sites of constant overlap and flux.[94] Faced with sinking cities and rising seas, architects are increasingly coming to eschew this folly and are also embracing what Berman calls a "new culture–nature continuum." In doing so, they also draw on insights emerging from ecology that see human and nonhuman actors as enmeshed in complex, fluid networks.[95] This is shaping new practices of design, including the Living Breakwaters project, the first of the Rebuild by Design prize-winning proposals to be implemented.[96] As one of the judges who awarded Living Breakwaters a "Socially Responsible Design" award from the Buckminster Fuller Institute wrote, the project "is about dissipating and working with natural energy rather than fighting it."[97]

Designed by a team led by SCAPE Landscape Architecture, with collaborators in fields as diverse as hydrodynamic modeling, marine biology, public education, and oyster restoration, Living Breakwaters investigates and responds to the challenges of urbanization, contamination, sediment starvation, and sea level rise in shallow ecosystems in the waters around New York City.[98] These problems are faced by many other coastal communities around the world, but they are particularly grave in the New York region. This was made clear when beachfront communities on Staten Island, once protected from inundation by a shallow offshore shelf known as the "West Bank," were devastated by the storm surge produced by Hurricane Sandy. Dredging, pollution, and the diminishment of natural and farmed oyster reefs off the coast of Staten Island have left beaches in the area exposed to eroding wave action over time, as well as to the catastrophic impact of periodic storm surges. Responding to these threats, the Living Breakwaters proposal calls for a series of exposed breakwaters anchored to the ocean bottom just offshore along the southeastern stretch of Staten Island's coastline. The team's proposal contrasts strongly with the traditional approach to beach protection: constructing a seawall. Such traditional measures cut off coastal ecosystems and communities from the ocean, starving shorelines of necessary water-borne sediments. While they might be attractive to communities that feel menaced by rising tides, seawalls ultimately are doomed to catastrophic failure, either when storm waters overtop the wall or when currents gradually erode the earth on the seaward side of the wall, eventually leading the wall to collapse. Breakwaters, by contrast, create a "thickened edge" designed to absorb wave energy, diminishing waves by as much as 4 feet during storms like Hurricane Sandy as well as reducing base flood elevations, according to studies conducted by the Living Breakwaters team.[99] The calmer waters promoted by breakwaters also encourage sedimentation, which helps to replenish the beaches that offer vital protective barriers to beachfront communities.

As the first part of its title suggests, Living Breakwaters innovates on existing breakwater schemes by seeding the project's 13,000 feet of concrete and recycled glass composite barriers with baby oysters, known as oyster "spat." As these oysters create extensive beds that grow organically, it is hoped that they will expand the size of the underwater structures, further enhancing the barriers' ability to reduce wave energy. As the SCAPE team puts it, "conceived as living systems, [the breakwaters] build up biogenically in parallel with future sea level rise."[100] In addition, as filter feeders, the oysters would sift out pollution and toxins from the water, making it a more desirable habitat for other marine animals such as crustaceans and fish.

Raritan Bay is an extremely important fish spawning ground for the North Atlantic, home to officially endangered species such as the Atlantic sturgeon. The living breakwaters are designed to maximize habitat not just for shellfish and crustaceans, but also for fish species like the sturgeon that require rocky habitat and tiny pore spaces for shelter during their juvenile phase, before they venture out into the Atlantic Ocean as adults.

In addition to such important environmental benefits, Living Breakwaters is also designed to connect Staten Island communities more closely with the ocean waters that surround them. As the SCAPE team explains, the project aims "to reduce actual risk while increasing the perception of risk by building a landscape scale intervention that integrates aquatic habitat and community access."[101] In other words, reducing risks posed by sea level rise and potential storm surges is not simply a material endeavor. It also has an important cultural and educational component. The more seaside communities know about the ocean, the more likely they are to value, protect, and be aware of both the benefits provided by healthy waters as well as the risks posed by environmental degradation. Seaside communities are conceived of by Living Breakwaters as an integral part of the project, a link in the networks of human and nonhuman actors that maintain healthy waterfront ecosystems. The project consequently calls for the construction of specially designed "water hubs" along the beachfront, community centers where Staten Island residents and visitors will be able to watch birds, rent kayaks, garden oysters, or gather for events and educational initiatives. As part of this educational effort, the New York Harbor School, a SCAPE team member, is developing programs and curricula that treat the New York harbor as a classroom. Through its Billion Oyster Project, the Harbor School aims to introduce one billion live oysters to the New York Bay, restoring a keystone species whose reefs once covered more than 220,000 acres of the Hudson River estuary.[102] The Living Breakwaters project intends to engage Staten Island residents in this exciting project of ecosystem restoration, paving the way for a radical shift in the way community members conceive of coastal protection and rejuvenation. If it is successful, Living Breakwaters may transform approaches to coastal protection and restoration around the United States and the world.

Of all the Rebuild by Design projects, Living Breakwaters engages in the most radical and innovative rethinking of relations between coastal human communities and the delicate ecosystems they inhabit and all too often precipitously degrade. Although other proposals such as Hunts Point Lifelines use restored natural areas such as wetlands to absorb storm surges and to improve water quality and natural habitat, Living Breakwaters embraces what might be called natural engineering to a far greater degree and on a much larger scale. The project can also be seen as a scrappy underdog proposal: despite being the first proposal to be implemented, Living Breakwaters is focused on Staten Island, the borough that the rest of New York tends to forget, and received only $60 million in funding, 15 percent of the award money made available by the Department of Housing and Urban Development to the Rebuild by Design competition. Finally, by restoring the area's oyster beds, Living Breakwaters can also be said to revive an important piece of Staten Island cultural heritage: before the twentieth century, the waters around the island were famous for exceptional oyster production, a heritage that made the neighborhood of Tottenville, at the southeastern tip of the island, famous as the "town that the oyster built."

Despite the project's many strengths, Living Breakwaters is likely to be plagued by a number of problems that illuminate the deeper contradictions of efforts to engage in ecological architecture and urbanism in fragile landscapes. Despite all the talk in architectural circles of fluidity and flexibility, Living Breakwaters is still fundamentally devoted to fixing the landscape in a condition of relative stasis.[103] This is perhaps not surprising: retreating from the shoreline and leaving behind homes, memories, and communities remains an inconceivable prospect in the United States, at least on a large scale. The name of New York City's post-Sandy recovery program—Build It Back—clearly articulates the dominant position on coastal retreat.

Nevertheless, a number of Staten Island communities have embraced precisely such a radical response. Members of the Oakwood Beach Buyout Committee organized community members of a Staten Island beachfront community to lobby for funds from the federal government's Hazard Mitigation Grant Program, which is designed to reduce loss of life and property by bankrolling mitigation measures including resident relocation as well as flood-proof rebuilding. This community-led demand for subsidized retreat stands in stark contrast to the plan for evacuating portions of New Orleans following Hurricane Katrina, a top-down model propounded by elite groups that unsurprisingly elicited angry resistance from citizens faced with displacement.[104] Oakwood Beach residents, aware that their homes were located on wetlands that had been paved over early in the twentieth city for industrial uses to support the city port, pushed for a communitywide buyout by the state that would facilitate the return of the area to its original wetland condition.[105] Encouraged by the success of Oakwood, and by the dismal record of Build It Back in disbursing funds, a total of nine community buyout committees formed on Staten Island. Controversially, only three of them were successful in their efforts to lobby for a State-managed, federally funded buyout program. Under current conditions, the retreat program Oakwood residents benefited from remains difficult to implement on a large scale because of a lack of federal will to disburse funds adequate to relocate threatened communities.[106] Indeed, after the passage of the Biggert-Waters Act (designed to end generous federal flood insurance subsidies), the trend seems to be in entirely the opposite direction: to shunt responsibility for insuring flood-threatened homes onto the individual home owner, including in areas where building was ironically encouraged by the generous federally funded insurance policies of the last half century.

If large-scale managed retreat is not a politically feasible strategy at the moment, the Living Breakwaters project perhaps represents an attractive, ecologically sensitive alternative. Nevertheless, Living Breakwaters confronts a number of intractable environmental problems that are likely to make it unsustainable in the long term. First of all, although breakwaters are certainly more sustainable than seawalls, they do take an environmental toll on the dynamic beach systems into which they intervene: breakwaters preserve the beach up-current, but they also speed up erosion on the beach down-current of the breakwater. Whenever sand movement from north to south is restricted, there is a potential down-drift impact. In other words, over time, a breakwater relocates sand from one section of the beach to another.[107] Living Breakwaters is intended to spread halfway up Staten Island, from Tottenville in the far southeast corner to Great Kills Park halfway up the island. If similar dynamics apply to Living Breakwaters as have been observed in other locations where such projects have been built over extended spans, including the Netherlands, the scheme is likely to diminish sand flowing across the Raritan Bay to the beachside communities in New Jersey. Thus, while it seems to solve a pressing environmental problem in one place, Living Breakwaters actually moves that environmental problem elsewhere, and, in doing so, generates a political problem: why should residents of New Jersey suffer from mitigation measures implemented to protect New Yorkers? While the design team for Living Breakwaters was extremely scrupulous in developing deep links with local communities in Staten Island, their project raises significant questions about the geographical scope that should be adopted by projects seeking to intervene in delicate landscapes in a holistic manner.

Even more worrying, however, is the question of whether Living Breakwaters will be sustainable over a more extended temporal span. As we have seen, the project depends on oyster spat for its planned biogenic response to sea level rise. But these plans overlook one of the greatest impacts of anthropogenic climate disruption: the acidification of the oceans. The developed nations are pumping so much carbon dioxide into the world's oceans, which absorb about a third of emissions each day, that they are altering the chemistry of the world's waters fundamentally. Ocean acidity is projected to increase by a factor of five by the year 2100, according to the National Oceanic and

Atmospheric Administration.[108] The planet has not seen a transformation in the world's oceans this dramatic for 50 million years. In such acidic water, the shell of a common adult mollusk will dissolve in forty-five days. For oysters, scallops, and other shellfish, lower pH means less carbonate, which they rely on to build their essential shells. As acidity increases, shells become thinner, growth slows down, and death rates rise. Juvenile oyster spats stand no chance in such an environment. Oyster spat use a form of calcium carbonate that dissolves particularly easily in acidic waters and are consequently especially vulnerable to this transformation of the world's oceans.

But this is not just a problem for future generations. Scientists hypothesize that acidification is responsible for the crisis in the shellfish industry in the Pacific Northwest, where oyster seed production plummeted by as much as 80 percent between 2005 and 2009.[109] This has cost the oyster industry in the region hundreds of millions of dollars in recent years. Although scientists have only recently begun to study the impact of ocean acidification on shellfish populations throughout US coastal waters, one of the first comprehensive studies found that economic impacts to the shellfish industry are likely to be far more widespread than previously estimated.[110] Indeed, the Atlantic Coast is likely to be hard hit in coming years not simply because of the general acidification of the oceans caused by carbon emissions, but also because this acidification may also be exacerbated locally by eutrophication, when algal blooms, produced when sewage and chemical waste introduce certain nutrients into coastal waters, decompose and release yet more carbon dioxide into the water. As a recent study reports, the impact of eutrophication on ocean acidity has only recently been considered. The study concludes on a suitably ominous note: "These coastal processes are likely to tip coastal oceans past organism thresholds as atmospheric CO_2 uptake continues in the future."[111] In other words, oysters and other marine animals will be unable to survive in the acidic ocean waters of the near future.

It is not entirely surprising that the Living Breakwaters team neglected to factor ocean acidification into their plans. Scientific study of this issue has only recently taken off; indeed, half of the existing scientific papers on the topic have been published in the last four years.[112] Yet the crisis of the oyster industry over the last half decade has been clearly linked by scientists to increasing ocean acidification, suggesting that oysters are playing the aquatic equivalent of the proverbial canary in the coal mine. The determination of the Living Breakwaters team and their partners to restore the Raritan Bay and the waters surrounding New York City to the remarkably diverse marine habitat of the preindustrial era is certainly laudable. But it is growing ever more unrealistic to think that such pristine environmental conditions can be revived; perhaps the stable equilibrium presumed by concepts of resilience should be discarded. The oceans are now 30 percent more acidic than they were before the Industrial Revolution, and they will continue to become more acidic even if we cease emissions today because they will continue to absorb the carbon dioxide already in the atmosphere. Moreover, fossil capitalism has radically transformed the planetary environment over the last 200 years. This is true even of the vast, once apparently immutable oceans.

The perilous state of the oyster is a testament to the sweeping impact of anthropogenic climate disruption. To base the resilience of coastal communities on a delicate organism that is particularly vulnerable to intensifying processes of ocean acidification is tragically short sighted. As the oceans acidify in response to intensifying carbon emissions, a coastal sustainability policy based on the model of Living Breakwaters not only threatens to waste money that could be better spent on strategic resettlement of human communities from vulnerable shorelines. Living Breakwaters may also produce exactly the same effect as the BIG U: to inadvertently build up risk by creating a false sense of security and hope. This is the danger of even the most attractive schemes planned under the slogan of resiliency.

João Pereira de Araújo submerged in water, Taquari District,
Rio Branco, Brazil. Photo by Gideon Mendel, March 2015.

5

Climate Apartheid

A year and a half after Hurricane Sandy struck New York, I was invited to participate in Rethinking Home, a collaborative project linking disaster-affected communities in the Pacific Island nation of Samoa and New York.[1] Run by curators at the American Museum of Natural History and the Museum of Samoa, and premised on the idea that people living near coastlines are particularly affected by the ecological impacts of climate change, Rethinking Home explored the ways in which houses and ideas of home are changing as communities are displaced and dwellings are destroyed. The goal of project organizers was to open dialogue between islanders facing various forms of climate change–related displacement. Central to the project was the recognition that climate change is affecting communities in the deepest way. After all, homes are more than simply bricks and mortar: they are the physical sites where we engage in many of the rituals through which we establish our community membership. For this reason, to be deprived of one's home is to be rendered socially invisible.

In 2012, the year Hurricane Sandy hit New York, more than 32 million people around the world were forced—either temporarily or permanently—from their homes because of extreme weather.² Of that number, an estimated 776,000 people across twenty-four states in the US were displaced by Hurricane Sandy. Although smaller than the estimated one million people forced from their homes in the Gulf Coast region by Hurricane Katrina in 2005, the scale of displacement in New York is still shocking.

In a blog post written after one of the Rethinking Home group's meetings, Staten Island participant Leila Rassi summarized the feelings of the displaced with smoldering bitterness:

> We are tired. We are fighting every day for basic needs. We cope with uncertainty about the future of our houses and neighborhoods. We appeal to insurance companies, aid programs, charitable organizations, community foundations, and government agencies, begging for the assistance that will enable us to recover. Those of us who experienced the most severe flooding and the most extensive structural damage to our homes rely on the kindness of family and friends, which wears our relationships down: after 15 months of staying in the guest room, or sleeping on the couch, or using the air mattress, the temporariness of displacement feels unending.³

This account of displacement captures the way in which even the most intimate relationships, the ones that are most sustaining under normal circumstances, can be strained and soured by the extended dependencies catalyzed by disaster-related displacement.

Leila Rassi's experiences are anything but unique. In some communities, harrowing displacement was the norm after Hurricane Sandy, as Alex Woods, a resident of a beachfront adult care facility in Queens, recounted to *Sandy Storyline,* an online participatory documentary project that collects stories, images, and videos about Sandy's impact on communities.⁴ Woods was evacuated along with 160 other residents of the facility on the morning after the storm hit, ultimately spending over three months in temporary residences.⁵ Although the facility lay smack in the middle of a floodplain designated as a "Zone

A" mandatory evacuation area, no efforts had been made to relocate Woods and his friends before the storm. Woods ended up spending much of this period in a halfway house on the grounds of the Creedmoor Psychiatric Center, a ramshackle, partially abandoned psychiatric institution in an isolated area of Queens, where he and his friends had to cope with deteriorating conditions, including sporadic lack of heat and hot water.

The displacement of people following a natural disaster such as Hurricane Sandy is a particular challenge in New York since the region already has a systemic housing crisis. At the time of Sandy, more than 50,000 people were sleeping in city shelters or on the streets every night, a number that has grown significantly in subsequent years. Disaster-related displacement thus raises basic issues of social justice. Leila Rassi draws the lesson powerfully in her blog post for *Rethinking Home:*

> To discuss the effects of Sandy without giving prominent consideration to the need for sustainable, fair, and affordable housing in New York City would be to ignore the needs of the many low- and middle-income residents of the devastated neighborhoods. It would also ignore the reality that housing justice is a tangible and achievable outcome that is well within the capacity of governments to implement ... My purpose in sharing these concerns is to inform a wider audience of the ongoing man-made destruction of our communities.[6]

While the question of homelessness was particularly vexing following Hurricane Sandy, the issue of finding housing for displaced people is a growing national and international challenge as increasingly extreme weather threatens coastal cities as well as flood- and storm-prone plains. According to a report by the Internal Displacement Monitoring Centre (IDMC), extreme weather linked to climate change was the main cause of human displacement in 2012.[7] In its latest report, the IDMC asserts that "disasters displaced around 19.2 million people across 113 countries in 2015, more than twice the number who fled conflict and violence."[8]

As the numbers of those displaced by climate change–related disasters have grown, the question of how to represent those displaced people has also grown more pressing. This question was perhaps most clearly highlighted by the controversy over how to refer to displaced groups following Hurricane Katrina. Civil rights activist Al Sharpton was particularly acerbic in his criticism of the news media for its use of the term "refugee" to describe the displaced. "They are not refugees. They are citizens of the United States," he said. "They are not refugees wandering somewhere looking for charity. They are victims of neglect and a situation they should have never been put in in the first place."[9] In rejecting the term refugee, Sharpton sought to challenge the way that Katrina victims had not just been deprived of dignity but demonized using some of the most flagrant racial stereotypes.[10] Yet, as reporter Mike Pesca noted at the time, Katrina victims were indeed looking for charity: "The people who heeded warnings and had the wherewithal to leave town before Katrina hit were evacuees. These beleaguered people who had lost everything were something else."[11]

While he may have been right to bridle at the use of a term that implicitly stripped the predominantly African-American victims of Hurricane Katrina of their citizenship, Al Sharpton's comments raise vexing questions about the boundaries of sympathy extended to displaced people. One cannot be a refugee, he seems to assume, and be recognized as a person worthy of respect and rights. But is this the case, and should it remain so? Where should we draw boundaries of sympathy, both legally and imaginatively, as climate chaos accelerates? Should we feel empathy and responsibility solely for our fellow citizens, in other words, for those whom geographical borders and the state demarcate as belonging? Or should our sense of ethical and legal obligation extend more broadly in a world of border-blurring climate change? What forces militate against this more capacious sense of ethical obligation, and how might they be challenged?

The Convenient In/visibility of Climate Refugees

Speaking at the 2016 meeting of the United Nations Environmental Program in Nairobi, French minister of the environment Ségolène Royal attempted to rally attendees to decisive action to diminish greenhouse gas emissions by warning of a future of mass climate change migration.[12] Global warming, Royal warned, will create hundreds of millions of climate change migrants by the end of the century, mostly through the social turmoil and conflict that will ensue. "Climate change issues lead to conflict, and when we analyze wars and conflicts that have taken place over the last few years we see some are linked to an extent to climate change, drought is linked to food security crises,"[13] she said. Royal urged representatives of the 170 attending nations to begin implementing the Paris Agreement on Climate Change. "Today it is your responsibility to contribute towards implementing it," she implored.[14] For Royal, policies to stem anthropogenic climate change are critical for addressing the future humanitarian emergency of mass migration. Invoking the threat of climate-induced mass migration to goad developing nations into adopting the Paris agreement, Royal adopted what has become a common rhetoric among leaders of wealthy nations. For much of her audience, however, such exhortations must have sounded completely hypocritical.

This is because the Paris agreement is hollow. Although the agreement was celebrated by French foreign minister Laurent Fabius as a "historic turning point" in reducing global warming, it contains no mandatory mitigation measures.[15] The agreed-to restrictions on carbon emissions that will limit the increase in global average temperature to "well below 2 degrees Celsius" are purely voluntary. Furthermore, the agreement fails to address the root cause of the potential climate catastrophe: fossil capitalism. For instance, the agreement never mentions decarbonization of global infrastructure and ignores the need for economic restructuring to contain destructive patterns of growth such as the global real estate speculation that is driving planetary urbanization.[16] Above all, there is no acknowledgement of the climate debt owed by historically developed nations such as Britain and the United States to the vulnerable countries of the global South. As those who have been most responsible for polluting the global atmospheric commons as they developed economically, these nations have an ethical obligation to pay climate reparations. And it's also pragmatic for them to do so: absent significant funding for adaptation in developing countries, climate chaos is sure to catalyze massive disruption and displacement in both poor and rich nations. For African delegates to the United Nations Environment Programme (UNEP), Royal's rhetoric must have been infuriating, since they represent nations that are the least responsible for but most imperiled by climate chaos. Indeed, in the prenegotiations to the meeting in Paris, South African delegate Nozipho Joyce Mxakato-Diseko, who led the G77 + China group, offered a candid assessment of the negotiations: "It's just like apartheid. We find ourselves in a position where in essence we are disenfranchised."[17]

Mxakato-Diseko's observation doesn't just apply to the unequal nature of international carbon diplomacy. As environmental disruptions proliferate across the globe, a condition well described as climate apartheid is becoming increasingly apparent. Climate apartheid encompasses the hardening of borders and restrictions on the movements of those affected by environmental and social disruptions. It also describes the conditions of social and economic precariousness that make people the world over increasingly easy to exploit. The parallel with the form of racial capitalism established in apartheid South Africa is intentional. With the world gripped by an unprecedented refugee crisis that is, at least in part, linked to climate change, climate apartheid is becoming increasingly apparent.

According to the UN refugee agency, the number of people who fled their countries surged to 60 million in 2014, a "nation of the displaced" greater in number than any since detailed record keeping began, an exodus equal to the population of the United Kingdom.[18] The war in Syria has been the single biggest contributor to the swelling numbers of displaced people. In 2014, Syria displaced Afghanistan as the largest source of global refugees, with one in five displaced persons worldwide coming from Syria. The conflict in Syria is arguably the world's first climate change war.[19] In the decade before the war's outbreak, Syria suffered from a bout of intense drought that saw the country's total water resources drop by half.[20] The drought decimated Syria's farmlands, driving hundreds of thousands of people from predominantly rural Sunni areas into coastal cities traditionally dominated by the Alawite minority. The Assad regime was unable to maintain grain subsidies as a result of dwindling revenues from declining oil reserves when the price of wheat doubled in 2010–11. These shortages sparked public protests in Syria's overcrowded cities, dissent that eventually escalated into armed rebellion against Assad's indiscriminately violent crackdowns on protest. Ségolène Royal's comments at the UNEP forum occurred against the backdrop of violence in Syria and the resulting displacement of at least 4.8 million people from the country.

Of course, not all of those who have drowned in the Mediterranean in the last year were displaced by climate change. Many were fleeing countries like Afghanistan and Iraq, where the efforts of the United States and its European partners to promote "regime change" have led to the unraveling of entire societies. Many were also escaping decades of austerity imposed by international financial institutions like the IMF. But "complex emergencies" in which climate change factors as one of the key causative elements are increasingly common, and they are likely to become even more so in the future. As Christian Parenti has documented, the "tropics of chaos" that span the planet are sites where climate change interacts with other destructive factors such as the legacy of the Cold War, austerity programs, and neo-imperial interventions and their disruptive blowback to create social turmoil and mass displacement.[21] Contemporary laws are singularly ill-suited to deal with the current and impending refugee crises. Despite references by global leaders to climate-induced migration, no international convention currently recognizes the needs and rights of climate refugees. They are invisible in juridical terms, a condition that effectively nullifies their pleas for refuge.

The vast majority of contemporary refugees—nearly 9 out of 10—are living in developing nations.[22] Indeed, Syria's neighbors Turkey and Lebanon currently host the largest number and concentration of refugees, respectively, in the world.[23] More than a million Syrians have entered Lebanon, a nation of only 4 million people, where they reside in highly precarious conditions.[24] In stark contrast, the world's wealthiest nations, those with the greatest capacity to accept the displaced, are increasingly slamming their doors on refugees, with deadly effect. Just days before Royal made her statement before the UNEP, footage of a smuggler's boat capsizing in the Mediterranean with scores of migrants on board was widely televised. More than 10,000 people have died attempting to cross the Mediterranean to Europe since 2014.[25] One out of every two people crossing last year—half a million people—was Syrian.[26] Rather than providing safe harbor for such refugees, France and other nations of the European Union have increasingly resorted to criminalizing migrants.[27] Border controls surrounding "Fortress Europe," cordons consisting of sea, air, and land patrols, and a surveillance system of satellites and drones have been augmented. The Italian-run search-and-rescue operation in the Mediterranean known as *Mare Nostrum* was replaced in 2014 by *Operation Triton*, a border security effort directed by Frontex, the European Union's border security agency. In the year following this shift from humanitarianism to criminalization, the death toll in the Mediterranean was eighteen times higher.[28]

This refusal to grant refuge to people fleeing conflicts that the developed world at least partially caused was made possible only after they had been dehumanized. Policy makers and significant segments of the public in rich nations have not simply responded to this spectacle with a shrug of the shoulders but with policies that amount to the statement: "Let them drown."[29] This is of a piece with refusing to take significant action to mitigate climate change, a failure that consigns entire nations in the global South to perish beneath rising seas or searing droughts. Such disregard should be seen for what it is: a form of climate apartheid that accords full humanity only to the privileged and controls movement in an effort to maintain that privilege against all odds.

European nations are not alone in establishing increasingly militarized policies for the interdiction of migrants. Australia's "Pacific Solution" policy deports asylum seekers to prisons on island nations such as Nauru and Papua New Guinea. Many poor nations are emulating the wealthy countries by also adopting an increasingly exclusionary attitude toward refugees. Indeed, shortly before the UNEP summit at which Ségolène Royal spoke, the Kenyan government threatened to close all of its refugee camps, including Dadaab, the largest camp in the world, a move that would displace more than 600,000 people.[30] The Kenyan government justified this move by insisting that national security interests dictated the closure of the camps and by arguing that the international community must take responsibility for the refugees.

But if this move has elicited condemnation, the United States has indisputably established the paradigm for global apartheid. The United States deports nearly 400,000 people annually.[31] The US prison-industrial complex keeps over 2.3 million people in cages; on any particular day, 19,000 people are in federal prison for criminal convictions of violating federal immigration laws, and an additional 33,000 are civilly detained by the Immigration and Customs Enforcement (ICE) agency separate from any criminal proceedings. These "illegal aliens" are physically confined in special immigration detention facilities or in local jails under contract with ICE, with no recourse to legal representation.[32] Being constructed as "illegal" thus amounts to a form of civil death.[33] The United States justifies its system of exclusion and detention in the name of national sovereignty, but its practices extend far beyond the borders of the nation-state. This global detention and deportation regime is one of the three legs of today's transnational security state, the other two of which are devoted to counterterrorism and drug enforcement.[34]

The policies of the European Union illustrate the increasingly global character of these practices of apartheid. While the

Mediterranean Sea remains the great and deadly moat surrounding the wealthy nations of western Europe, border controls are not contiguous with the borders of the nation-states, even though countries rely on claims of territorial sovereignty to demarcate citizen from "illegal" and "criminal." North Atlantic countries like the European Union nations and the United States are increasingly shifting their border controls and detention spaces onto "transit states" like Libya, Turkey, Mexico, and Morocco. The goal is to turn back or cage migrants before they even set off for North Atlantic borders, creating a form of remote migration control.[35] The sovereignty of these powerful states thus extends even to distant nations, not simply in the form of walls and cages but also networked hubs of indefinite detention.

This war against the mobility of the global poor is most intense in urban spaces in the global South. These cities are often represented as "feral" zones, breeding grounds for various forms of contagion, whether it is literal pandemics such as Ebola, or more metaphorical threats such as insurgent uprisings, environmental destruction, and unchecked streams of migration. This means subjecting the extreme cities of the global South to surveillance and counterinsurgency, if the incipient threats that they are thought to contain are to be quelled. For all the (largely unfunded) talk about adaptation to climate chaos in international forums such as the United Nations Framework Convention on Climate Change, it is in the militarization of the world's cities that climate apartheid can be most plainly seen. This is not just true of cities like Baghdad and Kabul, targets of the War on Terror over the last decade; through a global web of private and public "security" consultants, arms dealers, and detention corporations, it is also true of cities like Los Angeles and New York. But the highest walls, the strongest cages, and the most sophisticated surveillance systems and counterinsurgency operations cannot stop people from fleeing when the environmental foundation for life is stripped from them. Freedom of movement in such conditions is not just a human right, it is also the only meaningful form of adaptation.

The idea of the environmental refugee has existed for decades. As early as the 1970s, Lester Brown, founder of the World Watch Institute, first invoked the potential for mass displacement of people by environmental disasters.[36] Brown conjured up the specter of migration resulting from humanity's degradation of nature in order to push for environmental conservation measures. Brown coined the term, but it was a paper written by Essam El-Hinnawi for UNEP in 1985 that put the idea of the environmental refugee into wide circulation among humanitarian organizations, the media, and international policy circles.[37] El-Hinnawi defined environmental refugees as individuals who are "forced to leave their traditional habitat, temporarily or permanently, because of a marked environmental disruption (natural and/or triggered by people) that jeopardized their existence and/or seriously affected the quality of their life."[38] This definition was shaped by a gathering awareness of global climate change and the social and economic disruptions it was likely to catalyze. Indeed, El-Hinnawi's paper was soon followed by reports quantifying the number of existing environmental refugees around the world and projecting shockingly large mass displacement in the near future.[39]

In 2008, Srgjan Kerim, president of the 62nd session of the United Nations General Assembly, predicted that there would be between 50 million and 200 million environmental migrants by 2010.[40] He was adding his voice to others warning of the human impact of climate change, from the British biologist Norman Myers, who predicted 50 million climate refugees by 2010, to the British government's *Stern Report* of 2006, to the Intergovernmental Panel on Climate Change (IPCC), whose early assessment reports projected that up to 50 million people would flee drought, rising tides, and spreading deserts in the coming decades.[41] These huge figures, perhaps intended to galvanize attention to environmental issues, achieved their shocking effect by conjuring up images of barbarian hordes massing at the gates. Beneath the veneer of environmentalism and humanitarianism, in other words, was a strong current of xenophobia. And there was another problem: refugees failed to materialize in the places predicted by the United Nations. In fact, some of the areas that the United Nations projected would be abandoned actually saw population increase. The United Nation's erroneous predictions were seized on by climate change deniers as evidence of environmentalists' purported efforts to generate a state of fear.[42] The idea of the climate refugee was, for climate deniers, invented to cow ordinary citizens into submitting to the oppressive power of international organizations such as the United Nations. Such conspiracy theorizing conveniently allowed deniers to shirk all ethical responsibility for those displaced by climate chaos.

But the deniers were pointing to a genuine problem: people's migration decisions are influenced by multiple factors. Since the UN made its initial predictions, it has become clear that it is extremely difficult to establish simple causal relationships between climate change and migration. This is in part a result of uncertainty about the specific impacts of global climate change on particular places. The lack of clarity about links between climate change and migration is also a product of gaps in knowledge about migration flows, particularly when such flows occur within nations rather than across national boundaries. Not surprisingly, such knowledge is particularly scarce in relation to migration patterns within countries of the global South, the places that are most likely to be grievously affected by climate change.[43] As a result of these uncertainties, recent reports by bodies such as the IPCC have backpedaled substantially on the question of climate refugees, arguing that "predictions for future migration flows are tentative at best."[44] Nonetheless, they still evince an abiding sense that environmental crises can interact with social, economic, and political factors to generate precisely the kind of "complex emergency" seen in Syria.

There are other reasons why the figure of the climate refugee haunts contemporary geopolitics. In late 2013, Ioane Teitiota tried to become the world's first official climate refugee. In a case argued before the High Court of New Zealand, Teitiota claimed that he should be granted refugee status because rising sea levels caused by anthropogenic climate change imperiled his ability to live in his home country, the Pacific island nation of Kiribati.[45] Teitiota's suit was unsuccessful. In rejecting his petition, Judge John Priestly wrote that Teitiota's refugee claim did not meet the country's legal standards for asylum since "by returning to Kiribati, [Teitioa] would not suffer a sustained and systemic violation of his basic human rights such as the right to life ... or the right to adequate food, clothing and housing."[46] In ruling against Teitiota, however, Priestly was not simply deciding an individual case, for he was also clearly aware of the global precedent that a positive ruling would set. Were Teitiota's asylum claim to be successful, it might serve as a model for other jurisdictions, and, Priestly stated, "at a stroke millions of people who are facing medium-term economic deprivation, or the immediate consequences of natural disasters or warfare, or indeed presumptive hardships caused by climate change, would be entitled to protection under the Refugee Convention."[47] For Priestly and many other legal scholars, it is not the prerogative of the court system to alter the terms of the UN Refugee Convention, which was approved by member states shortly after World War II. Yet if climate refugees cannot be said to be subjected to rights violations similar to those carried out by the Nazis, climate refugees undeniably are, as Andrew Ross has written, "living embodiments of the quandaries raised by climate debt."[48]

As Judge Priestly noted in rejecting Ioane Teitiota's asylum claim, no international convention currently recognizes the needs and rights of climate refugees. By retaining narrow definitions of refugee status linked to overt political persecution, international organizations such as the United Nations help ensure that climate refugees will not only be invisible but will be perceived as illegitimate and even opportunistic "illegal aliens." Climate refugees consequently face multiple forms of exclusion and displacement. After all, if the UN *Declaration of Human Rights* enshrines the right to leave a country to avoid persecution, it does not grant a corresponding right to enter another country. Nation-states retain the sovereign right to decide who may legitimately enter their territory, and therefore to discriminate between citizen and alien. The result is to create a category of people who, once stateless, do not have the right to have rights. As Hannah Arendt observed, shorn of the political institutions that create rights, people effectively cease to be human beings.[49] Member states of the United Nations sought to address this category of rightless infra-humans through the 1951 *Convention Relating to the Status of Refugees*, which obliged nations to provide asylum for people fleeing persecution. However, since nation-states retained the authority to determine whether applicants qualify as refugees, the category of asylum is fundamentally based on exclusion.[50] Asylum seekers remain "deportable aliens" until they can prove their right to refuge based on documentation of the threats they face in their countries of origin. The asylum seeker is consequently a person out of place, a figure whose mobility across state borders places him or her fundamentally outside the framework of territorially inscribed citizenship rights. Asylum law allows states to deny humanity to migrants systematically while appearing to respect humanitarian claims.[51]

But if the right to asylum is heavily restricted, the legal status of the climate refugee is downright nonexistent. As legal theorist Jane McAdam points out, a number of problems arise for climate change-displaced peoples from the UN Refugee Convention's definition of the refugee.[52] While people fleeing political persecution (for example, by the Nazi regime) clearly fit the UN definition, climate change is not usually seen as an equivalent form of persecution, as Judge Priestly's ruling in the Teitiota asylum case makes clear. This is partially because it is hard to establish direct causal links between particular natural disasters and the more general transformation of the environment resulting from greenhouse gas emissions. But it also stems from the fact that climate change, while it may play a role in generating particular spectacular disasters such as hurricanes and cyclones, is transforming the environment in a very gradual manner. Climate change could be seen as the ultimate form of what cultural theorist Rob Nixon has called slow violence.[53]

The notion of the climate refugee is also problematic, McAdam argues, since it is impossible to identify the perpetrator, and it is also impossible to identify specific personal traits (such as race or religion) for which climate refugees are being persecuted.[54] Yet McAdam's position, far more than the scientific question of causal links between particular disasters and climate change in general, lays bare not simply the outdated character of the Refugee Convention but also the ideological nature of the international legal system. It is quite simple, in fact, to determine relative responsibility for fossil fuel–derived carbon dioxide pollution, from 1750 onward, on a country-by-country basis. According to a clear itemization by NASA climatologist James Hansen, the United States and United Kingdom account for more than 50 percent of historical emissions, with Germany and Australia clocking in at third and fourth.[55] Responsibility for climate-displaced populations can easily be established using Hansen's itemization. There is, in addition, a long history of colonial exploitation and oppression, not to mention contemporary modes of resource extraction, which must be taken into account. But contemporary international refugee conventions conveniently obscure this history. Worse still, standard legal recognition would not necessarily address the predicament of climate refugees but may simply create another level of second-class immigrant status for migrants, dooming them to be quarantined in prisonlike refugee camps and detention centers. This is hardly adequate recompense for the displacement climate refugees have suffered. As climate debtors, the rich nations of the world owe climate refugees sanctuary and civil protection, although more just and adequate forms of restitution should also be demanded on their behalf.

In articulating a definition of the climate refugee, Essam El-Hinnawi and other environmental activists sought to challenge systematic forms of invisibility. These efforts dovetailed with broader shifts taking place around issues of poverty and security after the Cold War. In 1989, for example, political theorist Jessica Tuchman Mathews' influential article "Redefining Security" argued for an expansion of definitions of national security to include "resource, environmental, and demographic issues,"[56] such as food security or energy security. This view was also echoed in various UN reports, including the *Brundtland Report* of 1987 and the *Human Development Report* of 1994. The point was to adopt a more humanitarian approach to security, from precarious livelihoods to gendered violence to food security, faced by people the world over. This approach to "human security" led to increasing concern with "global poverty," concern that could be said to culminate in the promulgation of the Millennium Development Goals in 2005.

But there was already a long history of perceiving poverty as dangerous. During the Cold War, for instance, Robert McNamara and other key figures in the national security complex viewed poverty in Third World countries such as Vietnam as a breeding ground for communism.[57] This stance allowed him to shift almost seamlessly between advising successive presidents on imperial warfare in Vietnam to addressing world poverty at the helm of the World Bank. As a result, it has become all too easy to wage imperial wars for so-called "human security" and humanitarian interventions. In the post-9/11 writing of global poverty expert Jeffrey Sachs, poverty breeds terrorism: "unstable societies beset by poverty, unemployment, rapid population growth, hunger, and lack of hope . . . poverty abroad can indeed hurt us at home."[58] As Akhil Gupta argues in his critique of Sachs, the poor subject who was intended to be the center of the human security agenda has been turned into an anxiety-inducing figure who threatens the true subject of these discussions: the global elite.[59]

Like concepts of human security and global poverty, the figure of the climate refugee was intended to elicit humanitarian empathy and policy. In particular, predictions of climate change–induced migration aimed both to galvanize efforts at reducing carbon emissions and to mobilize support for displaced populations. But the climate refugee turned out not to be the main concern—rather, it was the security of the affluent citizen and nation that really mattered. As a result, Malthusian discourses of overpopulation, never far below the surface in mainstream environmental groups like the Sierra Club, made a strong reappearance in discussions of environmental refugees. Jessica Tuchman Mathews wrote of sub-Saharan Africa:

The land's capacity to produce is ebbing away under the pressure of rapidly growing numbers of people who do not have the wherewithal to put back into the land what they take from it. A vicious cycle of human and resource impoverishment sets in . . . The resulting economic decline leads to frustration, domestic unrest, or even civil war. Environmental refugees spread the disruption across national borders.[60]

No mention is made of the structural inequalities of the global economy that produce poverty and climatic disruption; instead, the behavior of the poor (labeled as dysfunctional) is seen as a threat. This is a transparent revival of colonial discourses that represented the colonized as too numerous and responsible for environmental degradation. If warnings about the coming climate migration were intended to mobilize diplomatic cooperation in response to environmental challenges straddling national borders, they were all too easily shifted to focus on exclusionary models of climate security. Talk of climate refugees, in other words, played into the hands of the imperial security state.

A Genealogy of Insecurity

In the introduction to *Indefensible Space,* architect and critic Michael Sorkin describes the transformation of urban space in downtown New York after 9/11.[61] The proliferation of blast barriers, sniffer dogs, and security cameras that litter the urban landscape around Sorkin's office in Manhattan are part of an architecture of fear that is remaking not just urban space but also the cultural mores of Americans, instilling a deep sense of fear that legitimates all-pervasive systems of surveillance. Sorkin's account of the deputizing of design by the National Insecurity State powerfully captures the climate of fear that saw blast-proof planters and phalanxes of bollards transform downtown New York after 9/11, making a presumption of risk into the cardinal principle for planning.[62] Yet it is important to note that discourses linking national security, immigration, and the environment were not only in circulation prior to 9/11 but were a key element in legitimating the transnational security state whose presence manifested itself so clearly in downtown Manhattan during the War on Terror.

In fact, anti-immigrant sentiment has been present in discussions about climate change and the security state for decades. It would be wildly inaccurate to say that migrants from poor countries were welcomed to the United States and Western European nations with open arms in the period after World War II, but shortly after 1945, a dearth of workers led to the establishment of agreements such as the Bracero Program in the United States, dedicated mainly to recruiting farm workers from Mexico, and the *Gastarbeiterprogramm* or Guest Worker Program in West Germany, which brought workers from southern Europe, North Africa, and Turkey to fill openings in Germany's booming industrial sector. Along with similar schemes established in other industrialized northern European countries, these programs permitted relatively free movement of people across national boundaries. This changed when anti-immigrant discourses began to gain real purchase during the economic and political crises of the 1970s, leading to a cascade of policy changes to restrict immigration.

In the context of what cultural theorist Stuart Hall and his colleagues, writing in their seminal work *Policing the Crisis,* called the "organic crisis" of capitalism in the 1970s, British people of Caribbean descent were scapegoated as the culprits for the social conflict that accompanied declining profit rates in industry and the heating up of class warfare we now know as neoliberalism.[63] A moral panic around the figure of the black mugger was used by British governing elites such as Margaret Thatcher to cement what Hall and his comrades called *popular authoritarianism*, a xenophobic British nationalism that saw immigrants and their putatively alien behavior and social mores as a fundamental threat to the society. Highly repressive policing procedures in majority-black urban neighborhoods in Britain were the most immediate and tangible outcome of this popular authoritarianism, but this ideological shift also saw the rise of Britain's racist National Front, the successful mainstreaming of this anti-immigrant rhetoric by the Tories under Thatcher, and the passage of a sweepingly exclusionary nationality act in 1981.[64] Similar changes were afoot in other European countries and the United States, changes that culminated in two momentous pieces of policy with broad implications for migration policy.

In the United States, 1992 saw the passage of the North American Free Trade Agreement (NAFTA) under the Democratic president Bill Clinton. Uniting the United States, Mexico, and Canada in a trilateral trade partnership, NAFTA decimated Mexican agriculture as protective tariffs against US farm products were phased out. Subsidized US corn flooded Mexico, and as many as two million Mexican farmers, bankrupted by these changes, left the countryside and headed to Mexican cities and across the US border in search of work. The response of US authorities was to massively militarize the border, criminalizing those who crossed successfully as "illegals" and forcing them to live underground. In 1994, the Clinton administration established Operation Gatekeeper, whose goal was to halt illegal immigration at the United States-Mexico border. Three years later, the budget of the Immigration and Naturalization Service had doubled to $800 million, there were nearly twice as many Border Patrol agents deployed to the border, the amount of fencing had doubled, and the number of underground sensors had tripled. As part of Operation Gatekeeper, an automated biometric identification system was introduced to help identify repeat offenders and "criminal aliens."[65]

On the other side of the Atlantic, in a move animated by the same economic calculus as NAFTA, the Schengen Convention was adopted in 1990, abolishing border controls among most of the member states of the European Union. Two years later the Maastricht Treaty was signed, creating the European Union and the single European currency. For European nationals these agreements meant freedom of movement in a newly constituted political and economic entity made up of twenty-six states and over 400 million people. But, as political theorist Étienne Balibar observed, Schengen also instituted a form of European apartheid since "foreigners"—those residing in Europe but not belonging as citizens to a European nation—were excluded from the new open-borders model of citizenship as well as from the social rights that pertained to EU nations.[66] Under Schengen, third-country nationals were inherently viewed not simply as aliens but as a security concern. The freedom of movement of EU members thus came at the cost of this excluded additional nation of non-Europeans. Balibar alludes to the colonial origins of these exclusionary policies, describing the contradictory impact of the Schengen Area as a "recolonization" of social relations in Europe.[67] As was true of moral panics around the figure of the illegal alien in the United States, racism became a common response against the dismantling of well-paying employment and social benefits that disempowered large swaths of people under neoliberal globalization. As Balibar puts it:

> Institutional racism is a means of reconstituting in the imaginary a sovereignty that is in fact mythical given globalization [. . .] National citizens can be persuaded that their rights do in fact exist if they see that the rights of foreigners are inferior.[68]

The establishment of free movement within Europe coincided with increasingly militarized controls over entrance into the European Union. Under these increasingly militarized policies around immigration, the figure of the environmental refugee was quickly assimilated within discourses of national security. In 1992, then-Senator Al Gore argued that the environmental crisis should be taken seriously as a security issue in his book *Earth in the Balance.*[69] The language of national security saturates Gore's account of the environmental crisis. For example, in his efforts to alert the public to the dangers of climate change, Gore adopts a military lexicon of local "skirmishes," regional "battles," and "strategic" conflicts.[70] Climate change, which Gore classifies as a strategic threat, is repeatedly compared to the challenge of nuclear weapons.[71] One of the key steps proposed by Gore to cope with the climate crisis is what he calls a "Strategic Environmental Initiative" modelled on the Reagan-era Strategic Defense Initiative (aka Star Wars).[72] Within this framework, environmental upgrades in areas as diverse as agriculture, energy, and building would economically benefit the United States.[73] Gore does not write at length about the issue of environmental refugees, but he does single out "stabilizing world population" as the major (indeed, the sole) contribution to be made by underdeveloped nations to the global Marshall Plan for which he calls.[74] Although his book is centrally concerned with climate change, a crisis for which the historically industrialized nations of the global North are responsible, Gore repeatedly alludes to links between population growth, environmental devastation, and political instability and conflict:

> The social and political tensions associated with growth rates like these [in nations such as Kenya, Egypt, and Nigeria] threaten to cause the breakdown of social order in many of the fastest-growing countries, which in turn raises the prospect of wars being fought over scarce natural resources where expanding populations must share the same supplies.[75]

Even though Gore does not draw out the implications of such conflicts for global geopolitics, others were eager to do so. In a 1993 book entitled *Environmental Scarcity and Global Security*, Thomas Homer-Dixon made precisely such connections.[76] Replicating Gore's Malthusian arguments concerning overpopulation, Homer-Dixon examines cases of what he terms environmental scarcity, a problem he argues results from a combination of population growth, resource depletion, and unequal access to existing natural resources, in a series of case studies focused exclusively on countries in the global South.[77] Although he writes using the tempered language of academic sociology, Homer-Dixon nonetheless issues some remarkably ominous warnings. "Environmental scarcities are already contributing to violent conflicts in many parts of the developing world. These conflicts are probably the early signs of an upsurge of violence in the coming decades that will be induced or aggravated by scarcity,"[78] he writes of his research findings. As is true for Gore, Homer-Dixon's case studies never mention any external factors driving environmental scarcity. True to dominant models of international affairs, the specific nation-states Homer-Dixon discusses in his case studies are treated as isolated and self-contained entities, with no apparent relation to global systems of power and inequality, past and present. Places such as the Philippines and Peru, for example, are profiled with no discussion of the history of imperialism and unequal development to which they have been subjected. As a result of this, conflict seems to emanate from factors purely internal to those societies.

But if these conflicts germinate almost totally in isolation, they do not remain isolated for long. Indeed, the second of Homer-Dixon's three key hypotheses is that environmental scarcity causes migration and, in turn, violent "group-identity" conflict.[79] Researchers like Essam El-Hinnawi had already drawn links between climate change and environmental refugees, but now Homer-Dixon was explicitly tying the question of the refugee to issues of conflict, violence, and security. For Homer-Dixon, "group-identity conflicts" unleashed by environmental scarcity and displacement unfold exclusively in the global South; he cites border conflicts between Bangladesh and India, centering on migration from the former country into the northeast Indian states of Assam, Tripura, and West Bengal, as a particularly portentous example.[80] But such conflicts, he argues, have implications for "international security." Climate-induced migration may lead to the "fragmentation" of countries as "their states become enfeebled and peripheral regions are seized by renegade authorities and warlords," triggering "large outflows of refugees."[81] Alternately, this fragmentation can be halted if a state becomes a "'hard regime' that is authoritarian, intolerant of opposition, and militarized"[82] and also prone to launching military attacks against neighboring countries in order to divert attention from internal grievances. Such authoritarian regimes, Homer-Dixon argues, could threaten the military and economic interests of rich countries. Deploying both notions of security that were popular the 1990s, he focuses on the humanitarian impact of what he terms environmental scarcity, pivoting to a far more traditional set of assumptions about "security" that aim to maintain the global hegemony of North Atlantic nations such as the United States and the members of the European Union. Environmental security and maintaining empire are what ultimately count in his work.

In 1994, Robert Kaplan's widely read essay "The Coming Anarchy" translated these arguments into lurid, patently xenophobic prose. Any pretense to humanitarianism drops away in what became, alongside Samuel Huntington's *The Clash of Civilizations*, the main ideological primer for a new bout of bellicose imperial assertion by neoconservatives in the United States and satellite nations such as Britain. The debt to Homer-Dixon (as well as the sensationalistic nature of the claims) is clear from the subtitle of Kaplan's essay: "How Scarcity, Crime, Overpopulation, Tribalism, and Disease Are Destroying the Social Fabric of the Planet." Kaplan's text is saturated with racist scaremongering. He begins the essay with an account of arriving at a bus terminal in the Ivory Coast city of Abidjan, where "groups of young men with restless, scanning eyes surrounded my taxi, putting their hands all over the windows, demanding 'tips' for carrying my luggage even though I had only a rucksack."[83] It is a depiction drawn straight from colonial discourses of decades past. The impact is not much different: the African youths in question are depicted as an undifferentiated, menacing mass. Indeed, Kaplan represents such young men as being at risk of imminent combustion: "In cities in six West African countries I saw similar young men everywhere—hordes of them. They were like loose molecules in a very unstable social fluid, a fluid that was clearly on the verge of igniting."[84] Although his fear of these threatening "hordes" of black youths is visceral, Kaplan legitimates his aversion with an anecdote: He has been told by an official in one of the African nations he visits, a man whose nostalgia for the period of British colonial rule apparently tells Kaplan nothing about his political orientation, that such young men have lost the cultural moorings that communal life in the rural hinterlands provided and have descended into criminality as a result of what Kaplan calls "the corrosive social effects of life in cities."[85] Drawing on this hackneyed view of the deracinating impact of urban life, Kaplan goes on to state that the anarchy he thinks he sees through the window of his taxi is a clear premonition of a global future. "West Africa," he states, "is becoming *the* symbol of worldwide demographic, environmental, and societal stress, in which criminal anarchy emerges as the real 'strategic' danger."[86]

Kaplan's account of emerging global anarchy draws directly on Homer-Dixon's arguments, which Kaplan suggests have illuminated the underappreciated environmental dimension in global affairs. But he takes these arguments to an extreme.

> The political and strategic impact of surging populations, spreading disease, deforestation and soil erosion, water depletion, air pollution, and, possibly, rising sea levels in critical, overcrowded regions like the Nile Delta and Bangladesh—developments that will prompt mass migrations and, in turn, incite group conflicts—will be the core foreign-policy challenge from which most others will ultimately emanate.[87]

The causal chains here are direct, unqualified, and unexamined: overpopulation and environmental degradation lead ineluctably to mass migration and savage internecine violence. If Kaplan amps up Homer-Dixon's environmental determinism,[88] he also makes crystal clear whose interests are threatened by the social disruptions he predicts:

> The environment, I will argue, is part of a terrifying array of problems that will define a new threat to our security, filling the hole and allowing a post–Cold War foreign policy to emerge inexorably by need rather than by design.[89]

It is as if he were speaking directly to members of the US policy and military establishment, telling them that the search for a new orientation after the disappearance of the communist threat will be supplied by the emergence of anarchic violence sparked by environmental refugees. By threatening "our" security, the anarchy Kaplan predicts conveniently offers a new rationale for the military-industrial complex.

But the new age of chaotic warfare, Kaplan warns, will not be like those of the past. Humanity will bifurcate into "the Last Man," the affluent inhabitants of nations like the United States and those of Western Europe, and those outside this metaphorical stretch limo, denizens of a

> rundown, crowded planet of skinhead Cossacks and *juju* warriors, influenced by the worst refuse of Western pop culture and ancient tribal hatreds and battling over scraps of overused earth in guerrilla conflicts that ripple across continents and intersect in no discernible pattern—meaning there's no easy-to-define threat.[90]

In this anarchic Road Warrior world, violence will be pervasive and even relished. This is because "physical aggression is a part of being human. Only when people attain a certain economic, educational, and cultural standard is this trait tranquilized."[91] War will be rife and will emanate exclusively from the uncivilized global poor. Never mind the long history of CIA-sponsored coups, counterinsurgency operations, dirty tricks, and proxy wars fought on the terrain of poor nations during the Cold War or the US campaign of "Shock and Awe" in Iraq, involving the use of overwhelming and spectacular displays of force to paralyze enemies and destroy their will to fight.[92] For Kaplan, poor people are simply intrinsically vicious and will be rendered more so by the coming environmental crises.

While he might claim to be well-versed in the writing of Joseph Conrad—the penultimate chapter of the book-length version of *The Coming Anarchy* offers a reading of Conrad's great novel *Nostromo*—Kaplan apparently neglects one of the novelist's key insights. For, as Conrad suggests in *Heart of Darkness*, his novella written as part of the campaign against the genocidal policies of the Belgian King Leopold II in the Congo, barbarous violence actually lies deep within the hearts of the Europeans who purported to be bringing civilization to Africa. The novella's protagonist Kurtz states that European emissaries such as himself must appear to the Congolese "in the nature of supernatural beings—we approach them with the might of a deity." Yet it is precisely this claim to superiority that legitimated colonialism and allows Kurtz—and the all-too-real Belgians on whom he was modeled—to engage in the most depraved forms of barbarity in the Congo. It should not be so surprising that Kaplan neglects Conrad's critique of imperial rapine. Although they are anchored in arguments about environmental scarcity, Kaplan's assertions about the poor of the global South are predicated on assumptions of superiority not unlike what Conrad described. And Kaplan's warnings about the coming anarchy have helped to legitimate "security" solutions not unlike those articulated by Kurtz. While Kaplan predicts a widespread collapse into anarchy in the global South, he is also clear that this anarchy, rippling across continents, will menace the rich nations. If Kaplan's Last Man is to survive the predicted onslaught of skinheads and *juju* warriors, the restless hordes who crowd around his stretch limo with their scanning eyes and pawing hands, what choice does he ultimately have but to annihilate them? Either defensively, by refusing to open the doors of his air-conditioned limo, or offensively, by military means. The shocking conclusion of the tract written by Kurtz for the *Society for the Suppression of Savage Customs*—"Exterminate all the Brutes!"—might be a fitting epigraph for Kaplan's essay.

By the dawn of the twenty-first century, the scenarios of environmental scarcity, mass migration, and anarchic violence adumbrated by Homer-Dixon and Kaplan had become common sense among members of the policy elite. Writing in the summer of 2001, for instance, Jeffrey Sachs intones with total assurance that

economic failure abroad raises the risk of state failure as well. When foreign states malfunction (in the sense that they fail to provide basic public goods for their populations), their societies are likely to experience steeply escalating problems that spill over to the rest of the world, including the United States. Failed states are seedbeds of violence, terrorism, international criminality, mass migration and refugee movements, drug trafficking, and disease.[93]

But it was in the lucrative world of defense department–oriented think tanks that the imperial fantasies regarding environmental crisis and mass migration reached their most elaborate embellishment. Typical of this climate change–military–industrial complex is Peter Schwartz and Doug Randall's *An Abrupt Climate Change Scenario and Its Implications for United States National Security* (2003), which predicted that gradual global warming could lead to a relatively abrupt slowing of the Atlantic ocean's thermohaline conveyor, causing a sudden drop in temperatures in Europe.[94] This scenario was taken to a ridiculous extreme in the Hollywood movie *The Day After Tomorrow* (2004), in which the cooling is so rapid that helicopters literally freeze in mid-air. Written for the Office of Net Assessment, the Pentagon's internal think tank, *An Abrupt Climate Change Scenario* speculates that nations will develop two strategies in the face of the abrupt climate change: defensive and offensive.[95] According to Schwartz and Randall:

> Nations with the resources to do so may build virtual fortresses around their countries, preserving resources for themselves. Less fortunate nations, especially those with ancient enmities with their neighbors, may initiate in struggles for access to food, clean water, or energy.[96]

Like Kaplan, Schwartz and Randall highlight mass emigration from poor nations as one of the principal upshots of abrupt climate change, arguing that climate refugees will have a direct impact on rich nations: "For some countries, climate change could become such a challenge that mass emigration results as the desperate peoples seek better lives in regions such as the

United States that have the resources to adapt."[97] Similar assumptions about the relation between climate change and environmental refugees, which are seen as "threat multipliers," are embedded in the US Department of Defense's 2010 and 2014 *Quadrennial Defense Reviews*.[98]

The most detailed, credible, and unnerving of the speculative narratives generated by the climate change–military–industrial complex, however, is *The Age of Consequences: The Foreign Policy and National Security Implications of Global Climate Change. The Age of Consequences* was produced in 2007 by the Center for Strategic and International Studies (CSIS) and the Center for a New American Security (CNAS).[99] Convening a panel of well-credentialed national security experts and climate scientists, the CSIS/CNAS charged participants with developing three scenarios for climate change and its global social impacts using the scenario reports published by the IPCC.[100] What distinguishes *The Age of Consequences* from the IPCC scientific projections is its prediction of far more chaotic future worlds. More extreme future scenarios are warranted, the authors of the report argue, because of the fundamentally conservative character of climate science. In fact, the recent history of climate change alone has tended to exceed the worst-case scenarios of IPCC projections. "When building climate scenarios in order to anticipate the future, therefore, there is a very strong case for looking at the full range of what is *plausible*,"[101] they write. Consequently, none of the three scenarios in *The Age of Consequences* contemplate the possibility of climate stabilization, efforts to reduce carbon emissions notwithstanding. Each of the scenarios looks at a world in which emissions to date tip the planet into a postequilibrium state rocked by varying degrees of turbulence.[102]

The first of their three projections, the "expected scenario," might also have been termed the "inevitable" scenario since, as its authors emphasize, "there is no foreseeable political or technological solution that will enable us to avert many of the climatic impacts projected here."[103] The effects of climate change projected for this scenario are based on the A1B greenhouse gas emission scenario of the IPCC's Fourth Assessment Report, which predicts "massive food and water shortages, devastating natural disasters, and deadly disease outbreaks."[104] The national security implications of this expected scenario are marked, first and foremost, by large-scale climate-induced migration, with conflicts sparked by resource scarcity in regions of the global South.[105] Like Homer-Dixon and Kaplan, the authors of this section, Clinton-era White House Chief of Staff John Podesta and Chief of Staff of the Center for American Progress Peter Ogden, survey different regions of the world and suggest that sub-Saharan Africa and South Asia will be the most disrupted by internal displacement and transnational migration. Reflecting the post-9/11 moment, *The Age of Consequences* also speculates on the possible collapse of the European Union, as tensions over immigrants from Africa and the Middle East lead to a reimposition of border restrictions and cascading social, political, and economic fragmentation.[106]

The second scenario, dubbed the "severe climate change scenario," is predicated on "massive non-linear events" in the global environment giving rise to "massive non-linear societal events."[107] This scenario is marked by environmental feedback effects such as the release of carbon dioxide and methane from thawing permafrost in Arctic regions, effects that generate environmental and social change that is abrupt and difficult to predict but whose likely impacts include extensive mass migration between poor countries (for example, from Guatemala and Honduras to Mexico) and from poor to rich nations, the collapse of democratic governance around the world, increasing tensions over scarce resources such as water, emergence of deadly pandemics, and, ultimately, a mass die-off of hundreds of millions of people. The scenario is based on contemporary understandings of change within ecosystems, which may be gradual until a certain threshold is reached, at which point a rapid shift to a new state takes place. In this scenario, the global system of nation-states will be threatened with collapse. The authors argue that "the internal cohesion of nations will be under great stress, including in the United States, both as a result of a dramatic rise in migration and changes in agricultural patterns and water availability."[108] In addition, the report predicts that flooding of coastal communities in the Netherlands, the United States, South Asia, and China will cause tension within regions and may even lead to the collapse of nations.

The political and moral implications of these changes are catastrophic. The report states:

> Governments with resources will be forced to engage in long, nightmarish episodes of triage: deciding what and who can be salvaged from engulfment by a disordered environment. The choices will need to be made primarily among the poorest, not just abroad but at home.[109]

The author of this section of the report, Leon Fuerth, was the national security advisor to Vice President Al Gore, and his conclusion is very clearly shaped by the events following Hurricane Katrina in New Orleans. He is remarkably candid in his assessment of an apocalyptic scenario in which major mass die-offs occur, and he is even more radical in his assessment of how this catastrophic scenario may be averted: "Globalization will have to be redirected. It cannot continue forever in its present form, based on an insatiable consumption of resources," he writes. "Levels of demand will have to be brought into line with the availability of resources. This can occur either as the result of the collapse of the present system, or by its purposeful reconfiguration."[110] Although Fuerth purports to be advocating a transformation of "globalization," it is clear from his subsequent description of an economic system based on "an insatiable consumption of resources" that he is actually describing capitalism, which is founded on a suicidal imperative to unbridled growth on a limited terrestrial resource base. Although the apocalyptic implications of a failure to abandon capitalism's growth imperative are clear, Fuerth's call for the "purposeful reconfiguration" of the system poses but fails to answer the question of whether this may necessitate revolutionary transformation.

Could things get any worse than this? The answer, according to the final scenario in *The Age of Consequences,* is that they can indeed. This scenario, entitled the "catastrophic scenario," projects a series of tipping points such as the melting of the West Antarctic and Greenland ice sheets that push the planet from the metastable climate regime we currently inhabit into one of apocalyptic systemic turbulence. As the author of this section, former CIA Director James Woolsey, suggests, these shifts produce exponential rates of change that beggar the human imagination.[111] As the report notes, "this catastrophic scenario would pose almost inconceivable challenges as human society struggled to adapt. It is by far the most difficult future to visualize without straining credulity."[112] Indeed, the future challenges articulated by Woolsey, which center on the links between climate change and terrorism, are remarkably tame in comparison with those discussed in the previous, less severe scenario. The lesson here may be that efforts to conjure up future worlds based on unknowable contingencies and discontinuous ramifications are defined and limited by the present-day investments and bugaboos of those engaging in such fantasies. The manufacturing of climate change security scenarios thus dovetails with the worlds of literary genres such as science fiction and its subgenre Cli Fi, where apocalyptic futures are really projections of the fears and fantasies, the dystopias and utopias, of the present.[113]

Feral Cities and Enterprising Mercenaries

The Mediterranean has become a mass grave, according to Doctors Without Borders.[114] This is so not because of any natural features of the sea, such as shifting tides or stormy weather, but rather because of EU border-control policies. As the report *Death By Rescue* documents, the deaths of thousands of people each year are directly linked to policies of deterrence deliberately implemented by EU leaders, despite warnings that placing the burden of rescue operations on ill-equipped vessels would lead to higher fatalities.[115] In adopting such policies, the European Union is following a precedent set by the United States, where the Border Patrol outlined the policy of "enforcement through deterrence" in 1994.[116] Here too the result was a sharp and enduring escalation in the number of deaths in the border zone between the United States and Mexico. Yet if mortality rates of migrants are particularly high in the border zones between rich and poor nations, borders need to be seen not as fixed in time and space but rather as fungible.[117] This is particularly apparent in the case of the European Union, where powerful nations such as Germany have not only devolved much of the refugee infrastructure to southern European countries like Greece and Italy, but have also turned the nations of North Africa and Eastern Europe into postcolonial wardens responsible for interdiction and the accommodation of refugees.[118]

The literature on environmental refugees provides a convenient Malthusian template for the current crisis. If analysts such as Homer-Dixon and Kaplan employ a thoroughgoing environmental determinism to link mass migration to conflicts sparked by overpopulation and environmental crises, they also specify the geographical site from which mass migrations are launched: the cities of the global South. For Kaplan, for instance, "desertification and deforestation—also tied to overpopulation—drive more and more African peasants out of the countryside," to cities that are "ecological time-bombs" where "surging populations, environment degradation, and ethnic conflict may be deeply related."[119] According to this reductionist logic, as displaced people flow into the cities of the global South, conflict will automatically follow, generating refugee flows. Indeed, if Western security discourse has increasingly focused on the figure of the environmental refugee as a global threat, this imperial gaze has gravitated to the cities of the global South as the locus where this threat germinates.

Robert Kaplan's *The Coming Anarchy* prefigures this focus on the city as the breeding ground of systemic collapse. For if Kaplan takes "West Africa" as "*the* symbol of worldwide demographic, environmental, and societal stress," the true geographical matrix of this "criminal anarchy" is the sprawling informal settlements that surround and stud cities in the coastal megalopolis that runs from Abidjan in the Ivory Coast eastward to Lagos in Nigeria. It is in the former city's "Chicago" shantytown that Kaplan encounters more of the "young toughs" like those he describes surrounding his taxi at the main bus station. Kaplan represents these slums not just as shockingly poor, but, worse, as sites of total degeneracy, the locus of what he describes as a "nightmarish Dickensian spectacle" in which physical decay reflects and catalyzes the degeneration of residents' souls.[120]

Kaplan may see life in African cities as a premonition of an anarchic global future, but his dystopian account in fact draws on long-standing Western urban discourses that hinge on binary distinctions between Euro-American cities and the cities of the global South. The bifurcated narratives of urban discourse have long represented Western cities as the home of modernity, of cultural, technological, and economic dynamism. The city, dominant urban theory argues, is the primary locus of innovation and entrepreneurialism.[121] Cities are capitalism's great laboratories of progressive change. Cities outside the West, in contrast, are typically represented as sites wholly outside modernity, places where "development" can take place only through imitation of the norms generated in the cities of "advanced" capitalist countries. Cities have thus played a pivotal role in articulating modern–nonmodern binaries with a fundamentally colonial lineage.[122] Reproducing colonial discourse that situates the colonized in a premodern time, cities that are spatially distant from the capitalist core are represented as temporal laggards, trapped in a static premodern vacuum.[123] As a consequence, global South cities are not just seen as lacking material affluence and the infrastructural networks that often come with it. Such a lack might, after all, simply be seen as a product of historically inequitable power relations between the global South and North. Instead, drawing on traditions such as that of the Chicago School of Sociology, such cities are represented as convulsed by forms of social breakdown and violence that follow from the disequilibrium between urban life and the fundamentally premodern values of migrants from rural hinterlands, or from the disintegration of the customs that sustained order in rural worlds.[124] There is a striking similarity between this dominant urbanist discourse, which sees global South cities purely in terms of lack and degeneracy, and Kaplan's account of moral depravity in the slums of Abidjan and other West African cities.

Kaplan's suggestion that these anarchic cities offer a vision of the future also replicates claims made in Western urban theory. In his work with Harvard's Project on the City, for instance, the influential architect and theoretician Rem Koolhaas argues that the chaotic street life he finds in Lagos presages the future of urban life in the developed world.[125] For Koolhaas, the urban worlds of Lagos exemplify forms of extra-state organizing that anticipate the endgame toward which neoliberalism is driving city life in general, where "new modalities of organization acting outside juridical, parliamentary, and 'moral' constraints are increasingly required."[126] Global South cities that were once represented, by virtue of their supposed tribalism, primitivism, and traditionalism, as mired in the West's urban past, are now seen as exemplars of an anxiety-inducing global urban future. The temporal dynamic is thereby inverted. But, as urban theorist Jennifer Robinson has argued, this inversion of a fundamentally colonial urban perspective does little to challenge ethnocentric and, indeed, flagrantly racist assumptions about poor cities.[127]

Such cities are still seen as lacking the features considered constitutive of healthy urban life in the global North. This is patently the case in Kaplan's account of African urbanism, which he clearly sees purely in negative terms. If there is social infrastructure to be found in such cities, it is that created by urban mafias and transnational criminal syndicates. If there is any dynamism and innovation to be found in these places, it is generated by violent bands of tribal guerrilla warriors and Islamic extremist movements. Like Koolhaas, Kaplan worries that this dystopian world of anarchic violence is spreading to cities in the United States, as "crime continues to grow in our cities and the ability of state governments and criminal-justice systems to protect their citizens diminishes."[128] Dystopian projections about urban life in the global South are thus linked intimately to fears about life in US cities. It is worth noting that *The Coming Anarchy* was published the same year as Congress passed the Violent Crime Control and Law Enforcement Act, a keystone of the New Jim Crow that instituted repressive measures such as "three strikes and you're out," expanded the federal death penalty, and lifted the ban on assault weapons.[129]

Spinning out this logic of urban degeneration to its end point, military theorist David Kilcullen argues that "feral districts" have emerged in some cities located in rich nations, paralleling the "feral cities" he and Kaplan see in countries of the Global South.[130] In *Out of the Mountains,* he suggests that warfare in coastal cities of the world is inevitable and that these cities will be the predominant site of conflict in the future. Military theorists must come down "out of the mountains" (that is, from places like Afghanistan), to the conflict shorelines of the world, which will be beset by the usual litany of problems: rapidly growing populations, collapsing infrastructure, rampant crime, vulnerability to natural disasters, and shortages of energy, food, and water. In such sites, Kilcullen argues, it is the environment itself rather than any single group within it that is the principal threat.[131]

Drawing on a corpus of theory on military operations in urban terrain, Kilcullen argues that the conditions in densely populated coastal cities largely neutralize the advantages conferred by advanced technology to imperial powers like the United States. Since the late 1980s, technological developments such as the invention of "smart bombs" have allowed US military commanders and policy makers to unleash devastating violence from a distance and by remote control.[132] The drone wars of the Obama administration (and its targeted extrajudicial assassinations) are the latest manifestation of this evolution of remote killing devices.

Given the difficulty of engaging in combat in urban terrain, shouldn't imperial powers simply avoid such anarchic cities? Kilcullen argues that the military indeed long sought to circumvent such sites. However,

> that won't be an option in the future, when the coastal zone of an entire continent may be one giant megaslum, when most of the world's population will be concentrated in coastal cities, and when the enemy will be wherever we go, in part because our very presence turns locals into enemies . . .[133]

But Kilcullen believes that such enmity can be overcome; indeed, he represents military occupiers as a kind of nongovernmental organization dedicated to collaboration and community capacity building, employing a "co-design model" in which, once superior firepower has established peace, "locals" are able to "get together and begin to work toward a consensus on the nature of their problems."[134]

The complete evacuation of politics in Kilcullen's account, which, after all, describes methods for generating support for armed imperial intervention in postcolonial nations, is nearly as remarkable as his appropriation of the idiom of horizontal, networked political organizing. Citing the anarchist scholar James C. Scott, Kilcullen argues that his expert teams "eschew the high-modernist absolutism of centralized planning or unilateral and ill-informed prescriptions of outside designers or (worse) military interveners" and apply collaborative methods that "can help us treat the coastal city as a system and allow people to look for intervention or impact points to move that system in a positive, more resilient direction."[135] Kilcullen's model of co-design might also be termed collaboration, since it hinges on persuading local informants to work with and generate data for occupying military forces.

Kilcullen's enthusiasm for such high-tech espionage is not purely academic. Apart from his work as a military theorist, Kilcullen is also the founder and chairman of Caerus Associates, a "strategic research and design firm that helps governments, global institutions, businesses, and communities build resiliency in conflict, disaster-affected, and post-conflict environments."[136] This benign-sounding description, with its voguish reference to resiliency, effectively obscures the genuine thrust of Caerus, which was one of three companies contracted by DARPA (the US Department of Defense agency tasked with adapting emerging technologies for military use) to develop Nexus 7, a military intelligence program that "ties together everything from spy radars to fruit prices in order to glean clues about Afghan instability."[137] Nexus 7 is perhaps the most secretive program in the Pentagon's broader effort to use "big data" gathering software to allow the military to forecast conflict and insurgency.[138] Nexus 7 evolved from spying programs initiated by the National Security Administration (NSA), which began vacuuming up the phone records and emails of millions of Americans after 9/11 and then using new algorithm-based computer programs to sift through these mountains of data. In 2006, the NSA applied these techniques to fighting insurgents in Iraq in a program known as the Real Time Regional Gateway (RTRG), which scooped up and analyzed information such as "phone conversations, military events, road-traffic patterns, public opinion—even the price of potatoes," combining this information with data from drones flying above the Iraqi landscape.[139] Although it is unclear how accurately RTRG was able to predict insurgent attacks, we do know that the predictive information that it generated was employed by the secretive Joint Special Operations Command and its "kill teams." In 2010, DARPA took over RTRG, rechristening it as Nexus 7 and integrating data in order to monitor villages in Afghanistan, determine their political allegiances, and predict insurgent attacks. And Caerus has continued these operations elsewhere, producing a report entitled *Mapping the Conflict in Aleppo, Syria,*[140] a "four-month hyper-local assessment of the conflict in the city," whose "goal was to understand Aleppo's urban security and the humanitarian impacts of the conflict."[141] The company's intention was to provide information to imperial policy-makers and military forces before they make an intervention and to make lots of money in the process.

There are direct links between these counterinsurgency forecasting projects of the imperial state abroad and the repression
of immigrant communities and communities of color at home.
Across the United States, for instance, police departments are
currently deploying "predictive policing" technologies in order
to project future crime sites, technologies that were often developed in imperial war zones. The founders of one of the main
purveyors of such technology, the PredPol company, obtained
initial funding to develop software from the US Army Research
Office, for whom they modeled patterns of "terrorist and insurgent activities" in Afghanistan and Iraq. In a 2009 report to the
US military, the University of California at Los Angeles profes-
sors who developed this forecasting software made explicit
comparisons between "terrorists" and groups in the United
States they defined as "gang members."[142] Deploying their algorithms in "high-crime neighborhoods" with the help of the Los
Angeles Police Department (LAPD), they assured their military
sponsors, would "provide the Army with a plethora of new
data-intensive predictive algorithms for dealing with insurgents
and terrorists abroad."[143]

This revolving door between the imperial war machine and
the domestic immigrant detention and deportation industrial
complex has deepened systemic injustice. In 2010, the LAPD
was given a $3 million grant from the National Institute of
Justice to pioneer "intelligence-led policing" practices, including
crime-prediction methods, and in 2012 LAPD officers began
employing the PredPol technology. Since then many other police
departments around the country have acquired the forecasting
software, and in 2015 Arizona moved to appropriate funds for
statewide adoption of predictive policing. Money to support the
program was slated to come from the Arizona Department of
Public Safety's Gang and Immigration Intelligence Team
Enforcement Mission (GIITEM).[144] The algorithms used by
PredPol and other similar forecasting programs use data drawn
from previous police dragnets, producing exactly the same
dynamic as that criticized by Stuart Hall and his colleagues in
Policing the Crisis: racialized immigrant communities are

perceived as a threat and are consequently subjected to heavy policing (often with arrest quotas), which generates high crime statistics that are in turn used to legitimate heavier future policing.[145] Furthermore, as Arizona's GIITEM suggests, by collapsing "gang activity" and "immigration enforcement" into one policing organization, migration is criminalized, and, simultaneously, with the deployment of PredPol, the technologies of imperial warfare directed at global South cities are linked to coercive policing strategies that target immigrant populations in the United States. It would be naïve to think that these repressive technologies would not be used on environmental refugees in the future when they are already being used on immigrants today. As police kit up with assault rifles, armored personnel carriers, drones, and other military-grade equipment recycled from imperial escapades abroad, domestic communities of color are treated like occupied and oppressed internal colonies.

Climate Apartheid

Some would-be defenders of the rights of migrants have sought to shift the discourse by describing migration as a form of climate change adaptation.[146] Humanitarian organizations seeking to promote this shift consequently speak not of "climate refugees" but rather of "climate migrants." This approach to migration as a form of adaptation has been articulated in neoliberal terms, with migration seen as a form of bootstrapping self-help. Migrants are cast as good entrepreneurial subjects who respond to difficult conditions in a way that increases their own economic capacity while also benefiting the rich nations to which they migrate, many of which face a looming demographic deficit as their relatively affluent populations age. For organizations such as the World Bank, climate migrants are also seen as bringing economic development to global South countries, often in the form of remittances from migrants, allowing them to dodge the issue of deepening economic inequality between developed nations and much of the global South.[147] Above all, this response to deepening climate chaos is represented as a form of managed migration by the International Organization for Migration, a new paradigm of neoliberal global governance that would allow people to see themselves as "honorable workers" rather than "helpless victims," while also benefiting destination societies in search of flexible labor.[148]

One of the most revealing publications to embrace these notions of climate migration as a form of adaptation is *Migration and Global Environmental Change,* a report published by the British government public policy think tank Foresight.[149] In contrast with commentators like Kaplan, Foresight rejects the notion of environmental refugees, citing the multiplicity of factors that drive both internal displacement and international migration. Nevertheless, the report emphasizes that the impact of climate change on migration patterns will necessarily increase in the future, and that "no migration is not an option in the context of future environmental change."[150] Migration will either be "well managed and regular" or "if efforts are made to prevent it, unmanaged, unplanned, and forced." This argument is clearly intended to challenge the notion of environmental refugees as a security threat. Foresight seems to insist on some sort of right to transnational mobility, and it presents this option as a "new strategic approach" to issues of migration and climate change.

Equally of note in the Foresight report is the insistence that equal numbers of people will migrate into and out of areas of high environmental risk. This is especially the case when people leave rural areas for environmentally vulnerable cities in the global South, particularly "low-lying urban areas in mega-deltas or slums in water-insecure expanding cities."[151] In such circumstances, new arrivals in informal urban settlements are particularly vulnerable to environmental hazards, and, lacking the resources to migrate elsewhere, may end up trapped in increasingly dangerous circumstances. Foresight argues that global South cities face a form of double jeopardy, as their populations of ill-housed migrants burgeon while their exposure to environmental hazards of various kinds, from scarcity of fresh water to land loss to natural disasters of various sorts, skyrockets.[152] The report suggests that it is crucial that the cities housing them engage in long-term planning to cope with such environmental hazards and that the needs of expanding informal settlements be taken into account. There is little to quibble with in such prescriptions, but the authors ignore the patterns of disinvestment that have both driven urbanization in the global South and impeded the development of long-term planning and upgrading of informal settlements.[153]

Rather than restricting migration, Foresight advocates schemes based on circular migration. "Migration can be seen as a transformational adaptation strategy, as opposed to a more static approach of trying to improve 'coping' in current locations to current climate conditions,"[154] states the report, and "greatly increases the longer-term resilience of individuals and communities alike to the threats of environmental change."[155] Like the World Bank, Foresight argues that money flowing from migrant populations in rich countries can be an economic boon to their communities of origin. The responsibility of rich countries and their institutions for funding adaptation—or in other words, climate debt—is thereby obscured. In addition, Foresight also suggests that managed migration may benefit the economies of "receiving locations," where "it can help to address skill shortages in key industries and public services, fuel entrepreneurship, and even provide scope for addressing demographic deficits linked to ageing populations."[156] An example of such "management" is provided by New Zealand, which ran a migration lottery for the residents of Tonga, an archipelago of Pacific Islands that is likely to be submerged during the current century.

The idea of a lottery to determine who will be entitled to escape the rising seas and who will be left to perish beneath the waves underlines the fundamental injustice of managed-migration schemes, particularly given the fact that a nation such as Tonga is virtually totally unresponsible for global climate change. Managed migration is a system that allows some to migrate—usually those whose skills are attractive to capital in the wealthy nations—but denies movement to the vast majority of people. It seems to support a right to freedom of movement but in fact opens a path to migration for only a select few. Far from a solution to the problem of climate-induced migration, it simply makes "illegal" all who don't "win" the lottery, those who businesses and wealthy nations do not want, and those who choose on their own to move.

Although Foresight presents the scheme of managed migration as a novel strategic approach, there is little that is new about its proposal. Policies encouraging "circular migration" have been common not only in the United States and in Western European nations after 1945, but also (and perhaps most tellingly) in South Africa during the apartheid era. Indeed, it is the latter's system of naked racial capitalism that is most exemplary of "managed-migration" schemes. Denied full citizenship in the nation by the Bantustan or "Homeland" system, members of the black majority in South Africa were granted rights of residency in the nation's cities only if they were engaged in manual labor in the diamond and gold mines or in domestic work in the homes of whites. The apartheid labor system depended not only on racialization of the black majority in South Africa, but also on exploitation and reinforcement of gender hierarchies, with women often banished from cities as a result of their role in unremunerated forms of labor like childcare. The apartheid system ensured that migrant workers would subsidize South African capital by pushing the cost of education, pensions, and social services, as well as the costs of feeding workers' families, onto the backs of the dispossessed.[157] And of course the apartheid system could only be justified through the systematic dehumanization of the majority black population in South Africa.

Today, the apartheid system of migrant labor has gone global, with the dispossession of millions in the global South directly tied to the insatiable demand for supplies of cheap labor in the global North.[158] The insecurity of the migrant ensures the security of capital.[159] The "new security paradigm" proposed by Foresight is often represented as the antithesis of xenophobic nationalism, but schemes of managed migration rely on selective legalization and therefore are always defined by the zone of illegality to which legal immigration is opposed. In addition, the social abjection of the migrant produced by xenophobic discourse is absolutely essential to the conditions of insecurity that characterize the system of racial capitalism that we inhabit today. Racist discourses of inundation by mass migration are crucial to establishing the forms of precariousness on which contemporary capitalism depends. For this reason, representations of climate refugees such as those articulated by figures like Ségolène Royal, Robert Kaplan, and David Kilcullen should be seen for what they are: an integral element of today's burgeoning system of climate apartheid. In this emerging regime of accumulation, those who are least responsible for climate chaos are made to pay the most dearly. Under climate apartheid, no acknowledgment of the climate debt owed to the people of the global South is made. And in a world of climate apartheid, the specter of climate-induced migration becomes the crucial stratagem of a disaster capitalism looking to make money off the apocalypse.

Abandoned house at Far Rockaway after Hurricane Sandy.
Photo by Anne McClintock.

6

Disaster Communism

Spectacular disasters have buffeted global cities with increasing frequency in recent years, from Hurricane Katrina in New Orleans (2005) to Superstorm Sandy in New York (2012) to the devastation inflicted on the Philippines by Typhoon Yolanda (2013). These disasters have made it clear that humans are becoming increasingly vulnerable to the cataclysm produced in large part by our own scientific and technological accomplishments. Within the scientific community, and even in publications such as the World Bank's *Turn Down the Heat,* the assumption is that the promises of international climate negotiators to maintain global warming below 2°C are hollow and that the world is already on a trajectory for at least 4°C of warming.[1] Fatih Birol, chief economist for the International Energy Agency, has warned that current global energy-consumption levels put the planet on an even more alarming path to warm by at least 6°C above preindustrial levels by 2100.[2] We are warming the Earth at a rate that is unprecedented, forcing changes in planetary systems at a speed and magnitude for which there is no geological record in Earth's past, including during the Permian mass extinction event, when 90 percent of all species were wiped out. We are, in fact, in the midst of the planet's sixth mass-extinction event, although climate change is still responsible for only a relatively small (but increasing) percentage of species loss.[3]

The climatic conditions under which human civilization came to dominate the planet—the era of relative environmental stability since the Neolithic revolution 12,000 years ago—are now behind us. We inhabit an epoch of increasingly perilous climate chaos. As cultural theorist Evan Calder Williams has suggested, global capitalism is characterized not simply by combined and uneven development, but also by uneven and combined apocalypse. The apocalypse is not a singular, instant event, but is "unfolding in slow motion with sudden leaps and storms," with zones of breakdown spread like irregular sinkholes across the terrain of capitalist societies the world over.[4] Climate change is already a current reality, not a future possibility. Today's fight is over how fast climate change will happen and how bad the future will be.

The age of disaster is also the age of the city. Indeed, the two are inextricably intertwined. Mike Davis writes:

> Heating and cooling the urban built environment alone is responsible for an estimated 35 to 45 percent of current carbon emissions, while urban industries and transportation contribute another 35 to 40 percent. In a sense, city life is rapidly destroying the ecological niche—Holocene climate stability—which made its evolution into complexity possible.[5]

If today's cities are one of the major drivers of climate chaos, they are also its principal victims. The storms of climate chaos are already breaking on human shores, and their devastation is most apparent in the planet's coastal megacities, where vulnerable infrastructures, massive economic resources, and human populations are concentrated in unprecedented quantities. The city is paradoxically the greatest expression, principal culprit, and most endangered artifact of our turbulent times.

The way we frame the disasters that befall the extreme city is a major impediment to coping with climate chaos. Etymologically, disaster suggests an "ill-starred event," an abnormal occurrence brought about by malign external forces. Yet it is not the heavens but human beings who are responsible for climate chaos. We are responsible for the onset of the Anthropocene Age, which gestures to humanity's collective capacity to transform the planet. But who is the animating subject of the Anthropocene? Social historians Christophe Bonneuil and Jean-Baptiste Fressoz have shown that the Anthropocene is not the product of the human species as a whole.[6] A more appropriate (if rather unwieldy) term for this epoch, they argue, would be the Oliganthropocene, the era in which a small fraction of humanity exploited the planet's fragile environmental systems, not to mention immense numbers of their fellow human beings, beyond the point of sustainability. The fossil capitalism that is driving planetary ecosystems toward a mass-extinction event was adopted for the profit of a miniscule but powerful global elite.[7]

Hurricanes Katrina and Sandy showed that urban disasters deepen the grooves of already-existing social inequality. The stories of postdisaster initiatives such as Rebuild by Design in New York demonstrate this dynamic anew. Disasters afflict communities that are highly stratified by neoliberal capitalism, which has generated increasingly yawning inequalities and stark vulnerabilities over the last three decades. While often invisible to insulated economic elites, this slow violence is rendered visible in the drowned buildings, floating bodies, and abandoned populations that surface after disaster strikes. Exploiting the shock created by such disruptions, what Naomi Klein calls "disaster capitalism" commandeers the rebuilding process to direct state and private aid to the well-heeled while further starving an already emaciated public sector.[8] "Recovery" efforts all too often exacerbate existing economic and social inequalities, as in New Orleans, where public housing was demolished and the public school system was privatized as part of post-Katrina rebuilding efforts. Similar forms of disaster capitalism played out in New York after 9/11, with massive state aid going to the rich in downtown while nearby working-class communities like Chinatown were deprived of resources.

But people also tend to discover a sense of collective purpose and solidarity in the midst of disaster, much as Shirley Nash-Chisholm of Red Hook Initiative (described in the Introduction) did. Rather than provoking selfish, antisocial, and even belligerent behavior, evidence suggests that even under extreme circumstances, most people tend to regain their self-control and become concerned about the conditions of those around them relatively quickly. As Rebecca Solnit argues in *A Paradise Built in Hell,* disasters momentarily suspend the established social order, generating fluid situations in which people often (if not always) react with empathy, care, and heroic concern for one another, rupturing the solipsism that is relentlessly encouraged by capitalist culture.[9] Disasters may thus provide a temporary reprieve from a daily life that has become increasingly atomistic, violent, and dispiriting. Events such as those Solnit surveys, from the earthquakes in San Francisco in 1906 and in Mexico City in 1985 to Hurricane Katrina in New Orleans (2005) and 9/11 in New York (2001), are grievous affairs that should not be wished upon anyone, but they can also inadvertently open a window onto another way of being. "The possibility of paradise hovers on the cusp of coming into being, so much so that it takes powerful forces to keep such a paradise at bay," Solnit writes.[10]

Disasters can often further strengthen capitalism and profit the rich, but they can also offer a glimpse of what radical political theorist Jodi Dean calls the communist horizon, the sense that the oppressive conditions of the present can be overcome and new forms of solidarity discovered. Capitalism no longer seems the only possible future. We may even begin to enact a different society based on human empathy and mutual aid.[11] Communal solidarities forged in the teeth of calamity can be seen as a form of disaster communism,[12] under which people begin to organize themselves to meet one another's basic needs and to collectively survive. This may spark a more long-term process in which a more just and ecologically sustainable society, based on genuine human needs, begins to come into view and becomes the goal of collective organizing. Admittedly, these instances of mutual aid can be stymied and coopted by states or private interests: the most corrupt people and institutions are often best situated to exploit disasters, against popular movements that seek to build a more just order out of the ashes.[13]

Nonetheless, climate chaos is likely to make disaster communism an increasingly potent force in cities around the globe. There are two principal reasons for this. First, climate chaos increases the likelihood of revolution. In a series of theses that explore the uprisings of the Arab Spring, geographer Andreas Malm argues that while climate chaos cannot on its own cause revolution, it will be an increasingly important factor helping to light the fuse.[14] Malm cites the Egyptian Revolution of 2011, which was sparked in part by increasing pressure placed on global grain prices by droughts in grain-producing countries such as Ukraine. There is a long history of bread riots catalyzing broader insurrections: when ruling regimes are unwilling or unable to provide adequate food for citizens, they are perceived less as a guarantor than as a threat to the bodily metabolism of the people, provoking a crisis of legitimation.[15] The most famous example is undoubtedly the French Revolution, one of whose earliest incidents was the March on Versailles led by market women protesting the high price of bread. Elites can for a time insulate themselves and even profit from these food crises, but the global poor, who depend on purchased food and have but a thin margin for survival, tend to feel these shocks immediately.[16]

Successful revolutions also increase the likelihood of survival in the era of climate chaos. In a time of emergency, the calculus of who lives and who dies is often a product of the strength of one's bonds with others and of how egalitarian these communities are.[17] Decades of research into community vulnerability has demonstrated that equal ownership of resources is the best protection against natural disasters.[18] As the disaster expert Ben Wisner has suggested in his seminal work on the topic, "only radical changes in the organization of production and in access to political power will affect in a large number of direct and indirect ways vulnerability to disaster."[19] Meanwhile, many of the adaptation schemes I have surveyed in previous chapters offer band-aid solutions and dispense some resources without addressing the roots of the crisis. Ultimately, these could worsen the forms of vulnerability bequeathed by the unrestrained capitalism of the last several decades.

The window for greenwashing and other forms of disaster capitalism has closed. According to Kevin Anderson, deputy director of the Tyndell Centre for Climate Research, to have at least a 50 percent chance of averting more than 2°C warming by 2050, "global energy-related emissions have to decrease by 10–20 percent per year, hitting zero between 2035 and 2045. Flying, driving, heating our homes, using our appliances, basically everything we do, would need to be zero carbon."[20] Solutions implemented through free market capitalism cannot cope with this crisis because market economics is premised on tinkering at the margins of the system rather than transforming it wholesale, he argues.[21]

But if capitalism offers no solution to the crisis, nor do the kinds of localized, horizontalist experiments in radical democracy that much of the Left currently favors. As I will discuss in the context of Occupy Sandy, the first moment of disaster communism can all too easily be dismantled and coopted by the powers that be. Making cuts of the depth that Anderson and other scientists are calling for requires a systemic transformation, one that, as Andreas Malm argues, includes measures such as

> demand rationing and requisitioning, warlike state management of all industries, premature liquidation of astronomic amounts of capital sunk in fossil infrastructure, centralized decisions on who can consume what goods in what amounts, and punishments of transgressors threatening the annual emissions targets.[22]

Allusions to "war communism" are certain to be controversial. Even the explicit anticapitalist stance taken by Naomi Klein in her account of the climate justice movement has provoked attacks from both conservatives and liberals.[23] But however the movement for climate justice is labeled, it will have to confront many of the dilemmas central to the communist tradition. Communism has engaged with the ideas of the collective and the commons that need rebuilding, and it has been marked by lineages of internationalism and solidarity that are particularly essential in times of cataclysmic change. Equally important, while critics might dismiss communism as a form of totalitarianism, it harbors a long legacy exploring the relation between the state and popular social movements. This may offer a way to think about the kind of nontotalitarian but nonetheless strictly regulatory state that is necessary to save humanity and the planet from mass extinction. For Bolivian vice president Álvaro García Linera, the state may find ways to support the evolution of society's autonomous organizing capacities, as the country's government under indigenous President Evo Morales has attempted to do, clearing the path toward an egalitarian communist society.[24] Whether or not one ultimately agrees with García Linera, it is crucial to at least consider how popular egalitarian movements can consolidate power on a scale that is commensurate with the threat of looming climate catastrophe.

Above all, disaster communism must stand for a rejection of the devotion to incessant growth that characterizes capitalism. This can be most readily seen in the extreme city, the principal force behind climate change, where climate chaos is most harshly experienced and where affected communities are already organizing in the face of environmental disaster. The struggle for a just city is consequently also a struggle for climate justice. Yet "the ecological genius of the city remains a vast, largely hidden power," writes Mike Davis.[25] Most recent urban social movements have in fact articulated themselves around the right to the city rather than around traditionally defined environmental questions, while the environmental movement has largely ignored urban struggles to climate justice, tending to see nature as the antithesis to the city. As sociologist Daniel Aldana Cohen notes, even Naomi Klein tends to focus her account of climate justice on the predominantly rural environmental movements against extreme extraction that she calls "Blockadia."[26]

Connecting these diverse struggles will be the central challenge of our times. The struggle for a just city is, as Mike Davis argues, also the struggle for the low-carbon forms of habitation that may enable our predominantly urban species to survive. And as urban social movements in the extreme city come to see themselves as being on the front lines of climate chaos, their struggles become increasingly entangled with those of "ecosystem people" in the global South and with climate justice more broadly.[27] But urban movements for environmental justice, organizing around principles of social solidarity and radical demands for adaptation to climate chaos, are already engaged in a war against fossil capital. The alternative to the extreme city, these movements suggest, is the revolutionary city.

Mutual Aid

On the morning after Hurricane Sandy hit the city, New Yorkers who had met and formed bonds during the Occupy Wall Street (OWS) movement fanned out across the city to see which areas had been hardest hit and where help was needed. OWS activists had stayed in touch for several days using social media and friendship networks. Now they were checking in on one another and finding out what could be done to help communities devastated by the storm. The orientation of Occupy toward issues of inequality meant that activists knew disaster would not affect the city equally: the people who would bear the brunt would be those already struggling to survive in the extreme city.[28] The poor and working class who inhabit the city's outer boroughs would be the ones left without electrical power. Occupy activists were clear even before the storm hit that whatever resources they could muster should be concentrated on such marginalized communities.

In a city whose extensive but decrepit public transportation system had been knocked to its knees, the bicycle became one of the principal modes of transport. Among the corps of two-wheeled militants heading to hard-hit neighborhoods was

Conor Tomás Reed, a City University of New York graduate student involved with one of OWS's offshoots, the Free University, an effort to take radical education to the city's parks and other public places.[29] After connecting by texting with other members of Occupy, Conor met some friends at the Park Slope Armory in Brooklyn and rode three miles to Red Hook, which had suffered extensive flooding during the storm. As they cycled through the waterfront neighborhood, they met local residents who told them that power had gone down in the neighborhood's public housing complex—one of the oldest and largest in the city—leaving residents without light, without the use of elevators in 15–20 story buildings, and, for those above the fifth floor, without running water. Most affected were senior citizens in the complex, many of whom were now dependent on neighbors for water, food, and essential medications. The neighborhood's high-end supermarket, part of a wave of gentrification lapping into Red Hook in recent years, was locked up and inaccessible. There were no relief organizations in the neighborhood, nor were city authorities of any kind in evidence.

By the early afternoon, Conor's crew had reached out to Occupy activists with connections to Red Hook Initiative, a local community center founded in the early 2000s in response to the severe health and social issues affecting the neighborhood (one of the city's highly polluted "special maritime and industrial areas"). Miraculously, the power had remained on at Red Hook Initiative, and staff members quickly agreed to become a distribution hub for whatever aid supplies could be ferried into the devastated neighborhood. Local residents brought food from their kitchens to make a giant pot of soup to feed those without power and food. By the evening, Occupy activists with deep experience in improvising communal provision of food and other needs from the weeks of occupation in downtown Manhattan's Zuccotti Park were working with community activists from Red Hook, who spread word about the disaster-relief hub through their community networks. Within days, the hub at Red Hook Initiative was making hundreds of meals. An intake crew had been established to organize the flood of donations that were beginning to arrive, a team of doctors was providing medical services to community residents, and a nimble network of volunteers took off from the disaster hub each day to canvass vulnerable residents of the neighborhood about their needs. In the glaring absence of official disaster relief—the Red Cross and Federal Emergency Management Agency (FEMA) did not show up until days later—Conor's crew worked with local activists to establish mutual aid structures, and Red Hook was able to weather the deadly aftermath of the storm.

From the guilds of medieval Europe to the neighborhood assemblies in Argentina after the economic crash of 1998, mutual aid efforts that involve sharing collective resources using nonhierarchical forms of organizing have been a constant feature of human societies. Over the last two decades, anger at the perceived failure of the state has added political urgency to these experiments in mutual aid. Rather than waiting for the state to save them, people have organized themselves into autonomous mutual aid groups that eschew the hierarchy implicit in representational government.[30] The mutual aid efforts Conor and his friends contributed to in Red Hook played out in many other neighborhoods across the city, filling the vacuum left by sluggish city and federal relief organizations. The movement that came to be known as Occupy Sandy created central relief hubs across New York City that in turn facilitated the creation of smaller centers in a network structure. Occupy's horizontal organizing philosophy meant that relief centers could be set up wherever and whenever someone identified a need and took the initiative to set up a site. As a result, smaller centers expanded around the central hubs with remarkable speed and flexibility. Soon, the movement had spread beyond the boroughs of New York and into the hurricane-affected coastal regions of New Jersey. Occupy Sandy established three main distribution hubs in the city ("Jacobi" in Queens, "Clinton" in Brooklyn, and "Red Hook" in Brooklyn) where it stored resources, conducted volunteer trainings, and coordinated regional operations. "Recovery" hubs were set up in areas particularly badly affected by the storm, including the Rockaways, the Lower East Side of

Manhattan, Staten Island, Coney Island, and Red Hook. Smaller recovery sites were also established in Canarsie, Sheepshead Bay, Bay Ridge, Gerritsen Beach, Long Island, and across New Jersey. Occupy Sandy very quickly became the key disaster-relief effort in the region.

It was not simply that established relief organizations didn't turn up in many of these places, although this was often the case; it was also that their operating guidelines prevented them from helping people where and when they needed it most. For example, some official organizations did not send workers into public housing complexes, where many aged and infirm people were trapped without heat, electricity, running water, and access to critical medications. The manifest failures of established relief organizations ensured that Occupy Sandy would become the primary relief organization in the city in the days and weeks after the storm. At its height, Occupy Sandy helped to coordinate the activities of nearly 60,000 volunteers, mobilizing resources four times greater in size than the Red Cross.[31] So effective was Occupy Sandy in getting emergency supplies to those most in need that official disaster-relief organizations and city authorities were forced to acknowledge grudgingly the movement's importance in the wake of the hurricane and to collaborate with Occupy activists. It should be recalled that it had been less than a year since the New York Police Department forcibly evicted the Occupy movement from Zuccotti Park, arresting hundreds of the same activists that authorities were now dependent on to get aid to those in need after Sandy.

Equally important was the creation of virtual networks that linked activists across the city and the region. Occupy Sandy made extremely creative use of social media, including new tools invented expressly for the purpose of coordinating disaster relief. According to activist Devin Balkind, who worked to develop some of these resources, Occupy Sandy created a kind of knowledge commons using social media.[32] The day the storm hit the city, a website called OccupySandy.net was established that provided information about how to receive updates from the network, how to volunteer, where to donate goods, and where to find emergency shelter.[33] The site offered sign-up forms for those wishing to volunteer and listed mutual support sites. Interoccupy, a working group that connected global Occupy movements, moved quickly following Sandy to create a website called the "Interoccupy Hub," which consolidated initial Occupy Sandy social media feeds with a WePay account through which relief donations could be made. Tech-savvy Occupy activists like Balkind populated Occupy Sandy's Facebook page and regularly sent out Tweets through @OccupySandy. In addition, each main relief hub set up its own Facebook and Twitter pages to keep up with the avalanche of donations and volunteers. Occupy Sandy also used Google Docs, short text messages, and text loops to share information, and it developed its own open-source software, called Sahana, to control its internal inventory. A week after the storm hit, Occupy Sandy's Facebook page had 10,000 likes and it had 5,000 followers on Twitter. The mutual aid network by this point had a roster of 700 volunteers and was serving 20,000 meals each day across the city.

One of the key characteristics that made Occupy Sandy so remarkably effective, and that differentiated it from the hide-bound practices of established, bureaucratic relief organizations, was the flexibility and spontaneous improvisation that characterized the movement. For example, soon after Occupy Sandy formed, it became evident to volunteers at the central disaster-relief hubs that many donated items were not needed. A volunteer at one of these hubs came up with the idea of setting up an Amazon.com gift registry and began using this registry to field requests from the various hubs for emergency supplies. As a result of this online resource, people around the world were suddenly able to participate in relief efforts in real time, with no intermediaries. The disaster-relief registry exemplified key characteristics of Occupy Sandy: individual ingenuity and spontaneous response to a need, following principles of mutual aid.

What was true in the realm of technology applied equally to other aspects of Occupy Sandy. After going through a very brief orientation, volunteers from across the region could plug into the organization in any way they wished, adapting their existing skills to the needs identified at the time and responding on the fly to emerging crises. Specialized teams formed up quickly as the immediate disaster passed and more long-term needs began to surface. The "Kitchen" made and served meals to thousands. Medical teams organized to canvass for dead bodies in homes and apartment buildings and to distribute prescriptions and medical equipment. Volunteers were trained to be part of Construction and Clean Up Teams, which removed water, mud, debris, and mold from homes and began the rebuilding process. Housing teams formed to connect displaced survivors with people willing to host them, and a legal team advised survivors on tenant rights, insurance issues, and negotiating the byzantine process of applying for aid.

Occupy Sandy didn't just see self-declared Occupy activists as capable of organizing themselves in creative ways that have become known in the global movements as "autonomous" (i.e., as independent of the state and other official relief organizations, which tend to be highly bureaucratic and top-down).[34] It also set out to challenge the idea that those who weathered Hurricane Sandy were passive "victims," whose only role was to survive until relief agencies and the government arrived with aid. In place of this disempowering attitude, which is how the city and established relief organizations predominantly viewed disaster survivors, Occupy was animated by values of care and mutual aid that envisaged survivors as capable and willing to help themselves and their neighbors to recover from the storm.[35] If research on disasters has shown that people's capacity to survive cataclysm is often determined by the strength of their social networks, Occupy Sandy was predicated on the idea that people would jump at the chance not just to tap existing social connections but to establish new networks and share resources when given the opportunity. This behavior goes very much against the grain of dominant neoliberal ideology. As Rebecca Solnit emphasizes in A Paradise Built in Hell, mutual aid challenges the idea of a savagely selfish human nature that not only animates the work of influential dystopian philosophers like Hobbes and Malthus, but that also features prominently in contemporary media depictions of disaster.[36] Think, for instance, of the ubiquitous representations of zombies in popular culture, who exemplify a plague of single-minded barbarity that, with few exceptions, leads to a violent anarchy that only a strong (and usually white male) hero is capable of beating back, also through hyperviolent means. As Solnit emphasizes, such accounts of baseline human selfishness offer a convenient narrative that benefits the powerful and wealthy, supporting the idea that there is no alternative to the unjust status quo. In place of such dystopian ideology, Occupy Sandy's principled practice of mutual aid constituted a form of disaster communism: collaborative, altruistic, and often improvised forms of collective provision echoing Marx's dictum "for each according to ability, to each according to need." Occupy Sandy thus offered a glimpse of the communist horizon.

As the Superstorm Research Lab pointed out in their study *A Tale of Two Sandys,* there were two radically different ways of approaching hurricane-related social crises after the storm: one approach, which typified city government and official relief organizations, saw the devastation as exclusively storm-related and simply tried to restore communities to prestorm conditions.[37] The other, which typified Occupy Sandy activists, viewed the storm as exacerbating a chronic crisis of inequality characterized by factors such as poverty, lack of affordable housing, precarious or low employment, and unequal access to resources. For Occupy activists, the official disaster recovery narrative of building communities back obscured fundamental questions of equity.[38]

There was also the issue of the timescale on which the disaster was approached. Because government officials tended to make hard-and-fast distinctions between the storm's effects and more long-term urban crises, their response took the form of technical fixes to short-term infrastructural problems generated by the storm.[39] Federal government programs typically had deadlines for aid, which implied that an urban crisis began the day the storm hit and would be satisfactorily resolved by an arbitrarily set date. But for chronic crises—which unfold over an extended time—a system of rolling deadlines, responsive to people's changing and often unpredictable needs, would be far more appropriate. This was precisely the approach adopted by Occupy Sandy, which developed a decision-making body called the Occupy Sandy Project Spokescouncil to manage the network's resources and make decisions for the allocation of funds to specific recovery projects using a rolling project submissions process. All spokescouncil meetings were open to the public and anyone could request funding for an idea. Occupy Sandy was criticized for expending less than half of the nearly $1.5 million it collected during the year after the storm, but such criticism ignores Occupy's orientation around an understanding of crisis over an extended timescale. To put this in context, the city's audit of state programs in 2015 revealed that the city's Build It Back Program squandered millions of dollars on consultants who set up an incredibly convoluted aid application process while completing virtually no home reconstruction.[40] Occupy Sandy avoided such corruption through its horizontal structures, which ensured that resources would be managed in a transparent, responsive, and equitable manner as they flowed in and as the relief operations unfolded into rebuilding efforts.[41]

Among the notable examples of Occupy Sandy's efforts to build community capacity through mutual aid was the restoration of the You Are Never Alone (YANA) community service center in the Rockaways, the Queens neighborhood on a barrier island near JFK airport that was severely damaged by floodwaters washing in from the bayside of the peninsula. Occupy Sandy activists rebuilt the space using sustainable techniques, turning it into a relief hub for the island that provided meals as well as legal counseling, housing advocacy, and medical treatment for a neighborhood that was initially largely ignored by city authorities and big relief agencies. Like the work of Occupy activists at the Red Hook Initiative, the rebuilding efforts at YANA stressed the creation of jobs for local people in a community that had been used to warehouse marginalized citizens ever since the days of Robert Moses's "Rockaways Improvement Plan."[42] As I discussed in Chapter 2, Moses and city authorities had bulldozed the summer bungalows that dominated the Rockaways before World War II and built tall apartment blocks marked by their stark isolation from the rest of the city. These areas of the city were among those hardest hit by the storm surge that accompanied Hurricane Sandy. They were also those whose suffering was most invisible and lasted longest. While power was quickly restored to affluent downtown Manhattan, the Rockaways remained disconnected from essential elements of the urban infrastructure for many weeks following the storm. As in Red Hook, many residents were trapped in public housing projects when the elevators went out during the hurricane, and in the storm's aftermath residents began grappling with mold and other relatively invisible forms of natural disaster. Occupy Sandy's work at YANA sought to counter not just the effects of Sandy but also this much longer history of social abandonment.

Sofía Gallisá Muriente, who acted as one of the Occupy Sandy field coordinators at YANA during the months after the storm, ran into this culture of abandonment following the hurricane. While attending a meeting of the city's Office of Emergency Management in Brooklyn, as part of an effort to get people in the Rockaways certified in disaster management, Sofía was told by one of the top officials present that it was official federal government policy that disaster victims should not be disaster responders.[43] The Office of Emergency Management, Sofía learned, had "no program, no ability, and no interest in training people to help others." Government authorities insisted on seeing their constituents as passive, both during and after disaster. Solnit argues that this construction is an essential component of everyday forms of disaster, in which our ideas of our collective possibility are whittled down and privatized by neoliberal capitalism.[44]

Challenging this idea through mutual aid, Occupy Sandy activists like Sofía also sought to combat the stigmatization of many residents of hard-hit neighborhoods like the Rockaways, whose encounters with city authorities and the state often primarily involved policing and punishment. Homeless people and undocumented immigrants, not to mention racialized communities in the United States in general, tend to shy away from people in uniforms under the best of circumstances thanks to policies of racial profiling, like New York City's Stop and Frisk. But most disaster protocols are written for relatively well-off people who have rarely experienced such harassment. The homeless, for example, may be unable or unwilling to evacuate to areas staffed by government workers, given their routine experiences of coercion at the hands of police officers bent on enforcing "quality of life" laws. Undocumented people, for their part, are often reluctant to offer information about their needs that may expose them to the US deportation regime.[45] According to a study conducted by the nonprofit Make the Road New York, 78 percent of immigrants living in New York–area disaster zones did not apply for disaster relief following Hurricane Sandy.[46]

During her time at YANA, Sofía Gallisá Muriente encountered many undocumented people who found themselves unable to navigate the disaster aid bureaucracy. For example, a woman from El Salvador who had taken in her two sisters and their families after their homes burned down during the fire that Sandy sparked in the Rockaways told Sofía that she'd travelled all the way to Yonkers by bus to get emergency food stamps. She was given a qualification card but found that she needed to activate it with a password. In order to get a password, she needed a phone. Since she didn't have one, she borrowed someone else's but then, after struggling to understand the recorded message, available only in English, she found that the password would be issued only after a Social Security number was keyed in. Since she was undocumented, the woman didn't have a Social Security number. The phone system was automated so there was no way of explaining her predicament to a human being. Thus, although the US Department of Agriculture explicitly prohibits discrimination on the basis of race, color, national origin, gender, religion, age, disability, political beliefs, sexual orientation, or marital and family status, even the most basic disaster relief became inaccessible to this woman. By contrast, Occupy Sandy sought to help people by offering aid with no questions asked, by establishing collaborative relationships with local organizations and leaders, and by mobilizing bilingual activists such as Sofía Gallisá Muriente.

Occupy Sandy activists also went places and did things that most established relief organizations refused to do. Some of the hesitations by established organizations had to do with legal protocols concerning liability, which for example discouraged aid workers from entering residential buildings to check on the elderly, infirm, and those with disabilities without permission. For similar reasons, these organizations were wary of prescribing medication to individuals trapped in their homes. But in some cases dominant aid organizations like FEMA and the Red Cross did not venture into specific areas because of the way they were represented as danger zones by the media. In the Rockaways, this was particularly deadly.

After two days at YANA, Nastaran Mohit, a union organizer and friend of Sofía's who had headed out to the Rockaways when she realized that her home neighborhood of East Harlem had not suffered much damage, ran into a representative from Doctors Without Borders who was looking for a base on the peninsula.[47] It was quickly becoming evident to Nastaran that the area around YANA was one of the most medically devastated parts of the whole city. The neighborhood's concentration of nursing homes, exploitative three-quarter houses (an ill-regulated form of outpatient substance-abuse treatment for the poor), and formerly incarcerated people meant that the majority of the population within a three-block radius was dependent on some form of medication.[48] Yet there were almost no medical facilities open in the Rockaways—and, with no functioning gas stations, almost no way to get off the peninsula. Half a year before Sandy hit, New York State had closed Peninsula Hospital, leaving the island with only one functioning medical center, which was massively understaffed even in the best of times. So the services of Doctors Without Borders were very welcome, and Nastaran quickly helped find the organization a space in the Ocean Bay public housing complex. But like many New

York City Housing Authority (NYCHA) facilities, Ocean Bay was without power for weeks after the storm and, in addition, suffered from long-term neglect. According to Nastaran, members of the Doctors Without Borders team were unnerved by rumors of people being stabbed and raped in the complex. When she tried to publicize the presence of a medical team in the complex, the organization denied her permission to put up a banner.

Frustrated by this unwillingness to work with the peninsula's neediest residents, and nonplussed that there was no help from FEMA, the city health department, or any other official entities, Nastaran used the Occupy Sandy Facebook page to issue a call for help from medical workers. The next day YANA was flooded with doctors, nurses, and social workers. The New York State Nurses Association coordinated a rapid response team that sent volunteers to the Rockaways as well as Coney Island and Staten Island. When the Doctors Without Borders delegation turned these nurses away, Occupy activists got permission from the owner of a furrier with a storefront opposite YANA to open an improvised medical clinic. An artist made a sign saying "YANA Medical Clinic," and local people began flowing in through the doors. Nastaran helped to coordinate the teams of nurses who went out canvassing local high-rises to see who needed medical help. In many cases, according to Nastaran, these canvassers were the first people to knock on someone's door in days. The YANA clinic sent a runner out on a motorcycle first thing every morning to get medical prescriptions, with a copy of President Obama's executive order mandating that pharmacies fulfil prescriptions tucked into his pocket.

Commenting on Nastaran's experience, Doctors Without Borders spokesperson Michael Goldfarb observed that although his organization did set up two clinics in the Rockaways, their operations were constrained by internal and state-mandated regulations.[49] For instance, an organization such as Doctors Without Borders must respect state medical licensing requirements. Given the overall lack of effective coordination of relief efforts in the Rockaways, Goldfarb said that his organization was faced with a tough decision: spend time vetting volunteer caregivers to make sure they were licensed or work with known providers to care for as many people as possible. Doctors Without Borders engaged in active lobbying of state authorities, Goldfarb stressed, calling for greater medical support in the Rockaways and better overall coordination of existing relief efforts.

As the days and then weeks and months went by, Nastaran grew increasingly incredulous that she and (as she put it) a group of ragtag anarchists were running one of the few functioning medical clinics in the Rockaways. Every day brought an exhausting new drama, but for Nastaran each day was also filled with ingenuity and love, providing living evidence of Occupy's autonomist ideology. And as official relief organizations and celebrity visitors began showering the wealthier, whiter portion of the island north of 116th Street with resources, Nastaran and her friends at YANA became more and more aware of the crucial importance of their work in the area south of this class- and race-demarcation line, and more determined to make the operation they were running out of YANA work. But Nastaran also became increasingly angry that city, state, and federal authorities, who she maintains knew that Occupy Sandy was almost alone in serving and canvassing the area, had left the vacuum that mutual aid was filling and that they continued to refuse to coordinate with Occupy Sandy once they arrived in the Rockaways. The establishment might have been willing to tap Occupy Sandy's deep knowledge of local needs, but Nastaran concluded they were unwilling to do anything that might legitimate the organization. Instead, according to Nastaran, FEMA, the National Guard, and big aid organizations would send representatives to YANA to ask what they should be doing, and to vacuum up the information that Occupy volunteers had been gathering about the needs of the community. Then they headed back up to the wealthier portion of the island. They were using Occupy Sandy to fill the gaps, their pretense of ignorance allowing them to continue marginalizing the already disempowered residents of the Rockaways.

The bitter lessons of Occupy Sandy activists in the Rockaways dramatize some of the key shortcomings of disaster communism and horizontalist organizing. Disaster researcher Charles Fritz (whom Rebecca Solnit draws on in *A Paradise Built in Hell*) argues that even if the experience of finding community in disaster changes participants for life by providing them a glimpse of social possibilities, the liberated communities they create are typically short-lived,[50] often persisting only until society regains some stability and becomes functional again. Often this takes only weeks or months in peacetime disasters, but it may take several years in the case of wartime or chronic and serial disasters. This helps explain why the state did not respond to Occupy Sandy with the severe repression it meted out to Occupy Wall Street. In the case of Occupy Sandy, officials were more than happy to let the network plug the gaps that would otherwise have consigned marginalized communities to a far worse fate, stepping in with forms of disaster capitalist reconstruction, like loans for well-connected corporations rather than decimated local small businesses, once emergency conditions had receded and a sense of normality was restored. For a neoliberal state, which has consistently outsourced risk to individuals and communities, the bootstrapping ingenuity of Occupy Sandy was actually a boon. This helps explain why the Department of Homeland Security, in its laudatory study of Occupy Sandy, could argue that Occupy Sandy had not only set an important precedent but that future disasters would likely be met with similar citizen-organized relief efforts.[51] Disaster communism—on a purely local scale—does not actually constitute an inherent threat to the capitalist social order.

But the bureaucracies of official aid and reconstruction efforts posed obstacles to Occupy Sandy. According to Nastaran, the mainstream aid organizations that visited YANA to collect information were utterly unwilling to share any of the results of their own canvassing efforts. Occupy Sandy activists in other parts of the city hit similar walls. Goldi Guerra, who directed Occupy Sandy's canvassing efforts in Staten Island, used the information collected by activists there to help establish the

borough's Long-Term Recovery Organization (LTRO), one of
the only such organizations in the city. Aid groups had come
together to provide relief to the devastated communities along
Staten Island's coastline quite effectively, according to Goldi,
but when it came to recovery, he was dismayed to find a far less
cooperative dynamic emerging.[52] Occupy Sandy freely contributed all of the data it had collected to establish the LTRO, but,
as Goldi discovered, in the NGO world, information is money,
and instead of pooling their records and forming an organization of organizations, the other groups in the LTRO took their
data back to their offices to use in the cutthroat competition for
grants. As a result, in addition to the problems of class and racial
hierarchy that come with the professionalization of disaster
relief, problems that lead to often-unacknowledged but stinging
forms of casual racism in the provision of relief as middle-class
white professionals parachute into devastated communities of
color, the recovery effort was also plagued by a silo effect: rather
than working together and placing the needs of people on the
ground foremost, aid organizations hoarded information with
the aim of snagging grant money to fund their well-paid senior
staff members.[53]

In the weeks and months after the storm, survivors trying to
rebuild increasingly ran into many of the same bureaucratic
mazes that left them bereft of resources and vulnerable to disasters in the first place. Occupy activists such as Goldi witnessed
aid organizations, from the relatively diminutive World Cares
group to the Red Cross–affiliated Coordinated Assistance
Network, raise massive funds for Sandy relief and rebuilding
and then send out case workers who, knowing nothing about
the communities to which they were dispatched, consistently
messed up the complex FEMA claim applications, failed to
contact families when problems arose in their claims, and
generally reproduced the gaping holes in the existing social-
safety net.[54] Occupy activists who had excelled at providing
hands-on disaster relief found themselves getting burned out as
they struggled to mitigate the various levels of state bureaucracy. As a report by the Occupy-affiliated Strike Debt group

revealed, the reassertion of the unjust status quo was particularly apparent in the mechanisms through which disaster aid was dispensed after Sandy.[55] Apart from the Byzantine complexity of the application process, federal aid programs required that survivors apply for loans before they could qualify for FEMA aid. Contrary to most people's expectations that FEMA will come to their aid following a disaster, the agency exists mainly to provide grant programs to restore infrastructure. Individual victims of disaster are predominantly offered loans that, as Strike Debt emphasized in its report, have many of the same features of the predatory subprime lending schemes that buried so many Americans under crushing debt in the years before Sandy. Wealthier (and generally whiter) individuals and communities were usually able to garner more of this loan aid and under better terms. Disaster "aid," Strike Debt argues, actually intensifies the inequalities that fractured communities before disaster struck, shifting the burden from the public to vulnerable individuals while moving money from the victims of disaster into the pockets of the unscrupulous loan servicers who make billions off disaster aid.

The efforts of Occupy Sandy to engage in rebuilding were also stymied by political fault lines that predated the storm. According to Goldi, for instance, residents of the predominantly white southern portion of Staten Island did not want to work in coalition with relief organizations that provided aid to homeless people living in the island's northern section. It certainly did not help coalition building efforts that politicians in the conservative borough saw Goldi (and Occupy Sandy in general, according to Goldi) "like an Iraqi insurgent."[56] Faced with such ridiculous rhetoric, Goldi decided that the LTRO would make more headway if he resigned from the board. While this did not spell the end of Occupy's efforts on Staten Island, it did mean that there was far less attention to issues of social and environmental justice in the recovery effort. For example, like the Rockaways, Staten Island has a large population of undocumented people, many of them from Mexico and Central America, who are almost without exception renters rather than property owners.

Recovery efforts on Staten Island did next to nothing to address their plight.[57]

Occupy Sandy activists ran into similar political obstacles in Red Hook. Although many outside observers lauded relief efforts in the neighborhood as exemplary instances of community self-empowerment and mutual aid, post-Sandy reconstruction efforts were marked by increasing inequality and marginalization.[58] A week or so after the storm hit New York, Zoltán Glück attended a meeting in the Red Hook loft apartment of one of the neighborhood's self-styled power brokers.[59] In addition to members of Occupy Sandy, representatives from the city police department, the National Guard, and Mayor Bloomberg's office were present. Most attendees, however, were small business owners. According to Zoltán, discussion among those present quickly made it clear that the meeting was intended to ensure business owners' access to the institutions that controlled the recovery effort. Given this not-so-hidden agenda, it was significant that Reg Flowers, an African-American activist, was the only person of color invited to the meeting.

The consolidation of these networks of power and patronage was evident when Mayor Bloomberg eventually visited Red Hook, more than a month after the storm ravaged the neighborhood. The mayor avoided Red Hook Houses, even though it is home to 8,000 of the neighborhood's 11,000 residents, but instead visited the upscale Fairway supermarket and attended a meeting of ReStore Red Hook, an organization formed by neighborhood business owners. It was to these business owners, rather than the residents of the crippled public housing complex, that the mayor posed questions about the community's reconstruction needs. And it was to them that the recovery grants and special low-interest reconstruction grants were offered.[60] For example, as Zoltán documented, ReStore Red Hook secured 80 percent of a large grant from the Brooklyn Community Organization by tapping personal connections to politicians connected to the speaker of the city council. While Red Hook's rapidly gentrifying business corridor was benefiting from the reconstruction, residents of the neighborhood's public housing were still struggling to get their heating system replaced.

As the affluent members of the neighborhood tightened their grip on reconstruction funds, they also moved to marginalize Occupy Sandy activists and their calls for a socially just reconstruction. Hypocritical appeals to "the community" and insider versus outsider labels were used to keep Occupy organizers out of meeting spaces and to challenge their legitimacy in public meetings and discussion listservs.[61] According to Conor Tomás Reed, the real breaking point came when Occupy activists attempted to organize the residents of Red Hook Houses to demand that NYCHA grant them a rent freeze or reduction for the month of November.[62] Local officials and business owners responded by charging Occupy Sandy with being interlopers in the community, even though activists were attempting to coordinate neighborhood assemblies so that public housing residents could meet with and speak directly to city officials and aid organizations. Not only did this campaign succeed in delegitimizing such efforts, but it also had the effect of dampening demands coming from the poorest, hardest-hit people in the neighborhood.[63] For Zoltán, the experience of Occupy Sandy demonstrated both the strengths and weaknesses of mutual aid and horizontalism.[64] On the one hand, Occupy Sandy was able to establish a disaster-relief network that was far quicker and more flexible than official aid efforts. Without deep and long-standing connections and alliances in the community, however, Occupy Sandy was vulnerable to the efforts of neighborhood elites to evict activists and their message of social justice. Successful efforts to resist what Zoltán terms "disaster gentrification" require a preexisting base of antigentrification organizing, something that was not necessarily lacking in Red Hook, but which Occupy Sandy activists were not able to connect with and mobilize effectively during the weeks after the storm.[65]

If natural disasters potentially open a communist horizon, the reconstruction process also offers an opportunity for elites to recapture and even intensify their power. In his account of the militant uprisings in the Bolivian city of El Alto during the early

2000s, political theorist Raul Zibechi argues that the popular insurgency adapted its radically horizontal movement structures from the already-existing rural communities or *ayllus* of Bolivian indigenous peoples, tight-knit social organizations that were refashioned and strengthened under the conditions of extreme deprivation encountered by migrants settling in El Alto.[66] Similarly, Occupy Sandy was able to generate a remarkably extensive and flexible social network in the midst of natural disaster. But Occupy Sandy was not able to consolidate its power into something more permanent. When the immediate crisis ebbed, reconstruction began and elite interests began to reassert themselves. Autonomously organized relief hubs and centers, although loosely connected, did not generate the kind of united leadership that was necessary to garner significant funding from city and federal organizations. Meanwhile, local elites, such as the businesspeople who formed ReStore Red Hook, linked up with one another and the citywide bureaucracy.[67] "There was no backbone or party or any other structure to lean on when people who wanted to push us out began to do so," said Zoltán.[68] In some neighborhoods, Occupy Sandy helped form alliances that endured long after the storm passed, like the Lower East Side's LES Ready!. But these alliances came together in neighborhoods with a history of radical organizing around issues such as environmental justice and immigrant rights. In parts of the city without traditions of organizing, or where new alliances were overwhelmed by existing elites and their new coalitions, disaster gentrification dismantled the revolutionary energies that coalesced under the banner of disaster communism.

Radical Adaptation

Occupy Sandy was not alone in its relief efforts; it was hardly the solitary protagonist in its fight against disaster capitalism. Occupy's mutual aid strategy was particularly effective during the immediate crisis thanks to the many partnerships with community organizations that activists were able to forge. In

January 2013, roughly three months after Sandy struck New York, a group of over forty environmental justice organizations, community-based groups, labor unions, and allies met to develop plans for a grassroots-led recovery process that would include the priorities of low-income people, communities of color, immigrants, and workers. This alliance came to be known as the Sandy Regional Assembly. Reports like *Shouldering the Costs* revealed that low-income communities of color were on the front line of the extreme city, and community-based organizations in the Sandy Regional Assembly stressed how their members had often been the first and last responders to disasters such as Hurricane Sandy.[69] They called for a just rebuilding, one that wouldn't simply restore the conditions of extreme inequality from before the storm, and insisted that the recovery process could not and should not focus on rebuilding infrastructure alone.

After Mayor Bloomberg's office published its infrastructure-focused rebuilding report in 2013 (*Special Initiative for Rebuilding and Resiliency*; SIRR), the Sandy Regional Assembly responded with a devastating critique of its blinkered and elitist conception of recovery. According to the groups in the Assembly, the SIRR failed to leverage the job creation opportunities offered by the necessary rebuilding of Sandy-damaged public housing.[70] These reconstruction projects should have been part of a "local resiliency jobs strategy," a New Deal–style public works and jobs program that would build on existing community-based planning projects oriented around environmental justice and social reconstruction like the Sunset Park Greenway-Blueway and the Bronx River Greenway.[71] In addition, the Bloomberg plan neglected the infrastructural needs of low-income communities of color, particularly those located in the city's highly polluted and highly vulnerable "Significant Maritime and Industrial Areas." These failures are not particularly surprising given the top-down nature of the SIRR, which, according to the assembly, engaged in relatively superficial "outreach" activities rather than in systematic community-based planning and research. Given the long history of progressive community-based alternative planning in New York, much of it directly linked to movements for environmental justice, the kind of tokenistic community representation that characterized the SIRR and other Bloomberg-driven blueprints for adaptation was clearly inadequate.[72] Instead, the assembly called for genuinely inclusive decision-making and community oversight.

One of the Sandy Regional Assembly's key demands was that the city should certify that any project initiated under the recovery program would not lead to a reduction in the supply of affordable housing for low- and moderate-income residents in disaster-affected neighborhoods. Based on the argument that resiliency is a product of social connectedness and community integrity, assembly members called on the city to fund community organizations' proposals for the establishment of Climate Adaptation/Disaster Relief Centers, which would educate vulnerable communities about climate change threats, help to reduce disaster vulnerability, and track community members with special needs. Finally, in a call that goes to the heart of questions of urban sustainability in the age of climate chaos, the Sandy Regional Assembly urged the city to establish overlapping, distributed, sustainable systems for critical energy, food distribution, and transportation networks. By issuing such demands for the transformation of urban infrastructures in the context of a blueprint for just rebuilding, the Sandy Regional Assembly highlighted the extent to which radical adaptation must confront questions of power, of conflicting interests, control, and ownership—as well as legacies of colonialism, racism, and class- and gender-discrimination—in the provision of resources such as energy, food, and transportation. Radical adaptation, in other words, necessitates a significant power shift.

The Recovery Agenda called for by the Sandy Regional Assembly drew on the deep experience of member organizations like El Puente, UpRose, and WE ACT for Environmental Justice. Many of these organizations had been struggling for years for what Mike Wallace, one of the city's preeminent historians, called a New Deal for New York, including fighting

against the injustices of the post-9/11 redevelopment of downtown Manhattan.[73] Many of the demands issued by the assembly in fact mirror the proposals summarized in Wallace's manifesto for a more just and sustainable post-9/11 Gotham.[74]

Highlighting New York's vulnerability to periodic economic
crashes as a result of the prominence of finance, insurance, and
real estate—the so-called FIRE sectors—Wallace argued for a
New Deal–style program of urban job creation in energy-saving,
cost-cutting, and ecologically sound green design, jobs that
would pay a living wage for workers who would transform the
city by installing insulation, solar panels, and green roofs, among
other measures.[75] Like the Sandy Regional Assembly, Wallace's
manifesto for a new New Deal also hinged on a renewal of the
city's commitment to affordable housing. In addition, Wallace
issued a series of ambitious proposals to revamp the city's transportation infrastructure, including upgrading the city's Moses-
era rail and shipping facilities. Although it is influenced by
nascent arguments for green urbanism, Wallace's manifesto was
clearly penned before climate chaos put the need for systematic
transformation of urban infrastructures on the agenda. It was
nevertheless ambitious enough that it necessitated federal
support. Wallace argued that such support, and the political
capital necessary to leverage it, could come from a coalition of
the disparate groups in the city who understood the burning
need for a sweeping civic transformation of Gotham.[76] Such an
urban coalition, Wallace maintained, could play a crucial role in
wresting back progressive governance on the federal level from
the neoliberal interests that captured the Democratic Party
under Clinton–Gore, whose control of the Democratic National
Committee moved the party rightward on a host of issues from
the mid-1980s onward. If radical coalitions could gain power in
the nation's cities, Wallace argued, they might stand a chance of
breaking this right-wing dominance through grassroots pressure on the party. This would in turn prepare the ground for a
revived progressive urban politics.

Despite the political efforts of the many organizations on
which Wallace's New Deal for New York drew, the post-9/11

reconstruction process was one largely led by and benefitting the interests of the FIRE sector.[77] This reflects the enduring strength of the city's elite neoliberal regime, an iron-clad hegemony over governance and development in Gotham that was established during the fiscal crisis of the mid-1970s and has subsequently endured.[78] Under Bloomberg, mayor from 2001 to 2013, a series of megaprojects put billions of dollars in the pockets of real estate developers and financiers while the city's working class continued to lose economic ground, increasing vulnerability of the city as a whole to climate chaos. "Social movements can make the costs of peace for one or another sector of the mayoral-business alliance high enough to win concessions. To put it on the defensive, force it to retreat, and wring concessions from it, much less break it up somewhere down the line, will require the sort of mass disruptive movement we haven't seen for some time," writes Kim Moody in *From Welfare State to Real Estate*, his magisterial survey of New York politics since the 1970s.[79]

Dismay at the apparent invincibility of elite interests in the extreme city, and bitter disillusion with the sham popularism of Obama on the federal level (evident in his appointment of Wall Street darling Tim Geithner as Treasury Secretary) helps explain the Occupy movement's wholesale repudiation of electoral politics following the economic crash of 2007. In this context, the infuriated cry raised in Argentina after that country's economic crash in the early 2000s—*¡Que se vayan todos!* ("They All Must Go!")—resonated with many in New York, not to mention around the country and around the globe.[80] This rallying cry expressed the anger of the 99 percent and helped prepare the ground for the mutual aid networks created by Occupy Sandy. But as reconstruction eclipsed relief work, Occupy found itself collaborating with a coalition that, rather than completely eschewing the city's various levels of governance, monitored and put pressure on elected officials using a variety of protest tactics, seeking to hold various scales of governance accountable for the many shortcomings of the rebuilding effort.

The Alliance for a Just Rebuilding, which included Occupy Sandy activists as well as many of the environmental justice organizations, community groups, and labor unions that were part of the Sandy Regional Assembly, built on themes articulated in the assembly's *Recovery Agenda*. Testifying at a meeting of the New York City Council's Committee on Public Safety, for example, members of the alliance argued:

> resiliency must mean more than immediate responses and storm barriers, although those are very important. To have a more resilient city, we need to create more equity and economic opportunity for communities that have been neglected for decades. Resiliency means things like access to good jobs, pathways to job training, real affordable housing, and stewardship of our environment.[81]

The alliance successfully lobbied the city's Organization of Emergency Management to support people displaced by Hurricane Sandy, including providing for undocumented immigrants and for uninterrupted access of poor communities to food stamps and other essential supplies.[82] The alliance also monitored the rebuilding process, issuing reports that demonstrated the massive inefficiency and corruption of Bloomberg's Build It Back Program.[83] This independent monitoring subsequently led to damning investigations by watchdog agencies such as the New York City Department of Investigation, which concluded that more than 90 percent of homeowners seeking help from the Build It Back Program had received no assistance two years after Sandy struck the city. In addition, the alliance also helped coordinate marches on City Hall, where community advocates made connections between rebuilding efforts after 9/11 and after Sandy. Bobby Tolbert, a member of alliance member organization VOCAL-NY, made the following argument at a rally held during the final months of the Bloomberg administration:

> A lot of precious post-9/11 disaster money ended up going to big real estate and financial institutions to help build luxury apartments in lower Manhattan that not even the firefighters and first

responders who valiantly rescued people when the towers fell could afford to live in. This cannot happen again. As Sandy money gets allocated, we need our new mayor to direct city entities, particularly the Economic Development Corporation, to put the needs of low-income and vulnerable New Yorkers first and ensure good jobs and affordable housing result from these new investments.[84]

"Economic development in post-Sandy New York must lift all boats, not only the yachts of the real estate industry," argued Pastor David Rommereim, a leader of the organization Faith in NY, at the same rally.[85] In *Turning the Tide,* a report directed as much at the incoming de Blasio administration as at the lame duck Bloomberg, the Alliance for a Just Rebuilding hammered home similar core social and environmental justice messages: the next mayor should ensure that Sandy recovery creates thousands of good local jobs; should restore lost affordable housing and create new affordable housing for displaced residents; should invest in clean, sustainable energy infrastructure; and should include and engage communities in planning the future of New York City.[86]

The arguments for a radical reconstruction of the extreme city laid out by the Alliance for a Just Rebuilding were starkly opposed to the proposals for adaptation on display in the city's elite cultural institutions. In events such as Museum of Modern Art's (MoMA) *Rising Current* exhibition, the BMW-Guggenheim *Urban Lab*, the *Undercurrents* exhibition at the Whitney, and MoMA/PS1's Expo 1, New York City was presented as a laboratory for experiments in urban resilience.[87] Forming part of the broader elite zeitgeist captured by the Rebuild by Design competition (discussed in Chapter 4), these various initiatives were premised on the belief that cities are key sites for governance in the age of planetary climate change, and they laid out ambitious proposals for eco-cybernetic management of urban systems.[88] Voluminous information was to be gathered about conditions in cities using computers, which would ensure the accuracy of urban climate-proofing efforts. The recurring theme of such exhibitions was that humanity must be reintegrated with the natural world, not simply by abandoning the overweening drive to master nature but by using smart design that allows the system as a whole to adjust to perturbations in real time. Resiliency was the key word in these various proposals, which were characterized by other buzzwords such as ecological urbanism, regenerative cities, and biophilic cities.

The idea behind all of these terms is to design cities in such a way that they will no longer destroy the environment, whether by installing enough solar panels that they no longer need fossil fuels to power themselves or by establishing zero-waste programs to prevent them from fouling their ecosystems. All the rage in design circles today, these proposals for making the city resilient primarily adopted a formalist approach.[89] The focus here is almost universally on engineering urban infrastructures using new technologies, rather than on transforming the social conditions of cities. While they gesture toward participatory planning, in other words, their overwhelming emphasis was on technocratic, postpolitical, and even machine-driven forms of management of the city, which is conceived of as a new field of biopolitical governance.[90] These various exhibitions generated great enthusiasm among New York's cultural arbiters, but at best they produce gated green enclaves in which ecological design becomes a component of elite branding campaigns.[91]

Such green branding may boost property values for urban elites and provide political capital for governing agencies, but it does little to stem the carbon emissions of the extreme city. And carbon emissions correlate closely to wealth. There can be no ecological city, and indeed no avoidance of the wave of mass extinction that is engulfing the planet, without challenging New York City's powerful interests or shifting away from its growth-oriented policies. In the absence of successful popular struggle to gain control of the urban growth machine, technological innovations will simply be folded into the existing system of heedless expansion.[92]

Movements such as the Alliance for a Just Rebuilding are the primary protagonists in struggles for radical forms of adaptation. This is because, as urban sociologist Daniel Aldana Cohen puts it, "anti-gentrification battles against displacement in relatively dense areas, and fights to build new public housing close to mass transit, jobs, and services—these are struggles whose very core is a battle for climate justice."[93] Such movements challenge the rule of capital by fighting to take land and housing off the market, to expand public services, to establish living wages for low-income communities, and to establish energy democracy and collective control over the resources of urban power generation. Simultaneously, they struggle to defend compact urban living arrangements that marry small carbon footprints with public amenities such as parks and libraries. The conjunction of struggles for urban social justice and for climate justice has not been adequately acknowledged.[94] This is partially because movements such as the Right to the City have historically not emphasized the fight for a low-carbon city in their struggles against gentrification and for urban social justice. But it is also a product of the enduringly antiurban bias of the environmental movement, a bias that makes even as canny a thinker as Naomi Klein give relatively short shrift to the politics of urban struggles for climate justice. While she is obviously aware that the transformation of urban life is important, she does not explain how the struggle for urban justice might be connected to the fight for climate justice.[95] The ecological genius of the city, as Mike Davis puts it, consequently remains "a vast, largely hidden power."[96] Yet, as we have seen, movements fighting for a democratic, inclusive urbanism are also the key protagonists of the struggle for the low-carbon cities of the future. While innovative forms of green design and technology must be a part of this struggle, far more important in this transformation, as Davis reminds us, is the priority given to public affluence over private wealth.[97]

Although it would be an exaggeration to say that the battle for a just rebuilding was singlehandedly responsible for the election of populist mayor Bill de Blasio, the coalition of groups that mobilized behind him certainly played an important role. The well-documented failures of Bloomberg's Build It Back

Program dramatized the elitism of his top-down development and reconstruction approach, and he was severely criticized when he visited areas such as the Rockaways, where residents of public housing were still struggling with mold and other storm-related destruction years after Sandy. De Blasio pledged to fix these shortcomings when he visited during his campaign, and, although he caught flak for the time it took for his administration to make good on his promises, when he released *OneNYC*, his update of Bloomberg's *PlaNYC*, it was perceived by members of the Alliance for a Just Rebuilding as the product of a genuine engagement with the organization's campaigns. Indeed, according to an alliance press release, the *OneNYC* plan incorporates many recommendations first proposed by the alliance report *How Sandy Rebuilding Can Reduce Inequality in the City.*[98] Most important, *OneNYC* introduced equity as the cardinal guiding principle for Gotham's sustainability frameworks. Although this principle is woven through the many specific proposals for upgrading urban infrastructure in *OneNYC*, the overarching emphasis on equity emerges from the perception that "for true climate justice to exist, resiliency cannot rest with 'bouncing back' to an inequitable system where people of color and low-income communities are disproportionately burdened," according to the New York City Environmental Justice Alliance (NYC-EJA).[99]

Recognizing that politics cannot begin and end with the ballot box, New York's environmental justice organizations and advocates for urban social justice have kept the heat on the de Blasio administration after the publication of *OneNYC*.[100] In its exhaustive review of the document, NYC-EJA summarizes the plan's strengths, its emphasis on equality paramount among them, and proposes concrete additional action plans in five interlinked critical areas: climate adaptation and mitigation; equity and infrastructure; public health; community preparedness; and community-based planning.[101] These critiques and proposals build on work by predecessor organizations such as the Alliance for a Just Rebuilding. For instance, under the heading of climate adaptation and mitigation, NYC-EJA calls on the de Blasio administration to invest more equitably in coastal protection, pointing to the fact that attention to integrated flood-protection systems has been greatest in Manhattan, leaving climate-vulnerable environmental justice communities behind, including the city's waterfront-based Significant Maritime and Industrial Areas in the South Bronx, Sunset Park, Red Hook, Newtown Creek, the Brooklyn Navy Yard, and the North Shore of Staten Island. Other proposals reflect new ideas developed within the city's many environmental justice organizations, including suggestions that the city create a zoned system for commercial waste hauling in order to lighten the disproportionate load still borne by the environmental justice neighborhoods through which garbage trucks race to dump their loads. The proposed zoning system would mean that city authorities would gain oversight of an industry that is currently almost totally unregulated, leading to much better standards in waste hauling. NYC-EJA also suggests that the city use a Power Purchase Agreement to commit to buy at least 100 megawatts capacity of offshore wind power off the coast of Long Island, relieving poor communities of the pollution spewed by backup generators installed by power companies to cope with peak demand periods, and that the city create a long-term public participation process to engage community-based organizations in the evaluation and implementation of *OneNYC*.

While continuing to engage with and put pressure on existing channels of urban governance, New York's environmental justice organizations are also developing their own, remarkably forward-thinking proposals for radical adaptation. For instance, in 2015 Harlem's West Harlem Environmental Action (WE ACT), one of the city's most venerable environmental justice groups, held a series of workshops during which community residents and organizations developed a climate action plan for northern Manhattan using a participatory planning process.[102] The 600,000, predominantly African-American and Latinx, residents of Northern Manhattan deal with a disproportionate amount of pollution and the health risks that come with it. WE ACT has long documented and fought against this environmental injustice, but, as the Northern Manhattan Climate Action Plan (NMCA) states, these long-standing inequalities were not simply dramatized but deepened by Hurricane Sandy.[103] The action plan helps build the movement to link urban social justice with environmental justice, which is in turn linked to global struggles for climate justice. "In order to protect NYC's most vulnerable people from climate change," the plan forthrightly "promotes environmental policies that also address the root issues of inequality. Conflicts in terms of class, race, gender, ethnicity, and age, need to be mitigated and overcome, not simply the impacts of rising sea levels." The action plan states clearly that it supports "the growing movement in NYC to recognize the crucial connection between climate change and social equality."[104] Reflecting the lessons learned by social movements in recent years, the action plan also is unequivocal in its insistence that mobilization must unfold both within civil society and by the state. "We must engage with the legislative process, while building our own systems of economic exchange and urban development that are not dependent on a faltering public sector," it states.[105] If the left has made impressive electoral gains through grassroots mobilization in Gotham, including the election of a progressive mayor like de Blasio, organizations such as WE ACT are clear that the struggle to transform and democratize the city necessitates continued mobilization on a variety of scales, from the neighborhood to the municipal level to the federal government and, finally, to all important transnational connections with other organizations fighting for climate justice.[106]

The Northern Manhattan Climate Action Plan sets out a series of proposals for radical adaptation in four key areas: energy democracy, emergency preparedness, social hubs or meeting places, and public participation. The proposals in each of these areas contribute to cutting-edge intersectional struggles for climate justice and urban equality. In the platform for Energy Democracy, for instance, the action plan underlines the challenge of energy poverty for residents of New York's low-income communities:

According to the US Energy Information Administration, New Yorkers pay the nation's second-highest energy prices. This manifests as a disproportionate cost burden for low-income New Yorkers, which threatens not only their ability to retain access to energy services, but also limits access to housing, healthy food, healthcare, and other costly necessities.

Access to adequate energy sources has long been a political issue in the global South, but as austerity bites deeper in impoverished communities in cities in the core capitalist nations, energy poverty is becomingly an increasingly pressing issue: poor people are paying more and more for power, and in some cases are even having their power cut off by companies whose only interest is the bottom line.[107] In order to combat this increasing crisis, the Northern Manhattan Action Plan calls for green energy projects that directly benefit low-income communities, rather than adding to property values in green enclaves like Battery Park City.

> This plan calls for all green energy projects to provide direct economic and environmental benefits to low-income residents. This may be achieved through local hiring agreements, investments in neighborhood companies/organizations, and creation of systems for tenants to lead change within their own communities.

In particular, the action plan points to the potential of forms of distributed energy generation such as microgrids, freestanding local energy systems that can operate independently of the main grid. The action plan hopes that such microgrids may help promote the shift from fossil fuels to renewable sources while also empowering local communities both economically and politically. It is not enough, in other words, simply to shift from fossil fuel–generated power to renewable sources: communities rather than big corporations must be able to control energy for real benefits to be seen on a local level. For the many neighborhood residents who participated in the workshops that led to the action plan, community-managed microgrid systems "can confer direct economic benefits on low-income residents by creating manufacturing, construction, and maintenance jobs while also providing savings." In order to ensure that such savings end up in the hands of tenants rather than landlords, the action plan advocates the formation of green energy coopera- tives, potentially building on existing tenant associations, that would give residents of public housing democratic control over the generation, consumption, and costs of renewable power generation. As in all other aspects of the action plan, in other words, the emphasis is on transforming urban infrastructures in a manner that challenges inequality and simultaneously deepens grassroots democracy.[108]

WE ACT has already taken steps to realize this vision by working with a number of different institutions, operating at various scales, including the City University of New York and the New York State Public Service Commission's Reforming the Energy Vision process. Demonstration microgrid projects installed in public housing complexes in Northern Manhattan will play an important role in pushing forward the city's and state's efforts to remove roadblocks to the expansion of distrib- uted generation technology. But the action plan is clear that this power shift will not take place through some smooth, techno- cratic, top-down process. Instead, it will require politicization of the question of the energy commons and a grassroots struggle for genuine energy democracy. After all, although the slogan "power to the people" has a long lineage in progressive circles, it can potentially be appropriated to promote a reactionary neoliberal agenda for a low-carbon transition, leading to a breakup of large state power monopolies that may ironically generate increased market competition and higher prices for consumers.[109] Ensuring that distributed generation is to be part of a radical power shift will take political struggle. Citing the words of the allied group Trade Unions for Energy Democracy, the action plan says that ultimately "the transition to an equita- ble, sustainable energy system can only occur if there is decisive shift in power towards workers, communities and the public."[110]

This power shift will require transformation of the growth-oriented, profit-driven capitalist system that currently controls the extreme city. Drawing on another ally organization, the action plan asserts:

> ... in making such a transition, we must confront what Energy Democracy Initiative recognizes as a fundamental "clash between the priorities of political elites and corporations on one hand, and the needs of the masses of people for a truly socially and environmentally sustainable society on the other."[111]

True energy democracy will thus require not just a transformation in the sources of energy provision but a socialization of production, ensuring equitable and universal access and helping facilitate a sea change in attitudes toward consumption.

The struggle for energy democracy outlined in WE ACT's Northern Manhattan Action Plan raises fundamental and inescapable questions about the organization not simply of infrastructure but of social relations in the extreme city. Genuine democratic control of energy production and consumption—whether at a community, municipal, or state level—will only be possible if the competitive market conditions under which public entities like power companies operate is transformed. Otherwise, the basic premise of competitive accumulation under which public initiatives are forced to operate will militate against social and environmental justice. In order to realize the many progressive initiatives—from social hubs to community-supported agriculture and participatory budgeting—being generated by community-planning projects such as WE ACT's Action Plan, a fundamental transformation of capitalist social relations must take place. Indeed, in order to avert mass extinction, we need a revolution that overturns the economic system (and the ideologies that sustain it) that is hurtling the planet toward the abyss. As Naomi Klein puts it:

> [O]ur economy is at war with many forms of life on earth, including human life. What the climate needs is a contraction in

humanity's use of resources; what our economic model demands to avoid collapse is unfettered expansion. Only one of these sets of rules can be changed, and it's not the laws of nature.[112]

Radical adaptation, in other words, is not simply a question of redesigning the city, of updating urban infrastructures using smart technology and top-down technocratic governance. Such changes are a necessary but not sufficient element of a new urban order. To transform the extreme city, we need to gain popular power over the deployment of social surpluses in the short term and over the conditions of production in the longer term. New forms of collective, democratic planning need to be developed that guarantee equitable and sustainable control over the planetary commons. In short, we need new forms of communism for disastrous times.

NYC Housing Authority's Red Hook Houses farm—the first farm built on public housing land in New York City, which grows and distributes roughly 5,000 pounds of organic produce each year. Photo by Saara Nafici, courtesy of Added Value Farms.

Conclusion

Urban Futures

Retreat, the Last Taboo

When Hurricane Sandy pushed a massive storm surge into the seaside neighborhood of Oakwood Beach on Staten Island, three people died. Nearly 100 homes were destroyed, and, weeks after the storm, most residents were still without power and heat. At a meeting held after the storm, Staten Island resident Joseph Tirone asked whether members of the community would be willing to relocate if they were offered the prestorm value of their homes.[1] Half the two hundred people at the meeting said they would. Tirone's question was prompted by news he'd heard from a local Federal Emergency Management Agency representative about the federal Department of Housing and Urban Development's Hazard Mitigation Grant Program, an initiative created to fund measures—including relocation—to reduce loss of life and property from recurring natural disasters. Oakwood Beach residents had a long history of trying to get the government to pay attention to their chronic problems with flooding; now they had an opportunity to see real change. In response to the initial interest in community relocation, Tirone and other community residents formed a group, the Oakwood Beach Buyout Committee, which canvassed the neighborhood,

275

speaking to friends and neighbors about the area's history of flooding, gauging interest in the buyout program, and mapping the areas where people felt threatened by rising seas. Rather than being imposed from above by callous bureaucrats, in other words, the relocation plan was driven by community members themselves and consequently garnered increasing support among Oakwood Beach residents. Weeks later, once it had near-unanimous community support, the committee approached the state. In January 2013, Governor Cuomo announced a buyout program that leveraged federal disaster-relief funds to purchase Oakwood Beach residents' homes at their pre-Sandy value. Soon, residents of neighboring oceanfront towns on Staten Island, frustrated with the paralysis of the city's Build It Back Program, began forming buyout committees and applying to the state for relocation funding. In the spring of 2014, however, the governor's Office of Storm Recovery put on the brakes by announcing that it had no intention to purchase the eastern shore of Staten Island in its entirety.[2] Ultimately, only three towns on the island were successful in their relocation efforts.

One of the main concerns that residents of Staten Island's Oakwood Beach community initially expressed about the relocation plan was that the land would simply be redeveloped after they left, exposing a new generation of residents to even worse hazards than those faced by current community members.[3] A guarantee that the area would be returned to its original wetland condition and that future construction would be prohibited was thus key in convincing community members to accept the state plan. This civically minded stance sadly did not extend to the city buyout program for homeowners seeking to relocate, which was announced shortly after the inception of the state plan.[4] Overriding the state plan, the city program offered participants a similar amount of money for their homes but retained the right to turn purchased land over to developers. Although the city program mandated that any new construction in vacated areas should be flood resistant, by shifting the basis of the program from retreat to redevelopment of an imperiled shoreline, the city transformed the meaning of the program.[5] Now aligned with the defensive stance that characterized the Build It Back Program, the city buyout program may have placated developers looking for new coastal property to build up but was less attractive to many New Yorkers who were concerned about their city's long-term sustainability.

As sociologist Liz Koslov has argued, *retreat* has many meanings, including a place of contemplation and spiritual refuge.[6] Retreat is also used in ecological discourse to denote the dismantling of hard coastal defenses such as seawalls to create more permeable borders, allowing for natural flux and for the flourishing of intertidal habitats such as wetlands and salt marshes. Prior to development in the mid-twentieth century, Oakwood Beach was precisely such a fluid terrain, and the state buyout program not only restored it to its original wetland state but also helped create a "soft" defense that would buffer surrounding communities from future storm surges. For landscape architects like Kate Orff, Anuradha Mathur, and Dilip da Cunha, an embrace of this definition of retreat involves shifting not just material boundaries but also conceptual ones.[7] As Bengali architect Kazi Ashraf argues, seeing a city through the new lens of "liquid urbanism" means beginning "from its wet edge, ushering a conception of a city that is integrated with the delta," rather than starting from the dry land at the core. "Here fluid dynamics structures the city, and its infrastructure and hydrological issues serve as starting points and frameworks for future urban planning and design decisions."[8]

As cities around the world struggle to cope with rising tides, this conceptual shift is catching on. Nowhere is this more evident than in Holland, a country famous for its successful battles not just to defend against the seas but to reclaim land from the ocean. The ability of the Dutch to cope with the threat of inundation is a product both of structures of governance such as the country's network of *waterschappen* or water boards (autonomous local groups that have monitored and repaired dikes for many centuries) and of the massive network of dams, sluices, locks, dikes, levees, and storm-surge barriers—collectively known as the Delta Works—built over a series of decades after the deadly North Sea flood of 1953.⁹ So successful has the Dutch struggle with the sea been that they have now become global consultants, advising cities from Jakarta to New York on how to keep back rising tides.¹⁰ Ironically, however, the Dutch are beginning to recognize that they are caught in a "control paradox": flood defenses such as the Delta Works decrease the likelihood of inundation, which makes protected areas more attractive for development, which can in turn lead to disastrous flooding.¹¹

As I explain in Chapter 3, recognition of this paradox has led the Dutch to begin experimenting with policies of strategic retreat inspired by ecological paradigms. Water is being let back in to coastal areas such as the Oosterschelde, where storm barriers erected after the 1950s cut off tidal movement, destroying shell fisheries. The new paradigm of "making room for the river" also means that cities are being opened back up to canals and other forms of amphibious urban design, motivated by the understanding that hard barriers can never completely contain climate change–swollen floodwaters, and that wetlands and similar "natural" features can function as sponges for such deluges. Yet acceptance of this new paradigm of the "wet city" is not universal, and the engineering efforts undertaken in the name of "making space for water" are generally still seen as "icing on the cake" of Holland's network of hard defenses.¹² As historian Tracy Metz argues, the Dutch have grown so accustomed to their country's iron-clad protection from flooding that many are not only hostile to efforts to make "room for the river," but also take the security provided by hard barriers for granted. There is consequently scant preparation for catastrophic failure of the existing flood protection measures. Holland for example has many high-water refuges for animals but none for humans.¹³

In the United States today, retreat is predominantly interpreted not as an exciting new approach to coping with the realities of climate change, but rather in military terms, as a mortifying defeat.¹⁴ The broader cultural zeitgeist of imperial masculinity that typifies New York since the launch of the War on Terror, for example, helped ensure that the Oakwood Beach buyout program was seen less as a successful community-led struggle for relocation, and more as a humiliating military rout, akin to the evacuation of the CIA station in Saigon in 1975 as Viet Cong forces advanced rapidly through the city. For Koslov, this dominant interpretation of the term retreat helps ensure that community relocation is never recognized as an important adaptation strategy. Politicians "tend to discourage retreat. It is not a viable adaptation option for them, but rather a useful threat to encourage alternative courses of action, such as mitigation or building levees and seawalls."[15] Such a negative reading of retreat dovetails with the bellicose stance that has informed mainstream public posturing since 9/11.[16] It also puts money in the pockets of developers and others looking to reap the economic windfall of climate chaos. As Koslov notes, on an international level, adaptation funding that flows through the hands of kleptocratic states is typically used either for corrupt development (aka resiliency) projects or for involuntary relocation projects that displace and disempower local people, as when, for instance, disaster-affected fishing villages are pushed off coastal land to make way for luxury tourist resorts.[17] Even when policies are not driven by such a cynical calculus, the current emphasis on protecting people in place will inevitably mean returning communities to increasingly perilous locations.

In the face of such negative depictions of retreat, communities around the world are struggling for alternative definitions of relocation from terrain particularly vulnerable to climate chaos, and for the democratically generated and socially just programs that would result from positive conceptions of retreat. Like the residents of Oakwood Beach, many community members have seen this struggle drag on for many years. The indigenous village of Shishmareff in Alaska made global headlines when it voted to relocate in the summer of 2016, for example. However, many villages in the area, threatened by the melting of sea ice and other effects of climate change that are particularly dramatic in the Arctic, have been voting to move for decades but have not received the economic support they need to do so.[18] On the Cartaret Islands in the Pacific, islanders became so fed up with waiting for help from abroad that they formed their own organization, Tulele Peisa ("Sailing the Waves on Our Own"), and created a voluntary relocation plan called the Carteret Integrated Relocation Project.[19] More recently, after fighting for thirteen years to garner resources for their community in the fast-dwindling bayous of Louisiana, the Isle de Jean Charles Band of Biloxi-Chitimacha-Choctaw Native Americans won a grant of $52 million from the Department of Housing and Urban Development's National Disaster Resilience Competition to relocate their community to a safe spot further inland.[20]

It is not just island-dwelling and coastal communities that have been fighting for support for community-led retreat plans. Flooding of rivers as a result of climate change-induced extreme rainfall is also generating immense challenges around the globe, affecting over 21 million people annually at present and likely to affect twice as many in the next decade or so, as a warmer atmosphere holds more moisture, leading to heavier down-pours.[21] As Virginia Eubanks points out, "It is not the affluent who are most vulnerable in river-valley cities and towns. Poor and working-class neighborhoods have historically developed where inland-flood risk is the greatest."[22] As climate chaos hits home, the question of retreat will become increasingly pressing, and what Eubanks calls *climate redlining*—the abandonment of flood-vulnerable poor communities not just on the coasts but also in older riverine cities like Buffalo, Pittsburgh, Louisville, St. Louis, Memphis, and Baton Rouge—may become the new normal. And then there are the booming megacities situated on deltas at the mouths of great rivers such as the Ganges, the Niger, the Nile, and the Yangtze, where climate chaos is a product of a combination of riverine and coastal flooding, as well as man-made and natural subsidence.

It is becoming increasingly clear that nations such as the United States may have to consider retreat not just from portions of the coastline but from entire cities and regions.[23] Yet as the failure to support community bids for planned relocation on Staten Island demonstrates (a failure that has played out throughout the region), retreat on any kind of significant scale remains a taboo topic.[24] Nonetheless, given scientific projections concerning the impact of climate change, discussions of retreat should be in progress for areas such as southern Florida and southern California, threatened respectively by too much and not enough water. At the moment, however, the interests of capital and political corruption prevent any mention of (let alone thoughtful planning for) retreat from such regions. Moreover, even absent the looming threat of climate chaos, the United States has no rational policy of regional planning across the nation.[25] Cities are instead pitted against one another in a competitive race to generate economic growth, the sole exception being the care taken by the military-industrial complex to spread its pork barrel procurement policies widely across the country in order to tie down the votes of legislators. Yet notwithstanding this apparent anarchy and the regional disequilibrium it helps perpetuate, it is worth remembering that the social geography of the United States is a product of conscious design. The suburban sprawl that typifies the nation, with its extreme segregation based on class and race, and its monstrously exaggerated environmental footprint, represents the triumph of a specific, exclusionary model of the good life, as well as the victory of elite economic interests.[26] The same can be said about the shift of population to the Sunbelt in the south and southwest of the country ever since the 1970s. Although the spread of air conditioning may make the migration of population to warmer southern states seem inevitable, in fact, like suburbanization, the federal government played a decisive role in this reorganization of US cities. It was not only that land was cheap in the south: the government also placed abundant military bases and research facilities in the Sunbelt, fueling growth in other sectors such as information technology. Most important, the failure to challenge "right to work" laws ensured that industries would move south in search of cheaper labor. Thus, while it was produced by political struggles rather than careful planning and democratic deliberation, the organization of the American landscape is nonetheless the result of intentional shaping. Likewise, the rise of extreme cities and their vast informal settlements on a global scale was driven by decades of neoliberal policies, imposed by institutions like the World Bank, that decimated local farming industries.[27]

As climate chaos strikes vulnerable regions of the United States with increasing frequency and severity, the current policy of encouraging coastal development and then dispensing funds for rebuilding following natural disasters will become untenable. Already efforts are underway to curtail the National Flood Insurance Program (NFIP), bringing it into line with our increasingly hazardous realities by raising insurance premiums to reflect true flood risks and requiring updating of flood-risk maps.[28] The Bigger-Waters Flood Insurance Reform Act of 2012 provoked howls of protest from coastal residents (including many in New York City) who very reasonably feared that they would not be able to afford the new jacked-up insurance premiums. The true problem with federal programs, however, has been that they have subsidized the maintenance of resort homes in risky locations by rich people.[29] Such welfare for the rich, which encourages them to build taxpayer-insured seaside megamansions and then pays them to rebuild them following disasters with emergency relief, must end. Our collective economic resources should be used to plan for and manage a retreat from flood-threatened communities along the nation's coasts and rivers, with the greatest aid being directed to the economically needy rather than to the wealthy.

What would a blueprint for just retreat look like? On an urban level, such a plan would include the creation of communitywide options for relocation. Despite the example of Oakwood Beach's successful mobilization as a united neighborhood, current federal voluntary relocation programs are individual rather than communitywide. These policies consequently contribute to the scattering of communities, continuing policies with a long colonial and racist lineage, from the forced removal of Native American tribes to the displacement of communities of color by urban renewal programs and gentrification.[30] To avoid replicating these terrible precedents, relocation would have to be driven by communities rather than imposed from above.

The kind of framework for adaptation developed by Native American villages in Alaska, collaborating with scientist and human rights attorney Robin Bronen, might serve as a model that could be scaled up to larger urban contexts. Working in communities such as Shishmaref, Kivalina, and Newtok, Bronen and her collaborators created assessment programs that integrate ecological and social monitoring mechanisms to gauge the impact of climate change on indigenous communities.[31] Since vulnerability to climate change is dynamic, varying not just across spatial and temporal scales but also according to economic, social, and cultural factors, Bronen generated a series of ecological and social indicators that can be used to assess community vulnerability and guide community discussions of adaptation measures and potential relocation initiatives. Among the factors this mechanism would measure would be the impact of climate change on community health, infrastructure, and livelihoods. Unlike government-mandated relocation programs, which are decided from above and according to metrics that often ignore specific community experiences of and attitudes toward climate change, the mechanism Bronen developed is based on community perceptions of risk and aspirations for the future. Relocation, when it takes place, is driven by the desire of communities to remain intact, to retain the kind of physical proximity that is essential to the maintenance of community. Particularly key is the fact that the process developed by Bronen involves collaboration between communities, scientific institutions, and state- and federal-level governance organizations, with local communities making decisions about how they will use outside consultants and state agencies.

In a large and often atomized urban setting such as New York, the kind of monitoring and dialogue proposed by Bronen would have to be anchored firmly in particular neighborhoods. New York is fortunate to have a strong network of community-based organizations. As Tom Angotti suggests, New York's system of community boards, along with parallel organizations such as the tenant-formed community development corporations, provide an important resource for progressive planning that challenges the reign of real estate developers and their backers on Wall Street, in the process strengthening community control over land.[32] Environmental Justice organizations such as WE ACT and Uprose also offer vibrant forums for community mobilization around struggles for urban sustainability in neighborhoods such as Harlem and Sunset Park. The network of social centers proposed in WE ACT's *Northern Manhattan Climate Action Plan* would be ideal places where the community dialogues for planning advocated by Bronen might unfold.[33] As described in the *Climate Action Plan,* these hubs are intended to foster the kind of community solidarity that has proven to be lifesaving during climate change–related disasters such as heat waves. But they can also provide a venue for community education and dialogue of the kind pioneered by Bronen in Alaska. Indeed, the *Climate Action Plan*, which was drafted through a series of planning meetings that drew together community members; environmental activists and organizations; and scientists, engineers, and architects from local academic institutions, such as Columbia and City College, offers a model for the precisely the kind of interactive future-planning envisaged by Bronen.

As unpalatable as it may be to discuss this today, coastal flooding is already ravaging communities around the country and the world.[34] As this dynamic intensifies in the coming decades, rendering certain coastal areas (and even entire cities) uninhabitable, relocation plans that allow people to move in advance of disaster will come to seem an increasingly sane alternative to sudden displacement. In addition, while some cities may balk at the idea of financing community retreat, fearing the costs of such a move and the loss of tax revenue, buying people out once is actually a far more thrifty means of flood protection than building and maintaining levees, seawalls, and other hard defenses, that will become obsolete as floods worsen and sea levels rise.[35] Community-led planning for just retreat is the best hope we have to avoid climate redlining and the abandonment of poor communities to climate chaos.

Toward a Just Transition

The question the world faces is not whether partial or even total retreat from coastal and riverine zones threatened with inundation will take place. It is under what conditions this retreat will unfold: Will we plan now for socially just policies of adaptation and retreat, when climate chaos is still in an incipient phase and our collective resources to cope are relatively great, or will such changes take place under conditions in which the most powerful save themselves alone and exploit the vulnerable? As Mike Davis has argued, since climate change will produce dramatically uneven effects across classes and regions, damaging the poorest and the least culpable most grievously, adequate worldwide adaptation "would necessarily command a revolution of almost mythic magnitude in the redistribution of income and power."[36] Rather than agree to such a redistribution, Davis argues, it is likely that elites will respond to growing climate chaos with ever more panicked efforts to wall themselves off from their fellow human beings.[37]

The victory of shockingly reactionary forces in the US presidential election of 2016, along with the crisis of European unity provoked by Brexit and the rise of right-wing regimes in once-progressive regions such as Latin America, has moved the world in the opposite direction from the revolution envisaged by Davis. While the obstacles to progressive efforts to cope with the climate emergency are certainly real and daunting in the short term, this fact should not eclipse efforts to organize alternatives to the status quo. Indeed, reactionary movements have been able to gain such traction precisely because genuinely radical alternatives have everywhere been eclipsed by the bipartisan status quo. Reactionary movements have asserted themselves successfully by promising a galvanizing and total repudiation of business as usual, even if this promise is based on phony populism and blatant climate change denialism that is certain to intensify the climate emergency.

It is precisely in order to head off such reactionary responses to the climate emergency that demands for socially just planning need to be articulated. These plans will evolve as communities and social movements adjust to changing conditions, but framing them in advance, through genuinely inclusive forms of community collaboration, will be a vital step toward overturning the atrophied sense of social solidarity that decades of neoliberalism have instilled. Planning for a just retreat and transition should be seen as an opportunity to rekindle our sense of collective purpose and potential. Time is of the essence. The further we slide into climate chaos without establishing a democratic and socially just response, the more likely we are to be forced to adapt under the sway not simply of disasters but of the authoritarian and inegalitarian powers to which emergency conditions often give rise.[38]

There can be no sugarcoating the incipient crisis. We face a baleful collective reckoning in the coming decades, when climate change, the disruption and potential collapse of global industrial agriculture, dwindling freshwater supplies, ocean acidification, mass species extinction, and ongoing planetary urbanization will provoke unforeseeable disruptions and transformations. As Mike Davis puts it:

> There is no historical precedent or vantage point for understanding what will happen in the 2050s when a peak species population of 9 to 11 billion struggles to adapt to climate chaos and depleted fossil energy.[39]

The future laid up by fossil capitalism will be wrenching and will likely necessitate not just retreat from some cities but also sweeping reconfiguration of the current geography of global cities, the great majority of which are located in coastal regions threatened with flooding. But rather than assuming that these transformations will produce the kind of anarchic violence unleashed in Hollywood spectacles such as *Mad Max,* the only reasonable stance toward the precarious future is a determination to fight for a just transition that rights the systemic wrongs of the present. Urban civilization and human solidarity will not endure the coming planetary crises without a revival of aggressively utopian thought and comprehensive planning. If we are to envision a just transition, we need to break the chains of ideology, moral apathy, and political despair. As Mike Davis puts it, "either we fight for 'impossible' solutions to the increasingly entangled crises of urban poverty and climate change, or become ourselves complicit in a *de facto* triage of humanity."[40]

As the extent of the coming calamity begins to sink in, calls for large-scale planning and mobilization are becoming increasingly frequent. Urgent pleas are no longer limited to radicals agitating for forms of Climate Maoism or war communism.[41] In "A World at War," climate activist Bill McKibben compares the devastation of climate change to the destruction sown by the Axis powers of World War II. "We're under attack from climate change," he argues, "and our only hope is to mobilize like we did in WWII."[42] Comparing droughts in South Africa and wildfires in California to enemy armies, McKibben writes that "Day after day, week after week, saboteurs behind our lines are unleashing a series of brilliant and overwhelming attacks," and suggests that "it's not that global warming is *like* a world war. It *is* a world war." What sort of mobilization would be necessary in order to win the war? Much of McKibben's subsequent discussion is devoted to the plan proposed by Stanford engineer Mark Jacobson to power the US economy with 100 percent renewable energy sources by 2050 and to the infrastructural transformations necessary to make this plan succeed. Drawing on Mark Wilson's *Destructive Creation,* which chronicles the pivotal role played by large-scale public investment and government regulation in the transformation of the United States into the "arsenal of democracy," McKibben argues that World War II mobilization offers an example of not just collective solidarity but also successful government planning on a massive scale.[43] Ironically, though, the success of wartime mobilization also sowed the seeds of neoliberal ideologies of deregulation and privatization, as US business elites organized campaigns that simultaneously publicized the importance of business contributions to the war effort and denigrated public-sector policies. Given the decades-long success of this corporate backlash, McKibben concludes that "it's reasonable to ask if we can find the collective will to fight back in this war against global warming, as we once fought fascism." Pointing to the change in the Democratic Party platform following Bernie Sanders's insurgent primary campaign in 2016, McKibben holds out hope that such collective will may yet be mustered. Despite the quashing of the avowedly socialist Sanders by party elites, the party platform asserted that "we are committed to a national mobilization [to fight climate change], and to leading a global effort to mobilize nations to address this threat on a scale not seen since World War II."[44]

Although the 2016 platform of the Democratic Party is a dead letter given the defeat of Hillary Clinton's presidential campaign, the call for national mobilization against climate change in the platform was the product of significant struggle by rank-and-file within the party and may offer a leverage point for future fights. Given the need to diminish carbon emissions and the consumption that generates them in the world's rich nations, policies of fair-shares rationing from the era of World War II certainly offer an inspiring precedent, one that might be retooled for the age of climate chaos.[45] Sharing equally within the straightened circumstances that climate chaos will ultimately impose on even the wealthiest nations is a far more attractive proposition than the forms of arbitrarily and unequally imposed austerity of today's neoliberal era. The specter of climate chaos dictates that citizens in the overdeveloped nations be weaned from the habits of overconsumption that capitalism has inculcated in us. The guardian state of the war era, which mobilized society using fairly distributed, universal forms of sacrifice in order to fight off fascism, is an attractive model to follow.[46] During World War II, the US Office of Price Administration rationed a huge variety of commodities, from automobiles and fuel oil to meat, milk, and coffee. While this may sound like privation, public health actually improved in countries like Britain where rationing was imposed, because everyone was able to gain access to a varied diet.[47]

Nonetheless, there is abundant cause for skepticism about calls for national mobilization modelled on World War II. It's easy to question the dedication of Democratic Party elites to the progressive environmental policies they publicly avow. Scarcely a month after the drafting of the party's platform, for example, the Obama administration quietly auctioned off thousands of acres of land for oil and gas drilling in national forests, opened up 119 million acres for offshore drilling in the Gulf of Mexico, and weakened the Endangered Species Act.[48] In addition, both Obama and Hillary Clinton were long unwilling to make a strong public declaration of opposition to the Dakota Access Pipeline, which is, as Bill McKibben has pointed out, the new Keystone XL: a struggle with massive symbolic significance concerning the intentions and integrity of political leaders regarding climate justice.[49] How seriously are promises about future opposition to fossil capitalism to be taken when both of these politicians are not simply unwilling to take a stand but are actively encouraging extreme extraction in the present?

Equally fundamentally, calls for a mobilization against climate change akin to that of World War II betray a fundamental misunderstanding of that war and of state power as it is presently configured. Part of the appeal of such analogies resides in the widely accepted representation of World War II as the "last good war." McKibben himself reiterates this perspective by writing that the United States was devoted to the single, all-consuming goal of defeating "a planetwide threat to civilization." But to see the Allied powers in general, and the United States in particular, as democratic and as waging a "good fight" for freedom is to forget that these nations were both capitalist and imperialist. Leaders like Winston Churchill talked a great deal about democracy while brutally denying even a modicum of self-determination to Britain's colonies, which covered a quarter of the globe at the time. Although the United States engaged in direct colonial rule of far fewer territories than European colonial powers like France, Holland, and Belgium, it used its control of international markets to dominate Latin America and was also riddled with systematic racism internally. When they sought to expand into Eastern Europe, North Africa, and Southeast Asia, the Axis powers, who arrived late at the colonial table, were at least in part seeking to catch up with the imperial territories controlled either directly or indirectly by the Western Europeans and the United States. World War II was thus to a certain extent an interimperial conflict fought for global hegemony.[50] It was also, however, a people's war against totalitarian oppression, one in which partisans in Western European countries like France, Holland, Poland, and Yugoslavia fought the Nazi occupation; Chinese guerillas fought the Japanese; and Soviet troops fought the invading German forces. In such places, the interimperial war and the people's war were in harmony, but in others—including in colonies like India, Indonesia, and Burma—the two conflicts were at cross-purposes, as liberation movements challenged the colonial rule of Allied forces. After the war's conclusion, these liberation movements were often savagely repressed by the victorious Allied powers.

If World War II was both an interimperial conflict and a people's war, so too is the current crisis over climate change. It is imperative that we keep these intertwined but nonetheless very different struggles distinct. For while large-scale mobilizing against climate change requires the participation of federal governments, it is not inherently in their interest to do so. Indeed, and contrary to the assumptions of activists who describe Democratic Party elites and by extension the United States itself as a willing if frustratingly reluctant ally in the fight against climate chaos, capitalist states and the elites who control them are not going to do the right thing unless they are forced to do so by mass mobilizations from below. The state is not neutral: it is an organized expression of elite class interests. As has been demonstrated throughout this book, some politicians will make concessions to maintain power and legitimacy, but at the end of the day, the state tends toward defending the rule of capital. Internationally, efforts to achieve a binding agreement for reducing carbon emissions have failed, precisely because leading world powers like the United States and emerging powers like Brazil, Russia, India, and China (the BRIC nations) are animated by their tendencies to increase their global power by expanding their economies. This involves continuing to pollute the global atmospheric commons. Under this framework of global competition, genuine international solutions to the climate crisis will be impossible. Indeed, the international negotiating process itself seems to be part of the slow violence of climate change.[51] Although everyone is aware that it is in no one's interest to continue polluting, no one is willing to step back from the brink until everyone does, and so this dysfunctional competition pushes the entire planet relentlessly toward oblivion. As the policies adopted by the Obama administration in its twilight days suggest, global powers are actively supporting a competitive global drive to control and exploit the world's remaining energy resources.[52]

The 2016 election dashed any hopes for enlightened leadership in the United States, but even if the election had turned out differently, it would have been naive to ignore the role of the state in cementing the power of the corporate oligarchy—and, with it, fossil capitalism. A dramatic transition away from fossil capitalism will require public control over and lockdown of roughly $20 trillion dollars in fossil fuel infrastructure around the world. Global elites are not going to give up these assets without a bitter fight.[53] Stripping them of these assets and keeping the oil in the soil will require the construction of a mass movement to continue pressing governments to act before it is too late.

This movement cannot be framed in nationalistic terms. If there was ever an international problem, climate change is it. A national mobilization along the lines of the one envisaged by McKibben is an important step forward, but it will not be enough to ward off impending climate chaos. Even as forward-thinking a document as Canada's *Leap Manifesto*, with its rousing references to the rights of the nation's Indigenous Peoples and its linkage of fossil capitalism to settler colonialism, is articulated within a predominantly national framework.[54] Although the *Leap Manifesto* does underline the necessity of providing harbor to refugees and migrants given Canada's contributions to global military conflicts and climate change, the document talks about economic and social rights such as a universal basic annual income solely within Canada.

Contrast this nationalist orientation with the explicitly international and anti-imperialist outlook of the *People's Agreement of Cochabamba*. Produced in Bolivia by an international conclave of grassroots climate justice organizations and activists in 2010 in response to the abject failure of international climate negotiations in Copenhagen that year, the *People's Agreement* is founded explicitly on a fight against carbon colonialism and for a just transition.[55] Although the document was a product of international social movements rather than nation states, the basic demands articulated in the *People's Agreement* offer a key baseline for the struggle for climate justice. First, it demands decolonization of the atmosphere. Advanced industrialized nations such as the United States and the countries of Western Europe that have benefited from two centuries of fossil capitalism (as well as emerging powers like Brazil and India that are following their lead) must commit to quantifiable goals of emissions reductions that return atmospheric concentrations of greenhouse gases to sustainable levels of no more than 300 parts per million. Second, the *People's Agreement* insists that these climate debtor nations must assume the costs and technology transfer needs of developing countries, which arise from the loss of development opportunities resulting from the rich countries' historical colonization of the atmosphere. Third, the developed nations must pay adaptation debt to vulnerable countries as they seek to prevent, minimize, and deal with damages arising from excessive emissions for which they are not historically responsible. Finally, the *People's Agreement* insists that the beneficiaries of fossil capitalism must assume responsibility for the hundreds of millions of people who will be forced to migrate as a result of the climate change caused by these countries, eliminating restrictive immigration policies and offering migrants a decent life with full human rights guarantees. Migration is, after all, the ultimate form of adaptation and retreat in the face of climate chaos.

If we are to win the struggle for a future of human solidarity rather than dystopian triage, adaptation to climate chaos will have to take place on a global as well as a national scale. Massive investment must therefore be made not simply to green the infrastructures of rich nations but also in schemes for adaptive mitigation in the cities and rural areas of poor and medium-income countries. Wealthy nations should be doing everything in their power to make sure that developing countries do not follow them down the unsustainable path of fossil capitalism. The rampant capitalist globalization that has helped to generate the extreme city on a global scale in recent decades has been overseen by a handful of transnational institutions—the International Monetary Fund, the World Bank, and even the United Nations—that are controlled by a few countries in the global North. Whether these institutions must now be tasked with undoing the present calamity or whether novel institutions such as the recently created Climate Adaptation Fund of the UN's Framework Convention on Climate Change should be charged with oversight, it is clear that an unprecedented program of investment by the global North in a wholesale strengthening of the world urban system, beginning with the most vulnerable cities, needs to be launched.

There are many ways in which such a global adaptation initiative could be funded. The obscenely bloated "defense" budgets of wealthy nations like the United States could be cut radically and redirected. A recent audit of the US Department of Defense by Office of the Inspector General revealed that the Pentagon cannot account for $6.5 trillion.[56] This is not a one-time error: an audit conducted during the Clinton administration revealed that up to a third of the Pentagon transactions examined could not be justified. A budget for people and planet would challenge war profiteering by corporations like Halliburton and

Blackwater, redirecting today's obscene giveaways to the military-industrial complex to adaptation initiatives that would create true foundations for global stability and peace.

The financial sector has in recent decades invented increasingly baroque and exploitative forms of debt creation that destroy our common wealth; its assets could be used to bankroll a shift to renewable energy generation. We came very close to bank nationalization during the financial crisis of 2008. Former Treasury Secretary Timothy Geithner wrote in his recent memoir that Lawrence Summers, head of the White House National Economic Council during the crisis, suggested to President Obama that his administration should "preemptively nationalize" banks such as Citigroup and Bank of America.[57] Given the lack of serious regulation since the Great Recession of 2008, it is only a matter of time before another economic crash once again raises the issue of bank nationalization. While public ownership of the banks would not automatically redirect flows of capital to climate adaptation efforts, it would politicize the question of finance and investment. Nationalization could open up discussions of how the common wealth of nations should be used. People's movements for climate justice could make strong arguments that a significant portion of public assets should be directed to securing the future of the planet.

It is also worth noting that fossil fuel companies are presently benefitting from global subsidies of $5.3 trillion a year, equivalent to $10 million a minute every day.[58] If we are to stand any chance of halting galloping carbon emissions, these subsidies must be terminated immediately, and the massive amounts of capital that are thereby liberated should be redirected to a transformation of the global urban system. Such a demand may seem like pie in the sky given present political conditions, but we should recall that the G7 nations have pledged publicly to eliminate all support for coal, gas, and oil by 2025.[59] Taking such pledges a step further, fossil fuel corporations like ExxonMobil, which have lied for decades about climate change, owe a massive debt above all to the people of the global South.[60] This debt must be discharged as climate reparation. The assets of such carbon criminals should be redirected as part of a planned global shift away from fossil fuels and to renewable, community-based energy generation. There is a long history of seizing fossil capitalist assets as part of anticolonial revolutions: early examples include the Soviet Union in 1918, Bolivia in 1937, Mexico in 1938, Iran in 1951, and Iraq in 1961. Such seizures usually took place in the name of national development and were not intended to end oil production. Today, however, seizure of fossil fuel assets could take place in the name of planetary survival, with the aim of bankrolling a swift transition to popular control of renewable energy generation.

Where can we look for the mass revolutionary potential that could spark a just transition in a time of climate chaos? In *This Changes Everything*, Naomi Klein points to the heroic resistance movements that she dubs *Blockadia*.[61] Indigenous water protectors at the Standing Rock reservation in North Dakota are part of a global network of movements fighting extreme extraction. The connections being made between them and other movements like Black Lives Matter are one of the most important and hopeful developments of recent years. Nonetheless, while these movements are capable of blocking the growth of the fossil fuel infrastructure, it is unlikely that their efforts will be sufficient to produce a new and transformed economic order. Blockadia must be join with insurgent struggles in the key locus of contemporary capital accumulation: the city.

There are pragmatic reasons for this: Trump's election victory in 2016 was also a victory for fossil fuel interests, with climate deniers, industry stalwarts, and corporate shills now commanding some of the country's most prominent political positions, at both the state and federal levels of government. It makes eminent sense to focus struggles for climate justice on the scale of the city, where progressives can still hope to win meaningful victories during a period of reaction. This strategic turn also makes sense since cities are responsible for the lion's share of carbon emissions globally.[62] We are fighting for the city as it may be rather than the city as it currently exists, the good city of the future rather than the extreme city of the present. From the transformation of such cities a new global order may be built. Planetary urbanization has ensured that the human condition is now an urban condition.[63] The fight for a more just social order will take place above all on urban terrain. The object of this struggle must be the radical transformation of today's extreme cities.

The extreme city is the product of global capitalism run amok. But cities are also the point of greatest vulnerability for the global 1 percent, not just because they possess symbolically resonant rallying sites for the dispossessed such as Tahrir, Tiananmen, and Syntagma squares, but also because they concentrate the accumulated assets of the world's wealthy in physical form.[64] The gleaming spires of global cities are not simply symbols of the power of contemporary elites: they are concentrations of capital in concrete form. As command nodes of the global economy, cities are sites of vulnerability for elites. Revolutionary movements of the past two centuries have almost always had an urban dimension, and it should be no different in a period of rapid urbanization. But cities are also potent symbols of collective identity. Far from harbingers of the good life, the shocking inequalities that beset cities today are visible testimony to a system that is fundamentally out of joint.

If planetary urbanization is a product of a massive round of capital accumulation, capitalism has also generated the social form of the extreme city: cities of glittering glass where traders move phantom fortunes of capital around using arcane digital formulas, cheek-by-jowl with refugees from capitalism's processes of creative destruction struggling to subsist in the shadowy spaces on the edge of the law. The struggle for the right to the city, for the right to remain in one's home and one's community, is also predicated on abolishing the capitalist system, which drives systematic dispossession in the extreme city. In their most potent instances, these struggles demand a revolutionary transformation of urban life toward greater equality and community.

Finally, the extreme city is also where climate chaos will have its most potent and devastating impact. Extreme cities concentrate large numbers of people and remarkably fragile infrastructure in overtaxed ecosystems that are under increasing stress. Environmental vulnerability in the extreme city is radically uneven, with disparities of class and race determining one's chances of surviving isolated events such as a hurricane or typhoon, but also impacting one's susceptibility to asthma and other chronic diseases of the urban poor. Efforts to challenge environmental injustice in cities thus hinge on the most basic questions of survival: who has the right to breathe clean air, to grow up in an environment free from toxic pollutants, to have access to healthy food?

Given the apparent ironclad hegemony of contemporary capitalism, the absolute political and intellectual domination of neoliberalism for nearly four decades, it may seem foolhardy to imagine that we can emerge from the present crisis by means of anticapitalist politics and philosophy. But such sentiments betray not simply the atrophy of political will and imagination in recent decades but a weak understanding of our present circumstances. The idea of the Anthropocene incorrectly suggests that humanity as a whole has become the author of its current planetary condition.[65] Against this fallacy, it should be remembered that it is capitalism, an economic system predicated on inexorable growth, that is determining our collective destiny. While it is an incredibly dynamic system, it is one that is organized around short-term profit rather than long-term sustainability. To hope, as some analysts of the current urban condition do, that the innovative capacity of the capitalist market system will power us through climate chaos—indeed, that cities will thrive in a hotter future—is to ignore the wreckage that is already piling up around us and to lay up even greater disasters to come.[66]

The Urban Future

Planetary urbanization is one of the defining features of the Anthropocene Era. In fact, it might be said that we inhabit the Urbocene. If the second half of the twentieth century was the era of the "Great Acceleration," a period of steeply increasing resource use on a finite planet, it was also the age of the city. In the period from 1900 to 2013, the world's human population expanded 4.5-fold, from 1.5 to 7 billion. During the same period the global urban population grew from 225 million to 3.6 billion, a 16-fold increase.[67] In tandem with this urban growth, world economic output grew by a factor of 40, fossil fuel use increased 16-fold, and human water use grew 9-fold.[68] Much of this vertiginous growth in resource consumption and waste outputs was located in cities. Urban consumption and degradation of nature characterizes our impact on the planet more than any other factor at present.

The cities of the world need a new material and moral foundation to weather the impending storms of the climate emergency. The upheavals of the last decade in cities such as Cairo, Istanbul, El Alto, and even New York made the yearning for a more convivial, more just urban order tangible. While this revolutionary tide has ebbed, the hopes for a better human condition that animated it have not died. Nor have efforts to transform the city. The idea of the city to come, one in which social and environmental justice are aligned and inextricably interwoven, offers hope in dark times.[69] It also offers a pragmatic site of intervention given the breakdown of efforts to address climate change on the international and national scale.

Utopian thought, from Plato to St. Augustine and Thomas More, has often imagined the site of utopia to be an ideal city, a concrete emblem of social order and harmony.[70] If such utopian aspirations to construct the good city could generate excesses of rigid top-down planning such as the modernist blueprints of a Le Corbusier, they also may be seen as inspiring the radical ecological critique of the modern city articulated by socialists and anarchists, from the dreams of English Guild Socialists like William Morris for garden cities to the radical experiments in communal living pioneered in Red Vienna during the 1930s.[71] While the extreme cities of the present will no doubt be buffeted by social upheavals and natural disasters during the age of climate chaos, the ideals of these utopian socialists for the city to come hold out a model for sustaining human solidarity and cultivating meaningful lives in the face of cataclysm. The ideal of a sustainable urban order for the whole planet, not just for privilege groups, may help rekindle the sense of shared purpose and collective resolve that can provide the moral and practical basis of life in an age of climate chaos. As the urbanist Ash Amin puts it, the notion of the good city can provide an ideal for a just transition: "This is," he argues,

> the city of modest consumption, shared goods and services, alternative technologies, reduced waste and recycling, taxed excesses, pooled technologies, public transportation, and standard housing, all defended as environmentally urgent.[72]

A just transition would mobilize the labor of the urban residents of informal settlements, and the all-but-forgotten rural poor in the global South, for the sustainable reconstruction of their cities, towns, and villages. All over the world there are already many such efforts, including the Brazilian city of Curitiba's bus rapid transit system, the "vertical gyms" built in the slums of Caracas by Venezuela's Urban-Think Tank, and social housing schemes designed by Elemental in poor communities in Chile.[73] As the self-built working-class communities of the Tupac Amaru movement in Argentina suggest, such experiments in bottom-up transformation can generate social and material infrastructures for significant portions of the urban fabric in the megacities of the global South.[74]

Still, these innovative experiments are piecemeal and inadequate to weather the coming storms. Neither isolated green enclaves in the global North nor tactical interventions in the cities of the global South are commensurate with the challenge our cities face. We need a global people's movement to battle climate chaos while generating work for the disenfranchised masses of the world, marshalling their creative energies to build the kinds of cities I discussed in Chapter 4, harnessing the schemes of contemporary architects and designers to genuinely radical and inclusive urban transformation.[75]

The foundation for the city to come must be a global shift to the creation of cities that are not simply sustainable but that replenish the Earth. As the urban ecologist Herbert Girardet puts it, "The urban metabolism, which currently operates as an inefficient and wasteful linear input-output system, needs to be transformed into a resource-efficient and regenerative *circular system*."[76] How might today's extreme cities diminish their exorbitant demands on the planet's resources and even contribute to their restoration? How, in other words, might extreme cities become ecocities? A number of key steps in this transformation of urban ecosystems are already clear. Cities the world over must end their reliance on fossil fuels, moving to truly renewable and democratically controlled energy sources with haste. New buildings in the city must contribute more energy back to the power grid than they consume, and older buildings must be retrofitted to similar standards. Cities must cease their profligate discharge of degraded resources by becoming zero-waste. Furthermore, cities must help heal the ailing habitats in which they are built by replenishing water tables and addressing water pollution, and by restoring biodiversity and healthy soils, both in the city itself and in its surroundings.[77] And of course cities must be built to work with natural systems in order to adapt as much as possible to the future impacts of climate change. Finally, reversing the trend towards extreme cities also entails reversing the deteriorating social and environmental conditions of rural areas so that people can choose to remain in the countryside without subjecting themselves to spiraling deprivation and dispossession.

The ways in which particular cities achieve these goals may be quite different. After all, cities around the world are located in very different ecosystems and embody very different forms of development. In particular, the world's wealthy cities—in Europe, the United States, and Australia—where urban growth over the rest of the twenty-first century will be relatively limited, need to engage in ecological retrofits. By contrast, in the cities of the developing world, where most of the world's urbanization is occurring, urban development must be shifted from the unsustainable forms inherited from the colonial and postcolonial era, as well as away from the path of extreme sprawl and resource consumption of cities in North America. Making these changes will necessitate a sweeping global investment program, one that will put massive numbers of people to work. This is, in other words, a plan for social as well as environmental transformation on a global scale.

Decarbonizing the urban realm is a key element and absolute necessity of the struggle for the city to come. Given the extent of fossil fuel resources already in production, we cannot dig any new coal mines, drill any new oil wells, or build any more pipelines if we are to prevent catastrophic warming,[78] but at the same time, climate justice must involve decarbonizing cities, including cutting emissions from buildings and urban transportation systems. The renewable energy revolution is already in motion. But we should be careful: not all urban environmental reforms promise systemic transformation. For example, New York City has trumpeted its leadership in efforts to decarbonize planetary urbanism not only by recording its carbon emissions on an annual basis, but also by seeking to cut them substantially. According to an inventory of greenhouse gas emissions published in spring 2016, New York cut emissions 12 percent from 2005 levels, even while the city's population and employment base grew.[79] Moreover, with its *80x50* pledge, the city has promised that by 2050, emissions will be 80 percent lower. Nevertheless, the diminished emissions the city recorded during this period were achieved almost exclusively by switching the urban electricity grid from carbon-intensive coal to natural gas, much of which comes from unsustainable fracking operations in the Marcellus Shale formations of Pennsylvania. Thus, even while elites caved in to a strong public campaign to ban fracking within New York State, the city has essentially outsourced its polluting energy infrastructure to a neighboring state. An honest and comprehensive assessment of the ecological footprints of cities—which extend far beyond their physical footprints—must be a key element of struggles to decarbonize the city.

In addition, celebratory talk of urban emissions cuts as a whole ignores yawning disparities among city residents. In New York, a mere 2 percent of the city's one million buildings use 45 percent of all of the city's energy.[80] These are New York City's largest buildings, over 50,000 square feet in size, which primarily consist of a mixture of luxury apartments, commercial buildings, and multifamily housing developments. New York City's elite emitters live in the most expensive buildings and are among the worst carbon polluters in our city, burning up massive quantities of carbon to heat and power their indoor pools and private fitness centers. These elite emitters must be placed squarely in the sights of the city's efforts to decarbonize. At present, New York programs to retrofit buildings to increase energy efficiency are voluntary, and consequently are projected to reach only 30 percent of large buildings by 2025. Such energy efficiency programs must be mandatory.

Finally, the *80x50* plan is notably vague about how its substantial projected cuts will be made given the slowing rate of reductions since 2012. The plan promises to devote significant effort to making buildings more energy efficient, but it does not include a commitment to large-scale and systemwide renewable energy generation using wind, water, and solar power, as envisaged by Mark Jacobson.[81] The city has picked the low-hanging fruit—converting from coal to natural gas and retrofitting buildings—and now is faced with the far more radical task of abandoning fossil fuels. While the Jacobson study suggests that this shift is technically feasible, building a sustainable global urban order hinges fundamentally on a political struggle against the massive vested interests—from energy corporations to public utilities to investment banks—that continue to back fossil capitalism. This is a struggle for popular control of the energy infrastructure that implies democratization of multiple other aspects of urban governance and sociality.[82]

But as essential as it is to kick the fossil fuel habit, the shift to clean energy alone will not save us. This is because combustion of fossil fuels accounts for only about 70 percent of all anthropogenic greenhouse gas emissions.[83] The other 30 percent of emissions come from things like deforestation, the production of building construction materials like cement and steel, and industrial agriculture, which degrades soils around the world to the point where they begin leaching carbon dioxide. Industrial livestock farming alone produces nearly 15 percent of global greenhouse gas emissions, more than all the world's cars, trucks, and buses combined.[84] The problem, in other words, is not just the source of the energy we use, it's what we are doing with that energy. How will societies organized by the capitalist imperative to generate compound accumulation behave after making the switch to 100 percent renewable energy sources like wind, water, and solar power? If they remain driven by the present economic system, with its demand for endless growth, forests will continue to be clear-cut, megacities will continue to be built, industrial agriculture will continue to expand, and landfills will continue to fill up with the detritus of consumer culture. Shifting to clean energy would in no way slow down the growth of the emissions from such activities.

As the anthropologist Jason Hickel argues, the climate movement makes an enormous mistake when it focuses simply on ditching fossil fuels rather than challenging something deeper: "the basic logic of our economic operating system."[85] We burn fossil fuels, after all, only in order to keep our economies growing. Economic growth, we are told, is the only way to generate more jobs and money to improve our cities, and to foster better livelihoods in general. But there is plenty of evidence that GDP growth does not reduce poverty and that happiness does not increase as a country's income rises.[86] Meanwhile, continuous, compound economic growth is the key factor producing high carbon emissions and unsustainable planetary urbanization, generating an over-accumulation of capital that gets sunk back into speculative real estate development bubbles.[87] In addition, the treadmill of growth also produces much of the social malaise that afflicts rich countries, including overwork, under- and unemployment, overconsumption, vertiginous inequalities, enduring gender inequalities, a lack of time simply to care for one another and to enjoy life, and, ultimately, the mass extinction crisis that haunts the Anthropocene Age.[88]

We need to step off this treadmill of ceaseless growth if we are to survive as a species. In order to do this, we need creative thinking about how to curtail key components of fossil capitalism such as extraction, production, and consumption dramatically and fairly. But while some form of rationing will probably be necessary for human survival, it may not be a good idea to characterize the spirit of a just transition in such terms. Along with cognate policies that are now known as de-growth, zero-growth, and de-development, rationing smacks far too much of the forms of austerity imposed under neoliberalism. These terms run counter not just to the hollow blandishments of consumer capitalism but to fundamental conceptions of human aspiration.[89] We need to characterize the just transition in language that links it to truer forms of progress than the incessant accumulation of more stuff that consumer capitalism offers as its goal. We must, in other words, invoke the positive virtues and feelings of uplifting solidarity that emerge in the struggle for human liberation as an alternative to the selfish pursuits and suicidal trajectory of fossil capitalism. There is no better place to rekindle the virtues of social solidarity than the city.

So in addition to being green, the good city must be a just city. It will include a radically less unequal distribution of wealth and income, reducing social divisions. Whatever reforms are set in place to achieve this must open a pathway to systemic transformation rather than leaving the capitalist order that has generated today's extreme cities intact.[90] Suggestions for how this might be achieved include not only increased wages but also the kind of reduced working hours that would free up time for building community, including efforts to climate-proof cities by growing local food, planting trees, restoring wetlands, and educating one another about how to survive natural disasters. A universal basic income, available to both permanent residents and transients in the city, would enable everyone to partake in the kind of spontaneous, self-directed activity that helps to make us fully human, rather than slaving away at unfulfilling jobs just to make ends meet.[91] Finally, steeply progressive taxes on individual expenditure, corporate profits, and financial transactions could help rein in conspicuous and extravagant consumption, including the mobilization of elite culture as a city branding strategy from Bilbao to New York to Abu Dhabi's Saadiyat Island Cultural District.[92]

But this is not a crash program of austerity—quite the opposite. Climate proofing cities for instance, can create huge numbers of potentially well-paying jobs for needy urban communities, if we are willing to insist on living wages and job-training programs. For example, the excessive carbon emissions generated by air travel must be terminated, which means we need to build new high-speed regional and continent-spanning rail lines. Recognizing that our current carbon-based energy infrastructure needs to be abandoned entails initiating plans to construct a new renewable energy infrastructure, with all the opportunities for employment and devolved democratic control of power (in both senses of the term) that this can bring about.[93] As I discussed in Chapter 6, vibrant movements for municipal energy democracy are already laying out blueprints for cities in which the power—in both senses of the term—is controlled by the people.

It is worth remembering that cities were once sanctuaries from a broader world bereft of rights and filled with violence. As the medieval German saying *Stadtluft macht frei* had it, breathing the air of the city made you free of feudal vassalage. Today that urban legacy needs to be invoked as part of a demand that cities extend an ethos of unconditional hospitality to all in need.[94] Strong countervailing movements to decouple citizenship from nationalism, community, and property already exist in the global North,[95] providing the basics of human existence to urban residents, both temporary and permanent. For instance, New York City has retained a commitment to the right to shelter for all,[96] while also expanding universal free education at all levels, quality public health care, and parks, libraries, and swimming pools that make life not simply bearable but enjoyable. Much of this is under threat, as the social safety net is gradually curtailed nationwide in favor of increasing privatization, and fear and xenophobia are crushing civic culture. Against this, cities must reanimate the basic elements of urban solidarity that have in the past made them symbols of the good life.[97]

There is much excitement over creative efforts to adapt cities to impending climate chaos, from new floodwalls along the bottom half of Manhattan to promises to reintegrate cities with their watery surroundings. But if these are not carried out according to values of justice and equity they will simply exacerbate the unsustainable social conditions and yawning vulnerabilities that characterize the extreme city. Preparing for the coming climate chaos requires considering both the environmental degradation of the extreme city, as well as the crushing material deprivation that is the dark underside to planetary urbanization. The good city cannot be a version of today's city newly embellished with green trimmings like bike lanes and ribbon parks in front of high-end condos. The good city will only heal the wounds of calamitous environmental degradation if it is rebuilt to overcome today's yawning economic and social inequalities.

Dramatic natural and social disasters such as Hurricane Sandy have unleashed significant creative energies galvanized by the need to adapt cities to the climate crisis. Yet few of these proposals dare to imagine an entirely different social order. Human survival—and the survival of many of our fellow creatures on Earth—demands that we imagine new forms of collective flourishing. The ideal of the good city in a time of climate crisis offers a paradigm for the kinds of human connection upon which our collective survival depends. Liberated from the imperative of incessant economic growth and the bankrupt culture of consumption that it fosters, denizens of the good cities of the future may discover new forms of human plenitude while helping one another weather the coming storms.

Acknowledgements

Thanks first and foremost to Andy Hsaio and Audrea Lim of Verso: Andy for generously and enthusiastically supporting this project since its inception and for making brilliant interventions at key stages of the writing; Audrea for amazing editorial work with the manuscript and all sorts of other support at every stage of the book's production. It was an absolute blast working with such a terrifically engaged and talented editorial team. Thanks also to Verso's Duncan Ranslem and Ida Audeh for help with copy editing and other aspects of turning the manuscript into a book, and to Anne Rumberger and Wes House for work on publicizing the book.

CUNY generously provided me with a year-long sabbatical leave that allowed me to do a significant part of the initial research for the project, and the Advanced Research Collaborative at the CUNY Grad Center gave me a semester-long leave that helped me complete the book on time.

I am also grateful to my wonderful colleagues at the College of Staten Island, who helped maintain a convivial spirit in the department and college as I completed my term as chairperson while working simultaneously on this book. In particular, I want to thank fellow chair, friend, union leader, and rabble rouser George Sanchez for his redemptive sense of humor and his unceasing fight to make CUNY a better place for students and faculty alike.

I am indebted to a series of talented research assistants at the CUNY Graduate Center: Micheal Rumore, Sarah Hildebrand, Stefano Morello, and Steven Herran. Thanks to you and to the students in my poco ecocriticism and poco urbanism seminars at the Grad Center for very generative conversations about some of the topics covered in this book.

Thanks to my friends Tim Watson of the University of Miami for inviting me to present some of the ideas in the book, and Colleen Lye of UC-Berkeley, who helped me gain access to the wonderful libraries at Berkeley, where I conducted crucial research on the book for a year.

This book would not have been what it is without the many interviews that I was fortunate to conduct with an immense variety of brilliant activists and intellectuals. I am very grateful to all those who took time out of busy schedules to speak with me: Kazi Ashraf, Devin Balkind, John Barry, Terri Bennett, Keren Bolter, Brett Branco, Robin Bronen, Hillary Brown, Craig Colten, Richard Condrey, Dilip da Cunha, Mark Davis, Jackie Di Salvo, Michael Elliot, Goldi Guerra, Kristina Hill, Denise Hoffman-Brandt, Maya Faison, Zoltàn Glück, Michael Goldfarb, Klaus Jacobs, Kristin Jacobs, Ilya Jalal, Joep Janssen, Mychal Johnson, Jennifer Jurado, Fred Kaufman, Aurash Khawarzad, Kimberly Kinder, Chris La Motte, Colin MacFarlane, Desmond Majekodunmi, Julie Maldonado, Rebecca Manski, Darragh Martin, Mike Menser, Tracy Metz, Nastaran Mohit, Priya Mulgaonkar, Daniel Mundy, Sofía Gallisá Muriente, Jim Murley, Shamsun Nahar, Sheryl Nash-Chisholm, Jayanatha Obeysekera, Koen Olthuis, Mike Orbach, Dusty Pate, Tony Perlstein, Lekan Pierce, Leila Rassi, Conor Tomás Reed, Hanna Ruszczyk, Catherine Seavitt, Tammy Shapiro, Doug Sheer, Maritza Silva-Farrell, Michael Sorkin, Phil Stoddard, Jenneke Visser, Harold Wanless, Leah Weston, and Adam Yarinsky. The good work done by each of you and the many organizations and social movements to which you belong provided a foundation of hope as I worked on a topic that might otherwise have fueled despair.

Many of the questions and preoccupations that animate this book originally germinated in the fertile terrain of seminar meetings at the Center for Place, Culture, and Politics during the period when the Center was led first by Neil Smith and then David Harvey. Although I wrote the book after my stints at the Center, the project drew inspiration at every stage from the colossal intellectual contributions and tremendous political integrity of Neil and David.

Thanks also to the wonderfully peaceful Blue Mountain Center writers' retreat, where I worked through some of the initial ideas for the project. BMC was an ideal refuge from which to gain some perspective on the extreme city. Thanks to Harriet Barlow, Ben Strader, and the many others at BMC for providing such a wonderful space for engaged thought and writing.

Special thanks go to the many friends and scholars who discussed the ideas that found their way into this book. I am particularly grateful to Anne McClintock and Rob Nixon for crucial support and inspiration. Your passionate dedication to the environment and to social justice, and your deep awareness that the two are inextricably intertwined, have been an enduring beacon to me and to so many others.

I am deeply grateful to my family for the unstinting love you have shown me over the years. To my parents Ann and Nigel and to my sister Ginny for your great generosity and kindness during difficult and happy times. To my older daughter Sofia for your patience and understanding as the writing took me away from you during your critical early college years. And to Sholeh, who was born and grew up with this book: you cannot know now how much time this project stole from you when you were small but I hope you will someday forgive me knowing that I wrote with hope in my heart that we adults will find a way to make a better world for you and all the other children of your generation.

Finally, this book is dedicated to Manijeh. You are my intellectual and emotional lodestar in too many ways to count. Every day I spend with you makes me believe more strongly in the strength and beauty of the human spirit.

Notes

Introduction: Extreme City

1. I agree with E. Ann Kaplan's analysis of Hurricane Sandy as a "border event." See E. Ann Kaplan, *Climate Trauma: Foreseeing the Future in Dystopian Film and Fiction*, New Brunswick, NJ: Rutgers University Press, 2016.
2. Fred Kaufman, "Personal Interview," 6 June 2015.
3. Sheryl Nash-Chisholm, "Personal Interview," 2 June 2015.
4. Alex de Sherbinin, Marc Levy, Susana Adamo, Kytt MacManus, Greg Yetman, Valentina Mara . . . Cody Aichele, "Migration and Risk: Net Migration in Marginal Ecosystems and Hazardous Areas," *Environmental Research Letters* 7: 4, November 2012, 1–14.
5. For a refutation of the new positivist urbanism that holds that city size determines virtually all aspects of the lives of those who live in particular sites, see Brendan Gleeson, *The Urban Condition*, Abingdon, Oxon, United Kingdom: Routledge, 2014, 60.
6. Mike Davis, "Who Will Build the Ark?" *New Left Review* 61, January/February 2010, 29–46.
7. Brian Stone, Jr., *The City and the Coming Climate: Climate Change in the Places We Live*, New York: Cambridge University Press, 2012, 14.
8. Uli Linke and Danielle Taana Smith, eds., *Cultures of Fear: A Critical Reader*, New York: Pluto, 2009.
9. Stone, *The City and the Coming Climate*, 66.

10. Simon Romero, "Taps Start to Run Dry in Brazil's Largest City: São Paolo's Water Crisis Linked to Growth, Pollution, and Deforestation," *The New York Times,* 16 February 2015.
11. Sandra Postel, "Lessons from São Paolo's Water Shortage," *National Geographic,* 13 March 2015.
12. Robert D. Kaplan, *The Coming Anarchy: Shattering the Dreams of the Post Cold War,* New York: Random House, 2000. For a more recent iteration of this security-oriented urban Malthusianism, see David Kilcullen, *Out of the Mountains: The Coming Age of the Urban Guerrilla,* New York: Oxford University Press, 2013.
13. See, for example, Edward Glaeser, *The Triumph of the City: How Our Greatest Invention Makes Us Richer, Smarter, Greener, Healthier, and Happier,* New York: Penguin, 2012; Doug Saunders, *Arrival City: How the Largest Migration in History is Reshaping Our World,* New York: Vintage, 2012; and Bruce Katz and Jennifer Bradley, *The Metropolitan Revolution: How Cities and Metros Are Fixing Our Broken Politics,* Washington, DC: Brookings Institution Press, 2014.
14. Typical, in this regard, is Matthew Kahn's *Climatopolis: How Our Cities Will Thrive in the Hotter Future,* New York: Basic Books, 2010.
15. For a celebratory take on tactical urbanism, see Pedro Gadanho, *Uneven Growth: Tactical Urbanisms for Expanding Megacities,* New York: MOMA, 2014.
16. Christian Parenti, *The Soft Cage: Surveillance in America from Slavery to the War on Terror,* New York: Basic Books, 2004.
17. David Harvey, *Rebel Cities: From the Right to the City to the Urban Revolution,* New York: Verso, 2012, 6.
18. Neil Smith, "There's No Such Thing as a Natural Disaster," *Understanding Katrina: Perspectives from the Social Sciences,* 11 June 2006.
19. On the history of US residential segregation, see Douglas Massey and Nancy Denton, *American Apartheid: Segregation and the Making of the Underclass,* Cambridge, MA: Harvard University Press, 1993. On mass incarceration, see Elizabeth Hinton, *From the War on Poverty to the War on Crime: The Making of Mass Incarceration in America,* Cambridge, MA: Harvard University Press, 2016.
20. Greg Beckett, "Haiti: From Alienated Hope to a Durable Future," *Social Text Online,* 26 January 2010,
21. Randal Archibold, "Already Desperate, Haitian Farmers Are Left Hopeless After Storm," *New York Times,* 17 November 2012.
22. Rob Nixon, *Slow Violence and the Environmentalism of the Poor,* Cambridge, MA: Harvard University Press, 2012.

23. Archibold, "Already Desperate, Haitian Farmers Are Left Hopeless After Storm."
24. Margaret Sattherwaite, "Partnering for Rights: Rebuilding Haiti After the Earthquake," *Social Text Online*, 26 January 2010.
25. Alex Dupuy, "Beyond the Earthquake: A Wake-Up Call for Haiti," *Social Text Online*, 26 January 2010.
26. Ibid.
27. "Combined and uneven development" produced a "drawing together of the different stages of the journey, a combining of separate steps, an amalgam of archaic with more contemporary forms." See Leon Trotsky, *The History of the Russian Revolution*, trans. Max Eastman, London: Pluto Press, 1977, 23.
28. Benedict Anderson, *Imagined Communities: Reflections on the Origin and Spread of Nationalism*, New York: Verso, 2006.
29. Max Page, *The City's End: Two Centuries of Fantasies, Fears, and Premonitions of New York's Destruction*, New Haven, CT: Yale University Press, 2008.
30. David Owen, *Green Metropolis: Why Living Smaller, Living Closer, and Driving Less Are the Keys to Sustainability*, New York: Riverhead Books, 2009.

Chapter 1. Capital Sinks

1. Phil Stoddard, "Personal Interview," 7 September 2015.
2. Ibid.
3. Organization for Economic Cooperation and Development, "Future Flood Losses in Major Coastal Cities," 19 August 2013.
4. Elizabeth Kolbert, "The Siege of Miami," *The New Yorker*, 21 December 2015.
5. Jeff Goodell, "Goodbye, Miami," *Rolling Stone*, 20 June 2013.
6. Rebecca Lindsey, "Climate Change: Global Sea Level," *National Oceanic and Atmospheric Administration*, 10 June 2016.
7. Jayantha Obeysekera, "Personal Interview," 10 September 2015.
8. Kolbert, "The Siege of Miami."
9. Jobeysekera, "Personal Interview."
10. Ibid.
11. Harold Wanless, "Personal Interview," 8 September 2015.
12. Ibid.
13. Ibid.
14. "Miami-Dade Agrees to $1.6 Billion Upgrade of its Sewer System to Eliminate Overflows," *US Department of Justice*, 6 June 2013.
15. Jenny Staletovich, "Miami Beach King Tides Flush Human Waste Into Bay, Study Finds," *Miami Herald*, 16 May 2016.

16. Oliver Milman, "Florida Declares State of Local Emergency Over Influx of God-Awful Toxic Algae," *The Guardian,* 30 June 2016.
17. Staletovich, "Miami Beach King Tides."
18. Quoted in Goodell, "Goodbye, Miami."
19. Jonathan Soble, "Fukushima Keeps Fighting Radioactive Tide 5 Years After Disaster," *New York Times,* 10 March 2016.
20. Christina Nunez, "As Sea Levels Rise, Are Coastal Nuclear Power Plants Ready?" *National Geographic,* 16 December 2015.
21. Goodell, "Goodbye, Miami."
22. Ibid.
23. Lizette Alvarez, "Nuclear Power Plant Leak Threatens Drinking Water Wells in Florida," *New York Times,* 22 March 2016.
24. Tim Elfrink, "Turkey Point Nuclear Plant is Pumping Polluted Water into Biscayne Bay," *Miami Times,* 8 March 2016.
25. Stoddard, "Personal Interview."
26. Goodell, "Goodbye, Miami."
27. "The Truth About Florida's Attempt to Censor Climate Change," *Got Science? Union of Concerned Scientists Publications,* April 2015.
28. Jim Murley, "Personal Interview," 9 September 2015.
29. Ibid.
30. Stoddard, "Personal Interview."
31. Murley, "Personal Interview."
32. Wanless, "Personal Interview."
33. City of Miami, *Revenue Manual,* 2016–17. On total tax revenue in the region, see "Miami-Dade Property Values Surge Nearly 9% in 2016," *Miami Herald,* 31 May 2016.
34. Kolbert, "The Siege of Miami."
35. Ibid.
36. Nicholas Nehamas, "How Secret Offshore Money Helps Fuel Miami's Real Estate Boom," *Miami Herald,* 3 April 2016.
37. Nicholas Nehamas, "Panama Papers: Secret Offshores Trace Back to Brickell Condo Featured on *Miami Vice*," *Miami Herald,* 4 April 2016.
38. David Stockman, "Flight Capital, Bubble Finance, and the Housing Price Spiral in the World's Leading Cities," *David Stockman's Contra Corner,* 2 June 2015.
39. Nehamas, "How Secret Offshore Money."
40. Ibid.
41. Ibid.
42. "Secret Buyers in Miami Could Be Exposed," *The Real Deal,* 13 January 2016.
43. Stoddard, "Personal Interview."
44. Ibid.

45. Orrin H. Pilkey, Linda Pilkey-Jarvis, and Keith C. Pilkey, *Retreat from a Rising Sea: Hard Choices in an Age of Climate Change*, New York: Columbia University Press, 2016, 78.

46. Ibid., 79.

47. Ibid., 89.

48. Ibid., 83.

49. Stoddard, "Personal Interview."

50. Ibid.

51. Ibid.

52. John Englander, *High Tide on Main Street: Rising Sea Level and the Coming Coastal Crisis*, Boca Raton, FL: Science Bookshelf, 2012, 3.

53. Ibid., 44.

54. Kate Taylor, "Bloomberg Hails Lower Manhattan's Revival Since 9/11," *New York Times*, 6 September 2011.

55. "Mayor Bloomberg Delivers Major Address on the Rebirth of Lower Manhattan Since 9/11," 6 September 2011, nyc.gov

56. Ibid.

57. Ibid.

58. *PlaNYC: A Greener, Greater New York*, 2007, nyc.gov.

59. New York City Panel on Climate Change, *Climate Change Adaptation in New York City: Building a Risk Management Response*, Annals of the New York Academy of Sciences, Vol. 1196, 2010.

60. *Vision 2020: New York City Comprehensive Waterfront Plan*, 2012, nyc.gov, 107.

61. Quoted in Doug Turetsky, "Seas Rise, Storms Surge, and NYC Presses Ahead With Waterfront Development Projects," *IBO Blog*, 21 November 2012.

62. NYC Special Initiative for Rebuilding and Resiliency, *A Stronger, More Resilient New York*, 2013.

63. New York City Department of City Planning, *Designing for Flood Risk*, 2013, nyc.gov.

64. New York City Department of City Planning, *Urban Waterfront Adaptive Strategies*, 2013, nyc.gov.

65. Pilkey et al., *Retreat from a Rising Sea*, 52.

66. Emily Manley, "Number of NYC Buildings at Risk From Flooding Has Tripled," *New York Environmental Report*, 7 November 2014.

67. Sydney Brownstone, "Bloomberg Unleashes Plan to Guide City into Climate-Change Future," *Village Voice*, 12 June 2013.

68. Pilkey et al., *Retreat from a Rising Sea*, 55.

69. Ibid.

70. Liz Koslov, "The Case for Retreat," *Public Culture* 28:2 (2016), 364.

71. David Harvey, *Seventeen Contradictions and the End of Capitalism*, New York: Oxford University Press, 2014, 222–45.

72. David Harvey, *The Enigma of Capital and the Crises of Capitalism,* New York: Oxford University Press, 2010, 28.

73. David Harvey, *The New Imperialism*, New York: Oxford University Press, 2003, 115.

74. As the urban theorist Henri Lefebvre presciently argued some four decades ago, "real-estate speculation becomes the principal source for the formation of capital." Henri Lefebvre, *The Urban Revolution*, Minneapolis: University of Minnesota Press, 2003, 160.

75. David Harvey, "The Crisis of Planetary Urbanism" in Pedro Gadanho, ed., *Uneven Growth: Tactical Urbanisms for Expanding Megacities*, New York: MOMA, 2014.

76. David Owen, *Green Metropolis: Why Living Smaller, Living Closer, and Driving Less Are the Keys of Sustainability*, New York: Riverhead, 2010.

77. Louis Story and Stephanie Saul, "Towers of Secrecy: Stream of Foreign Wealth Streams of Elite New York Real Estate," *New York Times,* 7 Feb 2015; Julie Satow, "Why the Doorman Is Lonely: New York City's Emptiest Co-ops and Condos," *New York Times,* 9 January 2015.

78. Mike Davis, "Fear and Money in Dubai," *New Left Review* 41, September/October 2006, 47–68. See also all of the essays collected in Mike Davis and Daniel Bertrand Monk, eds., *Evil Paradises: Dreamworlds of Neoliberalism*, New York: New Press, 2008.

79. Mike Davis, *Planet of Slums*, New York: Verso, 2007.

80. David Harvey, "The Crisis of Planetary Urbanism," in Pedro Gadanho, ed., *Uneven Growth: Tactical Urbanisms for Expanding Megacities*, New York: MOMA, 2014, and *Rebel Cities: From the Right to the City to the Urban Revolution*, New York: Verso, 2012.

81. Kevin Fox Gotham and Miriam Greenberg, *Crisis Cities: Disaster and Redevelopment in New York and New Orleans*, New York: Oxford University Press, 2014, 2.

82. United Nations Human Settlements Programme (UN-Habitat). 2011. *Cities and Climate Change: Policy Directions Global Report on Human Settlements 2011* (Washington, DC), 16.

83. Mike Davis, "Who Will Build the Ark?" *New Left Review* 61, 2010, 41.

84. Ruth S. DeFries, "Deforestation Driven by Urban Population Growth and Agricultural Trade in the Twenty-First Century," *Nature Geoscience* 3, February 2010, 178–81.

85. Davis, "Who Will Build the Ark?" 41.

86. Ibid.
87. As Davis puts it, "What often goes unnoticed in the moral inventories [of urban theorists] is the consistent affinity between social and environmental justice, between the communal ethos and a greener urbanism [. . .] The cornerstone of the low-carbon city, far more than any particular green design or technology, is the priority given to public affluence over private wealth." Ibid.
88. Ibid., 42–43.
89. Climate Works for All Coalition, *Elite Emissions: How the Homes of the Wealthiest New Yorkers Help Drive Climate Change,* November 2015.
90. Ibid., 4.
91. Andrew Sayer, *Why We Can't Afford the Rich*, Chicago: University of Chicago Press, 2014, xx.
92. On the environmental branding of what they term cities threatened by climate chaos, see Kevin Fox Gotham and Miriam Greenberg, *Crisis Cities: Disaster and Redevelopment in New York and New Orleans*, New York: Oxford University Press, 2014, 181–222.
93. Melissa Checker, "Wiped out by the 'Green Wave': Environmental Gentrification and the Paradoxical Politics of Urban Sustainability," *City and Society* 23:2, 2011, 210–29.
94. Thomas J. Lueck, "Bloomberg Draws a Blueprint for a Greener City," *New York Times,* 23 April 2007.
95. Benjamin Barber, *If Mayors Ruled the World: Dysfunctional Nations, Rising Cities*, New Haven, CT: Yale University Press, 2013.
96. For an extensive discussion of New York City and urban planning, see Tom Angotti, *New York for Sale: Community Planning Confronts Global Real Estate*, Cambridge, MA: MIT Press, 2008.
97. Alexandros Washburn, *The Nature of Urban Design: A New York Perspective on Resilience*, New York: Island Press, 2013, 103.
98. Julie Sze, *Noxious New York: The Racial Politics of Urban Health and Environmental Justice*, Cambridge, MA: MIT Press, 2007, 43; Angotti, *New York for Sale,* 61.
99. Matthew Gandy, *Concrete and Clay : Reworking Nature in New York City*, Cambridge, MA: MIT Press, 2002, 84.
100. For a fascinating discussion of Robert Moses's impact on the city, see Marshall Berman, *All That Is Solid Melts Into Air: The Experience of Modernity*, New York: Penguin, 1982, 294ff.
101. Jane Jacobs, *The Death and Life of Great American Cities*, New York: Random House, 1961. For a discussion of the conflicted legacy of Moses and Jacobs, see Scott Larson, *"Building Like*

Moses with Jacobs in Mind": Contemporary Planning in New York City, Philadelphia, PA: Temple University Press, 2013.

102. For a comprehensive anatomy of the fiscal crisis, see Kim Moody, *From Welfare State to Real Estate: Regime Change in NYC, 1974 to the Present*, New York: New Press, 2007.

103. David Harvey, *A Brief History of Neoliberalism*, New York: Oxford University Press, 2007.

104. Naomi Klein, *This Changes Everything: Capitalism vs. The Climate*, New York: Simon and Schuster, 2014, 31–63.

105. Peter Marcuse, "PlaNYC is not a 'Plan' and it is not for 'NYC,'" 2008, hunter.cuny.edu

106. Tom Angotti, "PlaNYC at Three: Time to Include the Neighborhoods," *Gotham Gazette*, 12 April 2010.

107. For an acute anatomy of the "Bloomberg Way," see Julian Brash, *Bloomberg's New York: Class and Governance in the Luxury City*, Athens, GA: University of Georgia Press, 2011.

108. Angotti, "PlaNYC at Three."

109. "Reduction in Greenhouse Gas Emissions and New Programs to Continue Progress," 30 December 2013, mikebloomberg.com.

110. Heather Rogers, "How Michael Bloomberg Greenwashed New York City," *Tablet*, 5 January 2015.

111. Scott Waldman and Bill Mahoney, "New York Increasingly Reliant on Natural Gas for Heat," *Politico*, 5 October 2015.

112. Mireya Navarro, "Pipeline Plan Stirs Debate on Both Sides of the Hudson," *New York Times*, 26 October 2011.

113. Rogers, "How Michael Bloomberg Greenwashed New York City."

114. On this long durée of the city, see Edwin G. Burrows and Mike Wallace, *Gotham: A History of New York City to 1898*, New York: Oxford University Press, 1999.

115. On capitalism's increasingly predatory character and accumulation by dispossession, see David Harvey, *The New Imperialism*, New York: Oxford University Press, 2005. On the IMF structural adjustment and food riots, see John Walton and David Seddon, *Free Markets and Food Riots: The Politics of Global Adjustment*, Cambridge, MA: Blackwell, 1994. On bread prices and the Arab Spring, see Rami Zurayk, "Use Your Loaf: Why Food Prices Were Crucial in the Arab Spring," *The Guardian*, 16 July 2011.

116. The best history of New York's environmental justice movement is Julie Sze's *Noxious New York: The Racial Politics of Urban Health and Environmental Justice*, Cambridge, MA: MIT Press, 2007.

117. The City of New York, *PlaNYC: A Greener, Greater New York*, 2007, 4.

118. Ibid., 4–6.
119. Ibid., 4.
120. On the history of "quality of life" and "broken windows" polic-
     ing, see Andrea McArdle and Tanya Erzen, eds., *Zero Tolerance:
     Quality of Life and the New Police Brutality in New York City*,
     New York: NYU Press, 2001, and, more recently, Jordan T.
     Camp, *Incarcerating the Crisis: Freedom Struggles and the Rise
     of the Neoliberal State*, Berkeley: University of California Press,
     2016, and Elizabeth Hinton, *From the War on Poverty to the
     War on Crime: The Making of Mass Incarceration*, Cambridge,
     MA: Harvard University Press, 2016.
121. *PlaNYC*, 6.
122. New York Building Congress, "Boat Tour Focuses on Waterfront
     Development Opportunities," *New York Building Congress
     Newsletter*, Winter 2003.
123. As Neil Smith observes in his anatomy of gentrification, "the
     frontier discourse serves to rationalize and legitimate a process
     of conquest, whether in the eighteenth or nineteenth century
     West, or in the late-twentieth century inner city." Neil Smith, *The
     New Urban Frontier: Gentrification and the Revanchist City*,
     New York: Routledge, 1996.
124. Julian Brash, *Bloomberg's New York: Class and Governance in the
     Luxury City*, Athens, GA: University of Georgia Press, 2011, 88.
125. Ibid.
126. On the role of the Real Estate Board of New York as "bulwark
     of the landed elite" and chief promoters of the real estate growth
     machine, see Angotti, *New York for Sale*, 39.
127. Kevin Fox Gotham and Miriam Greenberg, *Crisis Cities: Disaster
     and Redevelopment in New York and New Orleans*, New York:
     Oxford University Press, 2014, 218.
128. On the direct links between the Olympics bid and planning
     under Bloomberg, see Mitchell Moss, *How New York City Won
     the Olympics,* New York University, 2011.
129. City of New York, "Mayor Bloomberg Announces Deputy
     Mayor for Economic Development and Rebuilding Daniel L.
     Doctoroff Stepping Down at Year's End," 6 December 2007.
130. Cited in Kim Moody, *From Welfare State to Real Estate: Regime
     Change in NYC, 1974 to the Present*, New York: New Press,
     2007, 213.
131. Ibid., 215.
132. Ibid., 217.
133. Ibid., 118.
134. On the rebuilding of Times Square, see Samuel R. Delany, *Times
     Square Red, Times Square Blue*, New York: New York University
     Press, 2001. On the New York State prison boom, see Ryan S.

King, Marc Mauer, and Tracy Huling, *Big Prisons, Small Towns: Prison Economics in Rural America*, New York: The Sentencing Project, 2003.

135. Gotham and Greenberg, *Crisis Cities*, 114–18.

136. Ibid., 133.

137. Wayne Barrett, "All Wet," *The Village Voice*, 13 March 2007.

138. Cynthia Rosenzweig and William Solecki, "Climate Change and a Global City: Learning from New York," *Environment* 43:3, April 2001, 11.

139. Ibid., 13.

140. Ibid., 10.

141. Barrett, "All Wet."

142. Anthony Doesburg, "Car Parks and Playgrounds To Help Make Rotterdam 'Climate Proof'," *The Guardian*, 11 May 2012.

143. For a discussion of the ontological shift necessary in order to embrace fluid terrain, see Anuradha Mathur and Dilip Da Cunha, eds., *Design in the Terrain of Water*, Philadelphia: University of Pennsylvania Press, 2014.

144. Brian Stone Jr., *The City and the Coming Climate: Climate Change in the Places We Live*, New York: Cambridge University Press, 2012, 99.

145. Ibid., 103.

146. Katy Lederer, "Why Buy in a Flood Zone?" *New Yorker*, 6 July 2015.

147. *PlaNYC*, 21.

148. On the history of containerization, see Marc Levinson, *The Box: How the Shipping Container Made the World Smaller and the World Economy Bigger*, Princeton, NJ: Princeton University Press, 2006.

149. Ibid., 78–79.

150. Ibid., 90.

151. Robert Fitch, *The Assassination of New York*, New York: Verso, 1993, x.

152. Levinson, *The Box*, 98.

153. Sam Roberts, "Poverty Race is Up in New York City, and Income Gap is Wide, Census Data Show," *New York Times*, 19 September 2013.

154. Ellen M. Snyder-Grenier, *Brooklyn! An Illustrated History*, Brooklyn, NY: Brooklyn Historical Society, 1996.

155. Ibid., 161.

156. Douglas Massey and Nancy Denton, *American Apartheid: Segregation and the Making of the Underclass*, Cambridge, MA: Harvard University Press, 1993, 44.

157. Ibid., 54.

158. Angotti, *New York for Sale*, 77.

159. Ibid., 139.
160. Melissa Checker, "'Like Nixon Coming To China:' Finding Common Ground in a Multi-Ethnic Coalition for Environmental Justice," *Anthropological Quarterly* 74:3, July 2001, 135–46; Angotti, *New York for Sale,* 139–40.
161. On the painful paradoxes of successful environmental justice struggles and viable strategies for resistance, see Angotti, *New York for Sale,* 30.
162. On the discourse of *terra nullius,* see Mary Louise Pratt, *Imperial Eyes: Travel Writing and Transculturation,* New York: Routledge, 1992.
163. Real Affordability for All Coalition, *A Tale of One Housing Plan: How De Blasio's NYC Is Abandoning the Same Low-Income People as Bloomberg,* 2016, 1.
164. Paul Moses, "A New Colony," *Village Voice,* 10 May 2005.
165. Ibid.
166. Maritz Silva-Farrell, "Personal Interview," 19 October 2015.
167. Angotti, *New York for Sale,* 54.
168. For a critical assessment of de Blasio's *OneNYC,* see the New York City Environmental Justice Alliance's *NYC Climate Justice Agenda,* April 2016.
169. Wendy Koch, "Could a Titanic Seawall Save This Quickly Sinking City?" *National Geographic,* 10 December 2015.
170. Ibid.
171. On Dubai's architectural phantasmagoria, see Mike Davis, "Fear and Money in Dubai," *New Left Review* 41, September–October 2006, 47–68.
172. Koch, "Could a Titanic Seawall Save This Quickly Sinking City?"
173. KuiperCompagnons, "The Great Garuda to Save Jakarta," November 2015.
174. "Dutch Seawall and Development Plan for Jakarta Bay Well Received by Indonesia Authorities," *Dutch Water Sector News,* 3 April 2014.
175. "Objectives," National Capital Integrated Coastal Development, en.ncicd.com/ncicd/tujuan-ncicd.
176. Quoted in Wendy Koch, "Could a Titanic Seawall Save This Quickly Sinking City?"
177. Jochen Hinkel, Daniel Lincke, Athanasios T. Vafeidis, Mahé Perrette, Robert James Nicholls, Richard S. J. Tol, ... Anders Levermann, "Coastal Flood Damage and Adaptation Costs under 21st Century Sea-level Rise," *Proceedings of the National Academy of Sciences* 111:9, 4 March 2014.
178. Martin Lukacs, "New, Privatized African City Heralds Climate Apartheid," *The Guardian,* 21 January 2014).
179. Ibid.

180. Lekan Pierce, "Personal Interview," 20 November 2015.
181. Tolu Ogunlesi, "Inside Makoko: Danger and Ingenuity in the World's Biggest Floating Slum," *The Guardian*, 23 February 2016.
182. Martin Lukacs, "New, Privatized African City."
183. David McNeill, "Japan's Sea Wall: Storm Brews Over Plans to Construct Giant 5 Billion Pound Barrier against Tsunamis," *The Independent*, 6 March 2016.
184. "Editorial: Stop Jakarta's Sinking," *The Jakarta Post*, 10 October 2015.
185. Ibid.
186. Corry Elyda, "Sea Wall an Environmental Disaster: Study," *The Jakarta Post*, 7 October 2015.
187. Dyna Rochmyaningsih, "Jakarta Clips 'The Great Garuda' Wings," *SciDevNet*, 16 May 2016.
188. Ibid.
189. Elyda, "Sea Wall an Environmental Disaster."
190. Ibid.
191. Rochmyaningsih, "Jakarta Clips 'The Great Garuda' Wings."
192. Ian MacKinnon, "Four-Metre Floodwaters Displace 340,000 in Jakarta," *The Guardian*, 5 February 2007.
193. "Podomoro Land President Director Arrested by KPK in City Bribe Case," *Jakarta Globe*, 2 April 2016.
194. Catriona Croft-Cusworth, "This Week in Jakarta," *The Interpreter*, 29 April 2016.
195. Mackenzie Funk, *Windfall: The Booming Business of Global Warming*, New York: Penguin, 2014.
196. Joep Janssen, "Personal Interview," 4 April 2016.
197. Ibid.
198. "Accumulation by Adaptation" is a play on David Harvey's notion of accumulation by dispossession. For discussion of the latter concept, see David Harvey, *The New Imperialism*, New York: Oxford University Press, 2003.
199. Nancy Kwak, "'Manila's Danger Areas:' Clearing Urban Waterways Creates New Challenges for the City's Most Vulnerable Inhabitants," *Places Journal*, February 2015.
200. Amita Baviskar, "Cows, Cars, and Cycle-Rickshaws: Bourgeois Environmentalists and the Battle for Delhi's Streets" in Amita Baviskar and Raka Ray, eds., *Elite and Everyman: The Cultural Politics of the Indian Middle Classes*, New York: Routledge, 2011, 391–415.
201. Lalith Lankatilleke, "Urban Cleansing in Dhaka," *Urban Poor Asia Journal*, April 2002.
202. Christophe Girot, Paolo Burlando, and Senthil Gurusamy, "Reinventing Ciliwung: 'Central Park' of the East?" *The Jakarta Post*, 12 April 2016.

203. Matthew Gandy, *Concrete and Clay: Reworking Nature in New York City*, Cambridge, MA: MIT Press, 2002, 88.

204. Corry Elyda, "River Normalization to Cause More Evictions This Year," *Jakarta Post*, 10 January 2017.

205. Joep Janssen, "Personal Interview."

206. Ibid.

207. Quoted in Zubaidah Nazeer, "Saving Jakarta From Flooding: Studies Under Way to Clean Up Flood-prone Ciliwung River, But Squatters Won't Budge," *The Straits Times*, 20 March 2013.

Chapter 2. Environmental Blowback

1. Ted Steinberg, *Gotham Unbound: The Ecological History of Greater New York*, New York: Simon & Schuster, 2014, 243.

2. Ellen Kracauer Hartig, Vivian Gornitz, Alexander Kolker, and David Fallon, "Anthropogenic and Climate-Change Impacts on Salt Marshes of Jamaica Bay, New York City," *Wetlands* 22: 1, March 2002, 71.

3. New York City Special Initiative for Rebuilding and Resiliency, *A Stronger, More Resilient New York*, 2013, 13.

4. See Ty Wamsley, Mary A. Cialone, Jane M. Smith, John H. Atkinson, and Julie D. Rosati, "The Potential of Wetlands in Reducing Storm Surge," *Ocean Engineering* 37, 2010, 59–68.

5. Steinberg, *Gotham Unbound*, 334.

6. Kate Orff, "Cosmopolitan Ecologies," in Alexander Brash, Jamie Hand and Kate Orff, eds., *Gateway: Visions for an Urban National Park*, New York: Princeton Architectural Press, 2011, 53.

7. Ibid., 51.

8. H. J. De Vriend and M. Van Koningsveld, *Building with Nature: Thinking, Acting and Interacting Differently*, Dordrecht, The Netherlands: EcoShape, 2012, 9.

9. Herman Boschken, "Global Cities Are Coastal Cities Too: A Paradox in Sustainability?" *Urban Studies* 50: 9, July 2013, 1760–78.

10. James P.M. Syvitski, Albert J. Kettner, Irina Overeem, Eric W. H. Hutton, Mark T. Hannon, G. Robert Brakenridge, ... Robert J. Nicholls, "Sinking Deltas Due to Human Activities," *Nature Geoscience* 2, 2009, 681–86.

11. Justin Gillis, "The Flood Next Time," *New York Times,* 13 January 2014.

12. Syvitski et al., "Sinking Deltas."

13. Rafi Youatt, *Counting Species: Biodiversity in Global Environmental Politics*, Minneapolis: University of Minnesota Press, 2015, 26.

14. Sara Nelson, "The Slow Violence of Climate Change," *Jacobin*, 17 February 2016.

15. On environmental historians' failure to acknowledge urban environmental justice struggles adequately, see Richard White, "Are You an Environmentalist or Do You Work for a Living?: Work and Nature," in William Cronon, ed., *Uncommon Ground: Rethinking the Human Place in Nature*, New York: Norton, 1995, 171–85. Examples of scholarship that challenges this elision include Ari Kelman, *A River and Its City: The Nature of Landscape in New Orleans*, Berkeley: University of California Press, 2006, and Karl Jacoby, *Crimes Against Nature: Squatters, Thieves, Poachers, and the Hidden History of American Conservation*, Berkeley: University of California Press, 2014.

16. Nik Heynen, Maria Kaika, and Eric Swyngedouw, "Urban Political Economy: Politicizing the Production of Urban Natures" in Nik Heynen, Maria Kaika, and Eric Swyngedouw, eds., *In the Nature of Cities: Urban Political Ecology and the Politics of Urban Metabolism*, New York: Routledge, 2006, 2.

17. Patrick Joyce, *Rule of Freedom: Liberalism and the Modern City*, New York: Verso, 2003.

18. On geopower, see Christophe Bonneuil and Jean-Baptiste Fressoz, *The Shock of the Anthropocene*, New York: Verso, 2016, 184–90.

19. For some of the more thoughtful examples of such geo-engineering schemes, see Tim Flannery, *Atmosphere of Hope: Searching for Solutions to the Climate Crisis*, New York: Atlantic Monthly Press, 2015.

20. Environmental blowback is intended to designate forms of urban-based fragility and vulnerability that may seem to resemble what Ulrich Beck calls risk society. It should be clear that I disagree with Beck's narrative of a nonreflexive modernity followed by a dawning awareness of the side-effects of modernization in recent decades. As I show in my discussions of Jamaica Bay and New Orleans, development often occurred *in spite of* the impact on the vulnerable rather than without knowledge of that impact. See Urlich Beck, *World Risk Society*, Cambridge: Polity, 1998.

21. Daniel Mundy, "Personal Interview," 24 February 2016.

22. Lisa Foderaro, "Pilot Program Aims to Save Jamaica Bay's Shrinking Marshes," *New York Times*, 14 October 2015.

23. Ibid.

24. Vittoria Di Palma, *Wasteland: A History*, New Haven, CT: Yale University Press, 2014, 94.

25. Steinberg, *Gotham Unbound*, 193.

26. J. R. McNeill, *Mosquito Empires: Ecology and War in the Greater Caribbean, 1620–1914*, New York: Cambridge University Press, 2010.

27. "Warfare on Mosquitos," *New York Times*, 23 May 1903.

28. Steinberg, *Gotham Unbound*, 194.

29. "Jamaica Bay To Be a Great World Harbor," *New York Times*, 13 March 1910.

30. "Jamaica Bay Development," *New York Times*, 13 March 1910.

31. John Locke, *Second Treatise of Government*, Thomas P. Peardon, ed., New York: Liberal Arts Press, 1952, 22.

32. Quoted in Mark Fiege, *Nature's Republic*, Seattle: University of Washington Press, 2012, 93.

33. Ibid., 94.

34. Albert J. Beveridge, "In Support of an American Empire," *Congressional Record*, 56 Cong., I Sess., 1899, 704–12.

35. Jedediah Purdy, *After Nature: A Politics for the Anthropocene*, Cambridge, MA: Harvard University Press, 2015, 161.

36. Ibid., 171.

37. Thorstein Veblen, *The Theory of the Leisure Class: An Economic Study of Institutions*, New York: Macmillan, 1899. On the modern advertising industry, see William Leach, *Land of Desire: Merchants, Power, and the Rise of a New American Culture*, New York: Vintage, 1994.

38. "Fight Port Treaty as Harmful Bill: Mayor Says Foreign Interests Are Back of Project for Interstate Harbor," *New York Times*, 13 April 1920.

39. "To Make Newark Bay a Big Port: The Jersey Meadows Being Transformed into a Busy Spot, with Docks and Reclaimed Land," *New York Times*, 27 June 1915.

40. Marc Levinson, *The Box: How the Shipping Container Made the World Smaller and the World Economy Bigger*, Princeton, NJ: Princeton University Press, 2006.

41. On the broader collapse of the oyster population in New York's waters, see Mark Kurlansky, *The Big Oyster: History on the Half Shell*, New York: Random House, 2007.

42. "Jamaica Bay, Foul With Sewage, Closed to Oyster Beds; 300,000 Bushels Gone," *New York Times*, 30 January 1921.

43. Ibid.

44. Priscilla Wald, *Contagious: Cultures, Carriers, and the Outbreak Narrative*, Durham, NC: Duke University Press, 2008, 68–112.

45. Ibid., 91.

46. Kate Orff, "Cosmopolitan Ecologies," in Alexander Brash, Jamie Hand and Kate Orff, eds., *Gateway: Visions for an Urban National Park*, New York: Princeton Architectural Press, 2011, 57.

47. Matthew Gandy, *Concrete and Clay: Reworking Nature in New York City*, Cambridge, MA: MIT Press, 2002, 109.

48. On the history of the externalizing of nature in mainstream economics, which took off in the 1890s, see Christophe Bonneuil and Jean-Baptiste Fressoz, *The Shock of the Anthropocene*, New York: Verso, 2015, 212.

49. Gandy, *Concrete and Clay*, 85.

50. Bonneuil and Fressoz, *The Shock of the Anthropocene*, 212.

51. For diverse accounts of the metabolic rift, see John Bellamy Foster, *Marx's Ecology: Materialism and Nature*, New York: Monthly Review Press, 2000, ix, and Jason W. Moore, *Capitalism in the Web of Life*, New York: Verso, 2015.

52. John Bellamy Foster, *Ecology Against Capitalism*, New York: Monthly Review Press, 2002, 160.

53. Patrick Joyce, *The Rule of Freedom: Liberalism and the Modern City*, New York: Verso, 2003, 67–75.

54. On the disruption of the nitrogen and phosphorus cycles as key elements of the contemporary environmental crisis, see John Bellamy Foster, Brett Clark, and Richard York, *The Ecological Rift: Capitalism's War on the Earth*, New York: Monthly Review Press, 2010, 14–18.

55. Joanne Abel Goldman, *Building New York's Sewers: Developing Mechanisms of Urban Management*, West Lafayette, IN: Purdue University Press, 1997.

56. "Polluted Beaches a Danger to City Bathers," *New York Times*, 17 July 1927.

57. Michael Specter, "Sea-Dumping Ban: Good Politics, But Not Necessarily Good Policy," *New York Times*, 22 March 1993.

58. Ibid.

59. "Jamaica Bay Project," n.d., New York City Audubon, nycaudubon.org

60. "History of the Ecowatchers," Jamaica Bay Ecowatchers, n.d.

61. Brett Branco, "Personal Interview," 27 February 2016.

62. On the competitive growth imperative, see Thomas Adams, "Discussion," *Proceedings of the Seventh National Conference on City Planning, Detroit, June 7–9, 1915*, Boston, 1915, 160, quoted in Steinberg, *Gotham Unbound*, 188.

63. On the contradictions of the Regional Plan Association, see Tom Angotti, *New York for Sale: Community Planning Confronts Global Real Estate*, Boston, MA: MIT Press, 208, 68.

64. Regional Plan Association, *The Graphic Regional Plan: Atlas and Description*, Vol. 1, New York: Regional Plan of New York and Its Environs, 1929, 327, quoted in Steinberg, *Gotham Unbound*, 188.

65. Steinberg, *Gotham Unbound*, 190.

66. Ibid., 309.
67. Cathy Newman, "A Tale of Two Ponds: NYC Park After the Storm," *National Geographic News,* 27 April 2013.
68. Daniel T. Rogers, *The Work Ethic in Industrial America, 1850–1920*, Chicago: University of Chicago Press, 1979, 109.
69. Orff, "Cosmopolitan Ecologies," 65.
70. Jonathan Mahler, "How the Coastline Became a Place to Put the Poor," *New York Times*, 3 December 2012, and Carol P. Kaplan and Lawrence Kaplan, *Between Ocean and City: The Transformation of Rockaway, New York*, New York: Columbia University Press, 2003.
71. Jamaica Bay Environmental Study Group, *Jamaica Bay and Kennedy Airport: A Multidisciplinary Environmental Study*, Vol. 2, Washington, DC: National Academy of Sciences, 1971, 87.
72. Ibid., 89.
73. *Gateway National Recreation Area: Hearings Before the Subcomm. On Parks and Recreation of the Comm. On Interior and Insular Affairs . . . on S. 1193 and S. 1852*, 92nd Cong. 160, 1971, 141.
74. Jamaica Bay Environmental Study Group, *Jamaica Bay and Kennedy Airport*, Vol. 2, 90.
75. For a critique of Ansel Adams's photographs of iconic Western landscape, see Emily Eliza Scott and Kristen Swenson, "Introduction: Contemporary Art and the Politics of Land Use" in Emily Eliza Scott and Kristen Swenson, eds., *Critical Landscapes: Art, Space, Politics*, Berkeley: University of California Press, 2015, 1–16.
76. Alexander Wilson, *The Culture of Nature: North American Landscape from Disney to the Exxon Valdez*, Cambridge, MA: Blackwell, 1992, 229.
77. Purdy, *After Nature*, 154.
78. Wilson, *The Culture of Nature*, 227.
79. William Cronon, "The Trouble With Wilderness; or, Getting Back to the Wrong Nature," in William Cronon, ed., *Uncommon Ground: Rethinking the Human Place in Nature*, New York: Norton, 1995, 69–90.
80. Jamaica Bay Environmental Study Group, *Jamaica Bay and Kennedy Airport* Vol. 2, 90.
81. Mundy, "Personal Interview."
82. Orff, "Cosmopolitan Ecologies," 70.
83. Ibid.
84. Ellen K. Hartig and Vivien Gornitz, "The Vanishing Marshes of Jamaica Bay: Sea Level Rise or Environmental Degradation?" *Goddard Institute for Space Studies Science Briefs*, December 2001.

85. "Marsh Restoration in Gateway," n.d., Gateway National Recreation Area, nps.gov/gate/learn/nature/marshrestoration.htm.
86. Branco, "Personal Interview."
87. "Proposed Expansion of JFK Airport," n.d., NYC Audubon.
88. "Animal Rights Group Sues to Stop Gull Shooting at JFK Airport," *AP News Archive*, 11 August 1992.
89. US Army Corps of Engineers, *North Atlantic Coast Comprehensive Study Report*, January 2015.
90. Matthew Schuerman, "Inside or Outside: Two Ways to Protect Jamaica Bay," *WNYC News*, 19 March 2015.
91. Catherine Seavitt, "Personal Interview," 7 March 2016.
92. On the MOSE project, see Antonia Windor, "Inside Venice's Bid To Hold Back the Tide," *The Guardian*, 16 June 2015.
93. Branco, "Personal Interview"; and Seavitt, "Personal Interview."
94. Structures of Coastal Resilience, structuresofcoastalresilience.org.
95. Catherine Seavitt, "Experimental Research Studio: Jamaica Bay," *Urban Omnibus*, 28 January 2015.
96. Ibid.
97. Ecoshape, "The Delfland Sand Engine," ecoshape.nl.
98. Schuerman, "Inside or Outside."
99. Shripad Dharmadhikary, *Mountains of Concrete: Dam Building in the Himalayas*, International Rivers.
100. Mackenzie Funk, *Windfall: the Booming Business of Global Warming*, New York: Penguin, 2014, 195.
101. "Isle de Jean Charles Community To Receive $52 Million to Relocate," *Houma Today*, 21 January 2016.
102. "The History," *Coastal Resettlement*.
103. Richard Campanella, "Beneficial Use: Balancing America's (Sediment) Budget: What Can We Do About the Catastrophic Erosion of American Coasts?" *Place Journal*, January 2013.
104. Nathaniel Rich, "The Most Ambitious Lawsuit Ever: A Quixotic Historian Tries to Hold Oil and Gas Companies Responsible for Louisiana's Disappearing Coast," *New York Times Magazine*, 3 October 2014.
105. Campanella, "Beneficial Use."
106. Mark Davis, "Personal Interview," 1 February 2016 citing Mark Carney, the governor of the Bank of England. See Larry Elliot, "Carney Warns of Risks from Climate Change "Tragedy of the Horizon,'" *The Guardian*, 29 September 2015.
107. Richard Campanella, *Delta Urbanism: New Orleans*, Chicago: American Planning Association, 2010, 3.
108. Ibid., 4.
109. Anuradha Mathur and Dilip Da Cunha, *Mississippi Floods: Designing a Shifting Landscape*, New Haven, CT: Yale University

Press, 2001, and *Design in the Terrain of Water*, Philadelphia: University of Pennsylvania Press, 2014.

110. Richard Condrey, "Personal Interview," 1 February 2016. See also Richard E. Condrey, Paul E. Hoffman, and D. Elaine Evers, "The Last Naturally Active Delta Complexes of the Mississippi River (LNDM): Discovery and Implications," in J. W. Day, G. P. Kemp, A. Freeman, and D. P. Muth, eds., *Perspectives on the Restoration of the Mississippi Delta*, New York: Springer, 2014.

111. Campanella, "Beneficial Use."

112. John Barry, *Rising Tide: The Great Mississippi Flood of 1927 and How It Changed America*, New York: Simon and Schuster, 1997.

113. John McPhee, *The Control of Nature*, New York: Farrar Straus Giroux, 1989, 7.

114. Ibid., 13.

115. In this regard, think about the phenomenon that Bonneuil and Fressoz describe as the "shock of the Anthropocene," the experience of suddenly waking up to anthropogenic climate change, despite the fact (illustrated at great length by the authors) that previous generations were well-aware of such environmental transformations. See Christophe Bonneuil and Jean-Baptiste Fressoz, *The Shock of the Anthropocene*, New York: Verso, 2015.

116. E. L. Corthell, "The Delta of the Mississippi River," *National Geographic* 8: 12, December 1897, 353.

117. Campanella, *Delta Urbanism*, 78.

118. Campanella, *Delta Urbanism*, 73.

119. Campanella, *Delta Urbanism*, 146–49.

120. Ibid.

121. Oliver Houk, "The Reckoning: Oil and Gas Development in the Louisiana Coastal Zone," *Tulane Environmental Law Journal* 28: 2, Summer 2015, 186–296.

122. These impacts are described, with abundant citational support, in Oliver Houk's long essay "The Reckoning."

123. Ibid., 218–19.

124. Ibid., 206.

125. On New Orleans as a new Atlantis, see John M. Barry, "Is New Orleans Safe?" *New York Times*, 1 August 2015, and David Uberti, "Is New Orleans in Danger of Becoming a New Atlantis?" *The Guardian*, 24 August 2015.

126. Houk, "The Reckoning," 207, 209.

127. Quoted in Ibid., 208.

128. Quoted in Ibid., 209.

129. John M. Barry, "Personal Interview," 20 January 2016. On the levee board lawsuit, see Nathaniel Rich, "The Most Ambitious Lawsuit Ever."

130. For a detailed history of the complicity of Louisiana politicians with the fossil fuel industry, see Houk's "The Reckoning."

131. Ibid., 221.

132. Ibid., 223.

133. Ibid., 230.

134. For an extended discussion of the culture of oil in Louisiana, see Stephanie Lemenager, *Living Oil: Petroleum Culture in the American Century*, New York: Oxford University Press, 2016.

135. Nathaniel Rich, "The Most Ambitious Lawsuit Ever."

136. Craig Colten, "Personal Interview," 21 March 2016.

137. Houk, "The Reckoning," 269.

138. Ibid., 274.

139. Barry, "Personal Interview."

140. US Department of the Treasury, *RESTORE Act,* treasury.gov.

141. Coastal Protection and Restoration Authority, *Current Coastal Master Plan,* 2012.

142. Quoted in Uberti, "Is New Orleans in Danger of Turning into a Modern-Day Atlantis?"

143. Ibid.

144. Suzanne Goldenberg, "Lost Louisiana: The Race To Reclaim Vanished Land from the Sea," *The Guardian,* 14 October 2014.

145. Quoted in Ibid.

146. Michael Blum and Harry Roberts, "The Drowning of the Mississippi Delta Due to Insufficient Sediment Supply and Global Sea-Level Rise," *Nature Geoscience* 2, June 2009, 488–91.

147. Condrey, "Personal Interview." See also Condrey, Hoffman, and Evers, "The Last Naturally Active Delta Complexes of the Mississippi River: Discovery and Implications" in J.W. Day et al, eds., *Perspectives on the Restoration of the Mississippi Delta,* Springer: Dordrecht, 2014.

148. For details on the diminished quantity of sediment being carried by the Mississippi, see Campanella, "Beneficial Use."

149. Barry, "Personal Interview."

150. Changing Course, "Changing Course Has Brought Together Teams of the World's Best Engineers, Scientists, Planners and Designers to Show the Art of the Possible in Creating a Self-sustaining Delta Ecosystem," n.d., changingcourse.us/the-competition/about-the-competition.

151. Ibid.

152. Baird Team, *A Delta For All,* February 2015, changingcourse.us.

153. Ibid., T-21.

154. Studio MISI-ZIIBI, *Living Delta: Changing Course for the 22nd Century,* February 2015, changingcourse.us.

155. Campanella, "Beneficial Use."

156. The Mississippi River Delta Science and Engineering Special Team, *Answering Ten Fundamental Questions About the Mississippi River Delta*, 2012.

157. Ibid.

158. Richard Condrey, Email correspondence with the author, 11 April 2016.

159. Uberti, "Is New Orleans in Danger of Becoming a Modern-Day Atlantis?"

160. Craig Colten, "Personal Interview," 21 March 2016.

161. Ibid.

162. Ibid.

163. On post-Katrina injustices, see Cedric Robinson, *The Neoliberal Deluge: Hurricane Katrina, Late Capitalism, and the Remaking of New Orleans*, Minneapolis: University of Minnesota Press, 2011; Kevin Fox Gotham and Miriam Greenberg, *Crisis Cities: Disaster and Development in New York and New Orleans*, New York: Oxford University Press, 2014; and Naomi Klein, *The Shock Doctrine*, New York: Picador, 2008.

164. Studio MISI-ZIIBI, *Living Delta*.

165. Ibid.

Chapter 3. Sea Change

1. Eddie Yuen, "The Politics of Failure Have Failed: The Environmental Movement and Catastrophism," in Sasha Lilley and David McNally, eds., *Catastrophism: The Apocalyptic Politics of Collapse and Rebirth*, Oakland, CA: PM Press, 2012.

2. Eric Rignot, "Global Warming: It's a Point of No Return in West Antarctica. What Happens Next?" *The Guardian*, 17 May 2014.

3. Chris Mooney, "The Melting of Antarctica Was Already Really Bad. It Just Got Worse." *The Washington Post*, 16 March 2015.

4. Rignot, "Global Warming."

5. M. Morlighem, E. Rignot, J Mouginot, H. Seroussi, and E. Larour, "Deeply Incised Submarine Glacial Valleys Beneath the Greenland Ice Sheet," *Nature Geoscience* 7, 2014, 418–22, doi:10.1038/ngeo2167.

6. J. L. Bamber and W. P. Aspinall, "An Expert Assessment of Future Sea Level Rise from the Ice Sheets," *Nature Climate Change*, 6 January 2013.

7. Nicola Jones, "Abrupt Sea Level Rise Looms as Increasingly Realistic Threat," *Yale Environment 360*, 6 May 2016.

8. "Ice Sheet Tipping Points," ClimateNexus.

9. Dale Jamieson, *Reason in a Dark Time: Why the Struggle Against Climate Change Failed—and What It Means for Our Future*, New York: Oxford University Press, 2014, 4.

10. E. M. Fischer and R. Knutti, "Anthropogenic Contribution to Global Occurrence of Heavy-Precipitation and High-Temperature Extremes," *Nature Climate Change*, 27 April 2015.

11. Mike Davis, "Who Will Build the Ark?" *New Left Review* 61, 2010, 33.

12. James Hansen, Makiko Sato, Paul Hearty, Reto Ruedy, Maxwell Kelley, Valerie Masson-Delmotte … and Kwok-Wai Lo, "Ice Melt, Sea Level Rise, and Superstorms: Evidence from Paleoclimate Data, Climate Modeling, and Modern Observations That 2°C Global Warming Could Be Dangerous," *Atmospheric Chemistry and Physics* 16, 2016, 3761–812.

13. Rob Nixon, *Slow Violence and the Environmentalism of the Poor*, Cambridge, MA: Harvard University Press, 2012.

14. Stephen Gardiner, *A Perfect Moral Storm: The Ethical Tragedy of Climate Change*, New York: Oxford University Press, 2013.

15. Robert J. Lifton and Greg Mitchell, *Hiroshima in America*, New York: Harper Perennial, 1996.

16. Kari Marie Norgaard, *Living in Denial: Climate Change, Emotions, and Everyday Life*, Cambridge, MA: MIT Press, 2011, 6.

17. Slavoj Zizek, *Living in the End Times*, New York: Verso, 2011.

18. Evan Calder Williams, *Combined and Uneven Apocalypse*, New York: Zero Books, 2011.

19. Ibid.

20. Ashley Dawson, "Documenting Accumulation By Dispossession" in Emily Eliza Scott and Kirsten Swenson, eds., *Critical Landscapes: Art, Space, Politics*, Berkeley: University of California Press, 2015.

21. Christian Parenti, *Tropic of Chaos: Climate Change and the New Geography of Violence*, New York: Nation Books, 2012, 4.

22. Ibid., 8–9.

23. Mike Davis, *Planet of Slums*, New York: Verso, 2006, 15.

24. Eric Hobsbawm, *Age of Extremes: A History of the World, 1914–1991*, New York: Pantheon, 1994, 288.

25. Micahel Kinyanjui, "Development Context and the Millennium Agenda." In *The Challenge of Slums: Global Report on Human Settlements 2003*, revised and updated version, April 2010, Nairobi, Kenya: UN-HABITAT.

26. Davis, *Planet of Slums,* 19.

27. See, for example, Jennifer Robinson, *Ordinary Cities: Between Modernity and Development*, New York: Routledge, 2006.

28. Davis, *Planet of Slums,* 121.

29. Ibid., 137.

30. Ibid., 142.
31. Mahmood Mamdani, *Citizen and Subject: Contemporary Africa and the Legacy of Late Colonialism,* Princeton, NJ: Princeton University Press, 1996.
32. Gordon McGranahan, Deborah Balk, and Bridget Anderson, "The Rising Tide: Assessing the Risks of Climate Change and Human Settlements in Low Elevation Coastal Zones." *Environment and Urbanization* 19: 1, 2007, 17–37.
33. Judy L. Baker, *Climate Change, Disaster Risk, and the Urban Poor: Cities Building Resilience for a Changing World,* Washington, DC: World Bank, 2012, 15.
34. S. V. Lall and U. Deichmann, "Density and Disasters: Economics of Urban Hazard Risk," *Policy Research Working Paper 5161,* Washington, DC: World Bank, 2009.
35. Brian Stone, Jr., *The City and the Coming Climate: Climate Change in the Places We Live,* New York: Cambridge University Press, 2012, 12.
36. Herman Boschken, "Global Cities Are Coastal Cities Too: A Paradox in Sustainability?" *Urban Studies* 50: 9, July 2013, 1760–78.
37. R. J. Nicholls, S. Hanson, Celine Herweijer, Nicola Patmore, Stéphane Hallegatte, Jan Corfee-Morlot . . . Robert Muir-Wood, "Ranking Port Cities With High Exposure and Vulnerability to Climate Extremes: Exposure Estimates," OECD Working Papers 1, Paris: OECD Publishing.
38. Ibid., 3.
39. S. F. Balica, N. G. Wright, N. Meulen, "A Flood Vulnerability Index for Coastal Cities and Its Use in Assessing Climate Change Impacts," *Natural Hazards* 64: 1, 2012, 73–105.
40. Hong Van and Sebastian Moffett, "The Quiet Sinking of the World's Deltas," *FutureEarth Blog.*
41. Stephen Graham, ed., *Disrupted Cities: When Infrastructure Fails,* New York: Routledge, 2009.
42. "Power Grid Failure: FAQs," *Hindustan Times,* 30 July 2012.
43. Rajesh Kumar Singh and Rakteem Katakey, "Worst India Outage Highlights 60 Years of Missed Targets," *Bloomberg Business,* 1 August 2012.
44. Stone, *The City and the Coming Climate,* 68.
45. Ibid., 81.
46. Ibid., 14.
47. Ibid., 66.
48. Raymond Williams, *The Country and the City,* New York: Oxford University Press, 1975.
49. Nik Heynen, Maria Kalka, and Erik Swyngedouw, "Urban Political Economy: Politicizing the Production of Urban Natures"

in Nik Heynen, Maria Kalka, and Erik Swyngedouw, eds., *In the Nature of Cities: Urban Political Ecology and the Politics of Urban Metabolism*, New York: Routledge, 2006, 2.

50. Ulrich Beck, *World at Risk*, New York: Polity, 2008.

51. Stephen Graham, "When Infrastructures Fail," in Stephen Graham, ed., *Disrupted Cities: When Infrastructure Fails*, New York: Routledge, 2009.

52. Max Page, *The City's End: Two Centuries of Fantasies, Fears, and Premonitions of New York's Destruction*, New Haven, CT: Yale University Press, 2008.

53. Ibid.

54. Melinda Cooper, *Life as Surplus: Biotechnology and Capitalism in the Neoliberal Era*, Seattle: University of Washington Press, 2008.

55. Melinda Cooper, "Turbulent Worlds," *Theory, Culture and Society* 27.2–3 (2010), 179.

56. Quoted in Atlas, "Is This the End?"

57. Michael Sorkin, ed., *Indefensible Space: The Architecture of the National Insecurity State*, New York: Routledge, 2007.

58. Joseph Masco, "Engineering Ruins and Affect," in Uli Linke and Danielle Taana Smith, eds., *Cultures of Fear: A Critical Reader*, Chicago: University of Chicago Press, 2009.

59. For a critical discussion of the new urbanology, one that informs my analysis, see Gleeson, *The Urban Condition*, New York: Routledge, 2014, 59–71. For typical examples of the new urbanologists, see Charles Montgomery, *Happy City: Transforming Our Lives Through Urban Design*, New York: Farrar, Straus, Giroux, 2014; Anthony Townsend, *Smart Cities: Big Data, Civic Hackers, and the Quest for a New Utopia*, New York: Norton, 2014; and Jeb Brugmann, *Welcome to the Urban Revolution: How Cities Are Changing the World*, New York: Bloombury, 2009.

60. Neil Smith, *The Urban Frontier: Gentrification and the Revanchist City*, New York: Routledge, 1996.

61. According to his website, for example, Brugmann is a "social entrepreneur" and "urban strategy consultant," while Townsend is an "American technology consultant" and Montgomery is the principal of the Happy City consultancy. In addition to being a professor at Harvard, Edward Glaeser is a senior fellow specializing in urban policy at the Manhattan Institute. See jebbrugmann.com and manhattan-institute.org/expert/edward-l-glaeser.

62. Edward Glaeser, *The Triumph of the City: How Our Greatest Invention Makes Us Richer, Smarter, Greener, Healthier and Happier*, New York: Penguin, 2012, 1.

63. Ibid., 8.

64. Glaeser in fact attributes the decline in crime in US cities to higher incarceration rates. See *Triumph of the City,* 110–11. For a critical history of zero-tolerance policing, see Christina Heatherton and Jordan T. Camp, eds., *Policing the Planet: Why the Policing Crisis Led to Black Lives Matter,* New York: Verso, 2016. The definitive scholarly debunking of the broken windows theory is Bernard Harcourt, *Illusion of Order: The False Promise of Broken Windows Policing,* Cambridge, MA: Harvard University Press, 2001.

65. Glaeser, *The Triumph of the City,* 9.

66. Ibid.

67. Ibid., 74.

68. For the self-reported happiness surveys, see Ibid.

69. Ibid., 75.

70. Davis, *Planet of Slums.*

71. David Owen, *Green Metropolis: Why Living Smaller, Living Closer, and Driving Less Are the Keys to Sustainability,* New York: Riverhead, 2009.

72. Davis, "Who Will Build the Ark?," 41.

73. Climate Works for All Coalition, *Elite Emissions: How the Homes of the Wealthiest New Yorkers Help Drive Climate Change,* 2016.

74. Matthew Kahn, *Climatopolis: How Our Cities Will Thrive in the Hotter Future,* New York: Basic Books, 2010.

75. Ibid., 181.

76. Ibid., 186.

77. Ibid., 7.

78. Ibid., 178.

79. Ibid., 8.

80. Peter Hall, *Good Cities, Better Lives: How Europe Discovered the Lost Art of Urbanism,* New York: Routledge, 2013.

81. Elizabeth Braw, "Rotterdam: Designing a Flood-Proof City to Withstand Climate Change," *The Guardian,* 18 November 2013.

82. Russell Shorto, "How to Think Like the Dutch in a Post-Sandy World," *New York Times,* 9 April 2014.

83. Orrin H. Pilkey, Linda Pilkey-Jarvis, and Keith C. Pilkey, *Retreat from a Rising Sea: Hard Choices in an Age of Climate Change,* New York: Columbia University Press, 2016, 63.

84. Giovanni Arrighi, *The Long Twentieth Century: Money, Power, and the Origins of Our Times,* New York: Verso, 1994.

85. For an overview of this history, see Tracy Metz and Maartje van den Heuvel, *Sweet and Salt: Water and the Dutch,* Rotterdam: nai010 publishers, 2012.

86. On the history of the Delta Works, see Han Meyer, Inge Bobbink, and Steffen Nijhuis, eds., *Delta Urbanism: The Netherlands,*

Chicago, IL: American Planning Association Planners Press, 2010.

87. On neoliberalism and the fragmentation of public infrastructure, see Stephen Graham, ed., *Disrupted Cities: When Infrastructure Fails*, New York: Routledge, 2009.

88. Metz and Van den Heuvel, *Sweet and Salt*, 282.

89. On the Second Delta Commission, see Han Meyer, Inge Bobbink, and Steffen Nijhuis, "Introduction: How to Deal with the Complexity of the Urbanized Delta" in Meyer et al., *Delta Urbanism*, xiv.

90. On the Dutch Room for the River program, see Han Meyer, "Delta City Rotterdam: Where It All Comes Together," in Meyer et al., *Delta Urbanism,* 155–65.

91. For a detailed discussion of IJburg, see Kimberley Kinder, *The Politics of Urban Water: Changing Waterscapes in Amsterdam*, Athens: University of Georgia Press, 2015, 94–116.

92. Ibid., 96.

93. The report "IJburg: Guest in Nature" is cited in Ibid., 107. For an overview of key concerns relating to IJburg, see Ibid., 110–12.

94. Kimberley Kinder, "Personal Interview," 12 April 2016.

95. Joep Janssen, "Personal Interview," 4 April 2016.

96. Tracy Metz, "Personal Interview," 22 June 2015.

97. Han Meyer, "Composition and Construction of Dutch Delta Cities," in Meyer et al., *Delta Urbanism*, 90.

98. Koen Olthuis, "Personal Interview," 13 October 2015.

99. Ibid.; Metz, "Personal Interview."

100. Daniel Goedbloed, "Extreme Rainfall & Rotterdam," Rotterdam Climate Initiative, lecture, available on youtube.com.

101. Orrin H. Pilkey, Linda Pilkey-Jarvis, and Keith C. Pilkey, *Retreat from a Rising Sea: Hard Choices in an Age of Climate Change*, New York: Columbia University Press, 2016, 62.

102. Klaus Jacob, "Personal Interview," 7 January 2016.

103. Jochem de Vries and Maarten Wolsink, "Making Space for Water: Spatial Planning and Water Management in the Netherlands," quoted in Tracy Metz and Maartje van den Heuval, *Sweet and Salt*, 282.

104. Ibid.

Chapter 4. The Jargon of Resilience

1. Oliver Wainwright, "Bjarke Ingels on the New York Dryline: 'We Think of It as the Lovechild of Robert Moses and Jane Jacobs,'" *The Guardian*, 9 March 2015.

2. See Mohsen Mostafavi, "Why Ecological Urbanism? Why Now?" in Mohsen Mostafavi, ed., *Ecological Urbanism*, New York: Lars Muller, 2010, 12, and Douglas Murphy, *Last Futures: Nature, Technology, and the End of Architecture*, New York: Verso, 2015.

3. Mostafavi, "Why Ecological Urbanism?" 13.

4. Ibid., 17.

5. Charles Waldheim, ed., *Landscape Urbanism Reader*, New York: Princeton Architectural Press, 2006, 11.

6. Mostafavi, "Why Ecological Urbanism? 40.

7. On tactical urbanism, see Mike Lydon and Arthony Garcia, *Tactical Urbanism: Short-Term Action for Long-Term Change*, Washington, DC: Island Press, 2015; Richard Burdett, Teddy Cruz, David Harvey, Saskia Sassen, Nader Terrain, and Pedro Gadanho, eds., *Uneven Growth: Tactical Urbanisms for Expanding Mega-Cities*, New York: MoMA, 2014.

8. Jaime Lerner, *Urban Acupuncture*, Washington, DC: Island Press, 2014.

9. For a discussion of indigenous forms of tactical urbanism in contemporary South America, a hotbed of such initiatives, see Justin McGuirk, *Radical Cities: Across Latin America in Search of a New Architecture*, New York: Verso, 2015.

10. Bruce Braun and Stephanie Wakefield, "Inhabiting the Postapocalyptic City," *Environment Planning D: Society and Space*, 2014, societyandspace.com.

11. Igor Linkov, Todd Bridges, Felix Kreuzig, Jennifer Decker, Cate Fox-Lent, Wolfgang Kröger, ... Thomas Thiel-Clemen, "Changing the Resilience Paradigm," *Nature Climate Change* 4, June 2014, 407.

12. Brad Evans and Julien Reid, *Resilient Life: The Art of Living Dangerously*, New York: Polity, 2014.

13. Judith Rodin, "Preface," in Barry Bergdoll, *Rising Currents: Projects for New York's Waterfront*, New York: MOMA, 2011, 9.

14. On such complex, open systems, see Jane Bennett, *Vibrant Matter*, Durham, NC: Duke University Press, 2010, and William Connolly, *A World of Becoming*, Durham, NC: Duke University Press, 2012.

15. Julien Reid, "Interrogating the Neoliberal Biopolitics of the Sustainable Development-Resilience Nexus," *International Political Sociology* 7, 2013, 353–67.

16. Rebuild By Design, rebuildbydesign.org.

17. Lilah Raptopoulos, "Congress Allocated Billions for Sandy Relief," *The Guardian*, 8 December 2014.

18. The Rockefeller Foundation, Rebuild By Design.

19. Josh Bisker, Amy Chester, and Tara Eisenberg, eds., *Rebuild By Design*, Madison, WI: American Printing Company, 2015, 26.
20. Ibid., 239.
21. Ibid., 68.
22. Lilah Raptopoulos, "'Are We Safe? Of Course Not': Climate Scientist's Warning After Sandy," *The Guardian*, 5 November 2014.
23. Superstorm Research Lab, *A Tale of Two Sandys*, 2013.
24. Adam Yarinsky, "Personal Interview," 23 July 2015.
25. Jim Dwyer, "Still Building at the Edges of the City, Even as the Tides Rise," *New York Times*, 4 December 2012.
26. Charles Bagli, "Redevelopment of Manhattan's Far West Side Gains Momentum," *New York Times*, 19 June 2015.
27. Julie Sze, *Noxious New York: The Racial Politics of Urban Health and Environmental Justice*, Cambridge, MA: MIT Press, 2007, 81.
28. Ibid., 84.
29. Elizabeth Dwoskin, "Columbia Ignores Peril," *The Village Voice*, 1 October 2008.
30. Ibid.
31. Coalition to Preserve Community, "White Paper: FAQ's on the Proposed Biohazard Bathtub," bathtubtalk.typepad.com.
32. Richard Pérez-Peña, "On the Front Lines of the Virus War," *New York Times*, 31 October 2003.
33. Coalition to Preserve Community, "White Paper: FAQ's on the Proposed Biohazard Bathtub."
34. Bisker et al., *Rebuild by Design*, 147.
35. Ibid., 154.
36. Ibid., 158.
37. Ibid.
38. Ibid., 159.
39. New York City Environmental Justice Alliance, "Waterfront Justice Project," nyc-eja.org.
40. Caroline Spivack, "Bronx's Asthma Alley Protests Plans to Extend Power Plant Permits," *City Limits*, 12 November 2015.
41. Ibid.
42. Mychal Johnson, "Personal Interview," 7 January 2016.
43. Bisker et al., *Rebuild By Design*, 156.
44. Patrick Wall, "Bronx Gains Jobs and People, But Suffers from High Unemployment," *DNAInfo*, 12 July 2013.
45. Johnson, "Personal Interview."
46. See Bronx Environmental Stewardship Academy, ssbx.org/best-academy.
47. South Bronx Unite, *Principles for Private Development*, southbronxunite.org/principles-for-private-development.
48. Ibid.

49. Ibid.
50. South Bronx Unite, "State 'Priority Project'," southbronxunite. org/a-waterfront-re-envisioned/state-designation-as-priority-project-on-draft-open-space-plan.
51. Johnson, "Personal Interview."
52. Department of Homeland Security, *Welcome to the Centers of Excellence,* dhs.gov/science-and-technology/centers-excellence.
53. Department of Housing and Urban Development, *National Disaster Resilience Competition,* hudexchange.info/programs/cdbg-dr/resilient-recovery.
54. Judith Rodin, *The Resilience Dividend: Being Strong in a World Where Things Go Wrong,* New York: Public Affairs, 2014.
55. The World Bank, *Resilient Cities Program.*
56. Kathleen Tierney, "Resilience and the Neoliberal Project: Discourses, Critiques, Practices – And Katrina," *American Behavioral Scientist* 59.10 (Sept 2015), 1335.
57. C.S. Holling, Quoted in Timothy Beatley, *Planning for Coastal Resilience: Best Practices for Calamitous Times,* Washington, DC: Island Press, 2009, 3.
58. Andrew Zolli and Ann Marie Healy, *Resilience: Why Things Bounce Back,* New York: Free Press, 2012, 6.
59. Jianguo Wu and Tong Wu, "Ecological Resilience as a Foundation of Urban Design and Sustainability" in S.T.A. Pickett, M.L. Cadenasso, and Brian McGrath, eds., *Resilience in Ecology and Urban Design: Linking Theory and Practice for Sustainable Cities,* New York: Springer, 2013, 213.
60. *Report of the World Commission on Environment and Development: Our Common Future,* UN Documents.
61. Ibid., 20.
62. Ibid., 21–22.
63. Mike Davis, *Planet of Slums,* New York: Verso, 2006, 62.
64. Ingolfur Blühndorn, "Sustainability–Post-sustainability–Unsustainability," in Teena Gabrielson, Cheryl Hall, John M. Meyer, and David Schlosberg, eds., *The Oxford Handbook of Environmental Political Theory,* New York: Oxford University Press, 2015.
65. Joseph Schumpeter, *Capitalism, Socialism, and Democracy,* London: Routledge, 1994, 82–83.
66. On ecological resilience, see Jianguo Wu and Tong Wu, "Ecological Resilience," in Pickett, 215.
67. See, for example, Jane Bennett, *Vibrant Matter: A Political Ecology of Things,* Durham, NC: Duke University Press, 2010.
68. Isabelle M. Côté and Emily S. Darling, "Rethinking Ecosystem Resilience in the Face of Climate Change," *PLOS/Biology,* 27 July 2010.

69. Wu and Wu, "Ecological Resilience," 216.
70. Rodin, *The Resilience Dividend*, 3.
71. Kathleen Tierney, "Resilience and the Neoliberal Project," *American Behavioral Scientist* 59: 10 (2015), 7.
72. On the inextricably intertwined history of capitalism and climate change, see Andreas Malm, *Fossil Capital: The Rise of Steam Power and the Roots of Global Warming*, New York: Verso, 2016.
73. Naomi Klein, *This Changes Everything*, New York: Simon and Schuster, 2015.
74. Melinda Cooper and Jeremy Walker, "Genealogies of Resilience: From Systems Ecology to the Political Economy of Crisis Adaptation," *Security Dialogue* 42: 2 (2011), 146.
75. Ibid., 149.
76. Friedrich von Hayek, "The Pretense of Knowledge," *The American Economic Review* 79: 6, December 1989, 6.
77. Ibid.
78. Ibid., 7.
79. Paul Lewis, "The Emergence of 'Emergence' in the Work of F.A. Hayek: An Historical Analysis" (p. 4), *Social Science Research Network*.
80. Ibid., 6.
81. Ibid., 35.
82. Chris Zebrowski, "The Nature of Resilience," *Resilience: International Practices, Policies and Discourses* 1: 3, 2013, 166.
83. Hayek, The Pretense of Knowledge," 7.
84. Tom Slater, "The Resilience of Neoliberal Urbanism," *Open Security: Conflict and Peacebuilding Forum,* 28 January 2014.
85. Judith Rodin, "Realizing the Resilience Dividend," *Rockefeller Foundation Blog* (22 January 2014).
86. For a list of the foundation's "platform partners," see 100resilientcities.org/partners.
87. On Veolia and the global privatization of water, see Karen Piper, *The Price of Thirst: Global Water Inequality and the Coming Chaos*, Minneapolis: University of Minnesota Press, 2014.
88. Tierney, "Resilience and the Neoliberal Project," 12.
89. On corruption in post-Katrina New Orleans, see Vicanne Adams, *Markets of Sorrow, Labors of Faith: New Orleans in the Wake of Katrina*, Durham, NC: Duke University Press, 2013, and Naomi Klein, *The Shock Doctrine*, New York: Knopf, 2007.
90. Slater, "The Resilience of Neoliberal Urbanism."
91. For a discussion of Chicago School urban doctrines, see Andrew Ross, *The Chicago Gangster Theory of Life: Nature's Debt to Society*, New York: Verso, 1995.

92. Ila Berman, "From Inundation to Scarcity," in Anuradha Mathur and Dilip Da Cunha, eds., *Design in the Terrain of Water*, Philadelphia: University of Pennsylvania Press, 2014, 114.

93. Philip E. Steinberg, "Of Other Seas: Metaphors and Materialities in Maritime Regions," *Atlantic Studies* 10 :2, 2013, 156–69.

94. Anuradha Mathur and Dilip Da Cunha, "Waters Everywhere," in Anuradha Mathur and Dilip Da Cunha, eds., *Design in the Terrain of Water*, Philadelphia: University of Pennsylvania Press, 2014, 1.

95. See, for instance, Bruno Latour, *We Have Never Been Modern*, Cambridge, MA: Harvard University Press, 1993, and, more recently, Eben Kirksey, *Emergent Ecologies*, Durham, NC: Duke University Press, 2015.

96. "Governor Cuomo Announces $60 Million Living Breakwaters Barrier to Protect Staten Island Shoreline and Habitat," governor.ny.gov.

97. Bill Browning, *IDEA Index,* The Buckminster Fuller Institute, bfi.org/ideaindex/projects/2014/living-breakwaters.

98. Bisker et al., *Rebuild By Design*, 178.

99. Ibid., 184.

100. Ibid., 186.

101. Ibid., 185.

102. billionoysterproject.org.

103. On fluidity and urban design, see Mathur and De Cunha, "Waters Everywhere"; Timothy Beatley, *Biophilic Cities: Integrating Nature into Urban Design and Planning*, Washington, DC: Island Press, 2010; Neeraj Bhatia and Lola Sheppard, eds., *Bracket 2: Goes Soft*, Barcelona and New York: ACTAR, 2013; Bruno De Meulder and Kelly Shannon, eds., *Water Urbanisms East*, Zurich: Park Books, 2013; Chris Reed and Nina-Marie Lister, eds., *Projective Ecologies*, Cambridge, MA: ACTAR, 2014.

104. Anthony Fontenot, Carol McMichael Reese, and Michael Sorkin, eds., *New Orleans Under Construction: The Crisis of Planning*, New York: Verso, 2014.

105. Elizabeth Rush, "Leaving the Sea: Staten Islanders Experiment With Managed Retreat," *Urban Omnibus*, 11 February 2015.

106. Ibid.

107. Mary Kate Leming, "Dunes vs. Sea Walls: Stopping Sand Loss Is a Complicated Business," *The Coastal Star*, thecoastalstar.ning.com.

108. Lisa Fletcher, "Ocean Acidification is Killing Baby Oysters," *Al Jazeera*, 19 June 2015.

109. "Ocean Acidifications' Impact on Oysters and Other Shellfish," *National Oceanic and Atmospheric Administration*, pmel.noaa.gov.

110. Siri Srinivas, "Oysters, Clams, and Scallops Face High Risk from Ocean Acidification, New Study Finds," *The Guardian*, 23 February 2015.

111. Julia Ekstrom, Lisa Suatoni, Sarah R. Cooley, Linwood H. Pendleton, George G. Waldbusser, Josh E. Cinner . . . Rosimeiry Portela, "Vulnerability and Adaptation of US Shellfisheries to Ocean Acidification," *Nature Climate Change* 5, March 2015, 209.

112. Ulf Riebesell and Jean-Pierre Gattuso, "Lessons Learned from Ocean Acidification Research," *Nature Climate Change* 5, January 2015, 12–14.

Chapter 5. Climate Apartheid

1. American Museum of Natural History, *Rethinking Home Blog*.

2. Laura Gottesdiener, Rachel Falcone, and Michael Premo (for *Sandy Storyline*), "The Time In Between: Displacement After Hurricane Sandy," *Creative Time Reports*, 15 July 2013.

3. Leila Rassi, "We Are Tired," *Rethinking Home Blog*, 9 April 2014, American Museum of Natural History.

4. *Sandy Storyline,* sandystoryline.com.

5. Gottesdiener et al., "The Time In Between."

6. Leila Rassi, "We Are Tired."

7. Cited in Gottesdiener et al., "The Time In Between."

8. Internal Displacement Monitoring Centre, *Global Report 2016*

9. Mike Pesca, "Are Katrina's Victims 'Refugees' or 'Evacuees?'" *National Public Radio Reporter's Notebook*, 5 September 2005.

10. For additional discussion of the representation of Katrina "refugees," see Cedric Johnson, *The Neoliberal Deluge: Hurricane Katrina, Late Capitalism, and the Remaking of New Orleans*, Minneapolis: University of Minnesota Press, 2011.

11. Ibid.

12. Adam Vaughan, "French Minister Warns of Mass Climate Change Migration if World Doesn't Act," *The Guardian,* 26 May 2016.

13. Ibid.

14. Ibid.

15. Patrick Bond, "Who Wins From 'Climate Apartheid'?" *New Politics* 15: 4, Winter 2016.

16. Ibid.

17. Ibid.

18. Griff Witte, "New U.N. Report Says World's Refugee Crisis Is Worse than Anyone Expected," *Washington Post*, 18 June 2015.

19. Colin P. Kelley et al., "Climate Change in the Fertile Crescent and the Implications of the Recent Syrian Drought," *Proceedings of the National Academy of Sciences* 112: 11, March 2015.

20. Nafeez Ahmed, "Peak Oil, Climate Change, and Pipeline Geopolitics Driving Syria Conflict," *The Guardian*, 13 May 2013.

21. Christian Parenti, *Tropic of Chaos: Climate Change and the New Geography of Violence*, New York: Nation Books, 2010.

22. UNHCR, *Global Report 2015*.

23. Griff Witte, "New U.N. Report Says World's Refugee Crisis is Worse than Anyone Expected," *Washington Post*, 18 June 2015.

24. International Refugee Assistance Project, *IRAP Berkeley January 2016 Beirut Trip*, law.berkeley.edu.

25. "Refugee Deaths in Mediterranean Hit 10,000," *EurActiv*, 7 June 2016.

26. Amnesty International, "Syria's Refugee Crisis in Numbers," February 2016.

27. Kenan Malik, "Migrants Face Fortress Europe's Deadly Moat," *New York Times*, 21 April 2015.

28. Ibid.

29. Naomi Klein, "Let Them Drown: The Violence of Othering in a Warming World," *London Review of Books* 38: 11, 2 June 2016.

30. Peter Yeung, "Kenya to Close All Refugee Camps and Displace 600,000 People," *The Independent*, 8 May 2016.

31. A.J. Vicens, "The Obama Administration's Two Million Deportations, Explained," *Mother Jones*, 4 April 2014.

32. Peter Wagner and Bernadette Rabuy, "Mass Incarceration: The Whole Pie 2016," *Prison Policy Initiative*, 14 March 2016.

33. Jenna Loyd, Matt Michelson, and Andrew Burridge, "Introduction: Borders, Prisons, and Abolitionist Visions," in Jenna Loyd, Matt Michelson, and Andrew Burridge, eds., *Beyond Walls and Cages: Prisons, Borders, and Global Crisis*, Athens: University of Georgia Press, 2015, 8.

34. Gregory White, *Climate Change and Migration*, New York: Oxford University Press, 2010, 9.

35. Ibid., 7.

36. James Morrissey, "Rethinking the 'Debate on Environmental Refugees': From 'Maximalists and Minimalists' to 'Proponents and Critics,'" *Journal of Political Ecology* 19, 2012, 36–49.

37. Essam El-Hinnawi, *Environmental Refugees*, Nairobi: United Nations Environment Programme, 1985.

38. Quoted in White, *Climate Change and Migration*, 21.

39. Jodi L. Jacobson, "Environmental Refugees: A Yardstick of Habitability," *Bulletin of Science, Technology and Society* 8: 3, June 1988, 257–58.

40. "General Assembly President Says 'Climate Refugees' Are Already a Reality," *UN New Centre*, 24 June 2008.

41. Norman Myers and Jennifer Kent, *Environmental Exodus, An Emergent Crisis in the Global Arena*, Washington, DC: The Climate Institute, 1995.

42. Axel Bojanowski, "Feared Migration Hasn't Happened: UN Embarrassed by Forecast on Climate Refugees," *Der Speigel*, 18 April 2011.

43. Cecilia Tacoli, "Crisis or Adaptation? Migration and Climate Change in a Context of High Mobility," *Environment and Urbanization* 21: 2, October 2009, 513–21.

44. Fred Pearce, "UN Climate Report Is Cautious about Making Specific Predictions," *Environment 360*, 24 March 2014.

45. John Queally, "World's First Climate Refugee Rebuffed by New Zealand," *Common Dreams*, 26 November 2013.

46. Ibid.

47. Ibid.

48. Andrew Ross, "Climate Debt Denial," *Dissent* 63: 3, 2013.

49. Hannah Arendt, *The Origins of Totalitarianism*, New York: Meridian, 1958, 298.

50. Jill Williams, "The Spatial Paradoxes of 'Radical' Activism," *Antipode*, 13 January 2014.

51. Miriam Ticktin, *Casualties of Care: Immigration and the Politics of Humanitarianism in France*, Berkeley: University of California Press, 2011.

52. Jane McAdam, *Climate Change, Forced Migration, and International Law*, New York: Oxford University Press, 2012.

53. Rob Nixon, *Slow Violence and the Environmentalism of the Poor*, Cambridge, MA: Harvard University Press, 2012.

54. McAdam, *Climate Change, Forced Migration, and International Law,* 186.

55. James Hansen, "Letter to Kevin Rudd," 2008, columbia.edu.

56. Jessica Tuchman Mathews, "Redefining Security," *Foreign Affairs* 68: 2, 1 April 1989, 162–77.

57. Akhil Gupta, "Is Poverty a Global Security Threat?" in Ananya Roy, ed., *Territories of Poverty: Rethinking North and South*, Athens, GA: University of Georgia Press, 2015, 94.

58. Quoted in Ibid., 93.

59. Ibid., 95.

60. Mathews, 167–68.

61. Michael Sorkin, "Introduction: The Fear Factor" in Michael Sorkin, ed., *Indefensible Space: The Architecture of the National Security State*, New York: Routledge, 2007.

62. Ibid., xiii.

63. Stuart Hall, Chas Critcher, Tony Jefferson, John Clarke, and Brian Roberts, *Policing the Crisis: Mugging, the State, and Law and Order*, New York: Palgrave Macmillan, 1978.
64. See my book *Mongrel Nation: Diasporic Culture and the Making of Postcolonial Britain*, Ann Arbor: University of Michigan Press, 2007.
65. Joseph Nevins, *Operation Gatekeeper: The Rise of the "Illegal Alien" and the Making of the US-Mexico Boundary*, New York: Routledge, 2002.
66. Étienne Balibar, *We, the People of Europe? Reflections on Transnational Citizenship,* Princeton, NJ: Princeton University Press, 2004, 43.
67. Ibid., 44.
68. Ibid., 35–36.
69. Al Gore, *Earth in the Balance: Ecology and the Human Spirit*, New York: Plume, 1992.
70. Ibid., 28–29.
71. Ibid,, 34.
72. Ibid. 319–37.
73. Ibid., 335.
74. Ibid., 307–14.
75. Ibid., 309.
76. Thomas Homer-Dixon, *Environmental Scarcity and Global Security*, New York: Foreign Policy Association, 1993.
77. Thomas Homer-Dixon, "Environmental Scarcity and Violent Conflict: Evidence from Cases," *International Security* 19: 1 (Summer 1994), 9.
78. Ibid., 5.
79. Ibid., 20.
80. Ibid., 21–23.
81. Ibid., 36.
82. Ibid.
83. Robert Kaplan, *The Coming Anarchy: Shattering the Dreams of the Post Cold War*, New York: Random House, 2000, 5.
84. Ibid.
85. Ibid., 7.
86. Ibid.
87. Ibid., 20.
88. On the revived environmental determinism of popular authors like Kaplan and Jared Diamond, see Andrew Sluyter, "Neo-Environmental Determinism, Intellectual Damage Control, and Nature/Society Science," *Antipode* 35: 4, November 2003, 813–17.
89. Kaplan, *The Coming Anarchy*, 20.
90. Kaplan, *The Coming Anarchy,* 30. See Francis Fukuyama, *The End of History and the Last Man*, New York: Free Press, 1992.

91. Kaplan, *The Coming Anarchy*, 45.
92. Harlan K. Ullman and James P. Wade, *Shock And Awe: Achieving Rapid Dominance* (National Defense University, 1996), XXIV.
93. Jeffrey Sachs, "The Strategic Significance of Global Inequality," *The Washington Quarterly* 24: 3 (Summer 2001), 187–98.
94. Peter Schwartz and Doug Randall, *An Abrupt Climate Change Scenario and Its Implications for United States National Security*, Office of Net Assessment, US Department of Defense, 2003.
95. Ibid., 2.
96. Ibid.
97. Ibid., 4.
98. Department of Defense, *Quadrennial Defense Review*, 2014.
99. Center for a New American Security, *The Age of Consequences: The Foreign Policy and National Security Implications of Global Climate Change*, 2007.
100. On the history and significance of scenario planning, see Melinda Cooper, "Turbulent Worlds: Financial Crisis and Environmental Crisis," *Theory, Culture and Society* 27: 2–3, March/May 2010, 167–90.
101. Center for a New American Security, *The Age of Consequences*, 5–6.
102. On the concept of turbulence across financial and environmental realms, see Cooper, "Turbulent Worlds."
103. Center for a New American Security, *The Age of Consequences*, 55.
104. Ibid., 56.
105. Ibid, 6.
106. Ibid, 59.
107. Ibid, 7.
108. Ibid.
109. Ibid, 77.
110. Ibid, 78.
111. Ibid., 82.
112. Ibid., 7.
113. Angela Evancie, "So Hot Right Now: Has Climate Change Created a New Literary Genre?" *Weekend Edition Saturday*, 20 April 2013, npr.org.
114. Doctors Without Borders, *MSF Calls for Large-Scale Search and Rescue Operation in the Mediterranean*, 19 April 2015.
115. Charles Heller and Lorenzo Pezzani, *Death By Rescue: The Lethal Effects of the EU's Policy of Non-Assistance At Sea*, Forensic Oceanography/Architecture Project, University of York & Goldsmith's, University of London, 2015.
116. "Massive Deaths in Border Desert Caused by US Immigration Policy," *Buzzflash*, 3 February 2015.

117. For a brilliant discussion of the proliferation of borders on various scales, see Sandro Mezzadra and Brett Neilson, *Border as Method, or, the Multiplication of Labor*, Durham, NC: Duke University Press, 2013.

118. Ilker Ataç, Stefanie Kron, Sarah Schilliger, Helge Schwiertz, and Maurice Stierl, "Struggles of Migration as In-/Visible Politics," *Movements*, 1: 2, 2015, 1–18.

119. Kaplan, *The Coming Anarchy*, 17.

120. Ibid., 27.

121. See, for example, Edward Glaeser, *The Triumph of the City: How Our Greatest Invention Makes Us Richer, Smarter, Greener, Healthier, and Happier*, New York: Penguin, 2012.

122. Jennifer Robinson, *Ordinary Cities: Between Modernity and Development*, New York: Routledge, 2006, 5.

123. Johannes Fabian, *Time and the Other: How Anthropology Makes Its Other*, New York: Columbia University Press, 2002.

124. Robinson, *Ordinary Cities*, 5.

125. Rem Koolhaas, Stefano Boeri, Sanford Kwnter, Nadia Tazi, and Hans Ulrich Obrist, *Mutations*, New York: Actar, 2000, 632.

126. Koolhaas et al., *Mutations*, 715.

127. Robinson, *Ordinary Cities*, 91.

128. Kaplan, *The Coming Anarchy*, 49.

129. Michelle Alexander, *The New Jim Crow: Mass Incarceration in the Age of Colorblindness*, New York: New Press, 2012. On the globalization of US policing strategies, see Jordan T. Camp and Christina Heatherton, eds., *Policing the Planet: Why the Policing Crisis Led to Black Lives Matter*, New York: Verso, 2016.

130. David Kilcullen, *Out of the Mountains: The Coming Age of the Urban Guerrilla*, New York: Oxford University Press, 2013, 237.

131. Ibid., 30.

132. On military operations in urban terrain, see my article "Combat in Hell: Cities As The Achilles' Heel of US Imperial Hegemony," *Social Text* 25, Summer 2007, 169–80.

133. Kilcullen, *Out of the Mountains*, 265.

134. Ibid., 257.

135. Ibid., 259.

136. David Kilcullen Bio, New America Think Tank.

137. Roberto González, "Seeing Into Hearts and Minds, Part 2: 'Big Data,' Algorithms, and Computational Counterinsurgency" *Anthropology Today* 31: 4, August 2015, 15.

138. Roberto González, "Seeing Into Hearts and Minds, Part 1: The Pentagon's Quest for a 'Social Radar'" *Anthropology Today* 31: 3, June 2015, 9.

139. Ibid.

140. Caerus Associates, *Mapping the Conflict in Aleppo, Syria,* February 2014.

141. Caerus Associates, *Mapping the Conflict,* 3.

142. Darwin BondGraham and Ali Winston, "From Fallujah to the San Fernando Valley, Police Use Analytics to Target "High-Crime" Areas, *truthout,* 12 March 2014.

143. Ibid.

144. Ali Winston, "Arizona Bill Would Fund Predictive Policing Technology," *Reveal News,* 25 March 2015.

145. Hall et al., *Policing the Crisis,* 184.

146. Romain Felli, "Managing Climate Insecurity by Ensuring Continuous Capital Accumulation: 'Climate Refugees' and 'Climate Migrants,'" *New Political Economy* 18: 3, 2013, 337–63. See also Hedda Ransan-Cooper, Carol Farbotko, Karen E. McNamara, Fanny Thornton, and Emilie Chevalier, "Being(s) Framed: The Means and Ends of Framing Environmental Migrants," *Global Environmental Change* 35, 2015, 106–15.

147. Jon Barnett et M. Webber, "Accommodating Migration to Promote Adaptation to Climate Change," *World Bank Policy Research Working Paper,* No. 5270, 2010.

148. Jane McAdam, "Do Climate Change 'Refugees' Exist?", Professorial Lecture Series, University of New South Wales School of Law, July 2011.

149. Foresight/The Government Office for Science, *Migration and Global Environmental Change: Final Project Report,* 2011.

150. Ibid., 13.

151. Ibid., 67.

152. Ibid., 109.

153. This is the central thrust of Mike Davis's *Planet of Slums: Urban Involution and the Informal Working Class,* New York: Verso, 2006.

154. Foresight/The Government Office for Science, *Migration and Global Environmental Change,* 175.

155. Ibid.

156. Ibid.

157. The seminal essay in articulating this critique of the apartheid labor regime is Michael Burawoy's "The Functions and Reproduction of Migrant Labor: Comparative Material from Southern Africa and the United States," *American Journal of Sociology* 81: 5, 1977, 1050–87.

158. Susan Ferguson and David McNally, "Capitalism's Unfree Global Workforce," *Open Democracy,* 20 February 2015.

159. Felli, "Managing Climate Insecurity," 338.

Chapter 6. Disaster Communism

1. World Bank, *Turn Down the Heat: Why a 4° Warmer World Must Be Avoided*, November 2012.
2. International Energy Agency, *World Energy Outlook*, 25 November 2011.
3. On previous and current mass extinction events, see my *Extinction: A Radical History*, New York, O/R Books, 2016.
4. Evan Calder Williams, *Combined and Uneven Apocalypse*, Ropley: Zero Books, 2010. Williams's arguments interestingly parallel those made about African societies by James Ferguson in *Global Shadows: Africa in the Neoliberal World Order*, Durham, NC: Duke University Press, 2006.
5. Mike Davis, "Who Will Build the Ark?", *New Left Review* 61, 2010, 41.
6. Christophe Bonneuil and Jean-Baptiste Fressoz, *The Shock of the Anthropocene*, New York: Verso, 2016.
7. Andreas Malm, *Fossil Capitalism: The Rise of Steam and the Roots of Global Warming*, New York: Verso, 2016; Timothy Mitchell, *Carbon Democracy: Political Power in the Age of Oil*, New York: Verso, 2013.
8. On disaster capitalism, see Naomi Klein, *The Shock Doctrine: The Rise of Disaster Capitalism*, New York: Picador, 2008. In relation to rebuilding processes in New Orleans and New York, see Kevin Fox Gotham and Miriam Greenberg, *Crisis Cities: Disaster and Redevelopment in New York and New Orleans*, New York: Oxford University Press, 2014.
9. Rebecca Solnit, *A Paradise Built in Hell: The Extraordinary Communities that Arise in Disaster*, New York: Viking, 2009.
10. Ibid., 7.
11. Jodi Dean, *The Communist Horizon*, New York: Verso, 2012.
12. Out of the Woods Blog, "Disaster Communism, Part 1," 8 May 2014.
13. See, for example, Diane E. Davis, "Reverberations: Mexico City's 1985 Earthquake and the Transformation of the Capital" in Thomas J. Campanella and Lawrence J. Vale, eds., *The Resilient City: How Modern Cities Recover from Disaster*, New York: Oxford University Press, 2005.
14. Andreas Malm, "Tahrir Submerged? Five Theses on Revolution in the Age of Climate Change," *Capitalism Nature Socialism*, March 2014.
15. Ibid., 4.
16. Ibid., 5.
17. Eric Klinenberg, *Heat Wave: A Social Autopsy of Disaster in Chicago*, Chicago, IL: University of Chicago Press, 2003.

18. Malm, "Tahrir Submerged?" 7.
19. Ben Wisner, "Flood Prevention and Mitigation in the People's Republic of Mozambique," *Disasters* 3: 3, 1979, 305.
20. Kevin Anderson, "Climate Change Going Beyond Dangerous: Brutal Numbers and Tenuous Hope" *Development Dialogue* 61, 2012, 25.
21. Ibid.
22. Malm, "Tahrir Submerged?" 11.
23. For an overview of these liberal attacks, see John Bellamy Foster and Brett Clark, "Crossing the River of Fire: The Liberal Attack in Naomi Klein and *This Changes Everything*," *Monthly Review* 66: 9, February 2015.
24. For a discussion of García Linera's writings, see Bruno Bosteels, *The Actuality of Communism*, New York: Verso, 2011, 226–68.
25. Mike Davis, "Who Will Build the Ark?" 43.
26. Daniel Aldana Cohen, "The Urban Green Wars," *Jacobin* (11 Dec 2015).
27. Ramachandra Guha and Juan Martinez-Alier, *Varieties of Environmentalism: Essays North and South*, New York: Routledge, 1997, 12.
28. Peter Rugh, "Climate Change Lifts the Lid Off Inequality in New York City," n.d., *Occupy Wall Street*.
29. Conor Tomás Reed, "Personal Interview," 25 May 2015.
30. On mutualism and revolution, see Marina Sitrin and Dario Azzellini, *They Can't Represent Us! Reinventing Democracy from Greece to Occupy*, New York: Verso, 2014.
31. Homeland Security Studies and Analysis Institute, *The Resilient Social Network,* 30 September 2013, anser.org.
32. Devin Balkind, "Personal Interview," 10 June 2015.
33. For a synoptic overview of Occupy Sandy's use of social media, see Homeland Security Studies and Analysis Institute, *The Resilient Social Network*, 30 September 2013,
34. On autonomy and other anarchist precepts in recent global uprisings, see Sitrin and Azzellini, *They Can't Represent Us!*
35. Rana Jaleel, "Into the Storm: Occupy Sandy and the New Sociality of Debt," n.d., *Is This What Democracy Looks Like?*
36. Solnit, *A Paradise Built in Hell*, 7.
37. Superstorm Research Lab, *A Tale of Two Sandys*, 21 December 2013.
38. Ibid.
39. Ibid.
40. David Chen, "New York City Comptroller Cites Flaws in Hurricane Sandy Recovery Program," *New York Times*, 31 March 2015.

41. On horizontalism and other key concepts in Occupy, see Writers for the 99%, *Occupying Wall Street: The Inside Story of an Action that Changed America*, New York: O/R Books, 2011. For a critique of elements of the movement, see the essays collected online in the Social Text–curated collection *Is This What Democracy Looks Like?*, eds. A.J. Bauer, Cristina Beltran, Rana Jaleel, and Andrew Ross, what-democracy-looks-like.com

42. See Jonathan Mahler, "How the Coastline Became a Place to Put the Poor," *New York Times,* 3 December 2012; Lawrence Kaplan and Carol Kaplan, *Between Ocean and City: The Transformation of Rockaway, New York*, New York: Columbia University Press, 2003.

43. Sofía Gallisá Muriente, "Personal Interview," 16 June 2015.

44. Solnit, *A Paradise Built in Hell*, 8.

45. Nicholas De Genova and Natalie Peutz, eds., *The Deportation Regime: Sovereignty, Space, and Freedom of Movement*, Durham, NC: Duke University Press, 2010.

46. Make the Road New York, *Unmet Needs: Superstorm Sandy and Immigrant Communities in the Metro New York Area,* December 2012, 9.

47. Nastaran Mohit, "Personal Interview," 4 June 2015.

48. On the exploitative system of three-quarter houses, see Christopher Beall, "The 'Three-Quarter House' System We Need to Embrace," *Gotham Gazette*, 12 October 2015.

49. Michael Goldfarb, "Personal Interview," 14 April 2017.

50. Charles E. Fritz, "Disasters and Mental Health: Therapeutic Principles Draw from Disaster Studies," University of Delaware Disaster Research Center, 1996).

51. Homeland Security Studies and Analysis Institute, *The Resilient Social Network*, 69.

52. Goldi Guerra, "Personal Interview," 28 May 2015.

53. On the casual racism of professional relief organizations during Sandy relief, see Zoltán Glück, "Race, Class, and Disaster Gentrification," n.d., *Occupy Wall Street*.

54. Mohit, "Personal Interview."

55. Strike Debt, *Shouldering the Cost: Who Pays in the Aftermath of Hurricane Sandy*, 10 December 2012.

56. Ibid.

57. Ilya Jalal, "Personal Interview," 29 May 2015.

58. Glück, "Race, Class, and Disaster Gentrification."

59. Ibid.

60. Ibid.

61. Ibid.

62. Tomás Reed, "Personal Interview."

63. Ibid.

64. Zoltán Glück, "Personal Interview," 30 May 2015.

65. Glück, "Race, Class, and Disaster Gentrification."
66. Raul Zibechi, *Dispersing Power: Social Movements as Anti-State Forces*, Oakland, CA: AK Press, 2012, 2.
67. For an account of internal critiques by some Occupy Sandy activists, see Ari Paul, "Storm Troopers: The Legacy of Occupy Sandy," *Brooklyn Rail*, 4 September 2013.
68. Glück, "Personal Interview."
69. Sandy Regional Assembly, *Sandy Regional Assembly Recovery Agenda*, April 2013.
70. New York City Environmental Justice Alliance, "Sandy Regional Assembly Releases Analysis of Mayor Bloomberg's Sandy Rebuilding Report," 23 July 2013.
71. Sandy Regional Assembly, *Recovery Agenda—Recovery from the Ground Up: Strategies for Community-Based Resiliency in New York and New Jersey*, April 2013.
72. On New York's history of radical community-based planning, see Tom Angotti, *New York For Sale: Community Planning Confronts Global Real Estate*, Cambridge, MA: MIT Press, 2008, 131–52.
73. On this history of uneven redevelopment, see Kevin Fox Gotham and Miriam Greenberg, *Crisis Cities: Disaster and Redevelopment in New York and New Orleans*, New York: Oxford University Press, 2014.
74. Mike Wallace, *A New Deal for New York*, New York: Bell and Weiland, 2002.
75. Ibid., 39.
76. Ibid., 92.
77. See Fox Gotham and Greenberg, *Crisis Cities*.
78. The best analysis of the fiscal crisis of the 1970s and its legacy in New York is Kim Moody's *From Welfare State to Real Estate: Regime Change in New York City, 1974 to the Present*, New York: New Press, 2007.
79. Ibid., 291.
80. Dario Azzellini and Marina Sitrin, *They Can't Represent Us!: Reinventing Democracy from Greece to Occupy*, New York: Verso, 2014.
81. Alliance for a Just Rebuilding, "Official Comments on Sandy Legislative Package in Front of NYC City Council Committee on Public Safety," 20 June 2013.
82. Alliance for a Just Rebuilding, "To Strengthen Important Sandy Legislation, the New York City Council Should Require OEM to Do More for Displaced New Yorkers and Vulnerable Communities," n.d.
83. Gloria Pazmino and Laura Nahmias, "New Yorkers Affected by Hurricane Rally for Relief," *Politico*, 24 February 2014.

84. Alliance for a Just Rebuilding, "Sandy-Impacted Communities Unveil New Rebuilding Plan for Next Mayor, Turning the Tide Away from Inequality and Toward Justice," 31 July 2013.

85. Ibid.

86. Alliance for a Just Rebuilding, *Turning the Tide: How Our Next Mayor Should Tackle Sandy Rebuilding*.

87. MoMA, *Rising Currents*, 2009; BMW-Guggenheim, *Urban Lab*, 2011; Whitney Museum, *Undercurrents*, 2010; MoMA *Expo 1*, 2011.

88. For a discussion of these exhibitions and their postapocalyptic rhetoric, see Bruce Braun and Stephanie Wakefield, "Inhabiting the Post-Apocalyptic City," *Society and Space*, March 2014.

89. See, for example, Mohsen Mostafavi, ed., *Ecological Urbanism*, Zurich: Lars Muller, 2010; Herbert Girardet, *Creating Regenerative Cities*, New York: Routledge, 2015; Timothy Beatley, *Biophilic Cities: Integrating Nature into Urban Design and Planning*, Washington, DC: Island Press, 2011.

90. Eric Swyngedouw, "Apocalypse forever? Post-Political Populism and the Spectre of Climate Change," *Theory, Culture and Society* 27: 2–3, 2010, 213–32.

91. On green urban branding, see Fox Gotham and Greenberg, *Crisis Cities*, 208–21.

92. As David Harvey puts it, "There are many urban innovations around the world, but they have yet to converge on [a] singular aim of gaining greater control of uses of the surplus (let alone over the conditions of its production)." See Harvey, *Rebel Cities: From the Right to the City to the Urban Revolution*, New York: Verso, 2012, 25.

93. Cohen, "The Urban Green Wars."

94. Ibid.

95. Ibid.

96. Davis, "Who Will Build the Ark?" 43.

97. Ibid.

98. "Thousands of Sandy Survivors Respond to Mayor De Blasio's *One City, Rebuilding Together* Plan," rebuildajustny.org. For the report that influenced de Blasio's plan, see *How Sandy Rebuilding Can Reduce Inequality in New York City*, rebuildajustny.org.

99. New York City Environmental Justice Alliance, *NYC Climate Justice Agenda: Strengthening the Mayor's OneNYC Plan*, April 2016.

100. For a critique of the de Blasio administration's housing policies, see Ari Paul, "All That Is Solid Melts into Condos," *Jacobin*, 20 March 2014.

101. Ibid.

102. Aura Bogado, "The People of North Manhattan Are Fighting Climate Change On Their Own Terms," *Grist,* 25 November 2015.

103. WE ACT, *Northern Manhattan Climate Action Plan.*

104. Ibid.

105. Ibid.

106. On the links between local environmental justice organizations such as WE ACT and the transnational struggle for climate justice, see Ashley Dawson, "Climate Justice: The Emerging Movement Against Green Capitalism," *South Atlantic Quarterly* 109: 2, Spring 2010, 313–38.

107. James Angel, *Strategies of Energy Democracy*, Brussels: Rosa Luxemburg Stiftung, 2016, 20.

108. Aurash Khawarzad, "Personal Interview," 19 June 2016.

109. James Angel, *Strategies*, 11.

110. WE ACT, *Northern Manhattan Climate Action Plan.*

111. Ibid.

112. Klein, *This Changes Everything*, 21.

Conclusion: Urban Futures

1. Elizabeth Rush, "Leaving the Sea: Staten Islanders Experiment with Managed Retreat," *Urban Omnibus*, 11 February 2015.

2. Ibid.

3. Ibid.

4. Liz Koslov, "The Case for Retreat," *Public Culture* 28: 2, 2016, 377.

5. Ibid.

6. Ibid., 362.

7. See Kate Orff, *Toward an Urban Ecology: SCAPE/Landscape Architecture*, New York: Monacelli Press, 2016; Anuradha Mathur and Dilip da Cunha, eds., *Design in the Terrain of Water*, New York: Applied Research and Design, 2014.

8. Kazi Ashraf, "Water As Ground," in Anuradha and Da Cunha, *Design in the Terrain of Water*, 94.

9. On the long history of Holland's relationship to water, see Tracy Metz and Maartje van den Heuval, *Sweet and Salt: Water and the Dutch*, Rotterdam: NAi, 2012.

10. McKenzie Funk, *Windfall: The Booming Business of Global Warming*, New York: Penguin, 2014, 215–34.

11. Metz and van den Heuval, *Sweet and Salt*, 282.

12. Ibid., 285.

13. Tracy Metz, "Personal Interview," 22 June 2015; Metz and van den Heuval, *Sweet and Salt*, 283.

14. Koslov, "The Case for Retreat," 364.

15. Ibid., 361.

16. On post-9/11 public rhetoric and the transformation of space in Manhattan, see Michael Sorkin, *Indefensible Space: The Architecture of the National Insecurity State*, New York: Routledge, 2008.

17. Julie Koppel Maldonado, "A Multiple Knowledge Approach for Adaptation to Environmental Change: Lessons Learned from Coastal Louisiana's Tribal Communities," *Journal of Political Ecology* 21, 2014, 74.

18. On the Shishmareff relocation vote of 2016, see Christopher Mele and Daniel Victor, "Reeling From Effects of Climate Change, Alaskan Village Votes to Relocate," *New York Times*, 19 August 2016.

19. Robin Bronen, "Choice and Necessity: Relocations in the Arctic and South Pacific" *Forced Migration Review* 45, February 2014, 19.

20. Chris D'Angelo, "A Louisiana Tribe is Now Officially a Community of Climate Refugees," *Huffington Post,* 12 February 2016.

21. Tianyi Luo, Andrew Maddocks, Charles Iceland, Philip Ward, and Hessel Winsemius, "World's Fifteen Countries with the Most People Exposed to River Floods," *World Resources Institute Blog,* 5 March 2015.

22. Virginia Eubanks "My Drowned City is a Harbinger of Climate Slums to Come," *The Nation,* 29 August 2016.

23. Justin Gillis, "Flooding of Coast, Caused by Global Warming, Has Already Begun," *New York Times,* 3 September 2016. For a more systematic analysis of these issues, see Orrin H. Pilkey, Linda Pilkey-Jarvis, and Keith C. Pilkey, *Retreat from a Rising Sea: Hard Choices in an Age of Climate Change*, New York: Columbia University Press, 2016.

24. Leslie Kauffman, "Sandy's Lessons Lost: Jersey Shore Rebuilds In Sea's Inevitable Path," *Inside Climate News,* 26 October 2016.

25. Compare the United States's laissez-faire policy regarding regional development with those discussed in Peter Hall's *Good Cities, Better Lives: How Europe Discovered the Lost Art of Urbanism*, New York: Routledge, 2013.

26. For the searing discussion of the roots of this geography of inequality, see Thomas J. Sugrue, *The Origins of the Urban Crisis: Race and Inequality in Postwar Detroit*, Princeton, NJ: Princeton University Press, 2014.

27. The classic analysis here is Mike Davis's *Planet of Slums*, New York: Verso, 2007.

28. Brooke Jarvis, "Under Water: Along Parts of the East Coast, the Entire System of Insuring Coastal Property is Beginning to Break Down," *New York Times Magazine* (23 April 2017), 65–68.

29. Katherine Bagley, "Thousands of Homes Keep Flooding, Yet They Keep Being Rebuilt Again," *e360 Digest*, 29 August 2016.

30. Julie Maldonado, "Personal Interview," 4 May 2016.

31. Robin Bronen, "Climate-Induced Community Relocations: Using Integrated Social-Ecological Assessments to Foster Adaptation and Resilience" *Ecology and Society* 20: 3, 2015.

32. Tom Angotti, *New York for Sale: Community Planning Confronts Global Real Estate*, Cambridge, MA: MIT Press, 2008, 225–34.

33. WE ACT, *Northern Manhattan Climate Action Plan*, 27 July 2015.

34. Justin Gillis, "Flooding of Coast, Caused by Global Warming, Has Already Begun," *New York Times*, 3 September 2016.

35. Koslov, "The Case for Retreat," 363.

36. Davis, "Who Will Build the Ark?" *New Left Review* 61, 2010, 38.

37. Ibid.

38. For an extended consideration of the need for a planned transition, see Brendan Gleeson, *The Urban Condition*, New York: Routledge, 2014, 122ff.

39. Davis, "Who Will Build the Ark?" 41.

40. Ibid., 45.

41. See, for example, Joel Wainwright and Geoff Mann, "Climate Leviathan," *Antipode,* 17 July 2012, and Andreas Malm, "Tahrir Submerged? Five Theses on Revolution in the Era of Climate Change," *Capitalism Nature Socialism* 25.4, 2014.

42. Bill McKibben, "A World at War," *New Republic*, 15 August 2016.

43. Mark R. Wilson, *Creative Destruction: American Business and the Winning of World War II,* Philadelphia: University of Pennsylvania Press, 2016.

44. *The 2016 Democratic Party Platform*, 8–9 July, 2016, 40.

45. Stan Cox, *Any Way You Slice It: The Past, Present, and Future of Rationing*, New York: New Press, 2013.

46. Brendan Gleeson, *The Urban Condition*, New York: Routledge, 2014, 125.

47. Heather J. Creaton, "Fair Shares: Rationing and Shortages," Sources for the History of London 1939–45: Rationing, British Records Association, 1998, 85–86.

48. Steve Horn, "Obama Admin Quietly Enables Oil and Gas Drilling on Public Lands and Waters, Weakens Endangered Species Act," *Desmog Blog*, 29 September 2016.

49. Bill McKibben, "Why Dakota in the New Keystone," *New York Times*, 28 October 2016.

50. Donny Gluckstein, *A People's History of the Second World War: Resistance versus Empire,* London: Pluto Press, 2012.

51. Sara Nelson, "The Slow Violence of Climate Change," *Jacobin*, 17 February 2016.

52. Michael Klare, *The Race for What's Left: The Global Scramble for the World's Last Resources*, New York: Picador, 2012.

53. Vaclav Smil, "The Long, Slow Rise of Solar and Wind," *Scientific American,* January 2014, 52–57.

54. *Leap Manifesto: A Call for a Canada Based on Caring for the Earth and One Another,* leapmanifesto.org/en/the-leap-manifesto.

55. *People's Agreement of Cochabamba,* 22 April 2010, pwccc. wordpress.com/2010/04/24/peoples-agreement.

56. Office of the Inspector General, *Audit Report,* 26 July 2016.

57. Ian Katz, "Geithner in Book Says US Considered Nationalizing Banks," *Bloomberg*, 8 May 2014.

58. Damian Carrington, "Fossil Fuels Subsidized by $10m a Minute, Says IMF," *The Guardian,* 18 May 2015.

59. Karl Mathiesen, "G7 Nations Pledge to End Fossil Fuel Subsidies by 2025," *The Guardian,* 27 May 2016.

60. Suzanne Goldberg, "Exxon Knew of Climate Change in 1981, Email Says – But It Funded Deniers for 27 More Years," *The Guardian,* 8 July 2015.

61. Naomi Klein, *This Changes Everything: Capitalism vs The Climate*, New York: Simon & Schuster, 2014, 293–336.

62. Davis, "Who Will Build the Ark?"

63. See Gleeson, *The Urban Condition.*

64. David Harvey, *Rebel Cities: From the Right to the City to the Urban Revolution*, New York: Verso, 2012, 131.

65. Christophe Bonneuil and Jean-Baptiste Fressoz, *The Shock of the Anthropocene: The Earth, History and Us*, New York: Verso, 2016; Jason W. Moore, ed., *Anthropocene or Capitalocene? Nature, History and the Crisis of Capitalism*, Oakland, CA: PM Press, 2016.

66. I am thinking here of works such as Matthew Kahn's *Climatopolis: How Our Cities Will Thrive in the Hotter Future*, New York: Basic Books, 2010.

67. Herbert Girardet, *Creating Regenerative Cities*, New York: Routledge, 2015, 4.

68. Ibid.

69. I am thinking here not just of Mike Davis's seminal essay "Who Will Build the Ark?" but also works such as Susan Fainstein's *The Just City,* Ithaca, NY: Cornell University Press, 2010, and Girardet's *Creating Regenerative Cities.*

70. Ash Amin, "The Good City," *Urban Studies* 43: 5–6, May 2006, 1010.

71. Davis, "Who Will Build the Ark?" 43. On Red Vienna, see Helmut Gruber, *Red Vienna. Experiment in Working Class Culture, 1919–1934*, New York: Oxford University Press, 1991; Eve Blau, *The Architecture of Red Vienna, 1919–1934*, Cambridge, MA: MIT Press, 1999.

72. Ash Amin, "The Urban Condition: A Challenge to Social Science," *Public Culture* 25: 2, 2013, 204.

73. Richard Burdett, ed., *Uneven Growth: Tactical Urbanisms for Expanding Megacities*, New York: MoMA, 2014; Jaime Lerner, *Urban Acupuncture: Celebrating Pinpricks of Change the Enrich City Life*, Washington, DC: Island Press, 2016.

74. Justin McGuirk, *Radical Cities: Across Latin America in Search of a New Architecture*, New York: Verso, 2015.

75. Mike Davis's metaphor of the ark is a fitting alternative to Garrett Hardin's notion of the lifeboat.

76. Girardet, *Creating Regenerative Cities*, 8.

77. Girardet, *Creating Regenerative Cities*, 11. See also Timothy Beatley, *Biophilic Cities: Integrating Nature into Urban Design and Planning*, Washington, D.C.: Island Press, 2011.

78. Bill McKibben, "Recalculating the Climate Math," *The New Republic*, 22 September 2016.

79. City of New York, *Inventory of New York City Greenhouse Gas Emissions 2014*, April 2016.

80. Align NYC, *Elite Emissions: How the Homes of the Wealthiest New Yorkers Help Drive Climate Change*, 2015.

81. Mark Jacobson et al., "Examining the Feasibility of Converting New York State's All-Purpose Energy Infrastructure to One Using Wind, Water, and Sunlight," *Energy Policy* 57 (2013), 585–601.

82. James Angel, *Strategies of Energy Democracy*, Brussels: Rosa Luxemburg Stiftung, 2016.

83. Jason Hickel, "Clean Energy Won't Save Us—Only a New Economic System Can," *The Guardian*, 15 July 2016.

84. Rob Bailey, Antony Froggatt, and Laura Wellesley, "Livestock—Climate Change's Forgotten Sector," *Chatham House* (December 2014).

85. Hickel, "Clean Energy Won't Save Us."

86. Richard Easterlin, Laura Angelescu McVey, Malgorzata Switek, Onnicha Sawangfa, and Jacqueline Smith Zweig, "The Happiness-Income Paradox Revisited," *Proceedings of the National Academy of Sciences* 107: 52, 28 December 2010.

87. David Harvey, "The Crisis of Planetary Urbanization," in Pedro Gadanho, ed., *Uneven Growth: Tactical Urbanisms for Expanding Megacities*, New York: MoMa, 2014.

88. New Economics Foundation, *21 Hours: Why a Shorter Work Week Can Help Us All to Flourish in the 21st Century*, 13 February 2010.

89. Jason Hickel, "Forget 'Developing' Poor Countries, It's Time to 'De-Develop' Rich Ones," *The Guardian*, 23 September 2015.

90. On "nonreformist reforms," see Susan Fainstein's *The Just City*, 17–19.

91. For a detailed philosophical discussion of this and other components of the good life, and how to encourage it through social policy, see Robert Sidelsky and Edward Sidelsky, *How Much Is Enough: Money and the Good Life*, New York: Other Press, 2012.

92. Ibid., 206–10.

93. For a discussion of such a Prometheus Project, as well as a broader suggestive survey of urban transformations with an eye to social justice, see Mike Wallace, *A New Deal for New York*, New York: Bell & Weiland, 2002. On energy, jobs, and democracy, see Sean Sweeney, *Resist, Reclaim, Restructure: Unions and the Struggle for Energy Democracy*, New York: Rosa Luxemburg Stiftung, 2013.

94. Jacques Derrida, *On Cosmopolitanism and Forgiveness*, New York: Routledge, 2001.

95. See, for instance, Étienne Balibar, *We, The People of Europe?: Reflections on Transnational Citizenship*, Princeton, NJ: Princeton University Press, 2003.

96. "The Callahan Legacy: Callahan v. Carey and the Legal Right to Shelter," *Coalition for the Homeless*.

97. Amin, "The Good City," 1009–23.

Index